Concordia Historical Series

Edited by

W. G. POLACK, Litt. D.

Concordia Seminary

St. Louis

———————

VOLUME IV

GOVERNMENT

in the

MISSOURI SYNOD

GOVERNMENT

in the

MISSOURI

SYNOD

THE GENESIS OF DECENTRALIZED GOVERNMENT
IN THE MISSOURI SYNOD

by

Carl S. Mundinger, Ph. D.

CONCORDIA PUBLISHING HOUSE

Saint Louis, 1947

TO

Sophia Krato Mundinger

FOREWORD

For some years there has been a growing demand for a complete, thoroughgoing, and well-documented history of the Evangelical Lutheran Synod of Missouri, Ohio, and Other States. The Literature Board of the Synod at various times attempted to supply this demand by calling on competent students of the history of the Synod to prepare a work of this kind. However, for one reason or another, the task remained undone. When the Literature Board requested the present editor of this series to undertake the task, he suggested the publication of a series of monographs instead of limiting the work to one volume, since in such a series the vast amount of material could be more adequately treated. The Literature Board thereupon authorized such a procedure. A general outline of the series was agreed upon, and individuals were commissioned to write the monographs. As several monographs had already been prepared, or were in process of being written, as doctors' dissertations in several universities of our country, the editor asked that these be included in the series, requests that were graciously granted by the schools and the authors.

According to the plan agreed upon, the history of the Synod itself is to be covered in twenty-five year periods, from 1847 to 1947. Two volumes will deal with the immigration of the Saxons and their settlements in Missouri. One volume will present the work of the Rev. William Loehe and his missioners. In addition there will be individual biographies of C. F. W. Walther, F. C. D. Wyneken, and William Sihler. Another biographical volume will contain shorter biographies of men who in one field or another figured prominently in the history of the Synod.

At the present writing, twelve volumes have been arranged for; more will be added later. Since each volume will constitute a unit, no special attempt has been made to publish the volumes in chronological order, as this would mean holding up the publication of those now ready. Nor will the volumes be of equal size. In the very nature of the case some will be much larger than others. However, there will be uniformity in binding and format.

The editor is happy to be able to begin the series with this volume: *The Origin of Government in the Evangelical Lutheran Synod of Missouri, Ohio, ond Other States,* as its appearance will coincide with the centennial of the Synod. Originally this work, a Ph. D. dissertation at the University of Minnesota, was entitled "The Genesis of Decentralized Government in the Missouri Synod." Important statistics in the book were, at the request of the editor, brought up to date.

It is with a sincere prayer for divine blessing that we send forth the first volume of this series. We earnestly hope that the study of it and its companion volumes will lead many to a renewed interest in the life and work of the men who have, under God, worked together in the building of our Missouri Synod. It will be seen that they were men with all the failings and frailties our flesh is heir to, men who were as prone to make mistakes as are we in our day, yet at the same time men who were dedicated to a high and noble purpose, namely, the establishment and propagation on American soil of historic Lutheranism, Lutheranism as represented in the great Confessions of our Church. In the measure in which they and their successors hewed to the line, in that measure we may gauge the success of their labors. And, by the same token, in the measure in which the Missouri Synod during the second century of its existence, now looming on the horizon, adheres to these principles, in that measure will it remain true to its great evangelical heritage.   W. G. POLACK

May 1, 1947

PREFACE

On April 26, 1947, the Missouri Synod of the Lutheran Church was one hundred years old. Inconspicuous in its beginnings — only twelve congregations had voted to join the proposed body, eight of which were represented at the first meeting in Chicago by their pastors and three by their pastors and one layman each [1] — there grew up in and with America a typical immigrant body, at present composed of 4,428 pastors with 1,532,702 baptized members.[2] This group is important enough to merit the serious attention of historical research.

Immediately before and during the early years of its existence, from 1840 to 1865, church government was the foremost issue for the members of the Missouri Synod. Many articles and essays were written, pamphlets were published, sermons and speeches delivered, and debates conducted on various phases of church power. The big question was: Who has the power, and what is that power?

To my knowledge no effort has been made to trace back to their origins the forms of government that finally prevailed. When, therefore, Oliver Peter Field, S. J. D., Political Science Department, University of Minnesota, suggested that this be done, the present writer timidly declared his willingness to attempt the task.

During my investigations I received the help of many people. I owe a debt of gratitude to the Concordia Historical Institute, St. Louis, Missouri, and its president, Prof. W. G. Polack, for the

---

[1] *Erster Synodal-Bericht*, 1847. (Reprinted as a second edition, Concordia, St. Louis, Missouri, 1876.) Pp. 5—6, 24. In order to keep a balance in voting strength between pastors and congregations, the Synod invented the device of non-voting, advisory membership. Advisory members were pastors whose congregations could not yet be persuaded to join Synod. Ten pastors had joined as advisory members, six of whom were present. Some came late, and others left early. Probably never more than twelve pastors were present at one and the same session.

[2] *Statistical Yearbook of the Evangelical Lutheran Synod of Missouri, Ohio, and Other States* for the year 1945, pp. 140, 144, 184.

use of unprinted source materials — letters, minutes of meetings, and documents of various descriptions; to Old Trinity, St. Louis, Missouri, and its present pastor, Rev. R. H. C. Meyer, for extensive use of the congregation's minutes (which, by the way, are among the best written and best preserved minutes in the Missouri Synod); to Trinity Congregation, Altenburg, Missouri, and its present pastor, Rev. A. Vogel, for access to archival material; to Concordia Congregation, Frohna, Missouri, and its pastor, Rev. G. W. Hafner, for permission to search old boxes of archival materials; and to the Pritzlaff Memorial Library and its librarian, Paul E. Kretzmann, Ph. D., D. D., Ed. D., for the use of printed sources and rare books bearing on the subject. Two men, both sons of founding fathers — Ludwig Fuerbringer, D. D., president of Concordia Seminary, St. Louis, Missouri, and Theodore Buenger, D. D., president of Concordia College, St. Paul, Minnesota (1893—1927) — permitted me to use documents in their private possession. To George M. Stephenson, Ph. D., History Department, University of Minnesota, my adviser, who was of great help to me, I owe a special debt of gratitude. Likewise to E. G. Richard Siebert of Concordia College, St. Paul, Minn., who gave the entire dissertation a critical reading. For any and all deficiencies the gentle reader may blame me.

TABLE OF CONTENTS

INTRODUCTION
OBJECTIVES AND SCOPE

How did it come that the Missouri Synod, whose founders came from an oligarchically ruled Church in which the State played a large role, adopted and adhered to a decentralized form of church government? Had they made any demands for decentralization while still in Germany? Were desires expressed or attempts made to establish a so-called "Free Church," a Church independent of the State, before the emigration? If these attempts failed, was the failure one of the causes of the emigration? Was it ever used as such? This is one set of questions that the present study attempts to answer.

Furthermore, what effect did the new environment have upon the church polity of the immigrants? Did "they imbibe rather distinctly American democratic characteristics"? Was "their contact with a democratic environment responsible for a turn in doctrine and polity which differentiated it from its German prototype"? [3] Did the Lutheran Church already existing in America at the time of the immigrants' arrival affect the church polity of the immigrant body? If so, to what extent and in what way? This influence appears to have been rather insignificant and mostly negative.

Again, what is the nature of "Missouri's" decentralized govern-

---

[3] Mauelshagen, *American Lutheranism Surrenders to Forces of Conservatism*, p. 125. Compare also the fear expressed by a contemporary of the founders, Pastor W. Loehe, in a letter to the Synod, September 8, 1847: "Finally, we do not wish to keep you in ignorance concerning something which has cut us to the quick and which also is of importance for the seminary at Fort Wayne. We notice with growing concern ('mit herzlichem Bedauern') that your synodical constitution, as it has been adopted, does not follow the example of the first Christian congregation. We have good reason to fear that the strong admixture of democratic, independent, and congregational principles in your Constitution will do greater damage than the interference of princes and governmental agencies in the Church of our homeland." Printed in *Kirchliche Mitteilungen aus und ueber Nord-Amerika*, VI (1848), p. 44. In this letter Loehe gives the seminary at Fort Wayne to the Synod.

ment? Is it democratic? Are matters of church polity decided after the fashion of the New England Town Meeting? Is there any affinity between the peculiar church polity of the Lutheran immigrants and the congregationalism of the Baptist and the Congregational churches? The study will show a marked divergence of the decentralized government of the Missouri Synod from American congregationalism.

Finally, what has been the effect of other doctrines not immediately connected with church polity on the government of the Missouri Synod? For example, the doctrine of the divine inspiration of the Scriptures, the efficacy of the Word, and the Bible as the sole arbiter in matters of faith? While the influence of these doctrines on church polity is more elusive, the study will show that it was a factor.

An effort has been made in Chapter II to give a composite picture of church life in Saxony and surrounding German states during the first half of the nineteenth century. The ever-present danger of generalization, so graphically expressed in the story of the seven blind men and the elephant, was ever before me. The picture differs from the one usually given in that certain brighter colors frequently omitted have been used together with the darker hues.

The question may be raised: Why devote so much space to a study of Luther in the investigation of an American Church? Had not Luther been dead three hundred years when the Missouri Synod was founded? True; but so far as church polity is concerned, the Reformer was more alive among the Missourians in the 1840's than he had been among the Saxons of the 1540's. Without a knowledge of Luther, governmental forms of the Missouri Synod will be imperfectly understood.

As the title indicates, this study does not go beyond the origin of the Missouri Synod in 1847, nor does it dwell extensively on matters which have no connection with church polity.

GOVERNMENT IN THE
MISSOURI SYNOD

CHAPTER ONE

LUTHER'S CONCEPT OF CHURCH GOVERNMENT

THE HISTORICAL INVESTIGATOR will not get very far in his research of the Missouri Synod without coming upon the fact that Luther and his writings played a very important role in the formation of Missourian church polity. The *Erweckungsbewegung* of Saxony during the early decades of the nineteenth century, in which the founders of the Missouri Synod were deeply involved,[1] claimed to be, and in part was, a movement back to Luther.[2]

Martin Stephan, the father confessor and spiritual adviser of the future founders of the Missouri Synod, was deeply steeped in the writings of Luther. Time and again, with the utmost emphasis, he urged his followers, especially those among the clergy, to go back to Luther. His attitude toward Luther can be gleaned from a statement which he made to Pastor E. G. W. Keyl: "If we were allowed to pray to the saints, I would fall down on my knees before Luther."[3] Stephan's insistent emphasis upon the study of

---

[1] Hennig, *Die saechsische Erweckungsbewegung im Anfange des 19. Jahrhunderts*, pp. 27—28, 117, 119, 121, 206—207. Cp. also an article by the same writer in *Zeitschrift fuer Kirchengeschichte*, LVIII (1939), Nos. 1 and 2, pp. 142—166. W. Kohlhammer, Stuttgart. The article is entitled: "Die Auswanderung Martin Stephans." G. H. Loeber, later pastor of Trinity Church, Altenburg, Perry County, Missouri, was won over for Moravian pietism at the Herrnhut Pastoral Conference in 1823. K. F. Gruber, later pastor in Paitzdorf, now Uniontown, Perry County, Missouri, was an active corresponding member of the Herrnhut Pastoral Conference for several years. The Count of Einsiedel and Prince Otto Victor I von Schoenburg-Waldenburg, who saw to it that pastors "who believed in divine revelation" were placed in charge of parishes over which they had the right of appointment and through whose offices young Keyl, C. F. W. Walther, and E. M. Buerger got into their respective congregations, were outstanding lay leaders in the *Erweckungsbewegung*. The Muldenthal Pastoral Conference, which must also be classified as part of the *Erweckungsbewegung*, was split in two during the 1830's, Rudelbach leading the men of definitely orthodox tendency, and Keyl, the men of pietistic stripe. C. F. W. Walther, O. H. Walther, and E. M. Buerger went over to Keyl's side.

[2] *Op. cit.*, pp. 62, 67, 81, 89, 91, 129, 146. In its opposition to rationalism the *Erweckungsbewegung* stressed Luther's doctrine of original sin and the reconciliation of God with man. For pietism in Norway see T. Blegen, *Norwegian Migration to America*, 1940, pp. 131—174.

[3] *Zeitschrift fuer die gesamte lutherische Theologie und Kirche.* Heraus-

Luther explains in part the strong tendency toward stricter confessionalism among the Stephanites during the 1830's.

The ultimate effect of Stephan's exhortations to read Luther can be seen in one of his most obedient followers, Pastor Keyl. Especially in America, Keyl became a fanatical student of Luther. Not only did he frequently spend ten and twelve hours a day in his study of the Reformer, but he made copious excerpts of his writings. He studied with pen in hand. His *Register,* an index made up of statements copied out of Luther's writings, contained 8,800 entries and in addition 54,000 references to Bible passages used and explained by Luther. His motto was: *Nulla dies sine linea.* He published a magazine in which he explained his whole system and in which he urged others to follow his example.[4] His sermon material was taken exclusively from Luther's writings. He would take whatever Luther had said on a given text and rearrange it into a sermon. He wanted every young minister (and he writes parenthetically: "Why not every old one, too?") to use Luther exclusively in the preparation of sermons. During his presidency of the Eastern District of the Missouri Synod, 1854—1868, he urged the young ministers whom he ordained to study Luther as he did.[5]

Other founders of the Missouri Synod were perhaps not quite as fanatical, but they were just as sincere in going back to Luther as a source of their theology. G. H. Loeber, pastor of Trinity in Altenburg, Perry County, Missouri, instructor in the Altenburg Concordia and, together with Dr. W. Sihler, examiner of the theological candidates, published a volume of excerpts from Luther's writings which enjoyed a wide circulation.[6] During the

---

gegeben von A. G. Rudelbach und H. E. F. Guericke, III (1842), p. 99. The quotation is part of an article by Pastor Keyl entitled "Offene Bekenntnisse von Pastor Keyl," pp. 94—114.

[4] The magazine was called *Lutherophilus.* The first copy was printed March, 1854, in Baltimore, Maryland. The copy from which the above data are taken is in the private library of Dr. L. Fuerbringer. The magazine is printed in the form of letters. His system of indexing is described on pp. 17—24 of the fourth letter.

[5] Koestering, *Leben und Wirken des Ehrw. Ernst Gerhard Wilh. Keyl,* p. 120. In his MS. notes for the biography Koestering speaks of a young pastor who had to preach four times a week, teach school five days a week, and who was to do his stint of Luther every day. Koestering adds: "Armer Kerl!" (Poor fellow!) These MS. notes are wrapped up in a large bundle and are in the private library of Dr. L. Fuerbringer. I shall refer to them as Keyl MS.

[6] Loeber, G. H., *Gaben fuer unsere Zeit aus dem Schatz der lutherischen*

terrible turmoil that followed the expulsion of Stephan from
Perry County, Pastor Ernst Moritz Buerger naturally took refuge
in Luther's writings.[7] C. F. W. Walther's intense interest in Luther's writings dates back to an enforced absence from his studies
at Leipzig. During this period, in which he recuperated from
a serious illness, he read Luther's writings with avidity.[8] Later
in life he summed up his attitude toward Luther in these words:
"A pupil, and I hope to God a faithful pupil, of Luther, I have,
in all that I have publicly spoken and written in the past, simply
repeated in a stammering way the words of this last prophet." [9]
His book the *Church and the Ministry* [10] consists chiefly of quotations from Luther. The habit of Missouri Synod pastors to settle
theological arguments with a quotation from Luther's writings
is one of long standing. The tremendous amount of space devoted
to quotations from Luther's writings in essays delivered before
synodical conventions impresses one who goes through the files
of the synodical proceedings as peculiar. It shows the bent of
Missouri Synod minds. The juxtaposition of the words *Gottes
Wort und Luthers Lehr'* and the masthead of the *Lutheraner,*
portraying Luther as the angel of the Apocalypse, Rev. 14: 6-7, is
also highly significant.[11]

A unique attitude toward the person of Martin Luther is evident. He is called the "unforgettable and highly enlightened true
servant of God" ("dem unvergesslichen und hocherleuchteten

---

*Kirche und besonders aus Dr. Martin Luthers Geist- und Glaubens-reichen
Schriften.* 1834.

[7] Buerger, Ernst M. "Lebensgeschichte von Ernst Moritz Buerger, Pastor
emeritus, von ihm selbst beschrieben," p. 132.

[8] Guenther, *Dr. C. F. W. Walther — Lebensbild*, p. 12.

[9] *14. Synodal-Bericht der Allgemeinen Synode von Missouri, Ohio und
anderen Staaten,* 1869, p. 22. This was part of Walther's presidential address
to the General Synod at Fort Wayne, Indiana, September 1 to 11, 1869. The
major portion of the address was devoted to quotations from Luther's writings.

[10] *Die Stimme unserer Kirche in der Frage von Kirche und Amt.*

[11] *Der Lutheraner.* Issued fortnightly since September 7, 1844, is a popularly edited religious publication. Through it Walther shaped the religious
thinking of the Missouri Synod in its infancy. The masthead representing
Luther as the angel of the Apocalypse was first used in Vol. 6, No. 19, May 14,
1850. Changes in the masthead were made beginning August 25, 1857; October 1, 1871; January 9, 1900; January 11, 1921; but Luther as the angel of
the Apocalypse was always retained. The motto *Gottes Wort und Luthers
Lehr' vergehet nun und nimmermehr* (God's Word and Luther's doctrine pure
shall to eternity endure) has entered many thousands of homes every two
weeks for the past 103 years.

treuen Knecht Gottes").[12]   When the three-hundredth anniversary of Luther's death is observed, one gets the impression that
the most beloved man of the colony has just passed away.   The
church in Altenburg is draped with yards and yards of black
cloth.   A special preparatory service is conducted the week before.   On the day of the anniversary there is a morning service
at 10 and an afternoon service at 2.   In his announcements from
the pulpit Pastor Loeber calls Luther "our father who rests in
God, who has fallen asleep in the Lord." [13]   The habit of calling
Luther "our father" is widespread.   In short, there is a definite,
emotionally supercharged piety over against anything connected
with Martin Luther.   This attitude precluded a critical study of
Luther.   That Luther might have erred in a given instance or
that his statement might not apply to the case at hand or that
Luther did not take the same stand consistently, does not seem to
have been suggested by anyone.

   Men were lifted out of the slough of despond by a quotation
from Luther.[14]   Questions of church polity, as we shall see in
the chapter on the emerging forms of church government, were

---

[12] "Nachrichten an unsere Nachkommen." It is written after the fashion
of medieval chronicles and is not very critical. The entries were made in a
book bound in brown leather. The handwriting seems to be that of Teacher
Winter. It was started five years after the founding of the Perry County
colony.

[13] Pastor Loeber's "Vermeldungsbuch." This book, now in the archives
of Trinity Church, Altenburg, was first used by Pastor Loeber in Eichenberg,
Saxony. The first entries were made on the first Sunday in Advent, 1835.
Turning the book upside down and beginning at the back, Pastor Loeber used
the same book for his announcements in Perry County. The announcements
concerning the anniversary of Luther's death were made on Sunday Sexa-
gesima, 1846.

[14] Buerger, "Lebensgeschichte," pp. 133—134. After quoting a certain passage in Luther's Commentary on Galatians, he says: "These passages brought
streams of light into my soul. . . . I showed the passage from Luther to Mr. N. N.
Whether Pastor Walther [evidently C. F. W.] was directed to this passage by
Mr. N. N. or whether Walther in his ardent study and his persistent search
for clarity found the passage, I do not know. To God alone be glory and
honor! This much is certain: it was through this passage primarily that the
Lord brought streams of light into our dark souls. Endowed with brilliant
gifts, Walther knew how to use this gold mine to the utmost. No one of us,
least of all I, was his equal in the use of Luther." Compare also the statement
in J. F. Koestering's *Auswanderung der saechsischen Lutheraner im Jahre 1838*,
p. 53. The day when Walther cleared up the fundamental question of church
polity (What is the Church?) on the basis of Luther is called the "Easter day
of the sorely tried congregations." In its importance, as far as church polity
is concerned, Koestering compares the Altenburg Debate, April, 1841, to the
debate between Luther and Eck at Leipzig, 1519.

decided or received strong support by quotations from Luther. True, the authority of the Scriptures was never questioned; but so great was the emotional attachment to Luther that a doctrine of Scripture, when put in the words of Luther, seemed doubly dear and doubly authoritative.

To bring Luther's concept of church government to paper presents unusual difficulties. Forms meant so little to Luther. When codified in legal instruments, they might even stifle spiritual life.[15] Small wonder that he threw Pope Leo's bull and the Canon Law into the fire at the same time on December 10, 1520. Luther's interest centered in the spoken Word. That made Christians and thus built the Church. Any form of church government and any order of service that gave the spoken Gospel a chance was acceptable. In Sweden, where the Roman Catholic bishops went over to Luther's side lock, stock, and barrel, the episcopal form of church government might be retained. In Germany, where the bishops failed to co-operate, someone else must be sought to take over the task of administration, and we have an almost endless variety of *Kirchenordnungen*.[16] *Kleinstaat* ideals and the emphasis on individualism in constitutional matters are largely responsible for the multiplicity of *Kirchenordnungen* in evangelical Germany during the sixteenth century.

Luther's opposition to legalism shows itself in his concept of the origin of *Kirchenordnungen*. He was opposed to the ecclesiastical legislator who had an urge to hand down a ready-made

---

[15] *Luther's Works*, Holman Edition, VI, 131—300, "On the Councils and the Churches." This tract, dealing particularly with the problem of church government, was written in 1530. Luther does not like the word *church*, because it is obscure and confusing. It conveys a notion of externals, p. 265. He condemns the Pope's holiness, because it consists of "chasubles, tonsures, cowls, garb, food, festivals, days, monkery, nunnery, masses, saint worship, and countless other points about external, bodily, transitory things." P. 269. Compare also Emil Sehling's *Die Evangelischen Kirchenordnungen des 16. Jahrhunderts.* When Nikolaus Herman had written a constitution (*Kirchenordnung*) for Dessau, Luther advised him not to publish it for fear that it might assume the character of a legal instrument (Sehling, *op. cit.*, I, I).

[16] Sehling, *op. cit.*, I, p. IX. The word *Kirchenordnung* embraces more activities of religious life than the word *constitution*. The *Kirchenordnungen* of the Evangelical Church in Germany embody the rules for government, worship, liturgy, discipline, marital relations, education, eleemosynary work, and property rights of the Church. The best collection of these endless sets of rules is the one to which this footnote refers. Sehling has issued five heavy volumes, and he confines himself to the sixteenth century. Paraphrasing Lessing, one is tempted to say that every German has his own nose and his own *Kirchenordnung*.

constitution, binding the congregation or a group of congregations.[17] Haste and force are two elements that should be kept
out of constitution making. Sets of rules for the government of
churches should be a matter of growth and development. Let the
rules grow out of a given situation in which the church finds itself; and as the situation changes, the ordinances ought to change
with it.

The effect of this principle can be seen in the readiness with
which Luther gives up certain attitudes when historical circumstances demand a change. Luther was not a doctrinaire in the
matter of church government. It is true, there is a remarkable
consistency in certain beliefs about church organization. But his
opposition to legalism made it impossible for him to continue his
attitudes when the facts in a given case demanded a change. In
church government Luther practiced *Realpolitik*. His question
was: What action do the realities of the situation demand? To
the doctrinaire who wishes to have the same set of rules applied
to all situations such a policy is the height of inconsistency. This
much is certain, the student of Luther's writings on church polity
must constantly ask himself these questions: When did Luther
say this? Where did he say it? What were the circumstances
in the case?

As a general rule, the ideals of church government that were
formed during the period from 1519 to 1525 had to be recast and
in part discarded because of the experience gained through the
visitations made from 1525 to 1528. The visitors found conditions
in individual parishes that forced Luther to change his entire
church polity. The reports of the visitors were too convincing
to be set aside.[18]

---

[17] Luther, *op. cit.*, Holman, II, 226: "My ardent desire and urgent prayer
is that no one would make a law out of this order of service nor force others
to adopt it. Without burdening the consciences of their members let the
individual congregations decide how, where, when, and how long they wish
to arrange their order of service. We are not your masters or your lawgivers.
If anyone can make a better order of service, let him go to it."

[18] *Niedners Zeitschrift fuer historische Theologie*, 1863, No. 2, pp. 295—322,
by F. Winter, Prediger in Schoenebeck bei Magdeburg. The article written on
the basis of reports made by the visitors is entitled: "Die Kirchenvisitation
von 1528 im Wittenberger Kreise." Thirty-eight parishes were visited. The
work was done during October and November, 1528. The visiting committee
consisted of two theologians (Luther and Jonas) and three lawyers. They
were appointed by the Elector. The bishops were the persons who should
have taken care of this visitation. They had been approached several times,

Two things — and they are most fundamental in any study of church government — remain constant throughout Luther's writings: his concept of the Church (*una sancta ecclesia*) and his concept of the local congregation (*die Gemeinde*). Put the question to Luther at any place or at any time: What is the Church? and you will invariably get the same answer. Ask him: What is the local congregation? and he will never vary. Strange as it seems, these were the two points on which colossal confusion reigned among the fathers of the Missouri Synod during their first two years on American soil. Luther's answers to these two questions brought light to their troubled souls and proved to be the guidelines of their church polity.

The Church in the real sense of the word is the whole number of all believers.[19] This community of believers is nothing external.[20] The essence, life, and nature of the Church is not a bodily assembly, but an assembly of hearts.[21] It is separate from all temporal communities, because it is not anything external.[22] The Church is not bound to any city or to any place. Its boundaries cannot be fixed.[23] Being in the Roman communion does not necessarily make one a Christian and part of the Church, nor does being outside that communion make one a heretic or a non-Christian.[24] It is true that the Church has certain marks, namely, the preaching of the Gospel and the Sacraments, whereby one can tell where the Church is in the world.[25] Nevertheless, the Church is not a visible body constituted after the fashion of the organizations of this world. There is no one above or under another. The differentiation of rank, so common to the organized bodies of men in this world, is absent from the Church. The true Church, the communion of believers, has no head on earth.

---

but they refused to do the work. The man who had the *de facto* power was the Elector. Luther had already written his *Deutsche Messe und Ordnung* early in 1526. This, together with Melanchthon's *Instructions for the Visitors* (reprinted in Sehling, *op. cit.*, I, pp. 149—174), formed the framework for the visitation. These two documents have been called "the first Lutheran Pastoral Theology."

[19] *The Papacy at Rome*, 1520; W. A., 29. This pamphlet of Luther, published June 26, 1520, presents his teaching of the Christian Church. Koestlin calls it "one of the most important of his general doctrinal treatises in that period." *Martin Luther*, I, p. 299.

[20] Koestlin, *Martin Luther*, p. 291.

[21] *Op. cit.*, p. 293.

[22] *Op. cit.*, p. 294.   [24] *Op. cit.*, p. 301.

[23] *Op. cit.*, p. 297.   [25] *Op. cit.*, p. 301.

Neither bishop nor Pope can rule over it; only Christ in heaven
is the Head, and He rules alone.[26]

According to the doctrine of Rome eternal salvation is dependent upon membership in the Roman communion. The Church
is an institution outside which there is no salvation (*nulla salus
extra ecclesiam*). The properly ordained priest is the mediator
who throws out the lifeline and connects man with all the blessings of the ship of salvation. Luther, on the other hand, believed
that we are reconciled to God through the death of His Son. This
reconciliation was effected for all men; and the moment a man
believes this, he becomes a partaker of this reconciliation, whether
he be a member of the Roman communion or of any other communion or of no communion at all. The all-important thing, according to Luther, is faith in the heart. Membership in a man-
made communion, brought about by the mediation of a properly
ordained priest, is inconsequential.

In fact, every believer is a priest in his own right. He is a
priest not in the sense that he must effect a reconciliation through
a sacrifice brought on an altar made with hands. His function
as a priest is to inform his fellow men of the redemption accomplished once and for all by Christ on the Cross.[27] In their function as priests all believers are alike. There is no distinction of
rank and authority, nor does the priesthood confer any particular
holiness.[28]

All believers are priests, and yet all do not function publicly
as priests. Why not? Because of the disorder that would ensue.[29]
Therefore every congregation must select one from its midst and
ask him to perform the public functions of a priest in the name of
the congregation. Only one who has been thus asked by the congregation is to officiate publicly. "Because we are all in like manner priests, no one must put himself forward and undertake, without our consent and election, to do what is in the power of all
of us. For what is common to all, no one dare take upon himself
without the will and the command of the community; and should

---

[26] *Op. cit.*, p. 297.

[27] Sermon on October 10, 1522. W. A., 10, III, 395.

[28] *Ibid.*, III, 395.

[29] Sermon on October 26, 1522. *Ibid.*, III, 397: "If all would preach, we
would be like the women who go to market: all want to talk, and no one
wants to listen."

it happen that one chosen for such an office were deposed for mal-
feasance, he would be just what he was before he held office.
Therefore a priest in Christendom is nothing else than an office
holder. While he is in office, he has precedence; when deposed,
he is a peasant or a townsman like the rest." [30] The number of
believers who happen to be residing in a geographic area select
one from their midst whomsoever they think best qualified and by
vote transfer to him the task of publicly administering the office
of a Christian priest. [31] This is Luther's concept of the Church and
the ministry. As a principle, the priesthood of all believers remained constant throughout Luther's life. It shaped and colored
all his thinking about church government. Incidentally, this is
the doctrine of transfer (*Uebertragungslehre*), which C. F. W. Walther lifted bodily out of Luther's writings and with which he
brought order into the chaotic thinking of the fathers of the Missouri Synod in April, 1841. But more of that later.

This fundamental principle was not entirely forgotten even
when Luther was forced to desist from its strict application. In
the noise and turmoil of battle, when the grim realities of life
forced Luther to suspend this principle, at least for the time being,
you can still hear the overtone of the priesthood of all believers.
Even the appeal for help directed to the princes contains this
teaching. "Since, then, the temporal authorities are baptized with
the same Baptism and have the same faith and Gospel as we, we
must grant that they are priests and bishops, and count their office
one which has a proper and useful place in the Christian community." [32] The men who formed the government in his day were
confessing Christians. The electors of Saxony were intensely religious men. The same can be said of some of the men who were

---

[30] *An Open Letter to the Christian Nobility.* W. A., 6, 408. This is a
companion pamphlet to the one entitled *The Papacy at Rome.* It came off
the press on August 18, 1520. The permanent separation between Luther and
Leo X had just taken place. The German knights, who formed a patriotic
party, had promised Luther their support. They are included in the "nobility."
In these pamphlets Luther lays the groundwork for his reformatory work.
They are his manifestoes.

[31] *How Servants of the Church are to be Elected and Put into Office.* 1523.
A long letter written to the Christian community at Prague. St. Louis Edition,
X, 1597 f. "Select your own man, anyone you think is fit and able to carry
out the tasks. Then let the leaders among you lay their hands on him, thereby
confirming the appointment and commending him to the people of the congregation. Thus are men made bishops in Christian congregations."

[32] *An Open Letter to the Christian Nobility.* W. A., 6, 408.

princes of other areas that adopted the evangelical faith. They were the foremost members (*praecipua membra*) of the Church. As such, not as statesmen, Luther appeals to them.[33]

In trying to arrive at an adequate appraisal of Luther's decision to call upon the princes for help in the government of the Church one must keep ever in mind the chaotic conditions in the Church and in the State. From the end of 1524 to well into 1529 we have a period that was revolutionary in certain parts of Germany. Not only were people changing their faith and others steadfastly refusing to change their faith, but the very Church, the one institution in which the social and economic life of the people was bound up, was being uprooted and reconstituted. The reports of the visitors of this period are most revealing. The disorder was indescribable. The ignorance of the parish priests was profound. Their education and social life was close to that of the peasant. There was great irregularity in the income from parish lands. During the colonization period in the eleventh and twelfth centuries certain acres of land (*Hufen*) had been set aside in each parish to maintain the priest and to repair or rebuild the church when necessary. There was litigation about that now that the "Gospel was free." Lands and income-producing investments which pious men had willed to Mother Church for the celebration of masses after their death were contested. Many heirs were trying to get this piece of land or that mine from the Church, since no prayers were now being said for the dead. The tendency to withhold payments to the parish priests other than income from land endowments was gaining momentum. The income of monasteries and convents was being disputed. The care of men who had grown gray as monks and of women who had lost their bloom of life in convents had to be regulated. Parsonages had to be remodeled and salaries revised now that the priests were marrying and rearing families. In short, a new social order was being established. On top of all this, certain religious sects, which were gaining adherents fast, were opposed to all government. They

---

[33] Sehling, *op. cit.*, I, p. 150. This is a reprint of the *Instructions for the Visitors*, 1528. In the preface Luther tells how he had asked the Elector to inaugurate the visitation. In the appeal to the Elector, Luther stresses the fact that his sovereign is a prince appointed by God and that he is a Christian. As a prince he has no obligation to teach or preach or to govern the Church. But as a Christian he has the obligation of love to do what he can to restore order in the sorely afflicted congregations.

were not only heretics in the Church, but also enemies of the State.[34] One can see why Luther called upon the princes to help regulate the affairs of the Church. Whom else should he have called upon for help? The bishops? They were the logical men, but they refused to participate in the building of a new social order. So he turned to the most prominent lay members of the Church, the princes.

But, after all, when all is said and done and proper allowances are made for the chaotic conditions which followed the first onslaught of the Reformation, it must be stressed that Luther retained the fundamental concept concerning civil government that was held in the Middle Ages, namely, that civil government must serve Christendom and, with that, the Church. It is true theoretically, and at times practically, Luther sharpened the distinction between Church and State. He set more sharply defined limits to the spheres of activity for each. With his distinction between the mass of humanity ("Herr *omnes*," "der grosse Haufe") and the "assembly of hearts" inside the outer circle [35] he contributed to a better understanding of the function of the Church and the function of the civil government.[36] But the extremely

---

[34] *Niedners Zeitschrift fuer historische Theologie,* 1863, No. 2: "Die Kirchenvisitation von 1528 im Wittenberger Kreise." This article is based upon the findings of the visitors. See also Sehling, *op. cit.,* I, 142 ff. Sehling portrays the many sweeping changes in matters of administration and constitution that were ordered by the visitors.

[35] *Deutsche Messe und Ordnung gottis diensts.* Wittenberg, 1526. W. A., 19, 72 ff. Reprinted in Sehling, *op. cit.,* II, pp. 10—16.

[36] Diehm, *Luther's Lehre von den zwei Reichen.* The author collected a veritable array of passages from Luther which show the sharp division between the two kingdoms: the kingdom of this world, which is the civil government, and the kingdom of Christ, which is the assembly of hearts. Luther's abundance of terms is instructive: "twofold governments, earthly and spiritual" (W. A., 11, 251, 15; W. A., 19, 629, 17; W. A., 16, 352, 21); "kingdom of God or kingdom of Christ" and "kingdom of this world" (W. A., 11, 249, 25; W. A., 18, 292, 31; W. A., 30, II, 558, 26, 28; W. A., 32, 387, 8); "worldly and spiritual empire" (W. A., 10, III, 371, 19; W. A., 28, 281; W. A., 51, 238, 29 f.); "worldly and spiritual estate" (W. A., 30, II, 519, 20; W. A., 32, 387, 8; W. A., 31, I, 190, 11); "worldly and spiritual order" (W. A., 32, 374, 20); "worldly and spiritual government" (W. A., 6, 256, 12; 258, 32); "worldly and spiritual power" (W. A., 6, 259, 20); "empire of Heaven and Empire of the Kaiser" (W. A., 51, 533, 24); "spiritual and physical empire" (W. A., 34, II, 537, 18); "sword of the mouth and sword of iron" (W. A., 46, 736, 29); "office of the sword and office of the Book" (W. A., 49, II, 709, 24); "the kingdom of the left hand (civil government) and kingdom of the right hand" (W. A., 52, 26, 23). The distinction is exceedingly sharp and clean-cut in Luther: here the believers under Christ, there the unbelievers under the hangmasters and men who put offenders in stocks for Christ ("Henker and Stockbloecher Christi," W. A., 11, 251, 15; 11, 249, 27). Here, then, in the Church, is no sword except

accentuated distinction between Church and State which makes
some of the second and many of the third generation of Walther's
students avoid the "things of Caesar" is not found in the theory,
and certainly not in the practice, of Luther. Luther's concept en-
visioned the State and the Church working together for the good
of the people, each one in its own sphere, but both actually working.

Nor can Luther be cleared of all responsibility for the existence of a prince-controlled Church in evangelical Germany. The
Consistorium, with its theologians and jurists as an administrative
device for the control of the Church in the hands of a supreme
bishop (the *summus episcopus*), the prince — this is Luther's coun-
terpart for the medieval bishop.

Luther was indebted to princes for much help. In fact, his
Reformation would not have been possible without the German
Kleinstaat and the steadily growing power of its prince. This is
true particularly of Saxony. Frederick the Wise had protected
him over against the demands of Rome in 1521. The Wartburg as
a hiding place was the prince's idea. The Edict of Worms, which
demanded the eradication of the new doctrine, was never executed
in the Elector's territory. Through the influence of the Elector
the imperial government closed an eye to the spread of Lutheran
doctrine in other parts of the empire. As the years roll on, the
power of princes becomes more and more essential to Luther's
cause. The years 1525 to 1527 were fraught with danger. Foes
from within and foes from without, foes from below and foes from

the sword of the Spirit, which is the Word of God, and this must be used
exclusively; there, in the State, the sword of steel and the policeman's club
must hold sway. There is no need for the sword of steel in the assembly of
hearts, "because the men and women in this assembly have the Holy Spirit
in their hearts, who teaches them and keeps them from doing harm to their
fellow men" ("die weyl sie den heiligen geyst im hertzen haben, der sie leret
und macht, das sie niemant unrecht thun," W. A., 11, 250, 251). The civil
government must keep the disturbers of the peace who will not listen to the
Word (which includes heretics) in check with physical force, so that the
"assembly of hearts" can carry on the work of evangelization. The better
the civil government preserves order and cares for the physical well-being
of the people, the better chance the Gospel will have in building up the
kingdom of Christ in the hearts of men.

It is necessary for the understanding of Luther's position to note that he
makes these sharp distinctions whenever he is face to face with the attempts
of Romanists or enthusiasts to dull the power of the Gospel either by asking
the civil government to do things that should be done by the "assembly of
hearts" or by declaring that civil government in itself is a nuisance and
should be abolished. Luther was driven to his sharp differentiations by
Romanists on the one hand and by anarchists of various hues on the other.

above, were attacking Luther's cause. A well-organized, compact Church was an absolute necessity. Without it the cause was hopeless. Driven by the realities of the situation, Luther asked the new elector, John of Saxony, to inaugurate a visitation and to provide for competent priests in the parishes of his principality. This step of necessity led directly to the establishment of a rule of the Church by princes. The fall of 1525 — more specifically, November 30, 1525, the day when Luther asked John to bring order into the ecclesiastical chaos [37] — is the birthday of the rule

---

[37] *Letters*, De Wette, III, p. 51. This letter, written November 30, 1525, is a remarkable document. Luther is feeling his way. He must have more reliable priests. He makes suggestions to John. John is to appoint them through a committee. Luther's old idea of the priesthood of all believers is still evident. The people of each parish are to be consulted. Their wishes should be respected. But the prince is to be the leading actor. A sort of trial visitation of a few parishes was ordered by John and conducted early in 1526. The *consilium*, or advice, of one of the visitors to John is reprinted in Sehling, *op. cit.*, I, p. 35. This report suggests that the principality be divided into circuits consisting of a number of parishes. The pastor in the leading city should be the superintendent of the circuit (*Aufseher*). He is not to lord it over the other priests. When they make mistakes, he is to correct them gently. If they refuse to listen to the superintendent, he is to bring each case to the attention of the civil government. Then the government is to conduct the necessary hearings and impose the penalties according to its findings. Neither the superintendents nor the committeemen who conduct the visitations shall have the right to appoint or remove pastors, *episcopi* (*Aufseher*, or superintendents), or preachers. This right is reserved for the prince. The above report was made immediately after the trial visitation early in 1526. In the fall of 1526, on St. Elizabeth's Day, November 22, Luther wrote to John again. He used much stronger language and urged John to take up the visitation once more. The people are to be forced by the prince to maintain churches and schools even as they are forced to build roads and bridges. A committee of four should be appointed — two experts in economics ("die auf die Zinse und gueter verstaendig sind") and two experts in theology ("die auf die Lehre und Person verstaendig sind"). This letter is found in De Wette, III, pp. 135—137. John ordered the visitation February 13, 1527. There are no reports extant, but the instructions for the committeemen, dated June 16, 1527, are reprinted in Sehling, I, *op. cit.*, pp. 142—148. They reveal much. John is much more energetic. Old, incapacitated, and unfit priests as well as those priests still clinging to popish ceremonies shall be relieved of their office. They must be provided for. They should be paid either a lump sum (*Abfertigung*) or a regular pension as long as they live. Those who are teaching error must be corrected; if they refuse to desist, they must be chased out of the country. If a pastor's life shows indiscretion or immorality, it should be corrected according to the intensity of the sin. If the transgression is not too flagrant, he is to be transferred to some other parish. If a pastor does not agree with us in doctrine, he must give up his parish. While it is not our intention to command a man what he is to believe or not to believe, we must prevent damaging turmoil and pernicious disorder ("schedlicher aufruhr und andere Unrichtigkeit"). The committee is to inquire into the views of laymen, find out whether any sectarian views prevail among them. If they refuse to give up their sectarian views, tell them to sell out and leave the country. See whether there are enough schoolteachers; if not, remedy the situation. Economic problems bulk very large in these instructions. People

of princes in the Lutheran Church. The entire development of church government in Saxony shows that Luther, not the prince, took the lead; that Luther, not the prince, was the dynamic personality in the movement. Every once in a while the Elector shows a certain tardiness, which makes it necessary for Luther to prod him on. Whatever Elector John does he does in close collaboration with Luther. Luther approves every step leading to control of the

---

who refuse to pay their parish dues ("iren rechtschaffenen Seelsorgern ire rente, zins, tetzen und dergleichen gebuehr") or who pay them in bogus money or in spoiled grain or deteriorated wine or rotten meat are to be admonished and possibly punished. Inquire into the divorce cases that are pending. Many priests in times past have assumed the role of judges in granting divorces or in settling marital difficulties by separation. They are not able to handle these cases adequately. This must be done by our civil servant ("unserm Amptmann oder Schosser"). The pastors must take care of their work and not dabble in worldly affairs. Examine the morals of the people ("fullerei, sauferei, spil u. musigang, schandlieder auf den Gassen, Hurrerei, Unzucht"). Too many monks are still clinging to their monkery. Try to convince them of the error of their way. Help the monks financially until they can get back into a normal social and economic life. No long and detailed report of this visitation is extant, but a summary of the evils is found in 14 "Articuli," reprinted in Sehling, *op. cit.,* I, p. 37. Though only a summary, these "Articuli" shed abundant light on the situation as it prevailed in the summer of 1527. These articles reveal a tremendous interest in economic and social matters. Money and investments set aside by pious men for Masses are to be put into the common treasury of the parish ("gemeinen Kasten"), out of which churches are to be kept in repair and the poor and needy are to be fed and clothed. If the heirs of the deceased donor are poor, they are to receive part of the money, the remaining portion going into the common treasury. The landlords who are trying to kick the pastors off the land should be talked to and reminded of the value of preaching and soul care ("Seelambt"). The costly vestments and other ornamentation should be sold, and the money put into the common treasury to support the poor and needy. The peasants who have stolen the chalices and other costly utensils should be forced by the government to restore them. The old, incapacitated, and unfit, as well as the young totally unfit pastors are to be turned out of office. The young are to receive a lump sum, and the old are to be supported from the income of monasteries. In conclusion, the committee heartily indorses Martin Luther's conservatism in changing the masses. Go slow! Take it easy! There is no hurry about introducing a new order of service. The great difficulty in the visitations of 1526 and 1527 was that the committee did not have an adequate set of administrative rules ("ein Visitationsbuch") to go by. In the fall of 1527 Melanchthon worked out a set of administrative rules based upon the experience of 1526 and 1527. This is the *Instruction for the Visitors,* 1528 (*Unterricht der Visitatoren,* 1528). The whole book is reprinted by Sehling, II, *op. cit.,* pp. 149—174. Much discussion and study preceded the publication. Luther, Bugenhagen, and Melanchthon did the chief work. Special attention was given to marriage and the celebration of the Lord's Supper *sub utraque.* It is the first Lutheran pastoral theology, an instruction to ministers on how to conduct their office. It reveals Luther's, Bugenhagen's, and Melanchthon's concept of the Lutheran ministry. The prince is not quite so prominent. He is in the background. The *Unterricht der Visitatoren* was published March 2, 1528; and September 6, 1528, an orderly and thoroughgoing visitation of the parishes of Saxony was launched by the prince.

Church by the princes, and he wishes "that this blessed example might be imitated by all other German princes." [38]

The "blessed example" did find imitators. The other Lutheran princes were quick to follow the Saxon prince. The first Diet of Speyer, 1526, expedited the control of the Church by the princes in that it gave each prince the right to arrange religious affairs according to his own desires. It is true, they were not forced to adopt a church polity in which the prince was the *summus episcopus*. They could have adopted constitutions in which the local congregations had much more to say. The fact that they did not must be attributed to Luther. The case of Hesse illustrates the point. Lambert of Avignon had drawn up a constitution for Hesse. In this constitution the local congregation is dominant. In fact, Luther's principle of the priesthood of all believers receives full recognition. The congregation elects the pastor. There are regularly conducted synods, in which pastors of local congregations discuss their problems and exchange experiences. One such synod was actually held. A constitution was adopted by the synod at Homburg in the fall of 1526. Philip of Hesse, next to the Elector of Saxony perhaps the most prominent prince in the Protestant Church, was in favor of the constitution and voted thus. Why did Lambert's constitution fail? In January, 1527, Luther suggested to Philip that Lambert's scheme be given up. Philip listened to Luther, and a church polity with the prince as the *summus episcopus* was adopted in its place. The Great Commoner was not trusting commoners in 1527. To be safe, he wanted a rule that had punch.

The many passages, quoted at length by Harold Diehm,[39] in which Luther complains about the rule of the princes and declares

---

38 *Unterricht der Visitatoren*, 1528. W. A., 26, 199.

39 Diehm, *op. cit.* Of the many passages quoted by Diehm the following are most significant: "Before our Gospel came, no one knew how to preach about the civil government and say what a good thing it was. Now that we have praised and exalted the government through our Gospel, the princes want to be above God and above His Word. They want to command what we are to believe." This statement was made in 1534 in connection with the explanation of Psalm 101. W. A., 51, 246, 4. "We must destroy the *Consistorium*" ("Wir muessen das Consistorium zerreissen"). Under no circumstances dare we permit the lawyers and the popes in high places. The lawyers with their lawsuits dare not be tolerated in the Church. They are bringing the Pope back." W. A., 6, 344.

his readiness to destroy the *Consistorium* were written by Luther when he was beginning to see to what lengths caesaropapism was taking the Lutheran Reformation. By that time it was a case of: "Die ich rief, die Geister, Werd' ich nun nicht los." Luther started something on November 30, 1525, that culminated in a Roman Catholic king as the supreme bishop of the Lutheran Church in his beloved Saxony A. D. 1830.

CHAPTER TWO

A PASTORATE IN SAXONY, 1830-1840

THE ECCLESIASTICAL POLITY of the Missouri Synod was determined by the men that came from Saxony. While the group that hailed from Bavaria and settled in the Saginaw Bay region of Michigan may have had a higher percentage of better trained and more stable laymen (Loehe had selected them as Christian models for the heathen Indians of Michigan), they did not enjoy the clerical leadership nor the experience born of controversy in constitutional matters which would have enabled them to insist on the kind of church government that finally prevailed. For this reason a knowledge of the background of the social, economic, and religious life among the Saxons before their emigration will prove helpful.

What were the general spiritual conditions? In what kind of economic, social, and cultural soil were the clerical leaders rooted? What work did a pastor have to do? To whom was he responsible? How did the church government function?

The traditional way of describing the spiritual side of life in Saxony during the early decades of the nineteenth century is to call it the Age of Rationalism. Usually such adjectives as "dark," "bleak," "sterile," and "oppressive" are added to make the picture supposedly complete. Writers, particularly those in the Missouri Synod, assume that rationalism was exclusively dominant, that it was growing in power during this decade and that it was making life progressively impossible for those who wished to maintain a Bible-centered faith.[1]

---

[1] Hochstetter, *Die Geschichte der Evangelisch-Lutherischen Missouri Synode*, pp. 4—7. — Steffens, D. H., *Doctor C. F. W. Walther*, pp. 78—90. — Hanser, C. J. Otto., *Geschichte der Ersten Ev.-Lutherischen Dreieinigkeitsgemeinde zu St. Louis, Missouri*, p. 5. — Koestering, *Die Auswanderung der saechsischen Lutheraner im Jahre 1838*, pp. 1—4. — Koestering, *Leben und Wirken* of Keyl, pp. 47—49. — Dau, W. H. T., *Ebenezer*, p. 24. — Mauelshagen, *op. cit.*, p. 84. See also the moving picture of the Saxon Immigration, 1939, sponsored by the Publicity Department, Fiscal Office, 3558 South Jefferson Avenue, St. Louis. Missouri. — Incidentally, this was also the belief of many of the immigrants. In their "Brief Sketch of Emigration Regulations" (reprinted in *Ebenezer*, p. 8) they state the cause of the emigration in paragraph 2: "After deliberate and mature counsel they can, humanly speaking, see no possibility of retaining

Aside from the fact that it is frequently misleading and quite often inaccurate and unhistorical to call a certain number of years that have been deftly dated at both ends an "age" of something, rationalism in Saxony during the fourth decade of the nineteenth century was lacking in vigor. It was definitely on the decline. There were other movements in the religious world that were just as vital and daily becoming more so, and life still held much in store for those who wished to retain the traditional Lutheran faith.

What is rationalism? It is the last stage of a movement that began with the Enlightenment of the eighteenth century and that eventually made human reason the sole arbiter of Christian doctrine. In its emphasis upon human reason it went back to Pelagian optimism concerning the nature of man, and this in turn had made itself felt in the Renaissance, Arminian theology, the Cartesian philosophy of Holland, and in English Deism and French Naturalism. In its theological aspects and during its infancy and early development the movement was willing to grant a relatively large space to revelation. At the beginning of the nineteenth century, however, when the movement had crystallized, revelation was accorded less and less space and finally completely crowded out as contrary to reason and unessential to "practical" Christianity.

---

in their present home this faith pure and undefiled, of confessing it, and transmitting it to their posterity. Hence they feel in duty bound to emigrate and to look for a country in which this faith is not endangered and where they can serve God undisturbed in the way of grace revealed and ordained by Him." How did this view of religious conditions in Saxony come into being? It is based upon the description given by the pietists of the day and by men who needed a justification for their emigration. It is in the very nature of pietism to emphasize evil. The pietist wishes to feel his personal wickedness. He measures the sincerity of his repentance by the depth of his feeling concerning evil. He loves to wallow in the mire of his own unworthiness. From individual to social evil is but a short step. The world is bad, and the righteous must flee from it. Furthermore, the pietism of the early 1830's was still in conflict with rationalism, and rationalism emphasized the good in man. In battle conflicting beliefs are sharpened and overstated. On the other hand, Martin Stephan and his followers promoted this view of contemporary spiritual life in order to justify the emigration. (See Koestering, *Leben und Wirken* of Keyl, pp. 47—49.) Stephan exhibited a somewhat mystical attitude concerning the time when they were to leave Saxony. He was waiting for a suggestion from God (Vehse, *Die Stephansche Auswanderung nach Amerika*, p. 5). Stephan's trouble with the police of Dresden probably had more to do with fixing the exact time of departure than any other single factor. The reasons given for the emigration were not the real reasons. Many sincerely believed that they were, but these were only the ostensible reasons. They have been repeated by many, and thus it happens that the traditional picture of spiritual conditions in Saxony during the third decade of the nineteenth century is rather one-sided and incomplete.

The utilitarian principle of sound common sense ("der gesunde Menschenverstand") in its least vital form usurped the place of revelation and became the slogan of the day. The men of the movement conceived it their duty to remove the barnacles that had fastened themselves upon the body of Christian doctrine during the centuries. They did this not to destroy, but, as they sincerely believed, to purify the Church. They thought they were doing God, and especially man, a service. The miraculous and the mystical in dogma and life were removed. Christ was retained not as the Son of God and the Redeemer from sin, but as the great religious philosopher who reveals and interprets God to man. The pulpit descended to a purely "practical" choice of subjects for presentation: "The value of early rising"; "the value of feeding cows in the stable during the winter" (this on Christmas Day); "the value of vaccination against smallpox"; etc., etc.

Rationalism was late in coming to Germany, and in all the states of Germany it was perhaps least vital in Saxony. Mild in its methods and sober in its thought processes, it seldom went to extremes. It always retained at least a few grains of sober Lutheranism. The leaders of the movement (their number was not as large as is commonly supposed) professed a much-diluted orthodoxy and pursued a policy of denatured pietism.[2] They were decidedly churchly; that is, they wished to see the Church and its forms maintained. In fact, the religion of many rationalists had degenerated into dead formalism. They clung to the old. They

---

[2] Even von Ammon, who is often mentioned as the most vicious of all rationalists, sailed a zigzag course between the old and the new faith. This is particularly evident in his *Summa Theologica*, 1803; fourth edition, 1830. He has a good word to say for the famous 95 theses of Claus Harms, which were directed against rationalism in 1817. Largely for political and personal reasons (he was somewhat of a trimmer) von Ammon opposed the Prussian Union. After the fall of the Einsiedel ministry, brought about by the revolution of 1830, von Ammon became slightly more bold in his rationalistic pronouncements. But his days were numbered; and it is significant that the great pillar of Lutheran orthodoxy, G. C. Adolf von Harless, was made the successor of von Ammon in Dresden. This fact indicates the trend of the times in Saxony during the latter years of the first half of the nineteenth century. For the facts concerning von Ammon see Meusel, *Kirchliches Handlexikon*, I, p. 118. Meusel was a superintendent of the Lutheran Church in Rochlitz, Saxony. Sihler's reaction to von Ammon's preaching is instructive. He calls it "a stale dish of heathen hash, garnished with a little Christian sauce" (Sihler, *Lebenslauf*, I, p. 91.) *Religion in Geschichte und Gegenwart*, I, p. 303, calls von Ammon one of the chief exponents of "Offenbarungsrationalismus," a rationalism which still left room for a certain amount of revelation. Rationalism had lost its vigor. It was inert.

permitted pastors to be bound by the Augsburg Confession and the other confessional writings of the Lutheran Church.[3]

That the rationalistic pastors were interested in the maintenance and progress of the Church is shown by their interest in so-called special undertakings of the Church. They are members of Bible societies. They join groups to promote Christian missions.[4] They work hand in hand with men who are known to be confessionally conservative.[5] In short, the rationalism of Saxony was middle-of-the-road rationalism, which on the whole and as a movement did not possess sufficient vitality to take an extreme stand on anything.[6] The readiness to assume responsibility and to act which comes from deep religious experience was absent.

Why, then, was there so much talk about rationalism during the third decade of the nineteenth century? There were several reasons. In statecraft the men of the romantic *Restauration*, a movement headed by Metternich of Austria and deeply affecting the policies of the Saxon government, regarded the rationalists as allies and all antirationalists as disturbers of the *status quo*. There were steadily growing groups of antirationalists, who were becoming more vocal, more powerful, and more orthodox every day. Lutheran theology was coming into its own. Then there

---

3 Ziehnert, *Praktisches evangelisches Kirchenrecht*, I, p. 122. C. F. W. Walther branded as hypocrisy the oath of rationalists which bound them to the teachings of the Augsburg Confession. Cf. his *Lebenslauf* of Buenger, p. 33. And so it was; but the fact that the oath was taken from all pastors, regardless of their shadings of orthodoxy, gave the Bible believers among them support for their position, and it did permit them to preach fundamental Lutheran doctrine. See Buerger, E. M., MS., pp. 72—75. Buerger gives us the exact wording of his call. Not only the Unaltered Augsburg Confession, but also the Apology, the Large and Small Catechisms of Luther, the Formula of Concord, and the Smalcald Articles are mentioned in the call. Although Martin Stephan informed Keyl that the *Consistorium* was going to remove the oath by which they were bound to preach and teach Lutheran doctrine (Koestering, *Leben und Wirken* of Keyl, p. 48), there does not appear to have been a concerted effort to remove this obligation. The regular articles as well as the many book reviews in Rudelbach und Guerickes *Zeitschrift*, do not indicate that it was a burning question. Harless' *Zeitschrift fuer Protestantismus und Kirche* contains no articles on the subject. Nor do the men who later founded the Missouri Synod seem to have been engaged in such a controversy. Ziehnert, *op. cit.*, I, p. 132, speaks of individual voices that have been raised against the oath at all times in the Church's history, but the question does not seem to have been particularly acute. He adds: "If anyone does not wish to take the oath, let him stay out of the ministry."

4 Hennig, *op. cit.*, p. 126.

5 *Op. cit.*, pp. 15, 55.

6 *Op. cit.*, pp. 14—15.

were a few rationalists who took an extreme position and made themselves extremely obnoxious.[7]

The antirationalistic movement in Saxony was rather complex. It really consisted of several diverse and independent movements. Inside these movements there were various shades of opinion; some contained quite a bit of Lutheranism, some less, and some almost none at all. Some contained positively anti-Lutheran elements, while some were heavily pietistic and emotionally revivalistic, but they all met on a common ground of opposition to rationalism. There were strange bedfellows here. For want of a better name the movement was called the "Awakening" (*Erweckungsbewegung*).[8] The axis around which the many different groups revolved was the emphasis upon original sin and the reconciliation wrought by Christ on the Cross,[9] the very antitheses of rationalism. The movement began when the Enlightenment of the eighteenth century had lost its vigor and had degenerated into the "vulgar rationalism" of the early nineteenth century; and the end

---

[7] For the religious side of the Restoration movement see *Religion in Geschichte und Gegenwart*, IV, pp. 1994—1995. J. A. L. Wegscheider, the dogmatician of "vulgar rationalism," took an extreme position. He denied many of the traditional doctrines of Christianity. The same is true of the exegete of the rationalists, H. E. G. Paulus, who attempted to "purify" the New Testament and to "restore" the primordial Christianity (*Urchristentum*) of Jesus Christ. Young Hengstenberg in 1829 and Karl Hase in 1834 attacked Wegscheider so vigorously and so effectively that his reputation as a scientific theologian was ruined. As the representative of a movement he was dead from 1835 on, although his natural life extended to 1849. Karl Hase's criticism of Wegscheider was positively devastating. Hase was peculiar. He was a quasi-rationalist who yet recognized the significance of orthodox teaching for his contemporaries and delighted in defending orthodoxy against extreme rationalists. See Meusel, *op. cit.*, VII, p. 181; *Religion in Geschichte und Gegenwart*, IV, p. 1046.

The various cases cited by C. F. W. Walther on pp. 32—42 of his *Lebenslauf* of Buenger are cases of extremists and show how far certain leaders in Church and State had gotten out of touch with reality. As a matter of fact, these men were on their way out. The future in Saxony belonged to sound Lutheranism. Walther's description must be read in the light of the many and profound articles appearing in Rudelbach und Guerickes *Zeitschrift*, and also in the light of the excellent articles appearing in *Zeitschrift fuer Protestantismus und Kirche*. Keyl's "Offene Bekenntnisse," written in Perry County at the end of August, 1841, and published in Vol. III, No. 1, pp. 94—114, of Rudelbach und Guerickes *Zeitschrift* should not be set aside lightly. They fit in with other parts of the picture.

[8] Hennig, *op. cit.*, p. 9. The antirationalists themselves coined the phrase. The Church in their estimation had been brought to such a state that it was in a coma. They had been aroused and were now a part of the great awakening.

[9] Hennig, *op. cit.*, brings countless excerpts from letters and reports which describe this emphasis in the various groups.

of the movement came when it was absorbed by the vital Lutheran confessionalism of the 1830's and 1840's.

Which were some of the more prominent groups that initiated the movement? A rather important one was the German Society for the Promotion of Pure Doctrine and Holy Life, with branch societies all over Saxony and other parts of Germany.[10] More important in its influence was the Moravian activity known as the "Herrnhuter Diaspora."[11] In this same classification we must

---

[10] Hennig, *op. cit.*, pp. 28—29. The branch at Dresden, over which Pastor Martin Stephan gained complete control in the 1820's, was a kind of home office for all Saxony. Reports and religious problems were sent to the Dresden branch from various parts of Saxony. Hennig calls this branch the "primordial cell of Stephanism" ("die Keimzelle des Stephanismus"). On page 29 he speaks of the society as "the soil from which mission and Bible societies and Stephanism sprang" ("Mutterboden fuer die Missions- und Bibelgesellschaften und fuer den Stephanismus"). The object of the society was to promote pure doctrine over against rationalism, to foster Christian missions and child welfare, and in general to promote spiritual life through the publication of conservative devotional literature. Its official name was "Deutsche Gesellschaft taetiger Befoerderer reiner Lehre und wahrer Gottseligkeit." Finally the name was shortened to "Deutsche Christenthumsgesellschaft." Like so many other groups in the *Erweckungsbewegung*, the society crossed denominational lines in its early history. With the rising tide of Lutheran confessionalism in the late 1820's and early 1830's it lost its identity as far as Dresden and Saxony were concerned. It must be examined by all who wish to trace the origins of the Missouri Synod. Incidentally, the motto of Concordia Publishing House: "The Word of God endures to all eternity" (*Verbum Dei manet in aeternum*), was used in the first manifesto of the founders of the "Deutsche Christenthumsgesellschaft" in 1780. Besides K. Hennig, who devoted pp. 15—33 of his *Saechsische Erweckungsbewegung* to this society, W. Wendland has written an informative article on p. 1575, Vol. I, of *Religion in Geschichte und Gegenwart*. For an earlier account of the society see Meusel, *op. cit.*, I, 731.

[11] This activity of Count Zinzendorf's followers was based upon the assumption that there are real Christians among the nominal Christians of all denominations. Thoroughly conscious of their own unworthiness, these men and women have a strong feeling that they are God's children through the reconciliation wrought by Christ on the Cross. Their number, so the Moravians believed, is relatively small, but they are the salt of the earth. Because of their small number and lowly position in the midst of many nominal Christians who persecute them, they must, in the opinion of the Herrnhuter, be strengthened, and if possible, their number must be increased. The task of strengthening these scattered individuals belongs to the home base. From here specially trained men are sent to the homes of individual Herrnhuters. On page 41 Hennig presents the report of one such missionary. In the year 1838 this man — his name was Carl Friedrich Enkelmann — called on 1,500 individuals who were scattered over 200 villages and towns of western Saxony. In some spots where the number of "real Christians" was large enough, they were able to conduct private meetings and to effect a loose organization. The most important semiorganized group was in Dresden. Every year a conference of kindred-minded pastors met at Herrnhut to develop the conviction of sin and grace according to Moravian patterns. G. H. Loeber and K. F. Gruber, later pastors in Perry County, became members of the conference in 1823, Gruber advancing to the position of a corresponding member. However, by 1835 both had rid themselves of Moravian individualism and had adopted

place the various Bible societies and mission societies that sprang
into existence between 1810 and 1830.[12] And finally, among the
forces which opposed rationalism we must place individual men
who possessed influence because of their position in society and
because they were personally opposed to rationalism.[13]

Summing up, we get the following picture of spiritual conditions during the 1830's in Saxony: Two opposing sets of ideas
are striving for the mastery. In this "battle that is now raging in
the entire Christian world,"[14] there is general confusion and a
ferment of ideas.[15] However, Lutheran confessionalism is steadily
but surely advancing and gaining the upper hand. Since 1827 the
young and spirited Hengstenberg is gaining fame by whacking

Lutheran confessionalism. For a description of Herrnhut Diaspora activity see
Religion in Geschichte und Gegenwart, V, 2118—2122; Hennig, *op. cit.*, pp. 33—53;
also an article by Hennig in *Zeitschrift fuer Kirchengeschichte*, LVIII (1939),
Nos. 1 and 2, entitled "Die Auswanderung Martin Stephans." Hennig has
written a history of the Missouri Synod which is still in MS. He has not
been able to find a publisher. Meusel, *op. cit.*, III, p. 270, says that the Moravians rendered the Lutherans of the State churches a real service during the
period of enlightenment. Sihler, *Lebenslauf*, I, p. 106, speaks in a similar vein.

[12] The mere fact that Bible societies and mission societies came into
existence in Saxony during the second decade of the nineteenth century indicates a rising tide of interest in the Holy Scriptures. Why did men organize
these groups? They believed in the power of the Word, and they wished to
share the things which they had received. Many of these societies became
outspokenly antirationalistic soon after their organization. J. W. Volkmann,
a retired lawyer, a leader of the Leipzig Mission Society in the 1820's and 1830's,
wrote a book entitled *A Rationalist Can Be No Christian*. The copious
quotations from the writings of Volkmann and other men in Hennig's dissertation indicate the antirationalistic bias of mission societies and Bible
societies. The pattern of development is almost always the same. In their
early history these societies cross denominational lines. But toward the end
of the twenties and the beginning of the thirties they become decidedly
Lutheran in their confessional attitude, usually adopting the Unaltered Augsburg Confession as a statement of belief. Even the Society for Promoting
Christianity among the Jews, begun in Dresden, 1822, as a branch of the
parent society in London, was finally absorbed by the Evangelical Lutheran
Central Society for Mission Work Among the Israelites. See Hennig,
op. cit., p. 129.

[13] Such men were Count von Einsiedel, who was a cabinet minister in the
Saxon government for many years, and Prince Otto Victor von Schoenburg-
Waldenburg, an outstanding legal mind of Saxony. Both of these men had
the privilege according to Saxon law of placing pastors in the churches of
their respective territories. Pastors Keyl, Buerger, and C. F. W. Walther were
placed in their congregations through these political leaders. They invariably
chose men for their parishes who were known to be antirationalistic. Hennig
gives the religious views of von Einsiedel on pp. 150—162, and those of von
Schoenburg-Waldenburg on pp. 163—165.

[14] C. F. D. Wyneken, in his famous appeal, reprinted in Harless' *op. cit.*,
V, p. 136.

[15] A. F. C. Vilmar, writing in Rudelbach und Guerickes *Zeitschrift*, I,
No. 4, p. 1.

away with telling effect at rationalism in his *Evangelische Kirchenzeitung;*[16] Hase is writing his devastating books that put an end to the scientific reputation of Roehr and Wegscheider. As a member of the theological faculty at Leipzig, August Hahn is attacking rationalism as anti-Christian and demanding that every rationalist be put out of the Church.[17]   In Dresden, pamphlets are being handed out (February 2, 1832) stating that Dame Rationalism is dead and giving glory for her demise to the *Erweckungsbewegung.*[18] Rudelbach, the great Danish Lutheran theologian,[19] who has just (1829) been called by Prince von Schoenburg as superintendent and *Consistorialrat* in Glauchau, Saxony, is writing his masterpieces of Lutheran theology, first in Grundtvig's *Theologisk Maanedskrift,* then in Hengstenberg's *Evangelische Kirchenzeitung,* and finally in a *Zeitschrift* which he is editing together with another outstanding superintendent in Saxony, H. E. F. Guericke of Halle.[20] Young and staunch Adolf Harless is writing and speaking in behalf of confessional Lutheranism, first at Erlangen (1829) in near-by

---

[16] *Religion in Geschichte und Gegenwart,* II, p. 1796.

[17] *Religion in Geschichte und Gegenwart,* II, p. 1579; also Hennig, *op. cit.,* p. 94. Buerger, "Lebensgeschichte," p. 44, says: "Hahn used the language of the old orthodox theologians. He taught the simple doctrines of Luther's Small Catechism. I loved this man and had the good fortune to be his guest at the regular weekly social gatherings which he conducted for serious-minded Christian students in his home."

[18] Hennig, *op. cit.,* p. 122.

[19] Next to Harless, Rudelbach was the most learned Lutheran theologian of the nineteenth century. His productions are fit company for those of Martin Chemnitz, Johann Gerhard, and Andreas Quenstedt. His long series of articles analyzing the Lutheran Church of Denmark, begun in *Zeitschrift fuer Theologie und Kirche,* II, No. 1, p. 65, gives evidence of a keen analytical mind and is invaluable for our understanding of the spiritual conditions of the times, not only in Denmark, but also in Germany. He was called the Luther of his day. If we had no other indications, the files of Rudelbach und Guerickes *Zeitschrift* would be sufficient to show that this was no sterile period. Rationalism was sterile and was on the way out. Its very sterility contributed to its death. For the facts about Rudelbach see Meusel, *op. cit.,* V, 681—683; *Religion in Geschichte und Gegenwart,* IV, p. 2130. See also Sihler's description of Rudelbach, *Lebenslauf,* I, p. 112.

[20] Guericke should not be overlooked when the productive minds of Saxony in the 1830's are mentioned. Already at the age of 21, in 1824, he established himself as an instructor at Halle. His learning was spoken of far and wide. He was a positive Lutheran and an inveterate enemy of rationalism. He tried to get Walther out of the clutches of Martin Stephan and, according to Walther's own confession, warned him against the danger of idolizing a man. To which Walther replied: "Shall I forsake the man who by the grace of God saved my soul from perdition?" See the lengthy footnote in Walther's *Lebenslauf* of Buenger, p. 29.

Bavaria, then at Leipzig, and finally in Munich.[21] What a productive decade for Lutheran theology!

Spiritual conditions in the individual congregations seem to be at or near normal. Church attendance is good, at least at the main service. Prayers are said at meals in the individual homes. Hymns are sung every Sunday afternoon under the direction of Father and Mother. The extremely popular but somewhat piously rationalistic *Stunden der Andacht* by Zschokke [22] are read regularly in the family circle, followed by the morning and evening prayers of Luther's Small Catechism. Orphans are being cared for in private homes, and innumerable eleemosynary institutions are springing up all over Saxony. Occasional periods of famine and unemployment cause suffering, but there is a remarkable spirit of surrender to God's will and trust in His loving-kindness. Evidently the extreme radicalism of Paulus, Roehr, and Wegscheider is no longer having much effect upon the spiritual life of the average layman.[23] Looking back upon this decade, W. Sihler, for many years a leading spirit in the Missouri Synod, says: "It was a period of spiritual springtime. After a long and dreary winter, during which rationalism dominated the pulpit, the lecture hall, and the press, the Lord raised up men of valor, equipped with mental and spiritual power, who were happy to bear testimony on the platform and in the press. The hoarse cawing of the crows was gradually silenced. The voice of the turtledove was heard in the land. The lark and the nightingale were sending their sweet songs of praise upward to the throne of God's grace." [24] When the blindfold was finally taken from Keyl's eyes, he wrote to Rudelbach from Perry County: "What an impudent lie to claim that there was no hope for the Lutheran Church, none in Saxony, none in Germany, none in all Europe! Incontrovertible facts show the very opposite to be true. What an assumption to pass judgment

---

21 Gottlieb Christoph Adolf von Harless became a *Privatdozent* at Erlangen in 1829 at the age of 23. Seven years later, in 1836, his attitude was the prevailing one in the theological faculty of Erlangen. In 1838 he founded the *Zeitschrift fuer Protestantismus und Kirche*. Harless had the ability to get some of the best Lutheran theologians to write for his *Zeitschrift*. Such a man was W. Vilmar.

22 Meusel, *op. cit.*, VII, p. 390. Zschokke can hardly be called a rationalist, nor can he be called a pietist. His *Stunden der Andacht* went through many editions.

23 Hennig, *op. cit.*, p. 14.

24 Sihler, W., *Lebenslauf*, I, p. 90.

and condemn pastors and congregation members who still uphold the Confessions of our Lutheran Church!" [25] Of a truth, Lutheran theology was beginning to flourish, and men like Rudelbach sensed the dawn of a new day for the Christian Church.[26]

Now let us look at the Saxon pastor in the midst of these conditions. From what strata of human society did he come? Very frequently his father was a pastor, in some cases even his grandfather and great-grandfather.[27] The ministry was still perhaps the most honorable profession in the land. In Saxony the pastor was a representative of both the State and the Church, and it was very natural that another great source of supply for the ministry be the professional government employees other than the ministers.[28]

Born in Saxony, the future minister was baptized within eight days of his birth in the Lutheran Church according to the law.[29] In the elementary public school (*Volksschule*) he was under the influence of Christian teaching.[30] Luther's Small Catechism, the

---

[25] Rudelbach und Guerickes *Zeitschrift*, III (1842), No. 1, p. 107.

[26] *Op. cit.*, II (1841), No. 1, pp. 65—115.

[27] O. H. Walther and C. F. W. Walther were descendants of a line of pastors. Their father, grandfather, and great-grandfather had been pastors. The same is true of Ernst Moritz Buerger. See pages 3 and 4 of his unpublished autobiography. Johann Friedrich Buenger was the scion of a line of Saxon clerics that reached away back into the days of the Reformation. See C. F. W. Walther's *Lebenslauf* of Buenger, p. 23. G. H. Loeber was a twig of a family of Lutheran theologians. His father was superintendent in Cahla in the duchy of Altenburg, Saxony. Two other forebears had been superintendents in the same duchy. See *Der Lutheraner*, VI (1850), p. 145. Theodor Julius Brohm was the only son of a pastor in Kallenberg, kingdom of Saxony. See Pastor Loeber's "Vermeldungsbuch" for Palm Sunday, 1843. Loeber pronounces the banns of Brohm and "die geschiedene Frau von Wurmb."

[28] Ottomar Fuerbringer's father was a lawyer, who was an employee of the State. He is called a *Regierungs- und Consistorial-Advocat*. See *Der Lutheraner*, IXL (1893), p. 155. E. G. W. Keyl's father was the receiver-general of taxes in Leipzig, Saxony. See Koestering, *Leben und Wirken* of Keyl, p. 8.

[29] Ziehnert, *op. cit.*, p. 175. The law of August 2, 1817, stipulated any time within eight days of birth.

[30] The elementary school of the community was under the supervision of the pastor, not so much as a pastor but as a representative of the State. Meusel, *op. cit.*, VI, p. 102. The local pastor examined the schoolteacher and confirmed or rejected his appointment in that part of Saxony known as Lausitz. Ziehnert, *op. cit.*, I, p. 128. Reading, writing, and arithmetic were regarded as accessory subjects during the seventeenth and part of the eighteenth centuries and began to come into their own as essential subjects when the State began to be interested in the child as a citizen. Unlike other German states, Saxony arranged its public schools in the nineteenth century on a confessional basis. Constitutionally the schools belonged to, and were

Bible, and the hymnbook were the most important textbooks. At the age of ten or eleven the future pastor entered the Gymnasium (*schola, lyceum, collegium*).[31] This institution prepared boys for professional study in the best traditions of the Christianized humanism of Melanchthon. Latin, Greek, and Hebrew were the principal studies. There was no choice of subjects. The student took the same course, whether he intended to be a doctor, lawyer, or minister. About this time mathematics, the natural sciences, and German history and literature were beginning to receive more attention at the expense particularly of Latin.[32] The full course lasted nine years, embracing roughly our junior high school, senior high school, and junior college. At the age of about nineteen years the future pastor was ready for the beginning of his professional studies at the university.

Armed with the report and recommendation from the Gymnasium, he knocks at the door of the university to begin a course of professional preparation, which lasts for three years, two of which must be spent in a university of his homeland.[33]

The prescribed courses for the future minister in 1826 were dogmatics, symbolics, history (especially church history), homiletics, exegesis, pedagogy, pastoral theology, logic, and metaphysics.[34] Although the length of the course was three years, the student who wished to continue beyond that time was not only permitted but urged to do so.[35]

---

supported by, school communities (*Schulgemeinden*). These school communities were either Lutheran or Roman Catholic. See *Religion in Geschichte und Gegenwart*, V, p. 1695.

[31] C. F. W. Walther was nine years and nine months old when he entered the Gymnasium at Schneeberg. J. F. Buenger was thirteen years old when he entered the Fuerstenschule at Meissen, but he had attended some other special school before he came to the Gymnasium. O. Fuerbringer entered the third class (Quarta) at the age of nine years. He had been prepared by a private teacher in his home. See *Der Lutheraner*, IXL (1893), p. 155. W. Sihler entered the Gymnasium at the age of ten years. See his *Lebenslauf*, I, p. 12.

[32] *Religion in Geschichte und Gegenwart*, II, p. 1559. For an instructive contemporary article on changes in the curriculum of the Gymnasium see *Zeitschrift fuer Protestantismus und Kirche*, V, pp. 428—438.

[33] Ziehnert, *op. cit.*, I, p. 117. For a Saxon this meant Leipzig, Jena, Halle, or Wittenberg. Prussia removed this restriction in 1810. Bavaria made all three years compulsory at a university of the homeland. The two Walthers, Keyl, Buenger, and Buerger studied at Leipzig, Loeber at Jena, Sihler at Berlin.

[34] *Op. cit.*, I, p. 118. Also E. M. Buerger's "Lebensgeschichte," p. 41.

[35] Keyl was a man of sufficient means and continued his studies at Leipzig after the prescribed three years had been completed. See Koestering's *Leben und Wirken* of Keyl, p. 18.

Three months before he was to complete his formal study of theology the future pastor wrote a polite letter to the *Consistorium*. He enclosed his *inscriptio* and *testimonia diligentiae* in dogmatics, symbolics, and church history, which evidently were considered the chief subjects. He also enclosed a *testimonium morum* of the university council. In the letter he asked for permission to take the examination *pro candidatura et licentia concionandi*. The purpose of this examination was to show that he was able to take over a congregation. It also made it possible for him to preach either as guest or as substitute. For this his first big examination he had to bring his baptismal certificate, his Hebrew Old Testament, Greek New Testament, a Latin edition of the Lutheran Symbolical Books, and, if he lived in Prussia, a document which proved that he had completed his military service. Conducted through the medium of the Latin language, the oral part of the examination was open to the public. At the conclusion of the oral examination the superintendent or the court preacher assigned a text and asked the future pastor to furnish an outline for a sermon on this text either in Latin or in German, and several days later also a complete sermon worked out on the basis of this outline.[36] A part of this sermon was preached behind locked doors of the church, with the *examinator* as audience. Then several children of school age were brought in, and the examinee had to give a practical demonstration of his ability to conduct a class in confirmation instruction.[37]

Having passed the examination *pro candidatura*, the young man was now ready to take over a parish. But alas, the number of candidates was so great and the number of openings so small that he had to wait for years before he could hope to get a permanent appointment.[38] In the meantime he continued his studies

---

[36] In his "Lebensgeschichte," pp. 48—49, E. M. Buerger, later pastor in Perry County and in Buffalo, N.Y., tells how the celebrated Dr. von Ammon and Superintendent Seltenreich examined him for three hours — Dr. von Ammon on the condition of the soul between death and resurrection, and Superintendent Seltenreich on Old and New Testament exegesis.

[37] Buerger, p. 49, tells us how greatly relieved he felt after he had completed his examinations and received a grade of "gut" on his sermon and "sehr gut" on his catechization. Ziehnert, *op. cit.*, I, p. 119, tells the future candidate not to be frightened. If he has worked faithfully at the university, he will have no difficulty. Buerger says that Keyl postponed his examination for a full year because he was afraid of it.

[38] The number of candidates connected with Stephanism (Brohm, Buenger, Fuerbringer, Geyer, Goenner, Kluegel, Schieferdecker, Wege, and Wetzel) in-

privately and tried to earn his living as teacher in some special
school, or as assistant of a pastor, or (which seems to have been
most frequent) as private tutor in the home of some upper-middle-
class or upper-class citizen who could afford to give his children
a better elementary education than the public schools of Saxony
were offering.[39]   At the beginning of the third decade of the nineteenth century the candidates who professed a Bible-centered faith
were more fortunate than their fellows who did not.   For this
reason: Some Bible-loving baron or prince who had the right of
appointment over the parishes of his territory (*Patronatsrecht*)
would appoint only such men.[40]   Furthermore, there were several
outstanding superintendents, such as Rudelbach in Glauchau and
Guericke in Halle, who favored men of a strictly confessional
attitude.

But what was the candidate to do regarding a permanent
position?   Was he to wait until a congregation came to him with
an offer?   That would happen only in the few cases in which the
parish was outstanding and the man had previously demonstrated
unusual ability.   The normal thing for the candidate to do was
to watch for openings.   The moment one occurred which was to
his liking and for which he thought he was fit, he made application
to the *collator*, that is, either some member of the landed aristocracy
who had the right of appointment or the *Consistorium,* whichever
the case might be.[41]

dicates in a manner how many were present in the ministerial profession at
that time.   In his *Lebenslauf* of Buenger, p. 21, Walther speaks of a *Can-
didatenverein,* which conducted regular meetings.

[39] C. F. W. Walther was a private tutor in the home of Friedemann
Loeber at Kahla from Easter, 1834, to the end of November, 1836 (see
Guenther's *Dr. C. F. W. Walther,* p. 17). — Buenger did the same work, first in
the home of his parents, then in Pirna and in Dresden (see *Lebenslauf* of
Buenger, written by C. F. W. Walther, p. 22).

[40] Thus Keyl, Walther, Buerger, received permanent positions compara-
tively early in life.   Keyl was only twenty-five; Walther was twenty-six;
Buerger was twenty-seven.   Many had to wait until they were forty.   See
Koestering's *Leben und Wirken* of Keyl, p. 18.

[41] In the district of Dresden (Kreis-Directions-Bezirk) there were 173
parishes under private appointment of some baron or prince, and 107 under
appointment of the king through the *Consistorium.*   In the Leipzig district
239 pastors owed their appointment to some nobleman, and 114 to the king;
in the Zwickau district 205 to some nobleman and 104 to the king.   These
figures are for the year 1837 and are taken from the *Kirchlich-statistisches
Handbuch fuer das Koenigreich Sachsen,* Carl Ramming, Herausgeber, Dresden, 1838.   It contains a list of parishes of all Saxony with their pastors and
schoolteachers, length of service, place of service, and place and date of birth.

Custom had decreed certain rules which must be observed in all efforts to secure positions: Do not go after a place too soon after your graduation from the university. You had better wait at least two years. Do not go after the biggest and most desirable parishes. Besides making a bad impression, you are impeding your theological and scientific development, because your time and energy will be consumed by the routine duties of a large parish. Proceed cautiously. Visit the *collator*. Be very polite. Tell him the facts about your life, and ask for permission to preach a guest sermon in the church of his residence. Do not be too persistent; do not use flattery; and do not promise to marry his daughter or niece. The worst thing you can do is to offer him a bribe in money.[42]

After the candidate has received the approval of the *collator*, he is to inform the superintendent of the district to which the parish belongs of this happy event and ask for an opportunity to take the examination *pro ministerio* (sometimes called *pro munere*). The superintendent makes the arrangements, and the *Consistorium* conducts the examination. The subjects covered are much the same as those of the examination *pro candidatura*, but the purpose is to show that the examinee is now ready to take over a designated parish. For this reason the superintendent and the *collator* play a much larger role in the second examination than they do in the first.[43] In Saxony, Prussia, and some other German states the candidate must have reached the age of twenty-five years (canonical age) before he can take over a parish. If he has not reached this age but has an opportunity to get a parish, he must secure a dispensation from the king.[44]

The next hurdle for the candidate was the trial sermon and the trial catechization. Usually they were in the church before the en-

---

A supplement, inserted between pages 356 and 357 and called a "Tabellarische Uebersicht," presents the totals by districts, also the totals of the right of appointment. The copy in Pritzlaff Memorial Library is from the private library of C. F. W. Walther.

[42] Ziehnert, *op. cit.*, I, p. 122.

[43] The procedure was taken over from the Roman Catholic Church. In the Council of Trent the necessary stipulations were made. The bishop and two assisting examiners conducted the examination. Usually a larger number of men were examined at one time. Constitutionally and theoretically the bishop selected the man who had the highest rating. See Meusel, *op. cit.*, II, p. 340.

[44] Ziehnert, *op. cit.*, I, pp. 127—130.

tire congregation, and the *collator* and the superintendent were present. The representatives of the parish (called *Kirchenrat* or *Kirchenvorstand* or *Kirchenaelteste* or *Kirchenjuraten*) were asked individually whether they had any objections to the doctrine or conduct of the candidate. If not, the *collator* issued the call, duly notarized by the civil authorities.

The procedure in calling a pastor shows how little power the congregation possessed in Saxony. The local board went by various high-sounding names but had comparatively little authority. They represented the congregation over against the *Consistorium* and the *collator*. They kept the buildings in repair, supervised the janitors, administered the funds which came in through the plate collections (*Klingelbeutel*) on Sundays. In some cases they were appointed by the pastor in collaboration with the *collator*. As far as power over the ministry was concerned, the *Kirchenrat* was merely and mildly negative. Even where there was definite opposition to a candidate in a parish, he was advised to accept the appointment and win the hearts of his opponents. The congregation as such remained passive and inactive. It was the raw material upon which the pastor worked with the means of grace. Anything that resembled congregationalism was looked at askance.[45]

Nor do the letters and documents of those who later organized the Missouri Synod indicate a desire for constitutional changes in the direction of decentralization. These men gladly receive appointments from landed aristocrats.[46] They praise the piety of these landlords.[47] To be sure, they oppose certain superintendents and certain members of the *Consistorium*. However, this is done not for constitutional but for purely administrative reasons. There is

---

[45] Ziehnert, *op. cit.,* I, pp. 104, 127—134; Meusel, *op. cit.,* III, pp. 806—811; II, pp. 717—720; III, p. 646; *Religion in Geschichte und Gegenwart,* III, pp. 948 to 1045; Buerger, "Lebensgeschichte," p. 72.

[46] Buerger, "Lebensgeschichte," pp. 75—76. O. H. Walther, "Acta die Anstellung des Candidaten des Predigtamtes Otto Hermann Walther als Pfarr-vicar in Langenchursdorf und Lauenberg betreffend." Superintendentur Waldenburg, Litt. II, No. 9, Rep. II, Vol. Lec. 1. Concordia Historical Institute has typewritten copies of all the documents pertaining to this appointment. They were made in the archives at Waldenburg. C. F. W. Walther, "Auszug aus den Acten der Evangel. Superintendentur Penig bei Chemnitz betreffend Wahl, Ordination und Amtseinfuehrung des Predigtamtscandidaten C. F. W. Walther zu Braeunsdorf." E. G. W. Keyl received his appointment from the Count of Einsiedel. Walther received his appointment also from the Count of Einsiedel. Koestering, *Leben und Wirken* of Keyl, p. 19.

[47] Buerger, "Lebensgeschichte," p. 71, Fuerst von Schoenburg is called "very pious and Christian" ("sehr fromm und christlich").

no demand for a so-called "free church," a church independent of state control, in whose government laymen would have a voice. As a matter of fact, there is a strong tendency towards centralization of power in the hands of the ministry among the future Missourians. They were very ready to approve Martin Stephan's demands for the episcopal form of government.[48] Inside the group, power tended to gravitate to the ministers, particularly to Stephan. Stephan was all powerful. Rudelbach went so far as to call the behavior of the Stephanites over against Stephan "a deification of man." [49] Having come to his senses, Keyl called it "a new popery." [50]

[48] The minutes of the meetings in which constitutional and administrative measures pertaining to the emigrant society were discussed and voted upon by an executive committee are recorded in MS. They are known as Fasciculi III, IV, V, VI. Each fascicle is a bundle of papers. There are about 100 pages to each fascicle. The size of the page is 10 inches by 18 inches. There are no page numbers. Fasciculus III contains, among other things, the minutes of November 13, 1837. There was a long discussion concerning the care and attention which the company should give to the person of Pastor Martin Stephan. "His person," so they said in this meeting, "is of the utmost importance for the welfare of our souls and for the welfare of the whole Church. Every effort must now be made that the most reverend archbishop of the Lutheran Church be kept alive." In the meeting of December 6, 1837, there was a long discussion about the episcopal vestments, especially about the kind of headgear ("Kopfbedeckung") that would set the bishop off properly from the other clergy ("Auszeichnung des Bishofs zu bestimmen"). The spiritual court is to consist of one bishop and nine assistants ("Diakonen"). In the meeting of September 27, 1838, the chief discussion centered in the amount of money that was to be set aside for the care of the bishop and ruler ("Regent") of the entire united Lutheran Church during the journey to America. After a long discussion they finally fixed the sum at $1,500. The money was to be placed at his disposal. During the voyage on the *Olbers* Martin Stephan was officially requested on the 14th of January, 1839, to accept the honor of a bishop. O. H. Walther was the leader of the men who made the request. In St. Louis, on February 24, 1839, the entire company through its representatives, headed by Pastors Loeber, Keyl, O. H. Walther, C. F. W. Walther, and E. M. Buerger, declared and published a request that his Reverence institute an episcopal form of church government and that he accept the office of the first apostolic Lutheran bishop. This was their unanimous and most urgent prayer ("einstimmig und mit angelegenster Bitte"). They say that their soul's welfare is bound up in the episcopal form and that they will obey any and all commands issued by the Bishop. The signature of C. F. W. Walther is plainly visible on this document. The original is in Concordia Historical Institute; a photostatic copy is in my files. This petition reveals utter subjection to a man, a servility bordering on the Oriental. Rudelbach was not using hyperbolic language when he spoke of "deification." Even when the pastors had decided that Stephan must be expelled from the colony (May 30, 1839), no one wished to enter the room in which he was staying. The reason for this reluctance was the respect for the office ("Furcht vor dem Amte"). There was something morbid and superstitious about their attitude. See Vehse, *op. cit.*, p. 20.

[49] Walther, *Lebenslauf* of Buenger, p. 29.

[50] *Zeitschrift fuer die gesamte lutherische Theologie und Kirche*, III (1842), No. 1, p. 101.

The ministers took the lead in all efforts to concentrate power. There was no democracy in the baggage of the future Missourians when they put out to sea in November, 1838, even as there was no democracy in the State Church of Saxony.

What were the tasks of a pastor in Saxony during the 1830's? His chief activity, of course, was preaching. With its doctrine of the spoken Word as a means of grace, the Lutheran Reformation had greatly increased the emphasis upon preaching. This emphasis is clearly evident in Saxony. The superintendents lay great stress on preaching when examining and recommending candidates for parishes.[51] The outlines of trial sermons are recorded in the archives of the superintendents. At the end of each year the pastors were asked to send their sheaf of sermon outlines for the year to the superintendent, who in turn was to send them on to the *Consistorium*.[52] And there was plenty of preaching in Saxony. There was a sermon in the main service, with Holy Communion, every Sunday morning, beginning at seven o'clock in the summer and at eight in the winter, which according to law was not to last longer than one hour. There was a midday service with a sermon beginning at twelve noon. There was a vesper service with a sermon at two. This service was conducted chiefly for young people and servants. The three great holidays of the Church, Christmas, Easter, and Pentecost, were celebrated with three days of services each. From St. Martin's Day (November 10) until Easter there were midweek services with preaching, beginning at seven in the morning during the summer and at eight during the winter.[53] Sermons were preached in conection with all funerals, even those of poor people and paupers.[54] Some marriages were solemnized with and others without sermons.[55] And finally, there were sermons for

---

[51] As an example I should like to cite the action of Supt. Dr. Leo, of Waldenburg. When O. H. Walther resigned as his father's assistant in Langenchursdorf, August, 1838, there were six candidates for the position. Candidate Fuellkruss was chosen after careful investigation of all candidates. The records show that ability to preach weighed very heavily in every deliberation. See typewritten copy of the "Acta" in Concordia Historical Institute, Litt. LII, No. 11, Rep. II, Vol. Loc. 1.

[52] Ziehnert, *op. cit.*, I, p. 154.

[53] *Op. cit.*, I, pp. 155—163. General Art, III, rescript on March 9, 1708, fixed the maximum length of the main sermon at one hour and of the secondary and weekday sermon at forty-five minutes.

[54] *Op. cit.*, I, p. 167. Sometimes there were several funerals in one day.

[55] *Op. cit.*, I, p. 251.

3

military events and national holidays.   The pastor of Saxony was
a preaching parson.

In addition to preaching the pastor had to perform all baptisms
of the parish, conduct all funerals, solemnize all marriages, make
sick calls and administer private Communion, conduct confirmation
classes four times a week, hear confession for individuals at an
appointed time every week, supervise the school or schools of the
parish, keep an endless number of records, witness oaths, certify
documents on the basis of archival records, make various and
sundry reports, and listen to quarrels between husband and wife.[56]

What remuneration did the pastor receive, and how did he
get it?   First of all, he belonged to a class which gave him standing
("Standesperson") and privileges.   While Prussia glorified the
lieutenant, the captain, and the colonel, Saxony still honored the
theologian.   Insults offered to pastors were punished more severely
than when offered to others.[57]   Pastors could not be arrested and
put into jail for nonpayment of debts.   They were exempt from most
taxes, imposts, and services.   Normally they were exempt from all
military imposts and duties, including the obligation of housing
soldiers during war or army maneuvers.   They had to pay con-
sumers' taxes, but refunds were made to them either monthly or
quarterly.   While they were free from most internal taxes, including
the tax on beer, meat, and salt, they were not exempt from duties

---

[56] The above paragraph is based on Ziehnert's *Praktisches evangelisches
Kirchenrecht*.   There are long discussions, rules, and laws regarding all these
activities.   Some of these activities the pastors of larger parishes could delegate
to assistants; others could not be delegated.   There was a large body of laws,
rules, rescripts, observances, and customs governing the conduct of the ministerial office.   In a large parish the pastor needed to be something of an
ecclesiastical lawyer.   At any rate an opus like Ziehnert's with its laws,
rescripts, and observances was a handy book to have in the study.   The
amount of work varied with the size of the parish.   Most of the fathers of
the Missouri Synod were very young during their ministry in Saxony.   Their
parishes for that reason tended to be smaller; but even at that Buerger
singlehanded served a parish of 2,060 baptized members; Keyl, one of 1,340
members; C. F. W. Walther, one of 581; O. H. Walther, together with his
aging father, served the parish of Langenchursdorf, which numbered 2,687
members.   When young O. H. Walther entered the service of the parish in 1834,
there were 2,612 members.   Four hundred eighty-one were of school age
("schulpflichtig").   There were two schools in the parish.   Langenchursdorf ·
proper had 325 school children, with one teacher.   The schools were in bad
condition.   See the typewritten copy of the "Acta" pertaining to Langenchursdorf in Concordia Historical Institute.   All figures, with the exception of those
concerning Langenchursdorf in 1834, are for the year 1837 and are taken from
the *Kirchlich-statistisches Handbuch fuer das Koenigreich Sachsen*.   Carl
Ramming, Dresden, 1838.

[57] Ziehnert, *op. cit.*, II, p. 508.

on imported goods, particularly not on whisky, beer, silks, and satins.[58] The pastors living in the duchy of Altenburg, however, were free from the obligation of paying duty on victuals brought in from Bohemia. The reason given for this rule is their proximity to the land of the Czechs.[59] In all parts of Saxony pastors were exempt from inheritance taxes,[60] and in some parts they could use the highways (*Chausseen*) and bridges without paying toll.[61]

The actual income of a pastor came from divers and sundry sources. I know of no profession whose members were paid in so many different ways and so well. One begins to understand the German proverb concerning the cleric's bottomless bag. For the sake of convenience let us discuss his income in money and in kind. In the first place, if he served a rural parish (and he usually began there), he had a fixed annual salary of not less than two hundred taler per annum. While the old taler was worth three German marks, its purchasing power in 1830 was greater than the sum of several times three marks. In fact, in all cash computations of clerical incomes one must keep the purchasing power of the money constantly in mind. Otherwise comparisons between 1830 and the present time might be misleading. While the sum of two hundred taler was the minimum in rural and small-town parishes, there were men even in these classifications who were getting seven hundred taler as a fixed annual salary; [62] and, of course, the pastors in the larger cities received a much higher fixed cash remuneration. This money was paid out of the public treasury ("aerarium") and was largely the income from land that had been put out at rent or from

---

[58] *Op. cit.,* II, p. 504.   [60] *Op. cit.,* p. 507.

[59] *Op. cit.,* p. 504.   [61] *Op. cit.,* p. 505.

[62] The fixed annual salary in cash was decided by the *Consistorium* (Ziehnert, *op. cit.,* II, p. 462). The sum was not in the specified call. Evidently the candidate under consideration had a conference with the superintendent or the *Consistorium* or both. In this conference the annual cash salary was discussed and fixed. Nothing is said regarding this amount in documents pertaining to individual appointments. Occasionally parishes were divided. In those cases the income of the parish was one of the main points of discussion. Thus Dr. Meissner, Superintendent of the Waldenburg district, to which Langenchursdorf belonged, wrote a long report covering the fourteen typewritten pages found in the Concordia Historical Institute's copy of the "Acta," in which he discusses conditions in the parish and shows why he thinks it should be divided. In this report he states that Pastor G. H. W. Walther, C. F. W. Walther's father, was receiving an annual fixed salary of seven hundred taler. The report is dated April 6, 1835. In Hannover, where the tendency to convert payments in kind into payments in money had perhaps progressed a little farther, there were three classifications: 300 to 600, 600 to 900, 900 to 1,200 taler.

money that had been placed at interest.[63]   In some parishes it was
the income from mines.[64]   In country parishes this was decidedly
the smaller part of the pastor's income.[65]   In addition to the fixed
annual salary the pastor received a fixed land tax from the smaller
landholders and a species of poll tax from all cottagers.[66]   Under
the heading of cash remuneration we must also list the various and
sundry fees.   They are called accidental because neither the time,
nor the amount, nor the quality was fixed.[67]   The original idea was
that these payments should be left to the discretion and good will
of the parishioners.   Then a division was made into free-will and
compulsory fees.   The free-will fees were for baptisms, attendance
at confession, and participation in the Lord's Supper, while the compulsory fees were for the pronouncement of the marriage banns, for
the marriage ceremony itself, funerals, formal exhortations in the
case of oaths and of people who had fallen into gross sin, certificates
based upon archival records, and special reports on matters in dispute.   As time went on, all fees became compulsory, and a definite
schedule of fees was adopted by the legislative procedure of September, 1812.   Four times a year every person who had reached the
age of twelve years had to pay the pastor one penny ("Opferpfennig," also "Schwengpfennig");   and on certain Sundays and
holidays the entire contents of the plate offering was given either
to the pastor or to the schoolteacher.[68]

An important part of the pastor's remuneration consisted in
contributions in kind made by men who held arable land.   The contribution was called corn rent ("Fruchtzins") or corn tithe
("Fruchtzehend") and in some parishes consisted of a tenth, in
others of a fourth, a ninth, and in some only of a twelfth of all
small grains (wheat, oats, barley, and, in some parishes, flax) that

---

[63] Ziehnert, *op. cit.*, II, p. 466.
[64] *Op. cit.*, p. 483.   [66] *Op. cit.*, p. 466.
[65] *Op. cit.*, II, p. 466.   [67] *Op. cit.*, p. 467.
[68] *Op. cit.*, p. 469. The report of Dr. Meissen, Superintendent, in connection
with the Langenchursdorf parish, gives the income from fees for the year 1834
as follows: baptisms, twelve reichstaler and twenty-two groschen; confession,
fifty-eight taler; funerals, fifteen reichstaler and eight groschen; weddings,
six reichstaler and sixteen groschen; Opferpfennig, five reichstaler; formal
exhortations in case of oaths, one reichstaler; sick Communion, one reichstaler
and sixteen groschen; wheat contribution, thirty-six reichstaler; oats, sixteen
reichstaler and sixteen groschen; barley, twenty-seven reichstaler; pay out
of the church treasury, two reichstaler and nine groschen. The total income
from this source was one hundred ninety-two reichstaler and twenty-one
groschen.

was raised on individual landholdings inside the parish. In addition to the great tithe, which included wheat, oats, barley, and flax, there was the small tithe, which included vegetables, such as peas, beans, beets, onions, potatoes, cabbage, maize, hemp, millet, and orchard products. The grain was either delivered in bundles ("Garbenzehend") or threshed and delivered in sacks ("Sackzehend"). Any effort to deliver products of poorer quality was severely censured and was usually prevented by the fact that according to law the pastor or his representative was to appear in the field at harvesttime and select every tenth bundle. If the pastor or his representative did not appear at the time specified in the law, the landholder could engage two officials at the expense of the pastor. These men supervised the selection of bundles for the pastor. According to law no grain could be harvested without the pastor's knowledge. In some parishes the landholder had to bring the bundles or the sacks of grain to the pastor's yard; in others the pastor's representative had to go into the fields and get them. No fields could be left fallow or diverted to less gainful produce without the consent of the pastor. New land was exempt from both the great and the small tithe. To promote land development in Prussia, this exemption lasted for twelve years from the date that a certain piece was put under plow. In the parishes in which the grain was delivered in sacks the pastor kept the amount he needed for seed and for the use of his family and servants and sold the rest. Occasionally some parishes held tithe rights on certain pieces of land in other parishes. In those cases the pastor's representatives had to go and get his share. The men who held only yardlands or hides and did not pay tithes were obligated to pay hide breads ("Hufenbrote") instead of tithes. These loaves had to conform to a certain size and had to be conducive to the pastor's health. Cash could be substituted for bread at the rate of six groschen (groschen — a little more than three pfennig) per bread. In some parishes the pastor received a mixed tithe, or an income from the increase of domestic animals, such as calves, lambs, chickens, wool, milk, butter, cheese, honey, wax, etc. All claims for payments in kind were considered a prior lien at law and had to be satisfied before a change in possession could be effected.[69]

The chief part of a pastor's income, however, was derived from

---

[69] *Op. cit.*, II, pp. 476—478.

land which he held in his right as pastor and which he could either
cultivate himself through his servants or put out at rent.   This
was called a clerical living or a glebe ("Pfarrguth," "Widdem,"
"Widenmuth") and consisted of the yard with its houses for the
pastor, the renter, and the servants, and its barns, stables, sheds,
and pens.   In addition, there was the arable land, the meadow land,
the garden, the wooded lot, the vineyard, the pond for a fish
hatchery, etc.   In a few cases pastors were actual landlords, from
whom others held fiefs.   All buildings of the glebe were under the
supervision of the *Consistorium* and had to be built and maintained
by the parishioners at the direction of the *Consistorium.*   Special
attention had to be given to the health and social rank of the pastor
in the erection and maintenance of buildings.   Rental contracts of
arable land, meadows, vineyards, fishponds, etc., of the glebe had
to have the approval of the *Consistorium* in order to be legal.   This
stipulation was based upon the theory that the church owned them
and that the pastor merely had the use of them as long as he was
pastor of the parish.   If the wooded lot did not produce sufficient
wood for the pastor's needs, he had access to the community wood-
lot like every other landholder.[70]

Finally, in addition to all the payments in money and in kind,
there was a type of remuneration known as emoluments.   Under
this heading contemporary writers on church law in Saxony list
such things as bequests made to pastors personally by pious parishioners, New Year's gifts, engagement and wedding presents, special
allowances in wine, salt, venison, etc.   An interesting form of emolu-
ment was the special payment on beer that was brewed within the
diocese by professional brewers.   Originally pastors were free from
the payment of any tax on beer which they brewed for their own
use.   In 1748 a decree was issued that a duly ordained pastor was
to get forty groschen per barrel on a certain number of barrels of
beer brewed by professional brewers.   This special gratification was
called *Tranksteuerbeneficium.*   The superintendent received forty
groschen per barrel on eight barrels, the city pastor received the
amount on six, the rural pastor on five, the teacher of a boys' school
on two, and the teacher of a girls' school on one barrel of beer.
This money was paid out of the regular beer tax.   In 1819 the date
for the annual payments to the clergy was set at March 31.   The

---

70 *Op. cit.,* II, pp. 480—485.

privilege of private brewing by the pastor without payment of tax
was continued as before, the one restriction being that he could
brew only for his own use and not for sale.   On top of all this the
pastor's community rights in the pasture land, fishing ponds, and
orchards were those of any other member in the community.[71]

Summing up the remuneration of an average pastor in Saxony,
we get a picture something like this: His membership in a highly
privileged group makes life rather comfortable and entitles him to
exemption from taxes and imposts that are beginning to weigh
rather heavily on the backs of many of his fellow countrymen.   He
receives a fixed annual salary in cash of four hundred reichstaler,
which is augmented by approximately one hundred twenty-five
taler in fees.   Emoluments bring in, let us say, another twenty-five
taler.   Commuting into cash the various payments that are made
to him in kind, we get fifty reichstaler in bad years, seventy-five
in average years, and one hundred in good years.   His total income
from his parish, then, averaged six hundred taler.   Multiplying
this sum by two and one half when prices are high and by three
and one half when prices are low, we get a more adequate picture
of the purchasing power in terms of the American dollar of today.
For the sake of convenience let us call this his side income.   His
chief income, of course, is from the glebe.   It is his living.   While
his family is growing, it takes just about all that the glebe can produce to keep victuals on the table, shoes on the feet and clothes on
the backs of the children and other members of the household.
Servants must be maintained, and the amenities of life commensurate with his rank in society must be procured.   When the boys
have been educated and the girls have become willing victims of
successful suitors, the income from the glebe takes care of father
and mother quite adequately.   In good years it may even add to the
savings that have accumulated over the years from the income in
cash.   All in all, it is a remuneration that offers a rather attractive
security.

Why all this?   And what does it contribute to our understanding of church government in the Missouri Synod?   There were
definite and far-reaching implications in the fact that the men who
later founded the Missouri Synod came from the most highly privileged class in Saxony.   Accustomed to the enjoyment of favors and

---

[71] *Op. cit.*, II, 487—491.

to a mode of living that very few people in their homeland or in any other state of Europe could enjoy at that time, they were not likely to get or promote ideas of democracy either in Church or State. Outside of life on the moon they probably knew less about government by the people in the Church than they did of anything else. Of the difficulties involved in the task of establishing a Church independent of the State they were blissfully ignorant. If Luther could say: "I have not the people for it" (namely, for self-government in the Church), they could talk likewise and with the very same justification. The laymen who came to St. Louis in the winter of 1839 were as innocent as newborn babes about the task of establishing a Church independent of the State. Perhaps the only thing that they knew about such a Church was that it did not have a *Consistorium.* Only persons brought up on German paternalism, surrounded by a Metternich-created post-Napoleonic world, and blissfully inexperienced in matters of government could have fallen for the pipe dreams promoted by Martin Stephan. It required a cataclysmic event to tear them up by the roots and transplant them across the sea. The depth of their later disillusionment can be measured only by the height of their previous innocence.

CHAPTER THREE

—————

STEPHAN AND STEPHANISM

MARTIN STEPHAN, the Bohemian preacher who led a company of Germans to the backwoods of Missouri in the late fall of 1838, was an unusual man. His powers of persuasion were abnormally strong. Men of learning and men of ignorance, men of wealth and men of poverty, were hypnotized by the spell of his spoken word and were persuaded to part with things most dear to their hearts. Among his followers were lawyers,[1] clergymen,[2] school-teachers,[3] merchants,[4] government employees of high rank,[5] who were persuaded to give up positions that were bringing honor and yielding financial security. Women parted with their husbands, and mothers forsook their infant children in order that "they might follow Christ to America."[6] To some of his contem-

---

[1] F. A. Marbach, C. E. Vehse.

[2] E. M. Buerger, E. G. W. Keyl, G. H. Loeber, C. F. W. Walther, O. H. Walther. The following were candidates of theology: J. F. Buenger, T. J. Brohm, O. Fuerbringer, C. L. Geyer, J. Goenner, O. Kluegel, G. A. Schiefer-decker, B. O. Welzel, K. W. Welzel.

[3] J. G. Hellwig, F. Koch, C. A. Schuetzler, F. Winter, J. G. A. K. Zoege.

[4] A. H. Doederlein, P. H. Berje, H. F. Fischer, J. G. Hoehne, J. K. Hoehne.

[5] F. W. Barthel.
The above occupational data are taken from official ship lists. Gustave W. Polack, professor at Concordia Seminary, St. Louis, made photostatic copies of the originals in New Orleans, the port of entry for the company. The photostatic copies may be seen in Concordia Historical Institute, Concordia Seminary, St. Louis, Mo.

[6] Pleissner, *Die kirchlichen Fanatiker im Muldethale*, pp. 8—9. Minutes of Old Trinity Church, St. Louis, Missouri, March 14, 1842. In this meeting the congregation resolved to give Mrs. Nagel financial assistance so that she could go back to her husband and four children, who were still in Saxony. The Nagels had been members of Pastor C. F. W. Walther's congregation in Braeunsdorf, Saxony. She was a Stephanite; he was not. He brought suit against C. F. W. Walther. All documents in the Nagel case have been copied from the official records in Saxony and are on file in the Concordia Historical Institute. See also Rudelbach und Guerickes *Zeitschrift*, III (1842), pp. 94—114. This article by Pastor E. G. W. Keyl is entitled "Offene Bekenntnisse von Pastor Keyl." On page 110 Keyl says: "I was at fault that so many blinded and deluded people gave up their God-appointed callings and their fatherland, to which they owed so much and to which they could have been a blessing. I was at fault that wives left their husbands, to whom they had promised lifelong fidelity, that children left their parents, to whom they should have

41

poraries he was a saint, to others Satan incarnate,[7] to still others
a psychological riddle.[8]

Psychology may help us to understand him. Whatever attitude one may take toward the "guilt" or "innocence" of Martin
Stephan, this much is certain — his was a maladjusted personality.
There is evidence to show that he suffered from a feeling of inferiority and that, instead of meeting the problems of life head on,
he took the roundabout way of compensation through persecutory
delusions and the achievement of complete control over his
fellows.[9]

The present writer's interest in such an interpretation of
Martin Stephan's personality was first aroused by two chance remarks of the Bohemian pastor and by his peculiar teaching concerning suffering and persecution. The first remark was made
when he was beginning to reach the height of his power. In a
footnote to his postil he said: "I lost my parents very early in
life and was forced to fight through many a battle as a poor and

paid back the many favors and kindnesses which they had received in their
infancy, that these children left secretly and in a stubborn mood." Agnes
Buenger, who later married Rev. O. H. Walther and, when widowed by his
death, the Rev. O. Fuerbringer, had an excellent position in Saxony before the
emigration. She asked her brother Candidate J. F. Buenger whether she must
give up her position and follow Stephan to America. He answered. "If you
wish to go to hell, stay here; if you wish to be saved, go with us to America."
The above conversation was related to the present writer by her son, L. Fuerbringer, D. D., president of Concordia Seminary, in July, 1940.

7 F. Delitzsch, a contemporary and an admirer of Stephan, stated contemporary opinion concerning Stephan in his *Wissenschaft, Kunst und Judenthum*, p. 2: "Martin Stephan, a name of ill fame and disrepute among all the
unbelieving and heterodox groups of our day, is cursed by all enemies and
blessed by all friends of the Church. He is a clever and ingenious fellow.
The spirit of Martin Luther and the religious zeal of the blessed martyrs is
in him."

8 Vehse, *op. cit., Die Stephansche Auswanderung nach Amerika*, p. 1.
Vehse uses the term *psychologisches Raetsel*.

9 For the latest information that psychology offers concerning maladjusted
people the following were consulted: J. B. Morgan, *The Psychology of the
Unadjusted School Child*. See particularly Chapter II, "Underlying Causes of
Maladjustment"; Chapter V, "Defense Mechanisms"; Chapter XIII, "Compensation." See also the same author's *The Psychology of Abnormal People*.
Chapter V, "Delusions"; Chapter XV, "Compensatory Disorders." Weathered,
Psychology and Life, Chapter IX, "The Inferiority Complex." Sorenson,
Psychology in Education, Chapter V, "Feelings, Emotions, and Personal Ad-
justments." W. S. Sadler, *The Mind at Mischief*. Shaffer, *The Psychology
of Adjustment*, an objective approach to mental hygiene, Chapter VI, "Adjustment by Defense."

neglected orphan waif." [10] The other remark was made on the eve of his departure from Dresden for America. A wealthy friend had given him a costly fur coat as a farewell gift. He put it on and made this remark: "Behold the pastor of St. Miserable! What a guy he is getting to be!" [11] In both of these remarks there is a large dose of self-pity. The frequency and the manner in which he deals with the problem of persecution and suffering in his sermons excites curiosity. Not only does the subject of suffering bulk large in individual sermons,[12] there are also casual references to the subject in almost every sermon. The student of Luther's sermons who reads Stephan's *Der christliche Glaube* is inclined to say that the amount of space which Luther sets aside for the Pope is devoted by Stephan to the subject of suffering.

Equally striking is the un-Lutheran manner in which he speaks of suffering, apparently referring to affliction as a means of grace.[13] Hardships prepare a Christian for the proper reception of grace.[14]

---

[10] Stephan, *Der christliche Glaube.* The original language of this remark seems to bring out the idea of persecution more forcibly than can be done in translation. It is found on p. XII and reads: "Ich habe meine Aeltern fruehzeitig durch den Tod verloren und musste als arme und verlassene Waise durch viele Drangsale hindurchkaempfen."

[11] Vehse, *op. cit.,* p. 7: "Nun sehen Sie was aus dem Pastor zu St. Miserabilis noch fuer ein grosses Thier wird!"

[12] Stephan, *op. cit.,* pp. 140—156. About three fourths of the sermon is devoted to the subject of suffering. Half of the sermon is devoted to the importance of suffering in the spiritual life of children ("seine Wichtigkeit fuer die ganze Kinderwelt"). This sermon was delivered the Sunday after New Year. He had just devoted considerable time to the subject in his sermon for the Second Christmas Day, pp. 91—98. He devoted about one fourth of the sermon for the Sunday after Christmas to the subject, pp. 123—128. Almost half of the sermon for New Year's Day was used to acquaint his hearers with the sufferings and persecutions that might strike them during the coming year, pp. 134—138. The third part of the sermon for the Second Sunday after Epiphany is devoted to the problem, pp. 195—198. On Reminiscere Sunday he devoted two thirds of the sermon to the subject, pp. 345—359. Two weeks later, on Laetare Sunday, the subject consumes one fourth of the time. The sermon on Jubilate Sunday devoted one third of the time to the subject of suffering, pp. 562—567.

[13] *Op. cit.,* p. 14: "Various hardships are means to keep us more firmly with Christ" ("Allerlei Widerwaertigkeiten sind Mittel in uns, das Bleiben bei Jesu zu befestigen").

[14] *Op. cit.,* p. 17: "The sufferings of our past play an important role throughout our lives. They are to prepare our hearts for the enjoyment of God's grace. They make us able to adapt ourselves to the present and to the future. They are a school of wisdom in which we store up for the future a knowledge of humility, patience, circumspection, faith, and hope" ("Auch die Leiden der verflossenen Zeit behalten fuer unser ganzes Leben eine grosse Wichtigkeit. Sie sollen unser Herze bereiten zum Genuss der Gnade Gottes. Sie machen uns tuechtig, die Gegenwart und Zukunft besser anzuwenden.

Persecutions are signs that God may be planning to use us as instruments to perform great things. The remarkable thing about this attitude is that he speaks of it in the first person singular. In the early months of 1838, while the preparations for the emigration were going vigorously forward, he remarked to Dr. Vehse, "God possibly intends to do great things through me; therefore I must suffer so much disgrace and humiliation." [15] A hidden pride seems to be lurking in these words, even though they sound exceedingly humble. [16]

The millennium offers a way of escape from the sufferings of this present world, and so it does not surprise one to find chiliastic ideas scattered through the sermons of Martin Stephan. As a matter of fact, preoccupation with the ills of this world and schemes for a millennium go hand in hand. [17]

But let us proceed to examine the details of Martin Stephan's life. What was there that would give him a feeling of inferiority?

Sie sind eine Schule der Weisheit, in der wir fuer die Zukunft Demuth, Geduld, Vorsicht, Glauben und Hoffnung lernen"). P. 123: "Suffering is a necessary means of preparation for eternity" ("Das Leiden ist ein nothwendiges Vorbereitungsmittel zur Ewigkeit").

[15] Vehse, *op. cit.*, p. 5: "Gott hat eben vielleicht noch etwas Grosses mit mir vor; darum habe ich hier noch so viel Schmach und Demuethigungen erfahren muessen."

[16] In this connection Stephan's habit of identifying his sufferings with the sufferings of Christ should be noted. *Der christliche Glaube*, p. 33. In the year 1830 a massive cross with a halo was placed over the pulpit of Stephan's church in Dresden. Above this cross stood a Latin inscription in golden letters: "*Crux Christi Nostra Gloria.*" The sufferings which we endure for Christ are our glory. For a picture and discussion of this emblem see *Glaubensbekenntnis der Gemeinde zu St. Johannis in Dresden*, zugleich als Widerlegung der ihr und ihrem Seelsorger, dem Herrn Pastor Martin Stephan, in einigen oeffentlichen Blaettern gemachten Beschuldigungen. Druckerei von Ernst Blochmann, Dresden, 1833.

[17] Stephan, *Der christliche Glaube*, pp. 29—30: "The time will come in this present world when Christ will put an end to the defection and crush the man of sin, the child of perdition, who is in league with Satan and who uses manifold powers of deception and signs and wonders, and who spreads destruction in unrighteousness. The time will come when the kingdoms of this world will belong to the Lord and to His Christ. At that time there will be no more wars; and swords will be beaten into plowshares, and spears into sickles. No one will wound another, nor will he cause destruction. Not only will the multitude of the heathen enter the kingdom of Christ, but all Jewry will be converted to Christ and will be saved." In a sermon preached on Jubilate Sunday, 1831, and printed in pamphlet form by request (Dresden, 1831, Walthersche Buchhandlung) he gives a long and rather somber description of the terrible times through which they were passing; and then, speaking on page 23 of the great and general conversion of all men to Christ, he says, "We know that God still has glorious times in store for this present world. We find this particularly in the prophetical writings of the New Testament." In a footnote he quotes Rev. 20:1-6; Rom. 11:25, 27, 32.

He was born of a racial stock that was regarded as decidedly inferior by his German associates.[18] Both of his parents were Bohemians; and both had been Roman Catholics and had become Lutherans.[19] His father, who was a weaver, decided that his son should follow the same trade. However, his father and his mother died early, leaving their growing son behind as a neglected waif.[20] Without a home, and without the guiding care of a father and a mother, at a time when the lot of an orphan was generally a hard one, the boy's elementary schooling was scanty and desultory. His mother, whose memory he revered, taught him prayers which he remembered all his life.[21] Before his father died, he impressed, with the zeal of a recent convert, the importance of Bible study upon the young child's mind. The fear of God was burnt into his soul.

His early history made him obnoxious to the Roman Catholics of his early environment. He was hated as the son of a turncoat and renegade. The opposition of his early associates, on the other hand, tended to develop in him a despotic and contentious temper, which, if anything, became more pronounced as the years rolled by.

In order to escape the persecutions of his Roman Catholic environment in his homeland, he left Bohemia at the age of twenty-one as a journeyman weaver and came to Breslau in Silesia. In Breslau he was quick to join the local branch of the German Society for the Promotion of Pure Christianity, a Donatistic group of "awakened Christians" who were known as "the Germans" ("die Deutschen"). Their purpose was to wage active

---

[18] Even in America, with its ideals of the melting pot and its many sermons on racial equality, Bohemians are still called "bohunks," and many an immigrant's son has suffered from an inferiority complex on that account. Stephan never got rid of his Bohemian accent. It was quite noticeable in his German preaching. See Herzog-Plitt, *Real-Encyclopaedie*, Vol. 14, p. 671. Speaking of Stephan's later ministry at St. John's in Dresden, von Polenz writes in his book, *Die oeffentliche Meinung und der Pastor Stephan*, p. 19: "With a Bohemian accent and with faulty use of the German language this man [Stephan] boldly preached the foolishness of the Gospel to one of the most cultured cities of Germany."

[19] Not only did their former Roman Catholic associates regard them as turncoats, but the Lutherans, who were very proud of their Lutheran ancestry (and nowhere in the world were men more proud of their Lutheran ancestry than in Saxony, the fatherland of the Reformation), looked at them askance because they had once been Roman Catholics.

[20] Stephan, *op. cit.*, p. XII.

[21] Von Polenz, *op. cit.*, p. 7.

and relentless warfare against all forms of rationalism.[22]   His
sharply polemical spirit and his desire to lord it over his fellows —
both compensatory devices — were evident from the first moment
of Stephan's activity in Breslau.   In the regular meetings of the
group, conducted in the "House of the Three Carps," Stephan's
polemical spirit was rampant.   Having acquired a large fund of
Bible knowledge through his reading of the Scriptures, he was
a ready debater in a group which regarded the Bible as the sole
and absolute truth.   His unbending manner soon affected his
fellows.   These pious but uncultured men began to regard him
as an oracle on things Scriptural.[23]

Moved by the desire to bring the blessings of his stubbornly
defended faith to others and supported by the good will and the
gifts of his pietistic though intellectually limited friends, he decided at the age of twenty-five years to sit on the benches of
St. Elisabeth-Gymnasium in Breslau alongside boys of eleven and
twelve, in order that he might prepare himself for the study of
theology at a German university.   The extreme disparity in age
and size as well as his scant elementary schooling and only average
native mental equipment made it difficult for him to make the
necessary social adjustments.   The mere fact that he was twenty-
five years old and they were eleven and twelve was a constant
reminder of the fact that he was an underprivileged man.[24]   The

---

22 Hennig, *op. cit.*, pp. 15—16.   The original name of this society is rather
high sounding — "Die deutsche Gesellschaft edler und taetiger Befoerderer
reiner Lehre und wahrer Gottseligkeit."   Its purpose was to organize all
"the true Christians" ("die wahren Christen"), wherever they might be found
scattered among the various congregations.   The organization was a loose one.
Personal holiness, commonly known as practical Christianity, was the main
concern of these men and women.   Unlike the earlier pietists, however, their
theological position was much more orthodox.   The absolute authority of the
Scriptures was a prominent doctrine among them.   They were chiliastic and
looked upon rationalism as a sign "that the end of all things was at hand."

23 Von Polenz, *op. cit.*, p. 7.   He seems to have impressed the shoemaker
Valentin Eiser, who was the president of the local "Deutsche Gesellschaft
edler und taetiger Befoerderer reiner Lehre und wahrer Gottseligkeit."

24 Von Polenz, *op. cit.*, p. 8.   The tendency of these younger lads to make
fun of their abnormal classmate was largely checked by his huge physical
frame.   His promotion from Tertia to Secunda was accompanied by the note
"propter staturam."   The size of his body seems to have influenced even his
instructors.   When he reached the highest class, known in the German
Gymnasium as Prima, he was *Oeconomus*, a liaison officer between the administration and the students.   It was his task to direct students to their
classes, ring the bell, etc.   The position was clothed with a certain amount
of authority over his fellows.   Luetkemueller, *Die Lehren und Umtriebe der
Stephanisten*, p. 47, maintains that Stephan's strong will as well as his thorough

so-called *Schnellkurs* — of six years in two — at St. Elisabeth gave him a very inadequate preparation for his studies at the university and did not tend to remove his feeling of inferiority.[25]

His choice of a university and his selection of courses while at the university are highly significant. Halle, the university of his first choice, was intended by its founder to be a seat of tolerance for the Lutheran Church of Prussia. Consequently pietism, and later on rationalism, found a ready asylum within its walls. In the theological faculty the emphasis was on "practical Christianity" in preference to the fine distinctions of philosophy and "cold" science ("kalte Wissenschaft"). Even the rationalism of Halle at the end of the eighteenth and the beginning of the nineteenth century was heavily colored by pietism. Moralizing was connected in some way with almost everything that went on at Halle.[26]

knowledge of the German Bible impressed the rector of St. Elisabeth and moved him to accept the twenty-five-year-old man in spite of his meager native equipment and his very mediocre elementary schooling. Incidentally, Stephan acquired only an imperfect knowledge of Latin and a mere smattering of Greek while at the Gymnasium. His stay at St. Elisabeth must have increased his feeling of inferiority, even as it moved him to gain compensation by getting control over his fellows through force. In another connection von Polenz, p. 19, speaks of "his powerful, though rather clumsy physique." ("Ausser seiner kraeftigen nur etwas an das Plumpe streifenden Gestalt besass er [Stephan] auch nichts, was die Welt haette ansprechen koennen.")

[25] Stephan seems to have been conscious of his inadequate preparation throughout his life. Remarks in his sermons (*Der christliche Glaube*, p. 196) and elsewhere seem to indicate this. There is evidence of self-pity, which Leslie D. Weathered calls "the most disintegrating of all emotions" (*op. cit.*, p. 120). One thing he seems to have taken with him from his association with Scheibel, the head of St. Elisabeth, and that was an awakened Lutheran consciousness. He is convinced that pietism with its weak confessional attitude and its emphasis on redemption from the power of sin must be replaced by a militant Lutheranism with its emphasis on redemption from the guilt of sin. See the article by Karl Hennig on "Die Auswanderung Martin Stephan's," *Zeitschrift fuer Kirchengeschichte*, LVIII (1939), pp. 142—166, Verlag von W. Kohlhammer in Stuttgart. See also *Real-Encyclopaedie*, Herzog-Plitt, Vol. 14, pp. 670—676. This is a well-written article on Martin Stephan by Pastor Kummer of the City Church in Dresden. Kummer carried on extensive research for this article. The archives at Dresden and surrounding territory were at his disposal. Unfortunately the articles on Stephan in subsequent editions of Herzog-Plitt have been merged with the article on the Missouri Synod. Less space is given to Stephan, and the article is not as well written.

[26] *Religion in Geschichte und Gegenwart*, II, pp. 1586—1591. Also Meusel, *op. cit.*, III, pp. 139—140. Pleissner, on p. 71 of his *Die kirchlichen Fanatiker im Muldethale*, makes a special point of the fact that Halle was intellectually inferior to Jena and consequently tended to breed fanatics. Von Polenz, *op. cit.*, p. 9, stresses the fact that at Leipzig Stephan lived in a basement room ("in einer kellerartigen Wohnung") because of his poverty. The room had

Stephan was little interested in philosophy and in those strictly theological subjects which Germans call *wissenschaftliche Theologie* (dogmatics, textual criticism, critical exegesis, etc.). He referred to them as carnal sciences.[27] In their stead he preferred the study of ascetical writings, particularly those of the golden age of pietism. He was interested in church history and occupied himself extensively with the persecution of the Hussites in Bohemia and with the Thirty Years' War.[28] When Napoleon closed the doors of Halle in 1806, Stephan transferred his residence to the University of Leipzig, an institution that had repeatedly shown preference for Lutheran theologians of a more pronounced confessional character.[29]

Finally, after a year and a half of study at Halle and three years and a half at Leipzig, he was admitted to the examination which was to demonstrate his fitness to take over a parish. The usual medium in these examinations was the Latin language. Because of Stephan's limited knowledge of Latin, German was used almost exclusively in his case. In judging him, the examiners attached great weight to his "spiritual attitude" and his "flair for the practical" ("sein praktisches Talent").

His interest in ascetical writings and his tendency toward "practical Christianity" brought him his first appointment. The

---

to be lighted artificially even at midday. Von Polenz thinks that Stephan here laid the foundation for his later habit of staying up until the early hours of the morning.

[27] Vehse, *op. cit.*, pp. 1—2. Herzog-Plitt, *Real-Encyclopaedie*, Vol. 14, p. 671. Ludwig, *Das falsche Maertyrerthum*, p. 15. Von Polenz, *op. cit.*, pp. 9—11. Hennig, *Zeitschrift fuer Kirchengeschichte*, LVIII (1939), p. 145. Stephan had a complete concept of theology before he ever went to the university. This concept grew out of the meetings of "the Germans" in the House of the Three Carps in Breslau and out of his association with Scheibel, the rector of St. Elisabeth. He was very quick in his judgments on theological questions. In fact, his judgments seemed to be tailor-made and memorized. They were not the result of long-continued study and critical evaluation of all the factors involved. White was white, and black was black, and that was that. Brusqueness and oversimplification characterized his theological thinking. In addition to his homemade theology he had a highly developed sense of practical Christianity. This he had received from the pietists of Breslau and Halle. These preconceptions served to strengthen him in his opposition to the radical rationalism which was also rampant at Halle (Wegscheider, Gesenius) and to the mild rationalism at Leipzig (Keil, Johann August Wolf, Tittmann, A. Tzschirner, and Ludwig Cramer). His aversion to rationalism developed into a veritable hatred of all learned studies.

[28] Stephan, *op. cit.*, p. 144. Also his two sermons printed in pamphlet form *Herzlicher Zuruf an alle evangelischen Christen*, pp. 1—3.

[29] Herzog-Plitt, *Real-Encyclopaedie*, Vol. 14, p. 671.

parish was in Bohemia, and it was poor. He describes the place as a "school of continence." The name of the parish was Haber. He remained at the place for one year.[30]

His second and last appointment came because of his ability to speak the Bohemian language. It was a peculiar parish; it really consisted of two separate congregations, which used the same church building. The congregation of St. John's at Dresden consisted of descendants of refugees made homeless by the devastations of the Thirty Years' War. These people had been driven out of their homeland on account of their persistent adherence to the Protestant faith. At first the persecuted Bohemian Protestants had settled in Pirna, Saxony. In 1639, however, they came to Dresden. For ten years they were permitted to conduct services and special private meetings in the parsonage of their pastor. All this time they were hoping to return to the hills of their homeland at the end of the war. When this hope was dashed by the provisions of the Treaty of Westphalia, they set up a petition in

---

[30] Fischer, *op. cit.*, p. 16. Von Polenz, *op. cit.*, p. 9. In 1921 Dr. W. H. T. Dau, then professor at Concordia Seminary, St. Louis, Missouri, requested Pastor F. Hanewinckel, then pastor at Dresden, Saxony, to examine all the archives and libraries of Dresden for source material on the early history of Stephan and Stephanism. Hanewinckel sent Dau an exhaustive report covering 201 pages in Hanewinckel's own handwriting. This report contains very valuable material for an understanding of Stephan and Stephanism. Dr. Dau turned the report over to Dr. L. Fuerbringer, president of Concordia Seminary, St. Louis, who, in turn, was kind enough to lend it to the present writer. It will be quoted henceforth as "Hanewinckel Report." On page 44 Hanewinckel reports a letter written by Stephan December 20, 1809, from Haber to the *Stadtrat* of Dresden, to which he appends this amusing but also revealing signature: "Martin Stephan, Pastor of the Evangelical Congregation at Haber and senior minister of all evangelical ministers of the Augsburg Confession in the Kingdom of Bohemia." He had been in office just a few months. His parish was small and poor. Even in this signature he reveals his compensatory proclivity. The original reads: "Martin Stephan, Pastor der Evangelischen Gemeinde zu Haber und Senior der Saemmtlichen (*sic!*) evangelischen Geistlichkeit der Augsburgischen Confession im Koenigreich Boehmen." Incidentally, the "Senior of all ministers of the Augsburg Confession in the Kingdom of Bohemia" was reminding the good fathers of the *Stadtrat* that he could preach German and that he would not be averse to a call from a German-speaking congregation in the Kingdom of Saxony. (Er bittet den Rat, "dieselben wollen wir auch sothane deutsche Prediger Stelle aufzutragen geneigt geruhen. Durch ein pflichtgemaessiges und exemplarisches Verhalten werde mich beeifern, dieses schaetzbare Wohlwollen wuerdig zu machen und habe die Ehre mit groesster Hochachtung zu sein Ew. Wohlgeb. und Hochwl. gehorsamster Martin Stephan," etc.). Hanewinckel has placed "106, XXIII, 9" immediately after this letter. This seems to be a reference to the archives of the *Superintendentur* of Dresden. On previous pages Hanewinckel had referred to the volumes in the *Superintendentur* of Dresden.

4

which they asked the ruling prince of Saxony for citizenship and a church. The date of the petition was March, 1650. In May of the same year the rescript was published, and they were told that they might be citizens and that St. John's Church (a small church compared with the other churches of Dresden) was now at their disposal. Among other provisions the rescript contained the permission to conduct their public services in the Bohemian language, to elect their own administrative council consisting of men and women, to call their own pastor, and to pay their pastor's salary out of the income from funds which they had brought along from Bohemia and which they had deposited with the Saxon government. (At the time of their flight, in 1639, this had amounted to twelve thousand taler. By 1837 it had grown to fifty thousand taler. Only the interest was used.) The custom of conducting semipublic meetings in the parsonage was continued for almost two centuries. Stephan's predecessor, Pastor Petermann, who served the parish for forty-six years, was particularly zealous for these meetings. These house gatherings, the use of a foreign language, the custom of dividing the congregation into children, recent converts ("Neubekehrte"), and experienced Christians ("Fortgeschrittene"), and, above all, the peculiar type of church polity set Stephan's church apart from all the other churches of Dresden. His was a nonassimilable group in one of the most cultured cities of Germany.

At the same time the pastor of the Bohemian congregation was also the pastor of a congregation of Germans who lived among the Bohemians of the neighborhood. Both congregations used the same church building and enjoyed the services of the same pastor. Sermons were preached regularly every Sunday in both languages. The pastor had two calls. The call from the Bohemians was issued by the representative officers of the congregation without any interference of city or state officials. The call to serve the German congregation was issued by the city council of Dresden.[31]

---

[31] For the details concerning the two congregations see the pamphlet of fifty-two pages published by Stephan, Dresden, 1823. The pamphlet contains two sermons, one preached on Reformation Day, October 31, 1823, and the other on the first Sunday in Advent of the same year. The pamphlet is entitled *Herzlicher Zuruf*, etc. He records the history of the parish and defends himself against recent attacks made upon him in the press. Dr. L. Fuerbringer has a copy of this pamphlet in his private library. Another source

Stephan was not a great pulpit orator. The usual devices employed by the rabble-rouser to sway crowds were not used by the Bohemian *Bussprediger*. His voice was ineffective. Contemporary Germans called it hollow and monotonous ("hohl und ziemlich monoton"). His sentence structure was exceedingly simple, and his German grammar was not above reproach. Extensive gesticulation and extreme changes in pitch and speed were

for these details is *Glaubensbekenntnis der Gemeinde zu St. Johannis*, published in Dresden in 1833. This bound book of seventy-four pages contains a historical introduction and three documents called "Beilagen." One of the documents is an oath of allegiance to the Augsburg Confession and the other symbolical writings of the Lutheran Church, then demanded of every Lutheran pastor of Saxony, every teacher of a secondary school, and every professor of a university in Saxony. "Beilage I" is a reprint from the *National-Zeitung*, dated November 21, 1821. See also Ludwig Fischer, *Falsches Maertyrerthum*. Fischer quotes a long letter from Stephan's friend Franz Delitzsch. Delitzsch furnishes details about the two congregations at St. John's. Karl Hennig's account in *Zeitschrift fuer Kirchengeschichte*, LVIII (1939), Nos. 1 and 2, is the latest pronouncement on the subject by a German scholar. On pages 20 ff. Hanewinckel includes these documents in a complaint which the German preachers of Dresden brought against Martin Stephan in 1820. The German preachers go back to the original arrangement for German preaching in St. John's. The arrangement was first made in March, 1672. At that time there were six little villages just outside the Pirna Gate. The villagers complained of the difficulties which they encountered while attending services at the churches inside the city walls. For military reasons the gate was locked during the morning hours. Furthermore, the congestion at the entrance to the city churches was so great that tumultuous scenes took place. For these reasons the villagers petitioned the *Stadtrat* of Dresden to permit German services in St. John's Church, which was outside the Pirnaer Tor. On March 27, 1672, the *Stadtrat* gave the following answer: "Preaching services shall be conducted by the Bohemian preacher of St. John's in the German language to satisfy the needs of these villagers. The pastor shall receive a special call from the *Stadtrat*. He shall receive special remuneration for this work by taxes collected from the parish to which these six villages belong. The pastor shall not announce engagements of betrothed couples; he shall not perform marriages in the German language; he shall not administer the Sacraments except in cases of great emergency, when no German *diaconus* can be gotten from the city. The whole arrangement was a temporary one, but it continued right down to, and included, the ministry of Pastor Stephan. The city pastors, in their complaint of 1820, cite the conditions of the call which the *Stadtrat* had extended to Pastor Stephan on April 12, 1810. "You are reminded of the fact that you are in no wise to interfere with the rights of the city pastors, with the one exception, that of extreme emergency (which emergency, however, has been eliminated since a German-speaking *diaconus* has been appointed for the suburb of Pirna and the Pirna Gate is kept open day and night). We hereby reserve the right to cancel and annul this arrangement as the development of conditions may dictate, since the entire arrangement is a temporary one." Hanewinckel copied these documents from the archives of the superintendent in Dresden. Hanewinckel has placed at the head of this report: "Aus XXIII. 17, S. 1, Anno 1820, Stadtgeistliche vs. Stephan."

absent.[32]   One contemporary who heard him frequently referred
to his sermons as dry ("trocken").[33]

How, then, can we explain his great power over men?   A dis-
tinguishing mark of his personality was his great sensitivity to
people — a sensitivity to their hopes and fears and personality
tensions.   He studied men and the art of handling men.   He was
a past master in the art of counseling.   A doctor of jurisprudence
who was in Stephan's immediate environment for several years
put it this way:

> Through his extended and intimate acquaintance with people
> of highest as well as lowest rank he came into possession of
> a mass of interesting information about many people and
> many things.   This enabled him to acquire a rare and un-
> failing knack in estimating people.   This ability stood him

---

[32] Herzog-Plitt, *Real-Encyclopaedie,* Vol. 14, p. 671.   Also von Polenz,
op. cit., pp. 29—30.

[33]   Vehse, *op. cit.,* p. 9.   Von Polenz, who heard Stephan frequently,
writes the following on p. 19 of his *Die oeffentliche Meinung und der Pastor
Stephan:* "Not one per cent of the inhabitants of Dresden took cognizance
of the installation and the inaugural sermon of the insignificant Bohemian
pastor who was soon to become the topic of conversation throughout the city.
Aside from his powerful, though rather clumsy physical frame there was
nothing that might have attracted the world to Stephan, neither his delivery
nor his gesticulation, neither the fire and rapidity of his speech nor the
cleverness in the arrangement of his sermons ("Geschicklichkeit im Dispo-
nieren") nor any other means of pulpit oratory — the golden containers in
which colored and insipid water is offered as the sweet wine and milk from
the hills of the Lord to the masses of the half-educated.   With a Bohemian
accent and in defective German this man dared to set forth the 'foolishness
of the Gospel' to one of the most polished and educated cities of Germany."
A contemporary American, Dr. Benjamin Kurtz, was traveling through Germany in 1827, trying to raise funds for Gettysburg Seminary.   He spent
two weeks in Dresden.   He heard Stephan on two occasions; and this is
what he says of him in the *Lutheran Observer,* reprinted in *Concordia
Historical Institute Quarterly,* XII (1939), pp. 21—24: "Mr. Stephan was then
about fifty years of age, remarkably plain in appearance, and his countenance
and the contour of his head reminded us very forcibly of Dr. Dwight, the
late president of Yale College.   His sermon was plain, vigorous, and evangelic,
and well calculated to enlighten the mind and affect the heart.   There was
nothing like an attempt to show off to advantage, no playing of the orator,
no effort for applause — nothing of that kind.   Fancy a very plain, matter-
of-fact man, rather tall, somewhat inclined to austerity, with a slight tinge
of melancholy in his features, addressing a crowded and deeply interested
congregation in a most solemn manner on the awful interests of the eternal
destiny of man, holding up Jesus Christ as the only hope of a perishing world,
and demanding faith in Him and obedience to His precepts as one who in
the name of his Master has authority to insist on compliance with these
requisitions, and you will have a tolerably correct conception of one of the
most devoted and consistent and successful ministers then residing in the
Kingdom of Saxony."

in good stead in handling people who differed greatly in character. He was the very embodiment of tact, so that people came under his control without knowing it.[34]

His sensitivity to the hopes and fears of people guided him in his selection of the content of his sermons. Let us recall the fact that rationalism dominated many of the pulpits and many of the administrative offices in Saxony, and, above all, that it was a crystallized, formalistic, and dead rationalism.[35] In these pulpits there was no contact with the day-to-day life of the people. High-sounding philosophical dissertations on trivial matters were declaimed with great solemnity. A colossal indifference to the actual needs of men had paralyzed the pulpit as well as the private ministrations of the clergy. The Church was out of touch with the people. "The hungry sheep look up and are not fed." This fact gave Martin Stephan an entrance to many troubled souls. There was a definite pattern in his ministrations. First he stirred up a sense of sin in his hearers, and then he assured them of the removal of their guilt through the shed blood of Christ.[36] Every sermon on the 1,137 pages of his postil begins with the same salutation: "Through the blood of Christ dearly redeemed souls" ("Durch das Blut Christi theuer erkaufte Seelen"). These people had a strong desire to be sure of God's grace. Stephan satisfied this desire by preaching the doctrines of Martin Luther concern-

---

[34] Vehse, *op. cit.*, pp. 1—2.

[35] It is customary to speak of "dead orthodoxy." In the twenties and thirties of the nineteenth-century rationalism was moribund. The very term "awakened" ("Erweckte") predicates a spiritual condition of deathlike sleep believed to have been induced by the lifeless moralizing of rationalistic sermonizers. See Hennig, *op. cit.*, p. 9.

[36] The doctrine of original sin is very prominent in the sermons of Martin Stephan, even as it was in the discussion of all pietists of the day. In most of his sermons he mentions it, and in some he discusses it at great length. It is part of the basis of his theological structure. See his *Der christliche Glaube*. Weathered, *op. cit.*, pp. 121—122, points to the great value of the forgiveness of sins as a means of adjustment. "I think I could write a book on the therapeutic value of the received idea of forgiveness. I have seen men and women recover their health of body and mind when they realized what forgiveness means. It is not enough to know with the mind that you are forgiven; there is all the difference in the world between knowing a thing and realizing a thing. It is one thing to know that bereavement is sad, it is a very different thing to realize it. And some people find that they have to say it over and over again to themselves till it dawns on them like the glory of a summer morning, that what they knew as a fact of the mind all their lives has become, in one liberating moment, an experience of the heart." Stephan said it over and over again to people who were morbidly conscious of their sins.

ing sin and grace with all the warmth of Philipp Jakob Spener;
and he did it in season and out of season.

His sensitivity to the hopes and fears and personality tensions
of people was still more pronounced in his private and semiprivate
ministrations. Every Sunday evening he conducted semiprivate
meetings for troubled souls in his parsonage. In addition, "Bible
hours" and "consultation meetings" ("Sprechstunden") were conducted during the week. In the consultation meetings any man
or woman could ask him any question concerning faith and life.
Some questions were written, some were oral. Stephan answered
them in a way that showed wisdom and understanding and, above
all, sympathy.[37] The result was that people came to him from all
walks of life, from all over Dresden, from the villages round about,
and from many parts of Saxony. His correspondence grew. Especially students at universities who were suffering from unadjusted personality tensions and whose doubts and fears were driv-
ing them to despair came to Stephan or wrote him letters.[38]

---

[37] Von Polenz, *op. cit.*, pp. 20, 32, who attended these semiprivate meetings
and who, though he forsook Stephan, never became bitter in his judgments of
his erstwhile teacher, gives us the best description of the *Sprechstunden*.
He claims that Stephan was at his very best in these semiprivate meetings.
He was in his element. All the people present were his most intimate friends.
He craved love, and they gave him expressions of their love. He revealed
the innermost parts of his heart. Polemical work against hostile pastors was
most pronounced in this innermost circle. Hymns were sung that were not
to be found in the legally prescribed hymnbook. The meetings usually began
with a hymn, followed by a Scripture reading. Hereupon Stephan would
comment on the text in his best and freest style. Questions were asked and
answered without previous preparation. Opinions were tossed out to the
audience with utter abandon. The pressure of public opinion was removed.

[38] The experience of C. F. W. Walther is described in a footnote of his
Lebenslauf of Buenger, p. 29. C. F. W. Walther, a young Leipzig University
student, was in great spiritual distress. He poured out his heart to various
men who had the reputation of being conservative Lutheran theologians.
He found no rest. Finally these men advised him to go to Stephan. He wrote
Stephan a long letter, in which he described his trouble. Speaking of Stephan's
reply, Walther writes: "When I read his reply, I felt as though I had been
translated from hell to heaven. Tears of distress and sorrow were converted
into tears of heavenly joy. He directed me to the Good Samaritan and
showed me what faith in Christ means. Peace and joy entered my heart. . . .
He applied the Gospel to my own soul." A little later Dr. Rudelbach, superintendent in Glauchau, Saxony, was about to recommend C. F. W. Walther as
a private teacher for the children of a certain pious prince. Rudelbach
demanded, however, that the candidate first break off all relations with Stephan.
The young man promptly replied: "Shall I forsake the man who by the grace
of God saved my soul from destruction?" This experience shows how Stephan
could engender blind fanatical zeal, particularly in young people. Here was
a set of circumstances which favored Stephan and of which he made the
best use.

What effect did this avalanche of requests for advice and counsel have upon Stephan? Karl Hennig claims:

> Stephan did not raise his voice against the un-Christian pronouncements made from Lutheran pulpits because of a feeling of personal power and authority ("nicht aus eigener Machtvollkommenheit"), but because he felt that the duties of his office demanded such activity on his part. Stephan was not a one-sided, stubborn, willful man of power. It is true that the untoward experiences of his youth and the constant battles of his early manhood made a rather stubborn and emotional fighter out of him. This stubbornness was interpreted as arbitrary obstinacy by the Saxon people, who are known for their friendliness and politeness, particularly by the supranaturalists who were given to compromise in matters of doctrine and life.[39]

This interpretation hardly takes all factors into account. Especially does it fail to explain the utterly servile behavior of his followers toward his person,[40] the tremendous emphasis which

---

[39] *Zeitschrift fuer Kirchengeschichte,* LVIII (1939), Nos. 1 and 2, p. 146.

[40] Vehse, *op. cit.,* p. 11. Cf. the "Unterwerfungserklaerung vom Dampfboot 'Selma.'" The original copy of this pact, signed on the *Selma* in February, 1839, is in the Concordia Historical Institute. The present writer had a photostatic copy made of it. Vehse reprinted it on pp. 163—166. The behavior of the group is rather un-Lutheran and almost Oriental in its servility. A few quotations from the "Unterwerfungserklaerung" follow: "We promise that we will submit completely in Christian willingness and sincerity to every decree, regulation, or ordinance which His Grace shall make, whether such decree pertains to ecclesiastical or secular ('communlich') matters. We will not regard these decrees as an oppressive yoke, but as a means for promoting our temporal and eternal welfare." "On account of the many defamations and slanders suffered by our most revered Bishop as well as by his assistants among the clergy, we believe that we ought to make a declaration to the effect that we will at all times show him the proper respect and that we will not tolerate any defamation or slander, no matter with whom they may originate, mindful of the words of Jesus 'He that heareth you heareth Me, and he that despiseth you despiseth Me.' Every time we need correction or reproof on account of any or all transgressions we will accept such reprimands willingly and gratefully, whether they come directly from the Bishop or from one of his appointed agents. In general, we promise to conduct ourselves in a sincere and upright and obedient manner over against all men who are charged with the cure of our souls. Heb. 13:17: 'Obey them that have the rule over you, and submit yourselves; for they watch for your souls as they that must give an account, that they may do it with joy and not with grief; for that is unprofitable for you.'" "If wicked and malicious people should try to sow seeds of discord and strife among us, or if they attempt to create factions in our midst, we will resist them with all earnestness and energy and inform our superiors according to the express command of God, 2 Thess. 3:14: 'If any man obey not our word by this epistle, note that man [German: "den zeichnet an"] and have no company with him, that he may be ashamed.'" The forms which Stephan's followers used when addressing their master indicate a similar servility. Fasc. VI, now in Concordia Historical

Stephan placed on the office of the Christian ministry (*Amt*),[41]
and the hierarchical and autocratic dictatorship which Stephan

Institute, contains a letter from Gottlob Christoph Schwabe to Stephan, dated
February 25, 1838, at Neustadt. The writer begins the letter: "Dearest pastor,
most intimate friend, leader of my soul" ("Theuerster Herr Pastor, innigster
Freund und Fuehrer meiner Seele"). The minutes of the committee which
made arrangements for the emigration show at various places how the
Stephanites regarded the *person* of Martin Stephan as a means of grace. These
minutes are known as Fasc. III in Concordia Historical Institute. In the
meeting of December 13, 1837, the committee talked at great length about
the "care of the pastor's person" ("die Pflege der Person des Pastors").
They adopted a special order of care for his person ("eine Pflegeordnung").
In the meeting of February 27, 1838, Dr. Vehse was put in charge of "die
Pflege der Person des Pastors." In the meeting of February 15, 1838, some
committee members express the fear that the means of grace will be destroyed
because the pastor's health is in jeopardy.

The Stephanites had been warned against this servile behavior on many
occasions while still in Saxony. Dr. Rudelbach, one of the greatest and most
influential Lutheran theologians of the nineteenth century, had warned them
again and again. C. F. W. Walther tells how Rudelbach warned him personally.
See his *Lebenslauf* of Buenger, p. 29. Walther quotes Rudelbach as saying to
him: "Beware, I say beware, of all deification of man" ("Hueten Sie sich,
hueten Sie sich vor aller Menschenvergoetterung"). Furthermore, Rudelbach,
with nine other theologians of Saxony, had inserted a special announcement
in the *Leipziger Allgemeine Zeitung*, No. 273, September 30, 1838, which was
reprinted in Harless' *Zeitschrift*, October 21, 1838; also in Ludwig Fischer,
op. cit., pp. 200—204. In the first paragraph these theologians announce their
adherence to the Unaltered Augsburg Confession and to all the other confessional writings of the Lutheran Church. They begin the second paragraph
by saying: "Because of our adherence to the Confessional Writings of the
Lutheran Church we are compelled to protest against any and all kinds of
human authoritarianism in the Church of Jesus Christ. We honor the
reputation of true teachers, and we appreciate the blessed work done by men
who are filled with the Spirit of the Lord; but we regard it as extremely
dangerous to forsake the objective authority of the Scriptures ('der objective
Pruefstein') in the least. The adherents of Pastor Stephan are doing just that.
Instead of critically analyzing his statements in the light of the Scriptures
and the Confessional Writings of the Lutheran Church, they are accepting
them on the personal testimony and authority of the man himself. This is
the chief source of error among the Stephanites."

The clergymen among Stephan's followers were just as obsequious as
the laymen. In sermons which they delivered in behalf of the episcopal
arrangement for the colony they outdid themselves in extravagant statements.
Dr. Vehse, *op. cit.*, p. 13, quotes them: "The Church is dependent upon two
eyes, the eyes of Bishop Stephan" ("Die Kirche steht auf zwei Augen,
die Augen des Bishofs Stephan"). The episcopal kiss of the Bishop's hand
was performed by the faithful (Vehse, *op. cit.*, p. 13).

[41] The dignity of the ministerial office (*Amt*) accompanies Stephan
through life. It is part of the compensation for his inferiority. Already
as a student at St. Elisabeth in Breslau he would put on the ecclesiastical garb
(*Talar*) and preach a sermon of an hour or more in his room. See Polenz,
op. cit., p. 9. In his collection of sermons *Der christliche Glaube* there are
references to the dignity of the ministerial office, p. 367. The origin of his
overemphasis on the ministerial office and on the power and authority of
the minister is to be sought in Stephan's rather limited mentality. The
Scriptural emphasis on the Gospel as a means of grace was transferred to
the person who proclaims the Gospel. To what extremes a Stephan-inspired

set up within his own group.[42]   Nor does it take into account the feeling of inferiority which Stephan manifested at so many turns in his life.[43]

A more adequate interpretation of Stephan's life and a more accurate estimate of the contribution which he made to the system of church government in the Missouri Synod can be obtained by focusing one's attention on his constant attempts to overcome the feeling of inadequacy which dogged him all his life.   To what extent this feeling was justified is difficult to determine.   Society in the Saxony of his day had arbitrarily set up certain standards which he does not seem to have reached in his formal education. But other standards of achievement, which the society of his day had largely neglected, he attained.

Stephan's compensatory behavior was a matter of slow growth. His original urge to compensate was gradually stimulated by the increasing number of men and women who came to him for advice and counsel on moral and religious issues.   No matter how deficient he felt himself to be, there were others — and many of them — who were still more deficient than he.   By coming to him they put him on a higher plane than they put themselves.   They were devout men and morbidly conscientious.   Some of them were noblemen, some professors at German universities; many of them were pastors and candidates of theology; some were lawyers; and some were merchants of high standing.   Their constant coming must have gradually convinced him that he was of a nobler order than most people and that his person was indispensable to their

---

respect could lead people is best illustrated by the behavior of the men who were to go to meet Stephan at Wittenberg Landing, Perry County, and inform him that he should appear before a council of clergymen and defend himself against specific charges of misconduct with members of the opposite sex.   A subcommittee consisting of two clergymen put on their clerical vestments and appeared before Stephan.   They informed him of their mission and then withdrew.   Nobody dared to stay with Stephan because of their morbid fear of his ministerial office. (Vehse, *op. cit.*, p. 20.)   The original reads: "Hierauf zogen die beiden Geistlichen sich zurueck; niemand, auch nicht die staerksten Leute, getrauten sich in der Nacht bei ihm im Zimmer zu wachen, aus unbegreiflicher Furcht vor dem Amte."

42 See the minutes of the Committee on Emigration, known as Fasc. III; also Vehse, *op. cit.*, pp. 9—14.

43 At Breslau, when he entered the society of "the Germans" (von Polenz, *op. cit.*, p. 7); in his "Vorrede an den christlichen Leser" (*Der christliche Glaube*, pp. XV—XVIII); in the darkness of the storm on the ocean (Vehse, *op. cit.*, p. 8); at the time of his deposition in Perry County (Vehse, *op. cit.*, pp. 20—22).

well-being, if not to the well-being of the entire Church.[44] During
the early years of his ministry at Dresden there was comparatively
little compensatory behavior. It seems to have grown mightily
with the publication of his postil,[45] which his followers placed right
next to the Bible and the Lutheran Confessions. During the last
years of his ministry, and particularly during the ocean voyage
and his journey up the Mississippi and his first months in Missouri, his behavior abnormality approached the stage of paranoia.[46]

A brief summary of the steps which led to an overdevelop-
ment of compensation in the case of Martin Stephan will, we believe, help us to understand the man and the contribution which
he made to the polity of the Missouri Synod. He was born
August 13, 1777, of humble parents who had turned from the
Roman Catholic faith to the Lutheran faith and who died not many
years after his birth. To make a living, he learned the trade of
a weaver, a very common occupation in Bohemia and certain
parts of Saxony. In 1798, at the age of twenty-one, he came to
Breslau to live with his sister and ply his trade. Shortly after
his arrival he joined the German Society for the Promotion of
Pure Christianity and soon became a dominant figure in this group.
At the suggestion of and with the assistance of his pietistic friends
he entered St. Elisabeth Gymnasium in 1802 to prepare for the
study of theology. The years from 1804 to 1809 were spent at the
universities of Halle and Leipzig. At each university he showed

---

[44] When the pastors began to tell the people that the existence of the
Church was dependent upon Stephan (Vehse, *op. cit.*, p. 13), the expansion
of his ego had already taken several tremendous steps forward.

[45] Stephan, *Der christliche Glaube.*

[46] The present writer accepts the definition which John J. B. Morgan,
op. cit., p. 545, gives: "A mental disorder characterized by fixed and sys-
tematized delusions, usually of a persecutory and grandiose nature." P. 542
the same author says: "The person who compensates is concerned largely
with himself. He must take himself very seriously, or he would not be so
determined to overcome any handicap which may be thrust upon him.
Naturally he thinks that others are likewise vitally interested in his success
or failure. He covers his selfishness by picturing the tremendous loss that
will accrue to society should he fail. The person who compensates has failed
in some respect. . . . The failure need not be a real one. If the individual
falls short of an artificial standard which he has established, although this
may be regarded as anything but failure to others, it is viewed most dis-
consolately by the subject. No standard of success but his own has any
meaning for him. The person who compensates is not consistent. He will
not admit that he has failed, though he feels that he has. This inconsistency
is behind every compensation."

the fighting tendency that is inherent in compensation.[47] He let
university professors know that he had a homemade system of
theology and that his system was superior to any system the universities might have to offer.[48] After spending a year in the parish
at Haber in Bohemia he accepted a call to St. John's in Dresden.
From 1810 to 1816 there is apparently little disturbance; but as
his system of theology becomes better known and he begins to
reach over the boundaries of his parish and men and women of
other parishes begin to seek his advice and his services, especially
when they ask him to perform baptisms and administer the Sacrament of the Altar, the enmity of neighboring brethren of the cloth
begins to rear its ugly head. [49] In 1825 and 1826 he published
a collection of sermons.[50] Shortly thereafter he got control of the
Dresden branch of the Saxon Bible Society. In the early thirties
pastors of the Muldental who, while students at Leipzig University, had selected him as their father confessor and counselor,
began to call him into their congregations for special services.[51]
He coached them in their opposition to their rationalistic brother
clergymen. His protégés — Keyl and Buerger in the Muldental
and Loeber in Altenburg — increased their congregations almost
in direct proportion to their obedience to Stephan.[52] Men and
women from the parishes of "unbelieving" pastors walked miles
to put themselves under the ministrations of a Stephan-guided

---

[47] Morgan, *op. cit.,* p. 519: "Compensatory reaction is essentially a fighting
reaction, even though the fighting may take diverse forms. . . . Fighting is
a natural response to opposition or to threatened failure. It is found in the
most elementary organism, and varies in complexity rather than in fundamental nature as we advance in the animal scale. In most animal forms,
fighting is largely a physical demonstration; but when we come to human
beings, most of the fighting is done by means of mental processes rather than
by any external application of energy."

[48] Von Polenz, *op. cit.,* p. 9. The author maintains that Stephan got his
theology in the House of the Three Carps and that he merely polished his
theological weapons in combat with rationalistic theologians at the universities.

[49] *Op. cit.,* pp. 24—25. "The so-called Stephanites were Germans from all
sections and parishes of Dresden. Though they belonged to other parishes,
they partook of Holy Communion in St. John's. This gave the clergy of
Dresden legal cause for complaint." Von Polenz suggests that if the clergy
who brought suit against Stephan had succeeded in getting out an injunction
restraining him from preaching and administering the Sacrament of the Altar
in the German language, they would have reduced his income very materially,
since a large part of his income came from Communion fees.

[50] Stephan, *Der christliche Glaube.*

[51] Fischer, *op. cit.,* pp. 31, 25.

[52] *Op. cit.,* pp. 26, 32.

and Stephan-controlled "believing" pastor.[53]   In the legal chicanery and lawsuits which followed and which were instigated by rationalistic pastors Stephan's protégés remained faithful to their master.[54] He led Keyl, Buerger, O. H. Walther, and C. F. W. Walther away from Dr. Rudelbach out of the Muldental conference.   His control over the "faithful" became tighter and tighter, while the "faithful" became more blind in their allegiance.   He must have derived a great deal of psychic satisfaction from the fact that he was gradually becoming an oracle to men who were far superior to him in formal education and native intelligence.   His word was law, and by the fall of 1837 he was fast reaching a stage in his compensatory disorders that revealed a disintegration of his personality.   No one who has read the minutes of the committee that made arrangements for the emigration [55] can escape the impression that Stephan exercised an autocratic control over the committee as well as over the men and women who finally emigrated to Missouri.   There is something morbid about his autocracy and about the obedience of his followers.   In one of the earliest meetings of the committee, the one that took place on December 13, 1837, in Dresden, there is evidence of man worship.   The committee had been appointed by Stephan, and the men present were the lawyer Dr. F. A. Marbach, Dr. Stuebel, Candidate Brohm, Candidate Welzel, the merchant H. F. Fischer, the landed proprietor Gube, and Gustav Jaeckel.   The most important point under discussion in this meeting was the care of Pastor Stephan's person during the journey.   The attitude of the men can be gleaned from the following excerpts of the minutes for that day:

> Our interest in the general welfare of the Church as well as our own soul's welfare makes the care of the person of our pastor the most important object of our concern.   All effort must be concentrated on the task of preserving the most reverend archbishop of the Lutheran Church.   A subcom-

---

[53] *Op. cit.,* p. 59.   Pleissner, *Die kirchlichen Fanatiker im Muldenthale.*

[54] Buerger, *Sendschreiben,* p. 11.   See also, Hennig, *Die saechsische Erweckungsbewegung,* pp. 206—207.

[55] The original copy of these minutes is found in Concordia Historical Institute, St. Louis, Missouri.   The pages are sewn together, apparently by hand.   The covers are semistiff.   The title on the outer page is Fasc. III, No. 12. There is a note in Dr. L. Fuerbringer's handwriting: "Protokolle ueber die Vorbereitung zur saechsischen Auswanderung. Wichtig."   This is extremely valuable source material.   Significantly enough, the committee began to have meetings shortly after the arrest of Stephan at Hofloesnitz, November 9, 1837.

mittee of the general committee has the task of setting up a schedule according to which the preservation and care of our pastor will be carried out with the greatest degree of solicitude and efficiency. If feasible, these plans should be carried out at once. The schedule for his care during the journey of the Church should also receive our earnest consideration.[56]

In the meeting which took place on December 6, 1837, there are three items of special interest. The first pertains to the form of church polity which the Lutheran Church is to assume in America. "The chapter of clergymen is to consist of one bishop and nine deacons."[57] The second pertains to the official garb of the bishop:

Sacerdotal attire must be prepared according to the fashion that was revoked forty years ago. At that time the officiating clergyman wore a different garb for different functions. There was one garb for preaching, another for officiating at the altar. During the celebration of Holy Communion a special garb was used. There were special colors used in the robing of priests, even as we still have special colors for the service of dedicating a church. For Easter they had red, for Pentecost, green; and for Christmas blue was used. The goods for the vestments must be firm and of good quality. The alb must be added. The alb must be made of white linen trimmed with lace. The alb must have sleeves. Albs without sleeves are reminiscent of the Leipzig Interim. The headgear must be such that it distinguishes the bishop from all other clergymen.[58]

---

56 The original German reads as follows: "Die Ruecksicht auf das allgemeine Wohl der Kirche und auf unser eigenes Seelenwohl selbst macht diese Pflege zum wichtigsten Gegenstand; denn alle Aufmerksamkeit muss jetzt darauf gerichtet sein, dass er, der Hochwuerdigste Erzbischof der Lutherischen Kirche, erhalten werde. Dieser Abtheilung ist daher die Aufgabe gestellt, in gewisser Ordnung und mit moeglichster Zartheit die zweckdienlichsten Mittel zu bedenken und, so weit thunlich, schon jetzt anzuordnen, welche zur Erhaltung und Pflege des Herrn Pastors am zweckdienlichsten sind; es ist auch zugleich wegen der Entwerfung einer Pflegeordnung fuer denselben bei der Wanderung der Kirche das noethige zu besorgen."

57 The orginal reads: "Die Geistlichkeit duerfte in Zukunft aus einem Bischof und neun Diaconen bestehen."

58 The original reads as follows: "Die priesterliche Tracht ist herzustellen, wie sie seit etwa vierzig Jahren abgeschafft ist; man hatte damals fuer verschiedene gottesdienstliche Handlungen auch verschiedene Trachten; sie waren verschieden beim Predigen und Diaconieren und dann beim Consecrieren. Verschieden auch bei den verschiedenen Festen, wie noch jetzt bei der Kirchenconsecration. Ostern roth; Pfingsten gruen; Weihnachten blau. Priesterzeug muss fest und gut seyn. Hierzu noch die Albe, von feiner weissen Leinwand mit Spitzenbesatz, mit Aermel, denn die ohne Aermel erinnern an das Leipziger Interim. Kopfbedeckung wie sie angemessen zu bestimmen Auszeichnung des Bischofs zu bestimmen" (*sic!*). Vehse, *op. cit.*, p. 15, tells

The third item of interest in this meeting concerned the question who should be permitted to join the emigrating company. This was a highly mooted question, since some of the men differed with Stephan's rather liberal attitude on this point. The minutes read:

> The condition of participation in the emigration is that only such shall be permitted to join as have stood the test of a rigorous examination. They must first abandon every hope of earthly gain. The words of Ruth, chapter one, must be heard: "Intreat me not to leave thee or to return from following after thee; for whither thou goest, I will go. Thy people shall be my people, and thy God my God." This must be followed by Josh. 24:14. No heretics may be taken along, no people of ungodly conduct or who refuse to submit to church discipline.[59]

of the continued preoccupation of Stephan with clerical vestments. Masses of woolen goods and silk and satin and gold embroidery were purchased and taken along. Women were engaged to sew these garments under his supervision in his own house. A young artist was commissioned to make an exact replica of the vestments worn by the Roman Catholic clergy in Dresden. A special tailor was taken along from Leipzig to complete the work begun in Saxony. While the main vestments were not to be used before the dedication of the proposed cathedral in Perry County, the alb was introduced already in services conducted by the immigrants in Christ Church, St. Louis. The alb of the bishop was distinguished from the alb of the regular clergy by a heavy lace. In addition to the vestments a bishop's miter, a bishop's crook, and a bishop's cross were ordered made. The cross and the gold chain were exceedingly heavy. The faithful gave up their jewelry so that the necessary episcopal paraphernalia could be fashioned. During the time that the company was temporarily sojourning in St. Louis a Roman Catholic church was dedicated. Stephan ordered all clergymen to attend the service and observe the robes and episcopal insignia of the officiating Bishop Rosati.

[59] The original reads: "Bedingung fuer die Theilnahme ist, dass nur solche aufgenommen werden, die in Redlichkeit geprueft sind. Es muss zuvor jede irdische Hoffnung abgeschnitten werden, bis man hoert (*Vide* Ruth, I. Cap.): 'Rede mir nicht darein,' etc. 'Wo du hingehest, da will ich auch hingehen. Dein Volk ist mein Volk, dein Gott ist mein Gott,' etc.; und dass man folge, was Josua 24, 14 stehet. Nicht Ketzer koennen mitgenommen werden, nicht die im gottlosen Wandel sind, nicht die der Kirchenzucht sich nicht unterwerfen wollen." Minutes of June 25, 1838, show that every emigrant had to have Stephan's or Marbach's approval. The subject came up also in the meeting of May 18, 1838. Stephan is present, and he is speaking about a constitution for ecclesiastical and civil affairs. He is making a plea in behalf of the unconverted, and he asks that they be taken along. "Es darf nicht vergessen werden, bemerkte der Herr Pastor, dass nicht bloss wahrhaft bekehrte Christen, sondern auch Unbekehrte mitgenommen werden koennen, wenn diese sich nur in die vorgeschriebene Ordnung fuegen. Denn die Kirche ist nicht bloss Pflegerin der Geborenen, sondern auch Mutter, die da gebieret; darum darf man solche nicht zurueckweisen, die noch nicht bekehrt sind. Man muss die Kirche nehmen, wie sie eben ist. Es ist naehmlich in derselben nicht alles Krauth; sie hat auch Unkrauth, und das sind die

In the meeting of February 15, 1838, there was a long discussion on the question whether or not the time had come to act, that is, to begin the emigration. Pastor Stephan's well-being was their chief consideration. The civil as well as the ecclesiastical courts were again taking up the case against him. In other words, the ground was becoming hotter under Stephan's feet. Stephan had convinced his followers that he was their only means of grace. They believed that outside Stephan there was no salvation. "The question is: Shall we still remain passive, or shall we act at once and with energy?" [60] The minutes show their morbid concern for the person of Stephan:

> The investigation [viz., of Pastor Stephan] has begun anew. Witnesses have been heard concerning the events which have received sufficient investigation in the vineyard and prior to that in the courthouse. The end is not in sight. They will investigate for the purpose of indefinite postponement. Consequently the proceedings (as is customary in demagogic investigations) will never come to a close. The object is to starve the pastor and us — us spiritually and him also physically. The pastor is being ruined economically (only 400 reichstaler of income for his wife, eight children, and one grandchild, and a reduced standard of living) and physically (his usual methods of recreation have been omitted for a quarter of a year). For that reason his life is in danger; and we are scattered like sheep, everyone going his own way.[61]

Unbekehrten und auch die Heuchler; aber solches Unkrauth erstickt den Waitzen nicht, es laesst ihn wachsen; und darum soll man es auch nach Anweisung heiliger Schrift nicht ausreissen, sondern stehen lassen. Anders aber ist es mit den Dornen; sie ersticken den Waitzen und koennen daher nicht bleiben." Vehse, *op. cit.,* p. 5, claims there was much discussion on the subject of taking so many poor people along. The men on the committee tried to convince Stephan that the number of people without means, who therefore could not pay for their transportation, was altogether out of proportion to the number who had means. The members of the committee drew up a budget; they tried their utmost to convince Stephan, but he remained adamant. "The poor dare not be left behind." Vehse is of the opinion that Stephan wanted these people to be taken along because he knew that he could control them in any emergency that might arise.

60 The original: "Soll man sich nunmehr noch passiv verhalten oder vielmehr sofort pro energie handeln?"

61 The original: "Die Untersuchung hat jetzt erst wieder aufs Neue begonnen mit Vernehmungen ueber Gegenstaende die bereits auf dem Weinberge und vorher auf der Rathsstube genuegend eroertert worden sind. Das Ende ist nicht abzusehen — man untersucht so lange, als man nichts findet, folglich werden die Acten (wie bei demagogischen Untersuchungen) nimmer geschlossen werden. Man will P. und uns aushungern, uns geistlich und jenen zugleich auch leiblich. P. verdirbt in Wirtschaft (nur 400 Reichsthaler

In the minutes of this meeting one can observe the method which Stephan used to get these men to do his bidding. There is a display of spirituality that makes one a little skeptical:

For years the pastor has been so thoroughly convinced of the necessity of the exodus that he would not have raised a finger in behalf of a further stay if God's Word did not indicate that ofttimes the most important things hang as by a hair, and we must be guided by that fact. Stuebel makes several statements which indicate his misgivings about America. Other statements follow: St. Louis is indeed 10,000 miles distant. Transportation from here to New Orleans will cost about 50 reichstaler per person; from New Orleans to St. Louis it will be about the same as from Dresden to New Orleans; therefore one can say that the cost will be about 100 reichstaler per person. Character description of an American: He is greedy and indifferent. Public safety in America was formerly endangered by several million Indians. About 1826 there were left only about 300,000 of them. Their number is constantly decreasing. Just recently, in the year 1837, an entire tribe died of the black smallpox. As far as internal conditions of safety are concerned, it must be said that although Americans still take the law into their own hands, they do it only when title to a possession is at stake. Other legal affairs are entirely a matter for each independent commune. Incidentally, law and order are enforced just as strictly there as anywhere else. Stuebel replies: "The pastor has often said: God will provide a way and will indicate a path." Marbach replies: "If we make preparations, nothing is lost. If in the meantime God indicates a different way, we will take that way." Our pastor now says that waiting merely means a loss of time. "Why stand ye here idle? Go ye into the vineyard. The decision of the court may never come. If it comes, it will be late. If we wait for the answer of the court, it will be too late to act." [62]

Einkommen bei Frau, 8 Kindern, 1 Enkel und schlechtere Haushaltung) an Gesundheit (die gewohnten Erhohlungen sind seit schon ¼ Jahr weggefallen) und deshalb Leben in Gefahr. Wir gehn zerstreut wie Schafe, gehen ein Jeder seinen eigenen Weg."

[62] The original reads: "P. ist von der Nothwendigkeit des Auszugs schon seit Jahren so fest ueberzeugt, dass er *gar nichts* fuer das laengere Zurueck- bleiben gethan haben wuerde, wenn Gottes Wort nicht zeigte, dass oft das Wichtigste an ein Haar gebunden sei — und darauf muss geachtet werden. Auf St.'s bedenkliche Aeusserungen ueber Amerika folgen einige Notizen darueber: St. Louis ist allerdings beinahe 10,000 Meilen von hier entfernt. Das Fortkommen wird fuer eine Person bis New Orleans ca. 50 Reichsth., von da bis St. Louis eben so viel, im Ganzen ca. 100 Reichsth. per Person betragen. Characteristik des Amerikaners: Besitzgieriger Indifferentist. Die Aeussere Sicherheit in A. war frueher bei mehreren Millionen Indianern

The general trend of opinion favored immediate action. Dr. Stuebel was the one exception. He seems to have been a rather timid soul.[63] Marbach uses religious sanctions to remove the fears and misgivings of Dr. Stuebel:

> Stuebel can give no definite reasons for his position and for that reason is willing to submit to the pastor's opinion. Marbach replies: The pastor does not want that; every man should stand on his own feet. Stuebel replies: If a decision is to come, it were better to wait for that decision. He will not venture to say, however, Wait for the decision; it will come. He is not willing to assume the responsibility for the ruination that will take place if no decision is forthcoming — for the following are placed in jeopardy: the pastor's health and life and therewith the chief means of grace for us; the entire building of the Church of God, which is to take place through Stephan; the eternal welfare of all other people. Even if a decision should come, all these weighty matters dare not be put in jeopardy. Therefore Stuebel, having heard this, expressed his personal conviction that immediate action was necessary.[64]

---

gefaehrdet, ca. 1826 gabs deren nur noch ca. 300,000. Sie verringern sich immer mehr und erst im Jahre 1837 ist ein ganzer Stamm an den Schwarzen Blattern ausgestorben. Die innere Sicherheit betreffend, so besteht zwar noch Faustrecht, das aber immer nur ums Besitzthum gehandhabt wird. Die anderen Rechtsverhaeltnisse sind lediglich Sache jeder fuer sich bestehenden Commune, u. uebrigens besteht im Allgemeinen so strenges Recht als irgend anders. M.: Nach derselben Analogie, nach welcher man bisher Alles gethan hat um die Kirche . . . (?) zu erhalten, muss man nun alles thun, um sie hinaus zu bringen. Mit laengerem Anstande wuerde man wohl Gott versuchen. St. entgegnet: P. habe oft gesagt, Gott werde doch noch Bahn machen und den Weg zeigen. Darauf entgegnet M.: Mit Vorbereitung ist immer noch nichts verdorben; denn zeigt Gott inzwischen einen anderen Weg, so gehts allerdings darnach. *Jetzt* sagt P., das Warten sei jetzt nur Zeitverlust: Was steht ihr hier muessig, geht hin in den Weinberg. Entscheidung der Behoerde kommt vielleicht gar nicht, oder doch spaet. Wird das Responsum erst abgewartet, so ist es dann zu spaet zum Handeln."

[63] In Fasc. VI there is a rather long letter from Dr. Stuebel, dated September 10, 1839. This letter indicates that Dr. Stuebel had a feeling that Stephan was basically dishonest. He claims that he told Marbach about his misgivings concerning Stephan's conduct over against members of the opposite sex and over against the members of his own family, particularly since he left them to shift for themselves in Germany while he emigrated to America, and concerning his rather lighthearted departure from the congregation over which God had placed him.

[64] The original reads: "St. kann keinen bestimmten Gegenstand angeben und will sich deshalb P.'s Ansicht submittiren. M.: Das will P. nicht, es soll vielmehr jeder selbststaendig sein. St. entgegnet, kaeme Entscheidung dann waere es besser, sie abzuwarten, getraut sich aber nicht zu sagen: wartet auf Entscheidung, sie wird kommen, will auch nicht die Verantwortung auf sich nehmen wegen dem, was zu Grunde geht, wenn kein Responsum kommt — naehmlich, es steht auf dem Spiel: P.'s Gesundh. u. Leben, u. damit das

5

This passage shows how much power Stephan had over the outstanding men of his group and what the source of his power was. Stephan convinced these men and all who believed as they did that he and they were the Church, that outside of the Church so conceived there was no hope of salvation, that his person was their chief means of grace. Every movement of the committee, in fact, every movement of the whole emigrating company, must be viewed in the light of this conviction.[65] In the given instance the entire

---

Hauptgnadenmittel fuer uns, der gze. Bau der Kirche Gottes, der durch ihn geschehen soll, das Heil aller Andern! — Wenn also auch wegen Eintreffen eines Resp. es nicht klar ist, so ist doch dies Alles deshalb nicht aufs Spiel zu setzen. Daher auch St. spricht seine Ueberzeugung dahin aus, dass sofortiges Handeln nothwendig ist."

[65] This concept of the Church is the source of all the confused thinking of the Stephanites concerning emigration, concerning the authority of Stephan, concerning their attitude toward such as did not agree with them. It is written all over the Stephanistic movement. According to L. Fischer, *op. cit.*, p. 43, Pastor Keyl announced publicly: "He who does not cross the ocean is no true Christian" ("Wer nicht ueber's Meer geht, ist kein wahrer Christ"). The gist of the rather wordy and flamboyant *Glaubensbekenntnis der Gemeinde zu St. Johannis in Dresden*, Dresden, 1833, is this: Only we have the true doctrine. This has been given us by Martin Stephan. Only we are the true Lutheran Church. Cf. particularly pp. 50 and 57 of this book. Fischer, p. 40, reports a statement which he himself had heard a Stephanite make: "Whoever resists Stephan contradicts pure doctrine" ("Wer Stephan widerspricht, widerspricht der reinen Lehre"). Fasc. III, No. 12, Minutes of the committee that made arrangements for the emigration. December 13, 1837: "The Church will leave Europe." February 15, 1838: "The entire building of the Church of God is in jeopardy." Cf. footnote 6 of this chapter. J. F. Buenger said to his sister, who became the wife of Rev. O. Fuerbringer: "Stay here, and go to hell." The abnormal solicitude for the safety of Stephan's person, against which Dr. Rudelbach and eight other pastors protested publicly in the *Leipziger Allgemeine Zeitung,* September 30, 1838, can be properly understood only in the light of the Stephanistic-Donatist conception of the Church. This concept of the Church runs all through the so-called *Exulantenlieder.* These poems were composed by O. H. Walther, who became the first pastor of "Old Trinity" in St. Louis, the mother church of the Missouri Synod. These *Lieder* reveal the souls of the men and women who were about to leave their beloved Saxony. On the title page is printed the motto: *Crux Christi Nostra Gloria,* a motto that was written in large letters of gold over the pulpit of St. John's in Dresden. The title of the collection is "Exulanten Lieder auf dem Meer, eine kleine Beisteuer zum geistlichen Schiffsvorrath der um ihres allerheiligsten Glaubens willen mit den treuen Knechte Gottes und Zeugen der Wahrheit, Martin Stephan, aus Sachsen nach Amerika fliehenden apostolisch-lutherischen Gemeinde, den 31. Oktober 1838." The copy used in this study was the one which the author himself handed to Pastor Stephan in Bremen. On the outside cover there is a gold-stamped dedication: "Dem Hochwuerdigen Pastor M. Stephan in kindlicher Ehrerbietung und Dankbarkeit von O. H. W., Bremen, d. 5. Nov. 1838." This copy is in the private library of Dr. L. Fuerbringer, St. Louis. There are four poems. In the first one we have statements like these: "Praise God, the hour of deliverance is approaching for the Church of Christ. . . . God wills to liberate His people. . . . A wise servant of the Lord leads us after the fashion of Moses from Egypt to Canaan. . . . Do you hear the Church cry in agony: Make me free? Can you see your mother in chains

committee favored the opinion of Stephan with the exception of Dr. Stuebel. Stuebel was not a renegade, but he harbored some misgivings. Immediately heavy pressure was brought to bear on his timid soul. A procedure bordering on third-degree methods was used. Finally, when Stuebel capitulated, Marbach tried to create the impression that the pastor favored independence of thought on the part of the committee members. The fact was that Stephan could not tolerate any doubters on the committee. He wanted everyone to say, *"Ja."* And so Marbach and the rest of the committee members go to work on Stuebel until the poor man finally says, *"Ja."* They did not convince him; they wore him down. A dictator wants a *"Ja"* vote. A man who cannot vote *"Ja"* is a traitor, or, as Stephan would say, he is not "true" ("redlich").[66]

This passage from the minutes of February 16, 1838, also gives us occasion to pause for a moment and examine the method by which the ecclesiastical autocrat gained control over his followers. Let us remember that he was a pastor in Saxony, where pastors were surrounded with a certain halo. They were *Standespersonen.* As a member of a privileged class, his word carried weight. For years he had been giving his adherents advice and counsel in spiritual matters. They had accepted his advice as pure gospel. He became more and more important in their sight, and they became less and less aware of any doctrinal irregularities on his part. As they became emotionally conditioned, their thinking lost its keenness; in fact, it became dull and slightly deranged. In this state of affairs Stephan easily became God's elder brother in their estimation. The next step was easy. Whoever forsakes God's elder brother for-

---

of slavery?" . . . The second *Lied* is dedicated to the author's nephew Stephanus Keyl, who was born June 27, 1838, and who for many years was the Missouri Synod's immigrant missionary in the harbor of New York. After addressing himself to the four-months-old child, whose flight from Saxony to America he compares with the flight of the Christ Child from Palestine to Egypt, he goes on to say: "The Church is in dire straits. Herod would destroy it. For this reason we have fled from our poor fatherland out on the high seas." The fourth poem is entitled "Moses in the Basket" ("Moses im Rohrkaestlein"). In this poem the author compares the troubles of the emigrants to the plight of Moses and the children of Israel. He says: "From Pharaoh's blood-dripping hand in our German Egypt land, from lying and murdering and teaching of the devil, the Lord is delivering your soul. . . . Praise God, ye Christians, young and old! The dawn of a new day is not far off. Soon the little flock of the Christian Church will be made free from her chains of long slavery. . . . Sing and rejoice and praise the Lord! The name of the Church of God is 'Moses.' God drew her out of the water and put Pharaoh to shame."

66 Minutes, December 6, 1837.

sakes God, and whoever resists God's elder brother resists God. From time immemorial religious sanctions have been most powerful devices in gaining absolute control over men. The altar and the throne, the priest and the potentate, have stood side by side and worked hand in hand for the development of autocratic government. When the priest and the potentate are combined in one person, the effect is heightened.

Stephan's clever way with men is particularly evident in the handling of the committee. It should be noted, to begin with, that they were appointed by Stephan.[67] They were called in ostensibly for purposes of consultation.[68] Their opinions were solicited with great care. They were left under the impression that their opinions carried weight. Stephan graciously permitted them to do a great deal of talking; but the decisions he reserved for himself. Frequently he did not even attend the committee meetings. His absence did not make so much difference, for at such times his right bower, the lawyer Dr. Marbach, took care of the committee. If all the committee members agreed with the opinions which Marbach had previously ascertained from Stephan,[69] Marbach would let them

---

[67] Minutes, December 13, 1837. "The present critical state of the Evangelical Lutheran Church and the momentarily expected arrival of the time when the Church will be forced to leave Europe makes it necessary for several members of the Church about whose prudence and reticence and willingness to serve God there is no doubt to get together and to consult with one another on the measures which should be taken to meet the situation." (The original: "Die Gegenwaertige Noth der evangelisch-lutherischen Kirche und das sonach praesumtiv nahe Bevorstehen des Zeitpunktes, wo die Kirche Europa verlassen muss, macht es nothwendig, dass einige Glieder derselben, auf deren Vorsicht, Verschwiegenheit und Willigkeit, Gott zu dienen, zu rechnen ist, zusammen treten, um sich ueber die sogestaltene Verhaeltnisse zu ergreifenden Massregeln gemeinschaftlich zu berathen.") In the very next paragraph of the minutes the report goes on to say: "Our revered pastor has therefore determined that for the first the following men are to serve on this committee: Herr Advocat Marbach, Herr Dr. Stuebel, Herr Candidat Brohm, Herr Candidat Welzel, Herr Kaufmann Fischer, Herr Gutsbesitzer Gube, and their treasurer, Jaeckel (the undersigned)." The original reads: "Unser Verehrter Herr Pastor hat hierzu vorlaeufig bestimmt: Herr Advocat Marbach, Herr Dr. Stuebel, Herr Candidat Brohm, Herr Candidat Welzel, Herr Kaufmann Fischer, Herr Gutsbesitzer Gube, und deren Kassierer Jaekel (Unterzeichneter), welche sich saemmtlich heute zu einer Besprechung eingefunden haben." It was definitely stated that their honored pastor wanted them to function as a *Berathungs-Comite.*

[68] Minutes, December 13, 1837.

[69] Minutes, December 13, 1837: "Business is to be carried on by order of the pastor under the leadership of the lawyer Marbach." (Original: "Geschaeftsbetrieb wird nach Auftrag des Herrn Pastors unter Leitung des Herrn Advocaten Marbach gefuehrt.") Minutes of March 24, 1838: Marbach announces that he is about to go to Leipzig on a business trip. Doctors Vehse

decide the matter. If not, the decision would be postponed to a later date. An instance will illustrate the technique: In the meeting of September 20, 1838, Marbach presented rules and regulations for the journey of the group ("Reiseordnung"). There was some discussion about the weight and size of the baggage of each individual emigrant. The majority seems to have opposed Marbach's views. It was decided to ask for an audience with Pastor Stephan and to postpone the publication of the "Reiseordnung" until he had made his decision on the size and weight of each man's baggage.

Another illustration of Stephan's technique of control is revealed in the manner in which he got his way in the choice of routes. The question was whether to go to Missouri via New York or via New Orleans. In order to control the crowd, Stephan insisted on the all-water route via New Orleans. The matter was under consideration in every meeting from April 25 till June 25, 1838. The committee seems to have been overwhelmingly in favor of sailing via New York. Even Marbach favored this route. So Stephan permits them to gather information from every possible source. They write letters hither and yon. In the meeting of April 28 seventeen common-sense arguments are advanced in favor of New York. Here are some: "Many ships sail from German ports for New York, very few for New Orleans." "Since we have a greater choice of ships, we are more likely to get an adequate and safe ship." "In New York we have a reliable Christian friend."[70] "The Mississippi might freeze up in the regions around St. Louis. Going from New York to St. Louis, we can wait until after the equinoctial storms." "The climate of New York will cause us no difficulty. In New Orleans we must contend with climatic conditions and sicknesses" (yellow fever). "If we go via New York, we will embark at Hamburg. This means we can go up the Elbe from Saxony and reload at Hamburg. If we go via New Orleans, we will have to reload at Hamburg, go overland to Bremen, and reload at that port." "The

---

and Stuebel agree to wait on the pastor and receive any orders which he might have to give. (Original: "DD. Stuebel und Vehse erboten sich, die vorkommenden Geschaefte in Angelegenheit des Herrn Pastors und der Gemeinde waehrend M.'s Abwesenheit zu besorgen u. nahmentlich abwechselnd beim Pastor wegen etwaiger Auftragsertheilungen nachzufragen.")

[70] This was a certain Mr. Sproede. He joined the colony in St. Louis later on. He eventually got into long-drawn-out and disagreeable arguments with C. F. W. Walther and the members of Trinity Church in St. Louis. He died in St. Louis of apoplexy in 1843.

journey to New Orleans is eight or ten weeks." "If we journey
via New Orleans, we will have many additional and difficult arrangements to make. If we go via New York, Sproede will give us reliable information on everything. We will save money." "If we
go via New Orleans to St. Louis, there are relatively few points of
interest. If we go via New York, we will get to see the Lutheran
center of America, and we will pass through most of the American
States." "If we go via New York, we get to see Cincinnati. Cincinnati is a city of 40,000. We may wish to settle there in preference to St. Louis." These reasons were to circulate among the
members of the committee, and then they were to be presented to
the pastor for his decision.

In the meeting of April 28 there was a long discussion. Most
of the arguments of April 25 were repeated. If anything, they had
been reinforced and clarified by correspondence that had arrived
since the 25th. Marbach claims that it is next to impossible to get
reliable information about shipping possibilities and traveling conditions from New Orleans to St. Louis. Everyone seems to think
that the journey should be made via New York. Finally Dr. Vehse
is commissioned to set up a list of questions and to send them to
Sproede, who is in New York.

In the meeting of May 2 Pastor Stephan is present in person.
Some members of the committee present the old arguments for New
York, but not with the same degree of force. The pastor is present,
and he does not favor New York. After they have presented their
arguments for New York, Pastor Stephan joins the discussion and
says substantially the following: All the information we have received thus far is from Sproede. We are very glad to hear from
him, and we ought to give credence to what he writes. But you
will remember Sproede. He is a man who is quick on the trigger
in making plans. He is not a man of careful deliberation, nor has
he proved his worth ("Er hat sich ueberhaupt noch nicht be-
waehrt"). As for overland travel, I would not care for a journey
even for one mile with a multitude of people. There are chances
that 300 people will join us. There may be at least 80 children.
How are we going to keep a group of 300 people together? The
flock must stay together. Thereupon the decision was made by the
committee that any idea of traveling overland in America must
absolutely be given up. Seventeen points in favor of New York
and all the oratory and correspondence connected therewith went
by the board in a three-minute speech by Pastor Stephan. In the

very first meeting in which this matter was to come up for discussion Stephan could have instructed Marbach to say: The pastor wants to travel via New Orleans to St. Louis. Instead Stephan carefully avoided the semblance of dictatorship and permitted the committee members to do a great deal of writing and inquiring and talking. Finally he appeared in a meeting, to indicate the importance which he attached to the decision. In a speech in which he indicated how solicitous he was for the welfare of the entire flock he used the religious symbol of shepherd and flock so effectively that no opposition was manifested. There was a semblance of untrammeled investigation and free discussion on the part of all, but the decision was made by one. This is the pattern of Stephanistic control: the appearance of democracy and the essence of highly centralized government. The same pattern appears in the selection of a place for the colony,[71] in the adoption of the episcopal form of church polity,[72] in determining the exact time when the company

---

[71] There was much discussion on this point according to the minutes. In the meeting of May 11, 1838, Northern Illinois, Indiana, Ohio, Michigan, and Wisconsin were mentioned as possible locations for the colony. Missouri was not regarded as a particularly good place for colonization because of the prevalence of yellow fever and lazy fever. Another circumstance that argued against Missouri was that slavery was practiced, also that lynch law prevailed without hindrance. For the opposition to Missouri cf. also the minutes of April 14, 1838. "Fuer die Ansiedelung ist Missouri noch nicht definitiv (die Selbstgewalt des rohen Haufens gibt erhebliche Bedenken)." In the meeting of May 18 there was quite a bit of talk about locating in Chicago. The U.S. consul in Dresden had advised them to choose Chicago. In the meeting of May 19 they discussed the high cost of living in St. Louis. Vegetables, including kraut, were said to be particularly high in price. In the meeting of May 18 England and Australia were under consideration. But the Lutheran Church is only tolerated in England; and, furthermore, England will undergo a great political change in the near future. In Australia there is too much robbery. According to the minutes of April 14 it must be a place where a whole township can be bought. They wished to preserve their own civil government, and the township is the unit of local government. It contains 23,060 acres. The cost will be $1.25 per acre. They will need about $43,000 for this purpose. The company is to buy the entire complex of land and then resell to individuals. May 11: Wisconsin is out of the question because of the fierceness of the Sioux Indians. Arkansas is mentioned in the meeting of December 6, 1837. The river connections are good for Arkansas. Vehse, *op. cit.*, p. 3, has this comment: "People have been surprised that the spiritual despot chose the United States of America, the most free country in the world, for purposes of colonization. But whoever is acquainted with his deep-seated aversion to all interference on the part of civil government in the affairs of the Church will understand his reasons for the choice of a state which is in no wise concerned about the Church, but rather permits the utmost freedom in religious matters. Here he could execute his medieval hierarchical plans concerning church government, provided, of course, that the people who emigrated with him would tolerate such a procedure. Furthermore, America offers protection of life and property and the purchase of much land at unbelievably low prices.

[72] There is no reference to episcopal polity in his sermons. The only

thing to be found there on this point is perhaps a slightly exaggerated statement concerning the office of the ministry. In the minutes of the *Berathungs-Comite,* December 6 and 13, 1837, the episcopal form of church polity is taken for granted. By September 27, 1838, Stephan had come to be recognized by the group as the bishop of the whole Lutheran Church. This entire meeting was given over to the problem of establishing the amount of money that would be necessary for the bishop's personal needs while traveling to America. The complete minutes of this meeting read as follows: "Der Hauptgegenstand der heutigen Besprechung war die Bestimmung einer dem Herrn Pastor Stephan fuer seine derzeitigen Beduerfnisse aus der Creditcasse zur Verfuegung zu stellenden Summe. Nachdem man die verschiedenen hier einschlagenden Ruecksichten erwogen hatte und nahmentlich die Verpflichtungen, welche nicht nur die hiesige Gemeinde als gegen ihren Seelsorger, sondern ueberhaupt die saemmtlichen vereinigten Lutherischen Gemeinden als gegen ihren Bischof, den Regenten der Kirche, zu erfuellen haben, vereinigte man sich ueberzeugt haltend — dahin: dem Herrn Pastor Stephan zu seinen jetzigen Beduerfnissen fuer sich, seine Familie und bedienung aus der Creditcasse die Summe von **Eintausend und fuenfhundert Thalern** — zum [*sic!*] beliebigen Verfuegung auszusetzen, und diese Summe zur Verausgabung beim Kirchen Conto zu verweisen. Herr Kaufmann Fischer soll mitterst Zufertigung gegenwaertigen Protokolls zu Zahlung dieser Summe mit Anweisung versehen und durch ihn den Herrn Pastor Stephan hiervon benachrichtigt werde. Bemerkt von Jaeckel." In addition to Jaeckel the minutes of this meeting were signed by F. A. Marbach, H. F. Fischer, Dr. Carl Eduard Vehse, Theodore Julius Brohm, Johann Georg Gube, Johann August Staertzell, Johann Gottlieb Palisch, August Friedrich Maeder, Karl Wilhelm Welzel. On the 14th of November Stephan arrived at Bremerhafen, definitely disappointed because there was no formal cortege to meet him and to accompany him to the hotel. He complained bitterly of the slight which his adherents were showing his person. He issued a standing order that hereafter due cognizance should be taken of his office ("sein Amt"). He demanded the honor, he said, not for himself, but for his office ("sein Amt"). See Vehse, *op. cit.,* p. 8.

The minutes of the meeting which took place on the *Olbers,* January 16, 1839, contain an interesting note about the bishopric. The candidates of theology are to form an escort and a bodyguard for the bishop. Messrs. Klemm and Graeber are appointed to minister to his personal needs. Two days before, on January 14, 1839, Stephan took the necessary steps to have the episcopal polity legalized by the company. He gave his vicar, O. H. Walther, orders to draw up a document in which all pastors and candidates of theology, those on the *Olbers,* the *Copernicus,* the *Johann Georg,* and the *Republic,* should formally request him to assume the title and office of a bishop. He also commanded O. H. Walther to preach a sermon that evening on "The Necessity of Introducing the Episcopal Form of Church Government and on the Enslavement of the Lutheran Church in Germany." On the next day he had the people elect twelve delegates who were to second the request of the theologians. Note again the semblance of democracy. Vehse, *op. cit.,* p. 10, claims that he was standing with Stephan on the bridge of the ship shortly before supper when Stephan said: "It is necessary that I step on American soil as a bishop. You know me, and you know that I have no ulterior motives. Our whole debarkation would be a lame affair if I would not step on American soil as a bishop." The original copy of the petition in which Stephan was "requested" to assume the title and function of a bishop is found in Concordia Historical Institute. Incidentally, the theologians who had crossed the ocean on the *Copernicus,* the *Republic,* and the *Johann Georg* and who had preceded Stephan in the journey up the Mississippi signed "the request" in St. Louis without the least bit of hesitation. This is also true of O. H. Walther's brother, C. F. W. Walther. The laymen also elected twelve delegates in St. Louis, who dutifully signed the "request." The episcopal form of church government was legitimized because it had its roots in the wishes of the people. Note again the semblance of democracy.

should leave Saxony,[73] in the selection of the individuals who should be permitted to join the company,[74] in the purchase of land after they had arrived in St. Louis,[75] and in the building operations down

---

[73] Mystery surrounds the selection of the actual date of departure. Stephan pretends to be waiting for a sign from the Lord which would indicate that the hour of departure is at hand. Cf. minutes of the "Berathungs-Comite," February 15, 1838. In the meeting of May 11, 1838, it was stated that the pastor wished to leave in the coming fall, "otherwise everything will go to ruin — the congregation spiritually, and he physically" ("Der Herr Pastor hat sich dahin ausgesprochen, dass er jedenfalls im Herbst dieses Jahres fortzuziehen gedenke, weil sonst noch alles zu Grunde gehen muesse, die Gemeinde geistlicher-weise und er selbst dem Leibe nach"). In a footnote which Jaeckel added to the minutes of May 18, 1838, the following is stated. Pastor Stephan remarked how peculiar it was that all the people who had talked to him about the present state of affairs were of one mind. This, he said, was particularly true of heads of families, who said: "If things continue, or if they become progressively worse, we and our children will perish spiritually." The fact of the matter was that conditions were steadily improving during the 1830's from a confessional Lutheran point of view. Conservative Lutheranism was showing more and more power. From a soberly religious, common-sense point of view there was no need for an emigration. Had the Stephanites really faced the situation with realistic eyes and looked at things as they were, not as Stephan wanted them to see them, there never would have needed to be an emigration. That things were improving is proved by Walther himself. Reporting on a trip which he and Wyneken made in the fall of 1851, Walther writes, *Der Lutheraner*, VIII (1852), p. 100: "Ueberhaupt hatten wir schon waehrend der noch sehr kurzen Strecke unsrer Reise auf deutschem Boden deutlich gesehen, dass in Deutschland seit unserer Abwesenheit von da eine grosse Veraenderung, und zwar zum Besseren, [eingetreten ist]. Von immer mehr Orten, wo frueher der elendeste Rationalismus gehaust hatte, hoerten wir, dass da jetzt glaeubige Prediger wirken und dass auch unter diesen glaeubigen Predigern immer mehr zu der Ueberzeugung kommen, wie nothwendig ein treues und entschiedenes Festhalten an dem kirchlichen Bekenntniss und eine dem entsprechende Fernhaltung von kirchlicher Gemeinschaft mit Falschglaeubigen sei. Von vielen vormals hartnaeckigen Verfechtern der Union erfuhren wir, dass sie jetzt die Bodenlosigkeit und Ungoettlichkeit dieses Werkes immer lebendiger erkennen und dass sich daher immer mehr frueher nach unionistischen Grundsaetzen gegruendete Vereine theils gaenzlich aufgeloest, theils mehr und mehr auf kirchliche Basis gestellt haben."

[74] On this point there was much discussion. It appears from the minutes that the committee was quite unanimous in its opinion that the number of poor people who were to be taken along should be small. Stephan, on the other hand, wished to take a large number of poor people. In the meeting of May 2, 1838, he speaks of 300 people who will form the company. In the meeting of May 18, 1838, he speaks of their duty to take unconverted people along, "for the Church is not only the caretaker of those who are born, but also the mother of those who are to be born." For the complete quotation see footnote 59 of this chapter. Needless to say, a large number of poor people were taken. There was plenty of discussion on the part of the committee members, but the decision was made by Stephan. See also Vehse, *op. cit.*, p. 5.

[75] Shortly after the arrival of the company in St. Louis the Gratiot family, who owned 15,000 acres of fine land along the Meramec River about twelve to fifteen miles distant from the heart of St. Louis, offered this land for sale to the Saxons on very favorable terms. This land was close to a rapidly growing market; it had a good stand of timber on it, part of which could

in the settlement.[76] In fact, wherever one examines Stephan's activity, he will find a show of great solicitude for the people's welfare coupled with a most highly developed autocracy. This is undoubtedly what Dr. Vehse had in mind when he wrote:

> His ungodliness is exceeded only by his craftiness. . . .
> Through his intimate and extended association with the
> people of high and low degree he came into possession of
> a mass of knowledge concerning people and things. His
> ability to size up people of the most divergent character was
> almost uncanny. This in turn gave him the habit of handling
> people with the utmost tact, so that they got under his control
> without noticing his power.[77]

have been cut down as firewood and sold at $5.00 per cord; and, in addition, there were some valuable springs on the land. There was a sufficient number of building sites on the tract which would have insured the health of the colonists. Payments could have been arranged to suit the convenience of the company. Again there was much talk; a committee was appointed to inspect this land, etc. But the final decision was made by Stephan, and he decided to purchase land in Perry County, about 100 miles south of St. Louis. See Vehse, *op. cit.*, p. 35.

[76] The first building which Stephan planned to erect in Perry County was the episcopal palace. It was to have a front of seventy feet with a large porch. Vehse, *op. cit.*, p. 18.

[77] Vehse, *op. cit.*, pp. 1—2. The desire for personal power is also evident from the various constitutions ("Ordnungen") which Stephan drew up in consultation with Marbach. The original copies of the "Ordnungen" are to be found in Fasc. IV, No. 4, deposited in Concordia Historical Institute. In the "Reiseordnung fuer die mit Herrn Pastor Stephan nach den Vereinigten St. von N. Am. auswandernde Gemeinde" there is a special paragraph on the government of the association ("Gemeinde"). It reads: "The supreme administration of all of the association's affairs is in the hands of the first clergyman, who combines in his person the highest powers in both spiritual and secular affairs." ("Die oberste Leitung aller Angelegenheiten der ganzen Gemeinde fuehrt der erste Geistliche derselben, der sonach in seiner Person die oberste Gewalt in geistlichen und buergerlichen Sachen vereinigt.") Paragraph 6 of this "Ordnung" says: "The first clergyman is to be treated with the proper respect and honor commensurate with his high position and deep wisdom. He receives as his title: 'Most Honorable Lord.' Disrespect for this person and disobedience over against his commands are punishable with serious civil and ecclesiastical penalties. Only pastors and members of the assisting administrative committee have immediate and free access to the first clergyman. Passengers of the first class also have this privilege and those to whom it has been specifically given. All other members of the association must be duly announced before they may appear in his presence." ("Der oberste Geistliche ist allenthalben von den Gemeindegliedern mit der seinem hohen Amte und seiner hohen Weisheit gebuehrenden Ehrerbietung zu behandeln; er erhaelt den Titel 'Hochwuerdiger Herr.' Vergehungen gegen seine Person und Ungehorsam gegen seine Anordnungen sind mit ernstlichen buergerlichen und kirchlichen Strafen zu belegen. Den unmittelbaren u. freien Zutritt zu dem ersten Geistlichen erhalten nur seine Herrn Amtsbrueder, die Ausschusspersonen, auf den Schiffe auch noch die Kajuetenpassagiere und wem er es sonst ausdruecklich verstattet. Alle uebrigen Glieder der Gemeinde haben nur nach vorhergegangener Anmeldung vor ihm zu erscheinen.")

Martin Stephan suffered from a feeling of inferiority. At times this feeling reached the stage of persecutory delusions. He compensated for it by getting complete control over his fellows. But the story of his peculiar development would be only half told if the belief and the activities of many leaders in the Church and State of his day were not mentioned. He reached the height of his career during the post-Napoleonic era. The heavy pressure of the Corsican's magic power was removed.[78] The fall of the

---

Paragraph 9 is headed "Penalties." "Transgressions of God's commandments and of this constitution as well as resistance against the commands of the first clergyman and the assisting administrative committee and the appointed inspector are punishable in the first instance with severe reprimand; in case the offense is repeated, a most severe reprimand in the presence of the entire administrative committee is to be given. If this does not bring desired results, the culprit is to be expelled and removed from the association. Complete expulsion and removal from the association can be decreed only by the first clergyman." Fasc. IV, No. 4, also contains the constitution for a theocratic civil government. There are various provisions which give Stephan power over the civil government of the colony. "The 'Rath' (of the colony) must be governed by the Word of God, by the laws of the United States, and especially by the laws in that State in which the colony will eventually settle.... In order to vote and be elected, it is necessary that the citizen be twenty-five years old and that he be a communicant member in good standing in the Church." Paragraph 6: ". . . A member of the 'Rath' who during the time of his office has been suspended from Holy Communion must resign his position in the 'Rath' at once." Paragraph 13 is entitled "Book Commission." "Freedom of the press shall in no wise be curtailed. However, a copy of every new publication must be submitted to the Book Commission before it may go on sale. The Book Commission shall be composed of a deputation of ministers and of a deputation of citizens. Each of these deputations singly shall have the right to forbid the sale of any books as soon as it becomes evident that such books are directed against the existing ecclesiastical and civil ordinances or against the Confessions of the old Lutheran Church or against Christian morals." Paragraph 15 is headed "Resignation and Expulsion." . . . "Whosoever is expelled from the means of grace in the Church ceases to be a member of the civil community and must remove himself from the territory of the community."

[78] Stephan refers to Napoleon and his magic power in a sermon preached the Second Sunday in Advent, 1825, *Der christliche Glaube*, p. 21: "In the year 1810 many of the wisest men of our time predicted publicly that Napoleon's power and domination would continue indefinitely. It seemed impossible that such indescribable power should collapse. They estimated the tremendous resources at the command of this powerful ruler; they counted the soldiers of the vast army that willingly did his bidding, and they said: Such power will continue for a long time. Behold, how quickly all this was changed! Five years later the power of this genuinely feared man was demolished. He was captured, stripped of all power, and died a lonely man on an island. Who could have foretold this most remarkable development of recent history? And yet how instructive this event is for all times!" The Little Corporal's physical and mental decline, the persistent hostility of England, the awakened spirit of nationalism in Spain and Prussia — these and other factors which played a role in the downfall of Napoleon seem to have escaped the attention of Martin Stephan entirely at the time.

man who had risen so quickly to meteoric heights and who had
held all Europe in thrall was so sudden that millions believed
that only God could have brought it about. Sin-ridden and morally
indifferent, doubting Thomases became religious. The hand of
God was too visible to be denied. A movement known as the
Restoration gained momentum.[79] Ignoring the patent accomplish-
ments of the Revolution and the Enlightenment, this movement
yearned to go back to a certain something that was believed to
have existed before the Revolution and the Enlightenment. There
was a nostalgia, a *Heimweh,* for something in the past. Unlike the
Renaissance and the Reformation, the movement was purely re-
actionary and utterly unprogressive. We see it in the program
of the Holy Alliance, a return to the medieval idea of a unified
Christian society. The crowned heads of Europe regarded themselves as brethren in association with each other, but as family
fathers in association with their subjects. There was something
unreal about a paternalism that regarded the men who had covered themselves with glory in the Wars of Liberation as children.
Religion was looked upon by the men of power in Church and
State as a means to an end, particularly as an instrument in the
hands of a prince or of his government to preserve the *status quo*
over against all men who advocated change. There was a childish
fear of revolution. The "Red Scare" of the 1920's in the United
States, during which men looked under their beds at night to
see whether a Bolshevik might be lurking there, is an analogy.
When nine strong policemen of Dresden are commissioned to go
out and arrest Stephan on the night of November 8, 1837, in the
Hofloesnitz, and when one of the chief charges against the fifty-
nine-year-old grayhead who had been pastor of St. John's for
twenty-eight years was that he had been taking a walk with an unmarried woman after ten o'clock in the evening, one is provoked
to ask the question, Who was more psychopathic, Stephan or the
Stadtrat of Dresden? [80]

---

[79] K. Aner has written a scholarly article on the Restoration in RGG, IV,
1994—1995. Also Ernst Troeltsch, *Die Restaurationsepoche am Anfang des
19. Jahrhunderts, Gesammelte Schriften,* IV, 1925, p. 587 ff.

[80] Hanewinckel in his report to Dr. Dau has carefully copied all the documents pertaining to this arrest. They are found on pp. 52—85 of the Hanewinckel Report. The documents show that the government was moved by
fear and hatred. They feared that Stephan and his group might start a revolution. The nocturnal gatherings in the vineyard the government believed

In attempting to arrive at a factual estimate of the government's side in the Stephan case, one must keep in mind that the Stephanistic movement was part of the larger neo-pietistic *Erweckungsbewegung* of the early nineteenth century; that this movement was a protest against the *status quo;* that it made for separatism; that its leaders were violent critics of the existing *publica doctrina* and the *publicae mores*, which at this time happened to be rationalism; [81] that it was opposed to all Biblical criticism and had no understanding of critical theology; that the movement had a strong tendency to form groups, whose members experienced piety in company with each other and who renounced the world and all its evil, but found a substitute in these very groups for the world which they had renounced.[82] Nor dare one

were meetings in which revolutionary ideas were taking shape. Hence its constant attempt to support the charge of *Conventickelwesen* against Stephan and Stephan's equally strong effort to show that these meetings were not conventicles. Hanewinckel states that his report on the arrest is an *Abschrift* of D 129. The whole thing was done at the instigation of the *Koenigliche Saechsische Kreis-Direction*. The head of this branch of government was von Winterheim. The government of Saxony, the government of Dresden, and the Superintendent of the Ephorie Dresden co-operated. The charges against Stephan were three: a. conventicles; b. nocturnal gatherings; c. forbidden walks ("verbotene Spaziergaenge").

[81] Walter Wendland has written a long and scholarly article in RGG, II, pp. 295—303, on the *Erweckungsbewegung*. He points out that rationalism was trying to maintain the *status quo*, a fact which is often overlooked by students of the nineteenth century. Karl Hennig, in his Leipzig Doctor's thesis, *Die saechsische Erweckungsbewegung im Anfange des 19. Jahrhunderts*, lays great stress on the connection between Stephan and the neo-pietistic *Erweckungsbewegung* of the early nineteenth century. His thesis is that the Stephanites began as neo-pietistic "Erweckte" and developed into highly confessional Lutherans, who finally kept aloof from everybody and sailed to America to save their souls.

[82] Through its criticism of the public doctrine and public morals Stephanism incurred the hatred and wrath of many. The fact that it had no understanding of critical theology made it a target for jibes. In his autobiography Ernst Moritz Buerger tells of his experience in the parish of Lunzenau. "Enmity against me continued. On a street corner a pasquil was posted which began with these words: "Pastor Buerger and the devil are bosom pals" (Original: "Der Pastor Buerger und der Teufel sind wohl ohne allen Zweifel liebe Herzensbruederchen"). Buerger continues: "On the barn doors which my friends from Seelitz" (Note of the present writer: These were people who were particularly devoted to Stephanism and whom Buerger had made what they were) "had to pass on the way to my church many spiteful caricatures were drawn with the legend underneath 'Mystics' ('Mystiker') or 'Mummlers' ('Mucker'). My pious and God-fearing count informed me that the police had been commissioned to keep an eye on my movements and to prevent me from conducting conventicles in my house. On the reredos of the altar of the church at Lunzenau there was a cross with a serpent attached to it. Shortly after I had entered office, the *Stadtrat* suggested that the serpent be removed, since it was esthetically offensive. In my protest

overlook the fact that many adherents of the *Erweckungsbewegung,* including Stephan, were in favor of constitutional
changes which would give the Church a different position in the
state from the one which it was then occupying.[83] If one takes

---

against the removal I pointed to John 3: 14: 'As Moses lifted up the serpent,' etc.
Two or three years later the serpent was no longer on the cross, but it was
found lying in the corner of the sacristy broken in pieces. I succeeded in
punishing the perpetrator of this sacrilege. After we had established an
independent parish in Lunzenau, a church seal had to be purchased. I considered it wise to consult the superintendent concerning the figure to be
engraved on the seal. Undoubtedly he had heard of the sacrilege concerning
the serpent, for he suggested immediately that I select some prominent
symbol of the Church for the seal. That was enough for me. I had a serpent
on a cross engraved on the seal. No one dared to protest against this figure.
In the new Saxon Agenda, an abominable makeshift, the old and proper words
of absolution had been corrupted. The old reading was: 'I forgive you your
sins.' This was changed to: 'I announce the forgiveness of your sins to you.'
But I used the old form, both on the pulpit and in the confessional service.
I said: 'I forgive you your sins.' For this reason the city representative made
complaint at the *Consistorium.* I received an order from the *Consistorium*
to use the form of absolution prescribed in the new Agenda. In a written
defense of my action I cited the Scriptures, where Jesus says: 'Whosesoever
sins ye remit,' etc., and the Symbolical Books of the Lutheran Church, in which
the following statement is found: 'Do you believe that my forgiveness is God's
forgiveness?' I also cited the fathers of the Church, e. g., St. Ambrose. I soon
noticed that the *Consistorium* would remain adamant, and so I decided to
seek the advice of Pastor Stephan in this matter. Stephan stood in high repute
with us young and inexperienced pastors. We regarded him as a true and
expert adviser. We had great confidence in him. However, he gave me some
bad advice. He suggested that if I were forced to use the new form, I should
give in but say to the congregation: 'If the congregation does not wish to have
the proper form, it shall not have it.' It did not take very long before two
superintendents, sent by the *Consistorium,* came to me and demanded of me
that I use the new form. My conscience was disturbed, but I finally gave
the answer that Stephan, suggested. I even signed my name to a statement.
Oh, terrible shame when I promised solemnly that I would use the form of
the new Agenda! Until this very hour this shameful denial of my Savior
is a sting in my conscience, against which I can find comfort only in the
shed blood of Jesus Christ."

    83 Ludwig Fischer, a contemporary of Stephan and a careful and dis-
passionate student, admits, *op. cit.,* pp. 99—102, that Stephan was right when
he argued for a constitutional change which would give the Church, and
particularly the ministry, a more respected position in Saxony. Stephan
argued for a church government that would be less subject to the secular arm
of the government. The authority of the *Cultus-Ministerium* should be reduced. The power of the estates of the realm (*Landtag*) over ecclesiastical
matters should be annulled, since the representatives in the *Landtag* know
little or nothing about evangelical doctrine. Some of them even have anti-
ecclesiastical tendencies. The welfare of the Church demands an independent
administration, with a bishop at its head. Only then will the Church regain
its former standing and influence in Saxony. L. Fischer agrees with Stephan
and cites other men who favored a change in polity that would introduce the
episcopal system. Nowhere does Stephan advocate a greater participation
of the local congregation in the administration of the Church. In fact,
Hanewinckel, pp. 86 and 87, Abschrift Reg. Dresden, den 9. September, 1837,
portrays the type of congregational government that had developed under

all these factors into consideration, and the peculiarities of Stephan's Czecho-German parish, one can begin to realize how Stephan developed the peculiarly warped personality that was his.

Emphasis on sex in the study of an individual's development has perhaps been exaggerated in recent years. In their efforts to explain all abnormal behavior on the basis of sex maladjustments Freud and Adler have undoubtedly oversimplified personality problems. On the other hand, nineteenth century students of personal problems have overlooked important sources of information because they have neglected the factor of sex. A study of Stephan and Stephanism in the fourth decade of the nineteenth century would be incomplete without a reference to Stephan's sexual difficulties.

Stephan was a man of intense social longings. He craved the association of his fellows.[84] He was goodhearted and extremely friendly. Reference has already been made to his stubborn insistence upon a plan which embraced financial assistance to many poor people in their efforts to emigrate. He called the poor "his pearls."[85] His advice to a young lady with reference to dancing shows that his asceticism was not as narrow as one might suspect.[86] Ahead of his time in staid and proper Dresden during the third and fourth decades of the nineteenth century, he conducted a so-called "institutional church." He rented a hall in which the

---

Stephan's leadership. "Herr Friedrich Strumpfwirker, an elder, appears in the office of the *Stadtrat* and is told that he must produce a complete list of the names and addresses of the Bohemian congregation. He excuses himself by saying that the election of the elders (*Vorsteher*) takes place in this way: Every time there is a vacancy, the pastor and the elders discuss the men who might be suitable candidates for the position. As soon as they are agreed on the person, his name is reported to the congregation, and the congregation approves of the election." A typical "*Ja*" vote!

[84] Von Polenz, *op. cit.*, p. 28: "Stephan appreciated friends. In fact, as long as his infallibility was not questioned, he was an extremely pleasant and goodnatured fellow. Socially cheerful and pleasant, he would visit his friends among the clergy in country parishes. He would preach in their churches, and they would preach in his." Vehse, *op. cit.*, p. 2: "He fascinated and held me through his cordial conduct" ("Mich wusste er durch die, ich kann es versichern, liebevollste Begegnung ganz an sich zu fesseln").

[85] Vehse, *op. cit.*, p. 6.

[86] Von Polenz, *op. cit.*, p. 40. This young lady was a governess. The family whose children she was tutoring had invited her to attend a formal ball. Being a devoted Stephanite, she, of course, put the problem up to her master. He asked her, "Would you like to go?" She answered very quickly and decisively, "No." Thereupon he suggested, "Well, then go." In fact, he was very much averse to facial expressions of piety. The traditional frown or the sanctified look as expressions of holiness were discounted.

Handwerker of Dresden met regularly after working hours for purposes of recreation only. The men would play billiards or chess or indulge in other games. Beer and other refreshments were served. Stephan drew up a constitution for the club. The club was run by a president ("Vorsteher"). Members were accepted by majority ballot. No one was permitted to make critical remarks about government officials or ministers of religion. Once a month, usually on Sunday evenings, Stephan appeared in person at the meetings of the club. At such meetings the men were permitted to bring their wives with them. These were gala meetings and, unfortunately for Stephan's reputation, lasted until one o'clock in the morning. Naturally, the *Handwerker* of Dresden were attracted by Stephan's social arrangements, since the churches in their own parishes had nothing to compare with them, and these men were beginning to feel the need of social intercourse. The fact that loyal adherents of Stephan — men and women drawn from his own parish and other parishes of the city — would accompany him on the way from the *Lokal* to the parsonage in the early hours of the morning, and the further fact that an ill-famed section of the city lay between the *Lokal* and Stephan's parsonage gave the ministers of the city and the members of the *Stadtrat* plenty of ammunition to blast his reputation.[87]

In devoting so much energy to the social life of his people, Stephan was possibly finding sublimation for his sex instincts.[88] This seems all the more probable since the normal opportunities for the outlet of his sex energies were prevented by the unsatisfactory marital relations with his wife at this time. Shortly after his arrival at St. John's he had married a lovely young girl from

---

[87] Von Polenz, *op. cit.*, pp. 48—49, describes the arrangement in detail. At another place, p. 23, the intense hatred and bitterness of Stephan's enemies in Dresden is described. The worst construction was put on his actions. It was said that he was encouraging women to steal from their husbands so that they might contribute towards his *"Heilandskasse."* Every time a person was admitted to an insane asylum, every effort was made to prove that he had attended Stephan's meetings. Karl Hennig, in *Zeitschrift fuer Kirchengeschichte*, LVIII (1939), p. 149, describes the attitude of Stephan's enemies in Dresden. The *Stadtklatsch* of Dresden was indescribable. A student of Stephan's life and work might be misled by these rumors, even as the populace of Dresden was undoubtedly misled.

[88] Weathered, *op. cit.*, p. 109, defines sublimation as "directing the instinctive energies, the biological channels for which are for various reasons impossible, into some channel by which they serve the community and satisfy the soul."

one of the most respectable families of Dresden. Her refinement
and breeding tended to bring her husband's coarse ways and lack
of education into bold relief. She had spent her youth in a social
world that differed markedly from his.[89] Cultural and religious
differences, prolific sources of domestic discord, coupled with the
irritation of too many children born in rather rapid succession; [90]
the close connection between Stephan, who believed himself persecuted, and his followers, who believed themselves persecuted
on his account; the nocturnal gatherings of male and female followers in the clubroom and in a rented house out in the vineyard,
which at times were extended to the break of day; Stephan's
tremendous zeal in the discharge of the duties of his office, which
led him to forget the social needs of his family — this combination
of circumstances and events was bound to have its effects in the
disorganization of Stephan's personality.[91] His wife was spiritually
separated from him long before the physical separation took place.
Her hostile attitude toward his beliefs and activities was a source
of constant offense to the faithful. It is not necessary to prove
infidelity and actual adultery on the part of Stephan [92] to show

---

[89] Von Polenz, *op. cit.*, p. 28, makes a strong point of this: "According to
Schiller no man is great in the eyes of his valet. I might add, no man is
a saint in the eyes of his wife. Stephan experienced this fact. Shortly after
his call to Dresden he led a lovely girl from a very respectable Dresden
family to the altar. Her refinement of manners tended to accentuate his
coarse ways."

[90] *Op. cit.*, p. 29, mentions ten children. For various reasons it seems that
the account of the *Berathungs-Comite* is more accurate. They are trying to
arrive at a proper remuneration for the pastor during the journey. In the
meeting of February 19, 1838, they say: "This remuneration must take into
consideration the fact that he has served the Church for twenty-eight years
as pastor, and other very unusual circumstances, as well as his numerous
family, a wife and eight children: seven girls — three of whom are deaf-mutes —
and one boy; the youngest child is a deaf-mute girl of nine years."

[91] *Op. cit.*, pp. 28—29, gives a dispassionate account of Stephan's marital
difficulties.

[92] Hanewinckel has copied all the documents concerning Stephan's difficulty. The accusations brought by the authorities of Church and State as well
as Stephan's defense are on file. Nowhere did the officers of the law succeed
in convicting Stephan of actual adultery in Saxony. In fact, the records do
not show that the prosecution even made such an attempt. It tried to prove
only that these nightly gatherings were conventicles, that they were improper
("unzuechtig"), and that Stephan acted contrary to the law when he went
walking in the company of an unmarried woman after ten o'clock in the
evening. Later on, in Perry County, Missouri, three young ladies, on the
Sixth Sunday after Trinity, July 7, 1839, confessed to their pastor, Rev. Gotthold
H. Loeber, that Stephan had made improper sexual advances to them. They
asked Pastor Loeber to announce this from the pulpit and to ask the congregation to pardon them. The names of these young ladies were: Louise

that there was definite maladjustment.   When he left his wife and
children in Dresden while he emigrated to Missouri, even the
blindest should have sensed that something was wrong.[93]   How
much of the fault for the failure of this marriage should be charged
to the husband and how much to the wife is difficult to ascertain.
They were a couple that just did not fit together.

    The sex instinct in man is one of the most troublesome;   it

---

Karoline Voelker, aged 21 years, whose number was 37 on the *Olbers* and who
hailed from Mittelfrohna; Friederike Sophie Hoeschel, aged 28, whose number
was 68 on the *Olbers* and who hailed from Dresden; Wilhelmina Hahn, aged 27,
whose number was 106 and who also came from Dresden. Pastor G. H. Loeber's
"Vermeldungsbuch" contains the following announcement, which was read
from the pulpit.   "The unmarried women Louise Voelker, Wilhelmina Hahn,
Sophie Hoeschel, the first two being weak and confined to their bed, earnestly
and anxiously ask the congregation to forgive them the great sin which they
have committed against the Sixth Commandment with the man who was
recently ousted from our midst.   They recognize the fact that they have given
great offense, and they ask the congregation not to reject them utterly.   As far
as we can see, they recognize their sin and are thoroughly repentant.   It is
well known that they have made this unexpected confession of their own
accord, being troubled in their conscience.   They have submitted themselves
for further questioning and investigation.   In this investigation it has been
brought out that Louise Voelker has been more guilty than the other two,
but like the three fallen women she is particularly anxious to receive the
assurance of God's grace.   Her heart and conscience are filled with blessed
remorse and hatred against this sin.   After careful supervision and investigation of their souls we have gained the conviction [Note: the word *Zuversicht*
is crossed out, and another word is put above it.   This word seems to be
Gewissheit] that their repentance is genuine and that God, through the
proffered comfort of evangelical grace, has given them life and forgiven them
their transgression."   Then follows a long exhortation to the entire congregation to show mercy and to examine their own lives.   It should be noted
that these women by their own confession transgressed the Sixth Commandment, which in the Lutheran Catechism reads: "Thou shalt not commit
adultery" and that they are called "fallen women" ("die drei Gefallenen").
Von Polenz, *op. cit.*, p. 15, tells us that there was a rumor concerning sex
irregularities on Stephan's part before he ever came to Dresden.   He thinks,
however, that not much weight should be attached to this rumor.

    [93] Early in the deliberations of the *Berathungs-Comite* it was taken for
granted that Stephan would take his wife and children along.   In the meeting
of February 15 the number of children are mentioned in an effort to establish
the amount of money to be set aside for Stephan's personal needs on the
journey.   Even as late as September 27, 1838, the committee speaks of the
needs of Pastor Stephan and of his family on the journey.   But in these latter
minutes the needs of the family have already receded into the background.
The big consideration in setting aside $1,500 for the pastor's needs on the
journey is that he is the bishop of all the united Lutheran congregations and
the ruler of the Church ("der Bischof der saemmtlichen vereinigten lutherischen Gemeinden und Regent der Kirche").   Nothing is said about the needs
of the family in the discussion.   The resolution reads, that one thousand five
hundred dollars are set aside for the pastor, his family, and his servants and
that this sum be taken out of the "Credit-Casse" and charged to the "Kirchen-
Conto."   Only the son was taken along.

causes more neurotic trouble than any other.[94]   Apparently it led
to pretense and self-deception on the part of Stephan.   Had he admitted, at least to himself, that he had strong sex urges, that to
be hungry for sex experience is as natural as to be hungry at
dinner time, that his wife's attitude put him in a rather precarious
position, and that the thoughts of adultery which passed through
his mind were really such, and that he was no different from other
human beings, he would have spared himself the danger of pretense and self-deception.[95]

---

[94] Weathered, *op. cit.*, p. 115. Mrs. Harriet R. Mowrer, author of *Personality Adjustment and Domestic Discord*, was domestic discord consultant of the Jewish Social Service Bureau, Chicago.   In her consultations she would in-variably inquire into the sex relations of the people she was trying to help. P. 150 she says: "While conflict in response involves the whole realm of re-sponse relations, in its more restricted sense it is often thought of in terms of sexual conflict or sexual incompatibility.   The fact that the sex factor is so often present in domestic discord cases has led many students of the subject to speak of sex as the underlying cause of conflict in marriage relations. While it is true that sex conflicts are usually found in domestic-discord cases, sometimes even appearing in disguised form, the conflict is in most instances so complex as to involve every phase of the marriage relationship.   Sex cannot, therefore, be considered the basic factor any more than any other of the factors which make up the conflict pattern."

[95] Stephan's defense, "Hanewinckel Report," pp. 55—86, is not altogether free from guile. P. 67: "I do not go to the vineyard to talk with my friends, but to be alone and to rest. I do not go there to talk, but in order to avoid every occasion for talk. Because of my weak chest I must rest from talking at least once a week. Surely, I cannot forbid those who pay the rent for the cottage in the vineyard to take walks in the direction of the house. But I have not caused anyone to come, nor did I know whether anyone would come or not. That they happened to come on those weekday evenings on which I happened to be there is explained by the fact that there would have been absolutely no refreshments there for them on any other evenings. As far as talking is concerned, I spoke very little with them; after 10 o'clock never." Pp. 67—68: "Concerning the walks in the open air I should like to say that they are not forbidden. The thing that is forbidden is a gathering of several people while the walk takes place. For this reason I have taken these walks alone in recent weeks, oftentimes absolutely alone or in the company of one single person. This person, as I stated in the hearing, took care of my immediate necessities. In order to escape the suspicion of conducting a gather-ing, I went alone." P. 69: "Let me repeat the statement that by the decree of the city government I was forced to keep the number of those who accom-panied me to one person. If necessary, this could be a woman. It all de-pended on the person who offered to accompany me. I never urged anyone to accompany me but left it to each one's discretion or desire, whether he or she wished to accompany me. It seems, however, that when I tried to escape the Scylla of conventicles, I ran against the Charybdis of alleged immoral conduct. It was purely coincidental that I spent that night out in the open. I am old and no longer a spring chicken. It is easily understandable that I must sit down and rest and that occasionally I fall asleep while sitting down and resting." (Original: "Ich bin alt und kein Held mehr; und es ist daher be-greiflich, dass ich mich zuweilen setze, um zu ruhen, und dass mich der Schlaf dabei ueberfallen kann.") P. 70: "Policeman Mueller has made a state-ment to the effect that I hid behind a pile of sticks that had been used for

Martin Stephan, then, was a definitely maladjusted person who believed that he was being severely persecuted and whose beliefs were reinforced by the silly suspicions of revolution-fearing officials of Church and State. His maladjustments were exaggerated by domestic discord, which had its origin in cultural and sexual differentiations. He compensated for his feeling of inferiority by persecutory delusions and by getting absolute control over certain human beings and by social intimacy with his male and female adherents.[96]

---

the support of grapevines. The untruthfulness of this statement can be proved by the fact that on November 8 the sticks were still used to support the vines. They were not piled up, and there can be no talk of hiding behind a pile of sticks. Incidentally, this is the same policeman who in July, 1836, was accused of slandering my friends."

[96] The opinion which George M. Stephenson, *The Religious Aspects of Swedish Immigration,* p. 50, expressed concerning Eric Janson might be applied to Martin Stephan. "Eric Janson's character was not above reproach, but in the earlier stages of his religious activity he was undoubtedly an upright man. Ignorance and an overweening self-confidence, combined with stupid persecution, drove him to absurd extremes."

CHAPTER FOUR

CHAOS IN MISSOURI

THE PROCESS OF DISINTEGRATION so noticeable in the personality of Martin Stephan during the last years of his stay in Dresden was, if anything, accelerated after the emigrants had left their native soil. The adulation formerly given spontaneously by the faithful was now demanded of them as a matter of law.[1] Safe from the reach of a persecuting government and alone with the faithful in the ark on the high seas, Stephan began to conduct himself like an Oriental despot. Only *die Herrn Amtsbrueder,* as we have seen in a previous chapter, and those to whom he had specifically granted this high privilege had access to his person. In all places and at all times the emigrants were to go through a regular ritual in recognizing the high importance of his *Amt* and the profound wisdom that dwelt in the "Hochwuerdiger Herr." Transgressions of his commands were put on a level with transgressions of God's commands and were punishable with the same penalties. All powers in spiritual and secular matters ("in geistlichen und buergerlichen Sachen") were united in him.[2] Although the official legitimation of the bishopric on board the *Olbers* on January 14 and 15, 1839, does not come as a surprise, it does smack of love of personal glory and dishonesty on the part of Stephan.[3] After they had gone up the Mississippi River several hundred miles in the steamship *Selma,* the height of this bizarre despotism was reached in the "Unterwerfungserklaerung." Neither in Oriental literature nor in comic opera has the present writer met with anything that surpasses this "Erklaerung" in submissiveness and ser-

---

[1] Vehse, *op. cit.,* p. 8. The "Exulantenlieder" and the conduct of Stephan in Bremen show that a new era is about to begin in the emigration.

[2] All provisions mentioned in this paragraph are taken from the "Reiseordnung." This "Reiseordnung" was drawn up by Stephan and is now the property of Concordia Historical Institute, Fasc. IV, No. 4.

[3] Vehse, *op. cit.,* pp. 9—10. Stephan made it appear that the request for such power came spontaneously from the people, although he had previously given his *Amtsbruder* Otto Hermann Walther orders to draw up such a petition and have it duly signed by representatives of the clergy and of the laity. He also made it appear that this was necessary for the glory of the Church.

vility. The immigrants promise to submit themselves absolutely
to every ordinance of the Bishop, whether it concern an ecclesiastic or a secular matter ("in kirchlicher sowie in communlicher
Hinsicht"), and to do so in the conviction that such ordinance
and command on the part of the Bishop would promote their temporal and eternal welfare. Everyone signed this solemn document under oath.[4] After the formalities of landing in St. Louis
had been completed,[5] Stephan's first concern was to get proper
signatures from the men who had sailed on the *Republik,* the
Johann Georg, and the *Copernicus,* to the document legitimizing
the episcopacy.[6] Next in importance was the completion of the
ecclesiastical millinery,[7] and finally the purchase of land down in
Perry County.[8] In all these movements there was an accentuation of autocracy and an absence of plain common sense on the
part of the "Ehrwuerdiger Herr." Emotional motivation was taking
the place of reason. In other words, his personality was disintegrating.

On April 26, 1839, the Bishop, with his entourage, left St. Louis
on the steamship *United States* for Perry County. On Rogate
Sunday, the Fifth Sunday after Easter in the Lutheran calendar,
which in that year happened to fall on the fifth day of May,
Pastor G. H. Loeber, the oldest of the clergymen, who, together
with about one third of the company, had remained in St. Louis,
preached the sermon for the Lutheran group in the basement of
Christ Church Cathedral (Episcopalian). Shortly after the service
a young lady to whom Stephan had made improper advances

---

[4] Vehse, *op. cit.,* pp. 163—166, presents the "Erklaerung" in full. This
statement, demanded by Stephan of everyone on board the *Selma,* indicates
that there was trouble brewing, that some immigrants were beginning to have
misgivings regarding the wisdom of Stephan, and that, in general, Stephan
was beginning to lose his grip.

[5] Vehse, *op. cit.,* p. 12. The Bishop waited from dinnertime till dusk before he left the *Selma* for his luxuriously appointed dwelling in the Belle
Fontaine neighborhood of St. Louis. His arrival was the big event of February 19, 1839.

[6] Pastors and candidates of theology who had been aboard the other seagoing vessels signed the document in St. Louis, February 24, 1839. Carl Ferdinand Wilhelm Walther's characteristic signature is also to be found on this
document. A delegation, headed by the schoolteacher Johann F. F. Winter and
elected by majority vote, signed the document in behalf of the laity. Stephan
seemed visibly relieved after the episcopacy had been duly legitimized. The
character of this document and the importance of the signatures moved the
present writer to have a photostatic copy made.

[7] Vehse, *op. cit.,* p. 15.   [8] *Op. cit.,* pp. 34—35.

came to Pastor Loeber and confessed her illicit relations with the Bishop. That afternoon two others followed her example. During the week several others came and told of their misdeeds.[9]

After Loeber had gotten over the first shock of these revelations, he decided to confer with those of his *Amtsbrueder* who had remained in St. Louis. For the time being nothing was said to the laymen. The upshot of the clerical deliberations was to send the young and energetic Pastor C. F. W. Walther down to the colony to prepare the soil for the big eruption. Every precaution had to be taken to safeguard the title to the 4,472.66 acres of land that had just been purchased by the company in Perry County. At that time the title of ownership was still in the name of the trustees; and they, together with other leaders in the colony, had to be won over completely for energetic action against Stephan. There must be no uncertainty, nor must factions develop. The young emissary of the St. Louis clergymen, beginning his first big assignment, spent the week of the nineteenth of May fixing the fences in Perry County. All information was kept from Stephan, although he seems to have sensed something. He had reason to talk of a conspiracy. Finally, when all the leaders had

---

[9] The present writer bases his account on Vehse, *op. cit.*, pp. 17 and 144—145; on Teacher Winter's letter reprinted in Rudelbach und Guerickes *Zeitschrift*, II (1841), No. 3, p. 127, and the report of the hearing in connection with the arrest of Sophie Hoeschel on November 9, 1837. She was arrested behind a woodpile in the vineyard, together with Stephan. A copy of the report on the hearing in the Dresden police court is found in Fasc. VI, Concordia Historical Institute. An additional valuable source for this episode is the "Vermeldungsbuch" of Pastor Loeber, from which he publicly announced the confession of those three women together with their names and their request for forgiveness. This formal request was made on the Seventh Sunday after Trinity, which in that year fell on July 7. The claim that these women were so psychopathic that they confessed imaginary sins has not been sufficiently substantiated to date. In evaluating the testimony of this episode, the writer has kept in mind that at least three women confessed; that they confessed independently of each other; that a cool, experienced, just, and lovable man, such as Pastor Loeber was according to the common report, would hardly have made the confessions known from his public pulpit before the assembled congregation if he did not believe them to be substantially correct. Finally, it should be borne in mind that almost two months intervened between the day when the confessions were first made to Pastor Loeber and the day of the public announcement. If there was anything wrong about these confessions, it would have been brought out during this period. There is a possibility that *coitus* did not take place, since lusts of the flesh and especially improper advances by members of the opposite sex are interpreted as adultery in the Lutheran Catechism. This should be taken into consideration in any evaluation of the testimony. However, Dr. Vehse, a lawyer, claims to have seen the written, notarized ("unterzeichnet an Eides statt") confession in which one of the girls mentions the room on the ship in which the relations took place.

been lined up in favor of drastic action against their onetime lord and master, the young theologian returned to St. Louis. His return was the signal for large-scale preparations. Two river steamers, the *Prairie* and the *Toledo,* were chartered for a special trip. Everybody in the company who could possibly get away sailed for the big event down the river. The first boat tied up at the landing in the colony in the gray dawn, about four o'clock of the morning of May 29. The second boatload did not arrive until about five o'clock that afternoon.[10]

Just why the laymen went to all the trouble of chartering two steamboats or why they came all the way from St. Louis at all, aside from the social value of satisfying their curiosity, is not plain from the documents. This much is certain, they did not have a single thing to do in the entire procedure of deposing Stephan. The old German pattern of the Saxon State Church was followed in detail, even to the meaningless expenditure of lay energy in saying, *"Ja,"* when the representative of the clerics read the document of excommunication. The pastors did everything. They considered themselves a final court of trial. The whole procedure was based upon the medieval assumption that the Church consists of the clergy and that the laymen have no part in the government of the Church. So completely had Stephan schooled these men in centralized church government that the simple principles enunciated by Luther in the early fifteen hundred and twenties were completely ignored. When some laymen talked about getting the entire group together and investigating the affair, they were severely criticized and roundly condemned by the clerical leaders.[11] The first thing that had to be done, so they said, was to excommunicate Stephan. This could be done only by the clergy, since they only had the power of excommunication. Thus did the Saxon fathers demonstrate their utter obedience to hierarchical beliefs and their profound confusion on the most simple procedures of Lutheran church government. Keyl was right when he said:

> Repeatedly and most earnestly did Stephan recommend the reading of Holy Scriptures, the Confessional Writings of the Lutheran Church, the works of Luther and other reliable

---

[10] Vehse, *op. cit.,* p. 19; Winter's letter, Rudelbach und Guerickes *Zeitschrift,* II (1841), No. 3, p. 127.

[11] Vehse, *op. cit.,* p. 143.

Lutheran theologians; however, he got me into the habit of regarding his interpretation of the Scriptures as the only true and correct interpretation and to look at the writings of Lutheran theologians through glasses which he himself had colored. Thus it happened that I used the writings of Luther and other Lutheran theologians as a means for developing and intensifying Stephanism. Gradually and imperceptibly Stephan aroused mistrust of these Lutheran theologians in our hearts by pointing out certain defects in their writings. Whenever Luther's writings were in conflict with his teachings, he would say: "Luther must be taken in a different sense. At another place he has said something which shows that this statement must be taken in a different sense." Or he would say: "This does not suit our times." [12]

By unanimous vote of the clergy, without even a trace of participation on the part of the laymen aside from the conventional "*Ja*" vote, Stephan was excommunicated, deposed, and removed from the landed property of the colony — all on that eventful day of May 30, 1839. The fact that the laymen had previously gotten out a document in which they pleaded for participation of the laity in the action against Stephan and in which they pointed to the convention of laymen and pastors described in Acts 15 and that the pastors had resigned their commissions in Germany and were temporarily without calls — seemed to have no effect upon *die Herrn Amtsbrueder*. The request of the laymen for participation in the action against Stephan had the effect, if anything, of making the clergymen extremely chary about all such action. Henceforth and for a period of almost two years the colony was divided into a clerical and a lay group, both arrayed against each other, both striving for control of their brethren, and both giving proof of their utter ignorance and inexperience in democratic ways.[13]

---

[12] Keyl's "Bekenntnisse," published in Rudelbach und Guerickes *Zeitschrift*, III (1842), No. 1, p. 99.

[13] For the facts in the removal of Stephan the present writer is indebted to Vehse, *op. cit.*, pp. 19—23, 142—151; to Winter's letter in Rudelbach und Guerickes *Zeitschrift*, II (1841), No. 3, p. 127; to Keyl's "Bekenntnisse," published in Rudelbach und Guerickes *Zeitschrift*, III (1842), No. 1, p. 111. Somewhat later Keyl condemned the action of the pastors. At the time, however, he was caught in the same whirlwind of confusion. "When the secret sins of Pastor Stephan became known and I became aware of the fact that I had been indescribably deceived, I approved of the method of procedure against Stephan, in part by my failure to protest and in part by my active participation in the proceedings. I did not take time for consideration and deliberation,

While the removal of Stephan from the property of the colony solved very few, if any, problems, it did bring home with sledge-hammer blows to every soul the tremendous difficulties confronting the company, and it did throw the colonists into utter confusion. The structure of the colony was based upon a benign economic paternalism, with Martin Stephan as the all-wise and benevolent father in the center of things. The "Credit-Casse," for which Stephan, in co-operation with Attorney Marbach, had worked out an "Ordnung," provided many of the emigrants with a possibility of investing the capital gained from the liquidation of their European holdings. The earnings of the fund were to be distributed on an interest basis. While the "Ordnung" is a little hazy about some of the sources of the earnings, it seems that Stephan expected these earnings to come from the interest which poor people whose traveling expenses had been advanced from the fund would pay back into the fund as soon as they had established themselves in America. He also expected some revenue from concessions that would be sold to men who would set up their business establishments in the city that he would build on the communal holdings of the colony; and finally he hoped to realize an income from the resale of the 4,472.66 acres of land which he would buy as one large complex.[14] Many emigrants put their entire life's savings into the

---

and I lacked the necessary knowledge of procedure in a case such as Pastor Stephan presented." Significantly, C. F. W. Walther, in his *Lebenslauf* of Buenger, p. 53, uses the passive voice in describing the removal of Stephan. He makes no mention of the persons who did the removing.

[14] The "Credit-Casse Ordnung" is the first of the "Ordnungen" to be found in Fasc. IV, No. 4, Concordia Historical Institute. All contributions were voluntary. Loans were to be made from it for the erection of churches and schools, for the needs of the civil community, to individuals who wished to emigrate but did not have the necessary funds, and for the purchase of cattle and farm equipment. All loans were to bear interest. The rate of interest was to be the one that was conventional in the State in which they would settle. Loans were to be approved by a majority vote of the investors. In order to have the right of vote, an investor had to have at least 100 taler invested. All property of the colony was collateral for loans made from the fund. Mortgages were to be taken on parcels of land resold to individuals but not completely paid for by them. Losses were to be absorbed by the fund. Borrowers who through no fault of their own got into financial difficulties should be treated in a Christian and brotherly manner. It might be necessary to suspend the interest charges to some borrowers temporarily. Interest charges were to begin one month after the arrival in St. Louis. The "Credit-Casse" would also take money and valuables for safekeeping and transport them to America. No interest would be paid on such funds. The administration of the fund would be carried out by a board of nine persons elected by a majority vote of the participants in the fund. A special deputy, appointed by the Church and the community, would supervise all actions of the Board, in

"Credit-Casse." The investigation made by the clergy in connection with the removal of Stephan revealed the fact that the funds of the "Credit-Casse" had been exhausted by purchases of costly episcopal equipment; by the personal needs of the Bishop, which were rather extensive; by the loans which were made to the large number of *Unbemittelte* who emigrated in spite of the fact that they did not have the wherewithal to pay for their transportation; and by the purchase of the 4,472.66 acres of land in Perry County, none of which had been resold by May 30.

The shock which the participants in the "Credit-Casse" received when the actual status of the treasury was revealed to them is indescribable. Here they were, in the forest primeval of a strange land, without proper housing and clothing, with insufficient nourishment, troubled by a hot and humid climate, in which fevers and agues seemed to thrive, with their life's savings squandered, and the man upon whom they had built their hope of temporal and eternal happiness discredited and rejected as a rank deceiver and an archhypocrite. Naturally, accusations, recriminations, charges, and countercharges followed each other in rapid succession. Nor did it help the position of the clergy that they had spent the last years in such close proximity to the fallen idol. All *Amtsbrueder* were put in the same pot by the populace. The fact that each clergymen received out of the "Credit-Casse" one hundred dollars and that each candidate of theology and each schoolteacher received thirty dollars did not tend to help matters. (Cf. the order of Stephan that these sums be paid. The order was dated March 9, 1839, and was approved by the five ministers to whom the money was paid. Also the original receipt dated March 23, 1839, signed by the same ministers.) In his autobiography [15] Rev. Ernst Moritz Buerger re-

---

order that everything might be done in a Christian and God-pleasing manner. The deputy was to work out a set of rules and regulations in co-operation with the Board. These rules were to govern the administration of the fund. In matters of dispute the word of the deputy would be final ("zur Entscheidung"). A complete report of all transactions, and of the condition of the treasury was to be given until such times as the whole fund was liquidated. The report was to be given in the presence of the Board and the deputy of the Church and community. Liquidation should take place as soon as it became apparent that the fund was no longer needed. All funds accruing from liquidation should be regarded as profits. If the fund was unable to pay back all amounts that had been paid into it, these deficiencies should be regarded as losses.

[15] Buerger, "Lebensgeschichte," p. 130: "I had the greatest difficulty in this respect. There was a large number of people in the district assigned to me who had suffered great loss, and their indignation was commensurate with

veals the bitter hatred of the colonists in his district because of the
bankrupt "Credit-Casse."

The political life of the community, or, as the immigrants preferred to call it, the civil community ("buergerliche Gemeinde"),
which was just beginning to assume organized form, was thrown
into utter confusion by the removal of Stephan. While the Stephanites denounced Communism, and while they were very chary
about the wicked Democrats ("die boesen Demokraten"),[16] they
did plan a civil community based upon strict Christian principles
and reminding us of the Old Testament theocracy which John Calvin
tried to resurrect in Geneva. Martin Stephan had written two
constitutions for this Christian civic community ("christlich buergerliche Gemeindeverband").[17] The first was intended for the
period during which the colony would be getting settled, and is
called Constitution for Colonization ("Ansiedelung-Ordnung fuer
die mit Herrn Pastor Stephan nach den Vereinigten Staaten von
N. Amerika auswandernde lutherische Gemeinde"); the other was
to regulate the political life of the community after it had become
a going concern, and is called the Constitution of the Civic Com-

---

the sums which they had lost. Although I had nothing to do with the administration of the 'Credit-Casse,' which was in the hands of a true and faithful treasurer, I was roundly denounced as a deceiver and an author of all
their troubles and losses."

A picture of the housing conditions in the colony can be gotten from
a letter which Loeber wrote to Guericke, dated April 28, 1841, and reprinted
in Rudelbach und Guerickes *Zeitschrift*, II (1841), No. 3, p. 114. Loeber lived
in one of the better houses. He had received an inheritance from his parents
and was in a better financial situation than any of the other pastors. The
house he lived in was built with the aid of the congregation at Altenburg.
It had two rooms upstairs and a large basement. The basement was above
the ground and served as church and school. Pastor Loeber furnished the
money to buy the building materials from his own private funds. The congregation furnished the labor. He lists the people who were living in this
three-room house: G. H. Loeber, 44 years; his wife, Wilhelmine Sophie Loeber,
47; Christoph Heinrich, 12; Martha Maria, 10; Gotthilf Simeon, 6; Johanna
von Wurmb, 10; Theobald von Wurmb, 8; Sara von Wurmb, 6; Theodore
Julius Brohm, candidate of theology, who shortly after Palm Sunday, 1843,
married Mrs. von Wurmb, age 32. Pastor Loeber's sister, Christiana Magda-
lena, 45, was with them until just shortly before her death. Three adopted
children were also living in the house with Pastor Loeber. A servant also
lived with them. Altogether there were fifteen persons living in these three
rooms, five of whom were adults. Most of the other emigrants lived in temporarily constructed barns, or sheds, called "camps." The terrible housing conditions undoubtedly contributed to the chaotic thinking of the group.

[16] Koestering's *Leben und Wirken* of Keyl, p. 37.

[17] They are found in MS. form in Fasc. IV, No. 4, Concordia Historical
Institute.

munity ("Ordnung der buergerlichen Gemeinde"). The control of the Christian Civic Community was to be in the hands of the first clergyman ("Die Oberaufsicht fuehrt der erste Geistliche"). In case he was unable to serve, he might appoint a deputy from among the *Herrn Amtsbrueder*.[18] With the *erste Geistlicher* in complete disgrace and removed from the landed possessions of the colony by the *Herrn Amtsbrueder*, it does not take much imagination to vis-

[18] The two constitutions give us an insight into the concepts of government that prevailed among the Stephanites. While some forms of decentralized government are present — the "Rath" is elected by majority vote of the citizens, who either approve or disapprove of the "Rath's" action — it is very evident that all power is in some way derived from the first clergyman. Only men who have altar rights can vote and hold office. The moment a man is suspended from Holy Communion, he loses his right to vote; and if he is an officeholder, he must resign his office forthwith. The first clergyman supervises the election of the "Rath" and inducts the elected members into office. The "Rath" must be guided in all its actions (a) by the Word of God; (b) by the laws of the United States and of the State in which settlement is made; (c) by this constitution. The "Rath" is to appoint a subcommittee from its midst to act as a court and take care of all litigation. Decisions of this court are to be made on the basis of God's Word. The court is to get the approval of the ministerium, which decides whether the Word of God has been properly applied in each case. Freedom of the press shall prevail. However, a board of review and censure shall be appointed. This board of censure, called "Buechercommission," shall consist of a deputation of clergymen and a deputation of citizens. Each deputation has the right to confiscate any edition of a newly printed book or pamphlet or any printed matter. If the clerical deputation has confiscated a certain editon of a book or pamphlet, the publisher may appeal to a court consisting of clergymen. But if the lay deputation has seen fit to confiscate, the publisher must appeal to the regular court appointed by the "Rath." Whoever is excommunicated from the Church loses all rights and privileges, also as a citizen, and must be removed from the landed property of the community. Land shall be divided into strips, so that no one citizen may get only good or only poor land. The chief industry of the colony is to be agriculture. However, silk, wine, and bee culture and the growing of trees and special plants, such as *Rhabarber, Opium, Ricinus* (a castor-oil plant, to which certain medicinal qualities were attributed), are to be encouraged. No factories shall be permitted in the colony. The wholesale tanning and leather dressing shall be carried on as public utilities ("Commun-Sache"). Income from these operations shall be used to pay the expenses of public administration ("die Communallasten zu decken"). Laborers who are employed by the day are to work eight hours only. Working conditions must be sanitary. Theaters or dance halls are never to be erected in the colony. Lotteries, games of chance, and cards are strictly forbidden ("strengsten Dinges verboten"). But the following are permitted: Billiards, bowling, shooting at the popinjay, and other shooting games. All cursing and foul language as well as bitter and sarcastic remarks ("das lieblose Aufziehen und Bewitzeln") are specifically forbidden. As soon as possible, a recreation building with many rooms is to be erected. Children of parents who must work shall be cared for in a playground supervised by men and women who are incapacitated by age to do other useful labor. No house shall be higher than two stories. Every house must be clean, dry, and well lighted. The public buildings shall be erected in this order: First the church; then the *Rathhaus;* then the seminary, combined with a school for children; later on a hospital, an orphans' home, a rest home, etc.

ualize the chaotic condition of all political and social life in the community.

Far more disturbing than the economic and political chaos was the spiritual anxiety of the colonists. They were deeply religious men and women. They had emigrated because they believed that their faith could no longer be maintained in the Sodom of Saxony. To them purity of Lutheran doctrine and Christian living meant everything. Luther's teaching concerning the means of grace had taught them to honor those who proclaimed the Gospel and administered the Sacraments. For years Stephan had adroitly manipulated this doctrine so that very many of the colonists were of the firm conviction that Stephan was their chief means of grace ("Hauptgnadenmittel") and that outside, and apart from, him there was no hope.[19] He and, to a lesser degree, *die Herrn Amtsbrueder* were the basis of their spiritual life. Though misguided and utterly unscriptural, the respect which these people entertained over against the *Amt* was sincere. Overnight this *Amt* fell into disrepute, yea, stank to the highest heavens. The "hochwuerdigster Erzbischof," stripped of the last thread of his glory, had been put aboard a boat and, together with his concubine, had been shipped across the Mississippi, to a point near Kaskaskia, Illinois, there to shift for himself as well as he could. That men and women who had been so suddenly disillusioned should lose all confidence in the Church and in the clergy, yea, that they should make nasty accusations against the clergy, was but natural. Ernst Moritz Buerger and C. F. W. Walther lost their congregations and had to resign.[20] Loeber offered his resignation, but it was not accepted.[21] Keyl continued in office, although with a greatly troubled conscience and with doubts and

---

[19] Fasc. III, No. 12. Minutes of February 15, 1838.

[20] Buerger's "Lebensgeschichte," p. 137. See also his published *Sendschreiben*, p. 46. Concerning C. F. W. Walther cf. G. H. Loeber's letter, reprinted in Rudelbach und Guerickes *Zeitschrift*, II (1841), No. 3. The letter was printed together with a longer letter from Teacher Winter under the heading "Stimmen aus Missouri." Loeber's letter is dated April 28, 1841, a few days after the Altenburg Debate. "The congregation in St. Louis had lost its Pastor Walther, Sen., through an untimely but blessed death. The younger Walther, who has been sick almost continuously for a whole year and who has been released from office by his congregation, which has been dissolved for economic reasons and because they have lost confidence in the ministry ('Misstrauen gegen das Amt'), has been called as his brother's successor."

[21] Hochstetter, *op. cit.*, p. 29.

misgivings regarding the legality of his call.[22] Otto Hermann Walther, an older brother of Carl F. W. Walther, died of a broken heart on January 20, 1841.[23] The disillusionment and bitterness of soul among the colonists was commensurate with the spiritual blessings which they formerly believed were wrapped up in the person of Martin Stephan.

In the welter of confused opinion and of charges and countercharges that followed that eventful day of May 30, 1839, two distinct factions developed. For want of a better name, we shall call the one the clerical faction; and the other, also for want of a better name, we shall call the lay faction. The clerical faction was gradually headed by C. F. W. Walther and the lay faction by Dr. Carl Eduard Vehse, perhaps the most learned of the entire group. His brethren in arms were the merchant Heinrich Ferdinand Fischer and Gustav Jaeckel, who had formerly been the secretary of the "Berathungs-Comite."

Headed by C. F. W. Walther, who was ably supported by E. G. W. Keyl and G. H. Loeber, the clerical party wished to carry on under the "Ordnungen" of the discredited Stephan.[24] The old medieval, paternalistic, and hierarchical concepts of church government developed by Stephan had been drilled into these young men during the most formative period of their ministry. It was hardly

---

22 Keyl's "Bekenntnisse," published in Rudelbach und Guerickes *Zeitschrift*, III (1842), No. 1, p. 112.

23 Late in July, 1940, Dr. L. Fuerbringer, whose father later married the widow of O. H. Walther, told the present writer of the conviction of his mother that O. H. Walther died of a broken heart. The *Berliner Allgemeine Kirchenzeitung*, III (1841), p. 866, quotes a report of the *Bremer Kirchenbote* on the death of Otto Hermann Walther as follows: "Otto Hermann Walther, misled by Martin Stephan, died of a broken heart in St. Louis. On his sick- and deathbed he spoke no longer of the Church, but of the Lord Jesus and His love to all who call upon His name in order to be saved. At his grave a Lutheran candidate of theology and the Evangelical preacher Rev. Wall delivered addresses." Carl E. Schneider, *The German Church on the American Frontier*, p. 107, presents a photostatic copy of the MS. used by Rev. Wall on the occasion of this funeral. The funeral was held on January 24, 1841.

24 E. G. W. Keyl's "Bekenntnisse," printed in Rudelbach und Guerickes *Zeitschrift*, III (1842), No. 1, p. 112: "Unfortunately the removal of Stephan did not mean the removal of Stephanism from our midst. In continued blindness I clung tenaciously to most of the Stephanistic ideas." See also Winter's letter, reprinted in Rudelbach und Guerickes *Zeitschrift*, II (1841), No. 3, p. 128: "At this juncture I must announce that we did not recognize the sinfulness of the emigration immediately after the fall of Stephan, nor did we grasp the real essence of Stephanism." Most valuable for the study of government after Stephan's removal is Marbach's manifesto dated March 3, 1841, and entitled "An meine unter Pastor Stephan mitausgewanderten deutschen Landsleute." The original MS. is in Concordia Historical Institute, St. Louis, Missouri.

to be expected that they would cast them off at one fell swoop, after they had defended them so stubbornly for the past seven or eight years over against some of the best theological minds of the Lutheran Church in Europe. If such theological giants as Rudelbach and Guericke could make no dent in their line of reasoning, or rather 'n their line of emotional reiteration, how could a layman with no technical training in theology hope to overthrow them with a few doughty attacks? Furthermore, what alternatives did these clerics have? Go back to Europe? They were thoroughly discredited in the eyes of the Lutheran Church of their homeland. For years they had been issuing judgment after judgment upon that Sodom and Gomorrah, the State Church of Saxony. Furthermore, they had no funds with which to make the return journey. Should they give up the control of the Church to such unstable and inexperienced hotbloods as Vehse, Sproede, Fischer, and Jaeckel? It is one thing to talk about the rights of the laymen to take part in the government of the Church; it is quite another to set up a government in which the laymen actually participate or, as the lay party wished, actually do the governing. Even Luther talked a great deal about the participation of laymen in the government of the Church; but how much did he really do to put power into the hands of the laymen? Over a period of three hundred years the Lutheran Church had developed a government in which the laymen were having less and less to say. Would it be the part of wisdom and propriety that all government should suddenly be turned over to men who had had no experience and no tradition in governing? It does not surprise us, therefore, that it took till November 20, 1839, before the clerical party was willing even to talk about the possibility of abandoning further plans for the bishopric.[25] Men do not readily give up power which they have had for a long time, and theologians are no exception to this rule. A German proverb says that no matter how insignificant a *Pfarrer* may be, there is a Pope in him. The controversy dragged on all through 1839 and 1840.

On August 5, 1839, the lay party formulated a set of six "Zeugnisse ueber das Predigtamt," a kind of advance edition of a larger document. These "Zeugnisse," which Vehse later incorporated in a larger document and which consist almost exclusively of state-

---

[25] Vehse, *op. cit.*, p. 152.

ments from Luther's writings and from the writings of "other reliable teachers of the Lutheran Church," were handed to the clerics in St. Louis. On that same day Otto Hermann Walther issued a very polite letter in the name of the clergy who were still in St. Louis. It was rather noncommittal, since it stated only that they had read the "Zeugnisse" and that they would be guided by the Symbolical Books of the Lutheran Church.[26] A little over a month later, on September 9, 1839, the clerical party issued a joint statement signed by the five clergymen of the company. By this time the clerics had gotten together and discussed the "Zeugnisse." However, their answer too was noncommittal. They were still entertaining hierarchical ideas of an *ecclesia repraesentativa,* but they were not willing that this should be known. As far as can be ascertained from the records, they made no effort to elect a bishop; they said that what was needed was a bishop like Stephan. For the present the clerics merely announced that in all matters of church government they would abide by the Symbolical Writings of the Lutheran Church. At the time they saw no conflict between the Lutheran Confessions and their conception of the ministry and the Church. They do, however, warn their respective flocks against all such subversive activity as is being carried on by means of *Schriften.*[27] On September 19, 1839, the lay party issued a new and enlarged edition of their document. It contained bulky additions, mostly quotations from Luther and Seckendorf and Spener. In the final paragraph they make a formal and strong public rejection of the entire Stephanistic concept of church government and declare that they will have nothing to do with it in any way, shape, or form. They add a "Schluss-Zusatz" to their already elongated "Protestationsschrift," which is really a *Zusatz* to the "Zusatz." In this "Schluss-Zusatz," dated November 14, 1839, they accuse the clerics of trying to maintain the idea that the clerics are the Church and that the power to govern the Church is to be lodged only in the hands of the clerics. This "Schluss-Zusatz" harks back to the removal of Stephan. In tracing this removal and the events that followed it,

---

[26] The letter is printed by Vehse, *op. cit.,* p. 107. The minutes of the ministerium dated September 9, 1839, show that this same noncommittal answer was given by resolution of the clergy.

[27] This document is reprinted in Vehse, *op. cit.,* pp. 169—170, as "Beilage E."

7

the lay party shows how tenaciously the clerics were clinging to
the old Stephanistic idea that the power to govern rests in the
clergymen since they alone represent the Church. The lay party
presses its case with increasing force and, of course, always with
quotations from Luther. Finally, six days later, on November 20,
1839, the clerical party issues a written "Erklaerung," in which
they aver that they do not intend to continue the priest rule of
Stephan and that they have decided to give up the idea of the
bishopric, although many good things might be said for the episcopal form of church government. Their chief reason for giving
up the episcopacy is the achievement of peace and the restoration
of confidence.[28] Three days later, on November 23, 1839, the lay
party issues a letter in which they declare that they are not quite
satisfied, but they will await events. They will keep the peace,
but they hope that the clericals will make no secret insinuations
and accusations against them. Apparently the lay party thought
it had achieved a signal victory when the clericals, at least in
principle, gave up the episcopacy. However, if the lay party
hoped that the surrender of the episcopacy in principle would
mean the immediate introduction of a system of government in
which the laymen would participate, they were to be sorely disappointed. Giving up a system of government is one thing; sub-
stituting something for the thing which you give up is quite another. The fact is that there was no agreement even among the
clergy. G. H. Loeber's letter shows this very plainly. He and
Keyl, and seemingly Otto Hermann Walther and Ernst Moritz
Buerger, were for an all-out public confession of their great wrong.
They favored a solemn statement to be published in America and
Germany in which they would say that the emigration per se was
sinful and that the whole Stephanistic system of church government was an evil. "Some were opposed to such a procedure."
By a process of elimination we arrive at the conclusion that the
"some" was C. F. W. Walther.[29] The reason for Walther's re-

---

[28] This written "Erklaerung" is reprinted in Vehse, *op. cit.*, pp. 151—153.

[29] See Loeber's letter to Guericke, dated April 28, 1841, and reprinted in
Rudelbach und Guerickes *Zeitschrift*, II (1841), No. 3, p. 112. "Unfortunately
we have been unable to muster up the right kind of unity of the spirit so
necessary for a public confession of the entire company. Satan is sowing the
seeds of discord among us." In his "Bekenntnisse," dated end of August, 1841,
and reprinted in Rudelbach und Guerickes *Zeitschrift*, III (1842), No. 1, Keyl
shows how slowly the clergymen came to a full realization of the wickedness

fusal to join any all-out confession seems to have been twofold. He was not clear in his own mind regarding the wickedness of the emigration per se, and he feared the consequences of lay rule. The implications of a sudden switch from an all-out priest rule to an all-out lay rule were staggering.

The "Protestationsschrift" — that was the name of the final edition of the lay party's document — affords us a glimpse into these implications. What were the principles on which the lay party wished to see the government of the Church based? "All Christians are priests through Baptism by faith and must exercise the priestly office not only as a matter of right but as a matter of command." [30] "As spiritual priests, laymen have the right to judge all doctrine and to supervise all the activities of the clergy." [31] "The final decision in all disputes rests with the local congregation." [32] "The local congregation has the power and the duty to

---

of the Stephanistic form of church government. He cites his own case on p. 112. On p. 96 he cites the tremendous implications of an all-out confession and a change from priest rule to lay rule. Ernst Moritz Buerger writes in his *Sendschreiben*, p. 13: "It took a long time for us to awake from our jag ('Taumel'). We did not realize what we had become with and under Stephan. We continued to claim that the emigration was a work of God. We continued our work under the old constitution and in the old spirit; parishes were established, and each man received a group of people ('einen Haufen Leute') consisting mostly of such as had clung to him while he was still pastor in Germany. The land which my group received by lot ('durch das Los') was not conducive to the health of the settlers. They called me as their pastor, and I accepted the call. Terrible conditions burst upon my congregation. There was a shortage of food and much sickness. Many died, and still we were blind." In his unprinted "Lebensgeschichte," pp. 128—139, Buerger gives more details about the conditions in his parish and the manner in which he emerged from total blindness to light. Perhaps the first public confession to come from C. F. W. Walther was in the first issue of *Der Lutheraner*, September 7, 1844: "I too was caught in the net of various errors and held by them for a considerable time. God has had mercy on me and with endless patience has put me on the path which led me to the truth." It took almost twenty-five years before he made another public confession of his guilt in the emigration. In a sermon commemorating his twenty-fifth anniversary in the ministry, preached on the Second Sunday after Trinity, 1862, which was printed by August Wiebusch and Son, Walther makes a remarkable statement: "Standing before you in deepest humiliation, I must confess that when I entered the ministry, unworthy though I was, twenty-five years ago, I did not know what important task was put upon me. The result was that I not only administered my office in a faulty manner, but also that I permitted myself to be misled. With an erring conscience I cast the office aside, and together with a few members of my flock I emigrated to this our new fatherland. In this solemn hour I am deeply conscious of this great sin in my life" ("Lebendig steht mir heute diese grosse Suende meines Lebens vor meinen Augen").

[30] Vehse, *op. cit.*, pp. 55—56.

[31] *Op. cit.*, pp. 61—62.   [32] *Op. cit.*, pp. 62—63.

establish all rules regarding liturgy, ceremonies, and church constitutions" (*Kirchenordnungen*).[33] "The true Church is invisible."[34]
"It is dangerous to judge people as to doctrine and as to their
faithfulness over against established teachers. Equally dangerous
is the habit of extolling clergymen as a class ('den geistlichen
Stand'), because such a habit engenders servility and hypocrisy."[35]
"The best type of church polity is the one that prevailed during
the first two centuries of the Christian era. At that time individual congregations, some small and some large, existed independently side by side."[36] "The association of individual congregations is not necessary and may be harmful."[37] "Not much importance is to be attached to church polity. The less you have
of it, the better off you are."[38] "The concept of the *ecclesia repraesentativa*, i. e., that the Church is represented in the clergy, leads
to the Papacy and to a lack of interest in church matters on the
part of the laity."[39] "All pastors should be placed on the same
level and exercise the same power. The episcopacy develops love
of personal glory and leads to the Papacy."[40] "Rom. 10:17: 'Faith
cometh by hearing' does not apply only to men who have studied
and who are ordained. It applies to all Christians."[41] "In case
of an emergency a congregation may engage a man who has not
studied."[42] "Men who have not studied, yea, ordinary laymen,
may administer the sacraments."[43] "In judging clergymen the
chief stress, it is true, should be placed upon doctrine; but life,
the fruits of doctrine, should not be overlooked."[44] "Stephan
taught false doctrine concerning the Church, concerning church
polity, concerning secular government, concerning the office of
the ministry, concerning excommunication, and concerning the
cure of souls."[45]

The lay party, as these principles taken from the "Protestationsschrift" show, stood for an extreme congregationalism with
heavy emphasis on the individual. Like the Anabaptists, they
took certain isolated quotations from Luther's writings of the
early 1520's, tore them out of their life situations, and tried to
construct a new church polity. Had the lay party prevailed, the

---

[33] *Op. cit.,* p. 69.
[34] *Op. cit.,* p. 82.
[35] *Op. cit.,* p. 85.
[36] *Op. cit.,* p. 86.
[37] *Op. cit.,* p. 87.
[38] *Op. cit.,* p. 88
[39] *Op. cit.,* pp. 91—92
[40] *Op. cit.,* pp. 97—98.
[41] *Op. cit.,* p. 112.
[42] *Op. cit.,* p. 113.
[43] *Op. cit.,* p. 114.
[44] *Op. cit.,* p. 118.
[45] *Op. cit.,* pp. 131—136

church polity of the Missouri Synod would have been a highly in-
dividualistic congregationalism somewhat akin to the polity of the
Baptist Church in America. The fact that both the lay party and
the clerical party were authoritarians, that both went to Luther's
writings for their ammunition, made it difficult for the clerics to
defend their position. In fact, the clerics' authoritarian habit of
appealing to Luther had much to do with the collapse of their
hierarchy. In the battle of quotations the lay party seemed to
have the better of the argument. At times, it is true, Vehse and
his friends went to almost ludicrous lengths — of course, with the
aid of quotations from Luther — in their efforts to subordinate
the clergy to the laity. In all seriousness they advocate a subordinate position for the clergy in public processions, since the
laymen are more honorable than the clergy, and since St. Paul
directs his Epistles not to the bishops, as a rule, but to the congregations.[46] This striving for position and honor may be a small
matter, but it seems to indicate the spirit that was in Vehse and
his lay faction — and that seems to have been a pharisaical spirit.
People who make a big fuss about being called rabbi or master
are striving for personal glory, even though they may be criticizing
such striving in others. In fact, one gets the impression from the
entire "Protestationsschrift" that Vehse would like to have the
Gemeinde change places with Stephan, that the laymen should be
in the ship and the clergy out in the water. The fact that the
pastors are members of the Church and that long debates about
"Ehrenvorzug" are just as bad when carried on by laymen as when
carried on by the clergy seems to have escaped the good brother.
This extreme congregationalism, which decried all leadership on

---

[46] *Op. cit.,* p. 70. "Die Gemeinden haben als Gemeinden den Ehrenvorzug
vor den Geistlichen." It would be unhistorical to call Carl Vehse a second
Roger Williams. True, like Roger Williams, he was a troublemaker for the
clerics; like Roger Williams, he was much concerned about "the peril of over-
lordship"; like Roger Williams, he fought for an extreme individualism in
matters of religion. But the mind of Roger Williams was active and independent. He believed "in the competency of the soul." He faced the realities
of life and tried by experience to find the most adequate way of adjustment
to situations as he found them. He was a spiritual Robinson Crusoe. James
Ernst, *Roger Williams, New England Firebrand,* p. 208, calls Roger Williams
"a spiritual ancestor of Theodore Parker, Channing, and Emerson." Vehse,
on the other hand, tried to solve the problems of life by quoting Luther "and
other reliable teachers of the Church." For the Baptist view on church
government see William Roy McNutt, of Crozer Theological Seminary, Chester,
Pennsylvania, *Polity and Practice in Baptist Churches.*

the part of the pastors, frightened C. F. W. Walther and explains in part the fact that he stubbornly resisted an all-out confession on the part of the whole company as well as an all-out switch from priest rule to lay rule, a switch which never took place during the entire existence of the Missouri Synod. The future church polity of the Missouri Synod was being formed in the mind of C. F. W. Walther during the summer and fall of 1839 and during all of 1840. The clash between the lay party and the clerical party forced him into an extensive study of church polity. The death of his older brother and his subsequent call to the city church, Old Trinity in St. Louis, in a land in which the civil government grants the churches generally a free hand, gave him an opportunity to develop a church polity on a small scale which later proved so successful on the big stage of the Synod of Missouri, Ohio, and Other States.[47]

Though C. F. W. Walther opposed a public confession of guilt on the part of the emigrating company, he does not seem to have tried to keep individuals from making such statements. There was a regular epidemic of confessions during 1840 and 1841. His brother made one.[48] His brother-in-law, E. G. W. Keyl, made a lengthy one, which was published in Rudelbach und Guerickes *Zeitschrift*, III (1842), No. 1, pp. 94—114. G. H. Loeber also made a rather long confession, which he called "Renunciation of Stephanism" and

---

[47] In a letter to Guericke, dated April 28, 1841, and reprinted in Rudelbach und Guerickes *Zeitschrift*, II (1841), No. 3, p. 114, Loeber writes: "The younger Walther has done us a great service by means of his ability, his theological learning, and his recently acquired conviction [neu erlangte Festigkeit]." In his unprinted autobiography, p. 134, Ernst Moritz Buerger speaks of Walther's "diligent and persistent search for clarity" ("sein fleissiges Forschen und Suchen nach Klarheit") during this period. Speaking of the way Walther treated him in this controversy, Buerger writes in his autobiography, p. 138, on a special insert pasted onto page 138: "The valiant Walther certainly did not intend to do me wrong. He had to contend earnestly that the blessed Sacrament of the Altar was in our midst and that it should be celebrated. He had to oppose sharply all who denied the existence of the Lord's Supper in our midst and who confused consciences" ("Der theuere Walther hat gewiss mir nicht aus Bosheit und mit Willen Unrecht thun wollen. Er musste ja mit Ernst dafuer eifern, dass unter uns das heilige Abendmahl war und verwaltet werden durfte, und hart geisseln diejenigen, die es leugneten und die Gewissen irremachten").

[48] He made his confession in the form of a sermon which was printed in the *Allgemeine Kirchenzeitung*, XX (1841), p. 375. He confessed and attacked violently the Donatism that had been rampant among the Stephanites. "Wir werden nicht mehr auf andere herabsehen, sondern fein niedrig einhergehen. Wir werden nicht mehr in das Geschrei einstimmen: 'Hier ist des Herrn Tempel! Hier ist die lutherische Kirche! Hier ist wahres Lutherthum!'"

which he had his brother-in-law, the *Seminardirector* Zahn in
Meurs, Saxony, copy and send to prominent theologians in Ger-
many.[49] Pastor Ernst Moritz Buerger tells us that he made three
sincere and lengthy confessions in three different meetings.[50]
Among the candidates of theology, Brohm, who was living with
Loeber and later became his brother-in-law, felt the urge to write
a confession.[51] This was followed by a document of Magister
Wege, in which he is said to have been guilty of gross exaggera-
tions.[52] In addition to the "Protestationsschrift" of Dr. Carl Eduard
Vehse, already referred to at some length, Ferdinand Sproede, a
hotheaded and rather pugnacious fellow, a baker by occupation,
wrote a document in which he "gave the preachers a terrific
shellacking and unmercifully condemned their call and office." [53]

[49] G. H. Loeber's letter to Superintendent Guericke, reprinted in Rudelbach und Guericke, *Zeitschrift,* II (1841), No. 3, p. 112. In this letter Loeber
expresses the hope that another and more complete confession will be published in the name of the entire company. The present confession was going
out in his name only. "Damit nur einstweilen bis auf ein — Gott gebe! —
baldiges besseres Bekenntnis, zu unsrer weiteren Reinigung im Vaterlande
ein Anfang unter denen gemacht werde, welche am meisten darauf rechnen konnten."

[50] Buerger, E. M., *Sendschreiben,* p. 14. "In three different meetings I made
a sincere and extensive confession of sins and asked most humbly for forgiveness. I was deeply concerned about the grace of God, and therefore it was
comparatively easy for me to make these confessions." Since some of his
former Seelitzers were now living in St. Louis, he sent them a special document
confessing his sins. He reprints this document on pp. 14—16. Then he preached
a sermon in which he confessed his sins again. However, in this rather lengthy
sermon, reprinted on pp. 20—37, the old *Erweckungsbewegung* habits begin to
show up, as they did in so many of these confessions. Though he confesses
his own sins, he devotes ninety-nine per cent of his time and energy to induce
his hearers to confess their sins. In this sermon he takes up every one of the
Ten Commandments and shows how they had broken them in emigrating
from Saxony.

[51] Teacher Winter refers to Brohm's confession as "written, but not
printed." Cf. Winter's long letter (which, by the way, might also be classified as a confession) in Rudelbach und Guerickes *Zeitschrift* II (1841), No. 3,
pp. 116—134. Brohm divided his confession into three parts: "The roots, the
branches, and the fruits of Stephanism." Winter says that "Brohm did not
quite hit the mark with his document" ("ohne jedoch die rechte Mitte zu
treffen").

[52] Teacher Winter's letter, p. 128.

[53] Teacher Winter's letter, p. 128: "Eine Schrift, worin er furchtbar auf
die Pastoren donnerte und ihre Berufung, Amt usw., verwarf." F. Sproede,
a baker by trade, had been one of Stephan's most intimate and trusted adherents. In fact, Stephan had sent him on ahead to New York in 1836. He
received regular instructions by letter from Stephan. He persuaded Pastor
Oertel of New York and a large part of his congregation to leave New York
and go to Perry County. These are the "New Yorkers" often referred to in
contemporary literature. When Stephan was unfrocked, Sproede became one
of the most violent anticlerics in the settlement. He called the clergymen

These confessions reveal the utter chaos that prevailed in the minds of many during the summer and fall of 1839 and during all of 1840. They also show how utterly stupid and psychopathic the followers of Stephan were in their complete obedience to the Bohemian *Bussprediger*. The enormity of their folly seemed to burst upon them. Without understanding all the implications, they confessed and confessed. One thing they were sure of — they had sinned. What sin they had committed they did not know, nor could they agree among themselves concerning the specific sins which they had perpetrated. The more active a Stephanite had been in fighting the battles of Stephan, the more keenly was he aware of having done a great wrong. Many of them were completely upset in their religious thinking. Poor Pastor Buerger! He was completely befuddled. For a while he quit preaching altogether. Then he agreed to read some sermons from Luther's *Postille*. That did not seem right; so he agreed to write his own sermons; of course, on the basis of what he had read in Luther, preach them, and perform baptisms, but not to administer the Lord's Supper. For a while he went out to a barn in a wooded area some twenty miles southwest of St. Louis. He hoped to get relief and clarity in solitude. As was to be expected, he took Luther with him and meditated upon his writings. After his return it seemed as though he was straightened out, at least for the time being. But it did not take long before he was again completely confused. Buerger was beyond a doubt the most pathetic person among the clergy during this period. Part of the time he was on the side of the clerics and would sign their writings, and part of the time he was on the side of the lay faction and would make speeches in their behalf. Most of the time he did not know on which side he was. His unprinted autobiography and his *Sendschreiben* still excite sympathy for the man. Keyl

---

"spirits of the devil, thieves, robbers, murderers, and wolves, false brethren." In his document, which he claims circulated among the Saxons, he accuses the clerics of trying to conceal and cover up the real evils. He is particularly violent because they will not publish all-out confessions. He was a member of C. F. W. Walther's congregation in Perry County and in every way possible tried to prevent Walther from getting an honorable release in order to accept the call from Trinity Congregation in St. Louis. His argument was that they were no congregation and that therefore Walther had no call. He followed Walther to St. Louis and for about two years carried on a running battle in the columns of the *Anzeiger des Westens*, a German daily in St. Louis. His first contribution is in No. 28 of the *Anzeiger*, dated December 20, 1842. Back numbers of the *Anzeiger* are on file in the St. Louis Public Library.

was similarly confused. In the opening remarks of his "Bekenntnisse" he writes that he would have confessed earlier; but whenever he tried to commit his confessions to paper, new ramifica-
tions of his enormous guilt thrust themselves upon him, and he
would become aware of the fact that he knew his guilt only in
part.[54] Loeber writes in a letter accompanying his "Renunciation
of Stephanism" that he does not know where to begin in his confession. There is so much to be confessed, and there are so many
people whom he has wronged.[55]

On some points it was impossible to get unanimity among the
confessors. Things were confessed as sins which should never
have been confessed, and other matters were passed over in silence
which possibly should have been mentioned, since confessing was
the order of the day. One of the moot questions among the confessors was worded: "Was the emigration sinful?" The majority
seemed to think that it was. Had they put the question thus:
"Was the emigration per se sinful?" "Which factors connected
with our emigration were sinful?" the confusion would not have
been so great. Nowhere has the writer found a statement by
C. F. W. Walther that the emigration per se was sinful. After the
expulsion of Stephan everybody was agreed that the emigration
was not necessary from a religious point of view. Keyl was particularly violent on this point:

> What an impudent lie to claim that the Lutheran Church
> had come to the end of its existence, either in Saxony or
> in Germany or in all Europe! Quite the contrary, the facts
> show that many a theological leader and many a layman
> was faithfully devoted to the Lutheran Confessions.[56]

In his "Busspredigt" Ernst Moritz Buerger claimed:

> Our emigration took place in disobedience to God. That
> is our chief sin and the basis for a thousand others.[57]

---

[54] Keyl's "Bekenntnisse," in Rudelbach und Guerickes *Zeitschrift*, III
(1842), No. 1, p. 96. "Allein je mehr ich ueber die Art und Weise, wie ich dies
thun sollte, nachdachte, desto schwieriger wurde mir die Ausfuehrung selbst,
indem ich immer neue Verzweigungen meiner Schuld entdeckte, zugleich
aber sah, wie mangelhaft meine Erkenntnis derselben sei und, durch die Erfahrung belehrt, meine Erklaerung bald wieder aendern zu muessen."
[55] The letter is reprinted in Rudelbach und Guerickes *Zeitschrift*, II (1841),
No. 3, p. 112. "Aber freilich, wo sollen wir anfangen, um nach allen Seiten
hin zu bekennen, abzubitten und, soviel an uns ist, zu versoehnen und wieder
gutzumachen?"
[56] Keyl's "Bekenntnisse," in Rudelbach und Guerickes *Zeitschrift*, III
(1842), No. 1, p. 106.
[57] Buerger, *Sendschreiben*, p. 23.

Later on, as an old man, the same writer said in his autobiography:

> Although one can say that certain things justified our emi-
> gration, the whole thing must be written off as a colossal
> error. Of course, the guilt of the promoters and leaders is
> greater than that of the weak and simple Christians who
> followed the leaders because of their blind confidence in
> their leadership. In the first place, the pure doctrines of
> the Lutheran Church were confessed in Saxony officially
> and otherwise. We pastors were bound by oath to preach
> and teach and administer our office according to the Con-
> fessions of the Lutheran Church. Over against our ene-
> mies we could have pointed to our oath of office. We had
> been called by God. We should have stood our ground,
> resisted to the uttermost ("bis aufs Blut kaempfen") until
> the legally existing confessions of the Lutheran State Church
> were abrogated and destroyed or until we had been driven
> from our offices. Our emigration was premature. It was an
> attempt to escape persecution. It was evidence of a care-
> less and negligent attitude over against our divine call.
> In many respects it was a work of the flesh.[58]

All were agreed that the exaggerated homage paid to the person
of the Bishop was idolatry of the worst kind; that their Donatistic
view of the Church, according to which they alone constituted
the Church and all others were outside the pale of God's grace,
implied a very sinful aloofness and uncharitable heresy monger-
ing; [59] that all pastors had committed a grave sin when they urged

---

[58] Buerger, "Lebensgeschichte," pp. 117—118.

[59] Keyl's "Bekenntnisse," in Rudelbach und Guerickes *Zeitschrift*, III
(1842), No. 1, pp. 100—101; O. H. Walther's *Busspredigt*, reprinted in part in
Schneider, *op. cit., The German Church on the American Frontier*, p. 104;
Buerger's *Sendschreiben*, pp. 14, 34-35; G. H. Loeber's letter to Guericke, *Zeitschrift*, II (1841), No. 2, p. 111; Vehse, *op. cit.*, pp. 84—85. For the effect of
Stephanism see Koestering's *Leben und Wirken* of Keyl, pp. 35—38. The
roots for the excrescences of exclusivism found in the behavior of certain Missourians can be traced to the Donatistic views of Stephan and the Stephanites. In the minutes of the meeting of Trinity Congregation in St. Louis, dated
September 22, 1842, there is a very enlightening remark in connection with the
reception of new members. In the previous meeting the voting members had
decided to accept new members with a certain amount of ceremony. "Beschlossen, dass die Aufnahme eines stimmfaehigen Gemeindegliedes oeffentlich
und feierlich in der Gemeindeversammlung zur Erbauung des Recipienten
und der Gemeinde geschehen soll, darueber ist ein Paragraph in der Ge-
meinde-Ordnung zu machen." In the meeting of September 22 it was decided
to rescind this. The most significant thing about the motion to rescind is the
reason given for the motion: Such a ceremony might create the bad impression that their congregation was the only true one. ("Um nicht den boesen
Schein zu geben, als ob unsere Gemeinschaft die allein rechte sei.") This
reason plainly indicates a reaction against the Donatism of their Stephanite days.

wives to leave their husbands and husbands to leave their wives in order "to follow Christ to America." Just why it was sinful to be interested in the economic advantages of America,[60] or just why it was a great offense against God to change one's occupation or even one's address,[61] is difficult for an American of the twentieth century to understand, unless he accepts Luther's teaching that everyone must remain in the occupation and place into which God has put him.

The chaos that followed the removal of Stephan was also evident in the voters' meetings of Trinity Congregation, St. Louis. Though this congregation was in many respects a model congregation, its business meetings were not opened with prayer during the entire first year of its existence. Finally one of the laymen suggested that the meetings of a Christian organization ought to be opened with prayer. The chairman was asked to go to the pastor's residence and ask him to write out a proper prayer, which he, the chairman, read regularly at the beginning of the meeting. The reason no prayer was said was that the pastor was not permitted to attend the meetings of the voters, because the congregation was childishly afraid that it might become a victim of priest rule if the pastor were tolerated in the voters' meetings. On the 22d of August, 1842, the question arose whether it would not be proper to permit the pastor to attend the voters' meetings. One member had scruples of conscience, and the decision was postponed indefinitely.[62] As far as the minutes show, the pastor was never legally permitted to attend the business part of the voters' meetings.

[60] Keyl's "Bekenntnisse," p. 107. *Zeitlicher Wohlstand* was a motive which helped convince some people of the advantages of emigration. Keyl seemed to think that such economic motives or the use of economic motives to convince others was sinful. Buerger, *Sendschreiben,* p. 26: "Wir machten die fleischliche Ruhe, Gemaechlichkeit, die fruchtbaren Felder in Amerika, eintraegliche Wirtschaften, gutes Einkommen, irdische Genuesse, die wir in Amerika zu finden hofften, zu unsern Goettern."

[61] Buerger, *Sendschreiben,* pp. 32—33. "Stephan trod every holy and God-ordained profession and relationship under foot, and we joined him in this activity. Everyone of us had a divinely appointed occupation in the fatherland. . . . We forsook our inheritance, our homes ('Hausstand'), our offices into which God had placed us."

[62] See minutes of Trinity Congregation, St. Louis, Missouri, August 22, 1842. "Beschlossen, dass eine Entscheidung ueber das Erscheinen oder Nichterscheinen des Herrn Pastors in der Versammelung wegen eines Scrupels eines Gemeindegliedes noch aufgeschoben werde." At the close of this meeting it was announced that there would be a meeting the following Wednesday evening to "discuss the scruples of the member." In the meeting of August 23,

Extreme though the chaos was which permeated the religious, the economic, the political, and the social life of the colonists, a system of church polity emerged during that chaos under which a church body grew from a handful of immigrants to a corporation of well over a million members * in less than a hundred years.

1842, it was decided not to incorporate anything in the minutes regarding the presence or nonpresence of the pastor in the voters' meetings: "Beschlossen, dass ueber das Erscheinen des Herrn Pastors in der Versammelung nichts protocolliert werde." Evidently the voters had run into some trouble with the man who had conscience scruples about the presence of the pastor in the voters' meetings.

* EDITOR'S NOTE. — Statistics of 1945: souls, 1,532,702; communicants, 1,056,240. W. G. P.

CHAPTER FIVE

EMERGING FORMS OF CHURCH POLITY

CARL VEHSE left St. Louis December 16, 1839. Evidently he was so discouraged that he saw no future either for the colony or for himself. He sailed on the *Johann Georg* from New Orleans for Bremen.[1] If, however, any of the clerical party entertained the hope that things would quiet down after his withdrawal, they were doomed to disappointment. For one thing, Vehse wrote letters to his friends in America, and he published a book in which he told all.[2] Furthermore, Lawyer Marbach, who seems to have receded into the background during the latter half of 1839, now came to the fore again, and, of course, Johann Friedrich Sproede was still active. Shortly after Pastor Buerger had been formally called by his congregation and had preached his initial sermon on the First Sunday in Advent, 1840, his unruly conscience caused him to doubt the legality of his call. He wrote a *Sendschreiben*[3] in which he questioned every call that any of the congregations of the company had extended. He tried to show that the congregations were not legally competent to call pastors and that those pastors who had accepted such calls were continuing a sinful relationship. He now sought the association of the men of the lay party whom he had previously avoided as troublemakers and disturbers of the peace.[4] Not only that — after a conference with the clerics he parted company with them and renounced any and all connections with them.[5] Buerger's move was almost fatal to the cause of the clerics. It affected many in the colony. The

---

[1] Vehse, *op. cit.*, p. 26.

[2] *Die Stephansche Auswanderung nach Amerika*, Dresden, 1840. The book has 183 pages and came off the press April 11, 1840. Rudelbach gave it a very critical review in Rudelbach und Guerickes *Zeitschrift*, I (1840), No. 3, pp. 133—144.

[3] Buerger, E. M., *Sendschreiben*, pp. 17—18. Cf. Winter's letter in Rudelbach und Guerickes *Zeitschrift*, II (1841), drittes Quartalheft, p. 129.

[4] Buerger, *op. cit.*, p. 19.

[5] Winter's letter, *op. cit.*, p. 129; Buerger's *Sendschreiben*, p. 19; and especially the "Protokoll" of the conference in Dresden shortly after March 3, 1841. This "Protokoll" is not specifically dated, but there are indications that the meeting was conducted shortly after March 3, 1841, the date of the appearance of Marbach's manifesto. The "Protokoll" is merely dated "Maerz 1841."

old doubts which some of the clerics thought had been definitely laid to rest came back with sevenfold fury. Here an ordained pastor, one who had served one of the largest, if not the largest, Stephanite congregation in Saxony and who was known for his exaggerated sense of righteousness, publicly announced and denounced the sinfulness of the calls extended by any and all erstwhile Stephanite congregations.

The immediate result was that under Marbach's leadership the lay party assumed new life and that in addition to Buerger, Candidate Kluegel and Candidate Brohm began to straddle. So the lay party now had professional theologians on its side. Things were drifting into a terrible muddle. On March 3, 1841, Marbach issued a manifesto, in which he charged that their whole church polity ("Kirchenwesen") was built upon a sinful foundation and that until this old foundation was completely demolished, no church polity on which they could expect the blessing of God could be established. This manifesto of Marbach seems to have created a great disturbance. Teacher Winter claims that both Buerger and Marbach were the cause of much confusion ("Verwirrung"). Shortly after Marbach had issued his manifesto, a conference of the interested parties was held in Dresden, Perry County. Those present, according to the "Protokoll," [6] were Pastors Loeber, Keyl, Gruber, and Buerger; Candidate of Theology Brohm; Magister Wege; and Lawyer Marbach. C. F. W. Walther was not present, although he lived in the Perry County settlement and after his most unedifying quarrel with the baker Sproede spent most of his time at the home of his brother-in-law, Pastor Keyl, about three miles away from the scene of the conference. Otto Hermann Walther had been dead about five weeks and therefore is not mentioned in the "Protokoll." Marbach reiterated the claim which he had already put forth in his document of a few days before, viz., that the foundation of their church polity was sinful and that this sinful foundation must be destroyed before they could expect the blessings of God. By "destroy" Marbach meant a public confession of sin on the part of the whole company, coupled with a return to

---

[6] The "Protokoll" is to be found in Fasc. VI, C. H. I. It is written in Marbach's own handwriting. It is a most important document for the history of the Altenburg Debate, since it shows the weakness of Loeber and Keyl and presents Marbach's position unequivocally. It also reveals the fact that C. F. W. Walther was not present at this meeting.

Germany. Buerger, Brohm, and Wege agreed with Marbach — Brohm with reservations, Buerger and Wege without reservations. Buerger went a step farther. He was consistent in that at the close of the meeting he formally renounced all connection with local church matters (Marbach's minutes read: "Er sagte sich vom hiesigen Kirchenwesen los"). The minutes show that Keyl and Loeber cut sorry figures at this conference. They lacked that quality which Loeber calls *Festigkeit*. Neither of these two men could resist Marbach with any degree of force, since in their utter confusion they too were making a moral issue of the problem; and in this they were agreeing with Marbach. Two years after their landing in America, almost twenty months after Stephan had been ousted, Keyl and Loeber were still speaking of their support of Stephan and Stephanism as "the abominations that are present among us" ("die vorhandenen Greuel"). They spoke thus for three reasons: First, the leaven of Stephanism had not been entirely removed from the thinking of the Stephanistic clerics even at this late date; secondly, it was simpler to make a collective confession for the whole group; and, thirdly, they believed in the purging effect which a collective confession would have upon their souls ("Reinigung durch ein Bekenntnis"). In their estimation they had not cleansed ("gereinigt") themselves. There was much talk back and forth, but the clerics were getting nowhere fast, simply because they did not know what they wanted. (Marbach's minutes: "Nach langem Hinundherreden erklaerten die Pastoren Keyl, Loeber und Gruber, dass sie zwar zur Zeit diesen Punkt [a collective confession, coupled with a return to Germany] nicht widerlegen, aber auch nicht zugeben koennten"). Evidences of accelerated disintegration were piling up on all sides. At the end of March, 1841, the whole colony was fast approaching a state of complete disintegration. The spirit and influence of the clerics seems to have reached its lowest mark. Something had to be done, and that something had to be drastic and dramatic.

At this point C. F. W. Walther flashes into prominence. Just how much influence he had been exercising from behind the scenes during the previous months is not known. The behavior of Keyl and Loeber at the conference with Marbach indicates that they were under some pressure from Walther, who was beginning to feel the necessity of offering himself as the savior of the day. Walther was realistic enough to see that Vehse's theories, now espoused by Marbach and Buerger, had many adherents throughout the colony. Although Walther, together with the rest of the clerics, had disagreed violently with Vehse's premises and conclusions at the beginning of the controversy, back in September, 1839, he now saw that these premises could be purged of certain excrescences and used in an attempt to save the day. The chief excrescence of Vehse's polity that called for purging was that part which called for a return to Germany. In his effort to conceive a scheme that would save the day Walther had thoroughly familiarized himself with the many quotations from Luther which Vehse had incorporated into his document. He was now ready to put forth a plan that would appeal to the adherents of the fast-growing lay party as well as to the adherents of the rapidly diminishing clerical party.

To what extent Walther promoted the rising clamor for a full and free public debate of all the issues involved in the lay-clerical controversy cannot be ascertained with any degree of certainty from the documents at hand; but we do know that he had been sweating over the problems of the colony for over a year and that he had very good reasons for being unalterably opposed to a return to Germany.[7]

---

[7] Walther had been an extremely zealous Stephanite in Germany. His rabid Stephanism had gotten him into endless trouble with both the civil and the ecclesiastical authorities in Saxony. He had had repeated rows with his teacher. He had had a tiff with the school officials because he stubbornly refused to introduce certain new textbooks. Furthermore, he had broken up several homes by insisting that whoever was not a Stephanite was of the devil. He had been party to the kidnaping of his niece and his nephew, Theodore Schubert, aged 10, and Marie Schubert, aged 15. With the consent of their grandparents, Pastor and Mrs. G. H. Walther, and the connivance of Magistrate Piehter, C. F. W. Walther had removed these two orphans from the home in Waldenburg, where they were staying. He had taken them as far as the Saxon border city of Muehlau. There he had turned them over to Widow Buenger, who thereupon brought them to Bremen. In the meantime the guardian of these two children, a certain Mr. Engel in Waldenburg, brought pressure to bear on Magistrate Piehter in Waldenburg and criticized him bitterly for the loose way in which he handled the case. At Engel's insistence a warrant of arrest and extradition papers were gotten out for the two Walther brothers and Mrs. Buenger. The warrants for C. F. W. Walther and Mrs. Buenger were gotten out first. C. F. W. Walther had hurried on ahead to Bremen and grabbed the first sailing vessel of the five that he could get, in order to get out on the high seas, away from possible arrest. It happened that one of the Stephanites who was booked to go on the *Johann Georg* was willing to give up his place and go on the *Olbers.* The *Johann Georg* was just about ready to sail on November 3, 1838, when Walther arrived. He secured his place and escaped out on the high seas on November 3, 1838, shortly before the warrant arrived. Mrs. Buenger, on the other hand, was arrested on November 4, 1838, and held until December 11, 1838, when a certain attorney by the name of Krause, who was attending to the business of the Stephanites

Finally a public debate on the questions which had all but disrupted the colony was set for April 15 and 20, 1841, in Altenburg, Perry County. This public debate is a definite milestone in that it marks a turning point in the development of church polity in the colony. At all events, from that time on the colonists knew where they were headed. Whether it was really the "Easter Day" of the bedeviled colony, as one of the participants, the exuberant Schieferdecker, later called it,[8] may be questioned. This much is certain:

---

after they had left Dresden, succeeded in securing her release, so that, together with her daughter, Agnes, who later became Mrs. O. H. Walther, and her son, J. F. Buenger, candidate of theology, she traveled to St. Louis via New York to meet her other six children, who had traveled on ahead with Stephan. The warrant for O. H. Walther did not arrive until November 21. He had sailed on the *Olbers* on November 18. All stories connected with C. F. W. Walther's supposed sailing on the *Amalia*, as recorded in Martin Guenther, *Dr. C. F. W. Walther,* p. 33, and by Julius Friedrich, *Ebenezer,* p. 26, are edifying, but purely fictitious. The *Johann Georg* left fifteen days before the *Amalia.* The *Amalia* was not overcrowded, since she had only fifty-five passengers, with space for seventy-five. Walther's name appears on the list which the captain of the *Johann Georg* gave when he entered the harbor of New Orleans.

In addition to all this, Walther's release from his former parish was not entirely clean. While he received a formal release from the consistory, his obstreperous behavior as a Stephanite prevented him from securing an entirely clean release. All these factors made a return to Germany rather distasteful to the former Braeunsdorf Stephanite and explain why he applied the purge to Vehse's theory of the necessity for a return to Germany, much defended by Marbach. The above facts and the interpretation of them is based upon a letter of O. H. Walther to his parents, Pastor and Mrs. G. H. Walther, dated November 8, 1838, sent from Bremen to Langenchursdorf. This is one of the unbound letters stored in the Concordia Historical Institute. Walter Forster, graduate student of Washington University, St. Louis, has had a photostatic copy of this letter made. The present writer has a photostatic copy of this letter in his possession. In this letter O. H. Walther tells how his brother got out to sea, "entirely out of danger of yet being apprehended." Cf. Buenger's "Tagebuch" in possession of the Concordia Historical Institute; a copy of the legal documents in the case of Nagel versus Walther, in possession of the Concordia Historical Institute; a complete copy of the files of the Superintendency of Waldenburg in so far as they apply to Braeunsdorf and the ministry of C. F. W. Walther. The typewritten copy of the Nagel and Braeunsdorf document is to be found in C. H. I. Cp. also footnote 23.

[8] G. Schieferdecker, who in 1841 was a candidate of theology and as such attended the public debate at Altenburg, said some years later, in his second presidential address opening the second meeting of the Western District, *Proceedings,* 1856, p. 7: "The testimonies of the Holy Scriptures and of the fathers of the Church, particularly of Luther and Gerhard, were the arbiters ('Schiedsrichter'). With convincing clarity it was demonstrated that in spite of all our errors we still had the Lord Jesus, His Word, the blessed Sacrament, and the Office of the Keys, and that the Lord had His Church, His people, among us. Nothing more was necessary to free the hearts of men from the terrible pressure of anxiety that weighed so heavily upon them. It was the Easter Day of our sorely tried congregations. Like the disciples on their way to Emmaus, we beheld the light and power of God's grace and were filled with new hope. There are still many present today who recall that day with tears of gratitude to the merciful God. Several of the faithful champions

8

it did help to clarify the people's thinking, and it was definitely the making of C. F. W. Walther.[9]

Unfortunately, the minutes of these two important meetings have not come down to posterity. At least their existence is not known at the present writing.[10] We have, however, the notes ("Vorlage") which Marbach made in preparation for the meeting and the notes which he made either during or immediately after the first meeting.[11] We also have the theses which C. F. W. Walther,

---

of the cause of Jesus Christ and of His woefully disrupted flock are living today. The dear brother whom the Lord used as His foremost instrument in the battle is here." (The records show that C. F. W. Walther was present when this very fulsome eulogy was pronounced. This is a good example of the glorification of men by epigonous individuals, of whom the Missouri Synod offers a goodly number in its later history.) "I do not hesitate to say that as important as the Leipzig Debate of 1519 was for the cause of the Reformation, so important was the Altenburg Debate for the development of the polity of the Lutheran Church of the West. It saved us from spiritual pride. We no longer regarded our Church — nor any denomination for that matter — as the only saving Church. It also saved us from denying the existence of the Church in those organizations in which the Word of God is mixed with error."

9 From this day on, Walther is the leader of the Lutheran group. His personality dominates and overshadows all its thinking and speaking. He takes the place of the fallen Stephan. The Saxons again have a man around whom they can rally, a *Fuehrer* who knows what he wants and why he wants it. The authoritarian principle shattered by Stephan's removal is re-established.

10 There were official minutes. Marbach refers to them in his notes as follows: "In our discussions I have permitted the pastors to write the final wording of the 'Protokoll' ('Bei unserm Gespraech habe ich den Herrn Pastoren die Fassung des Protokolls ueberlassen')." This statement is taken from the notes which Marbach made after the first meeting. He calls these notes "Erklaerung zum Protokoll," to distinguish them from the notes he jotted down in preparation for the first meeting, which he calls "Vorlage." The "Vorlage" he evidently read to the meeting; and after he had read it, he made comments on it. Fasc. VI of the Concordia Historical Institute contains letters written to Marbach and copies in his own handwriting of letters which he wrote. It is in this fascicle that the notes on the Altenburg Debate are to be found. Since the minutes of the debate are not available, these notes are invaluable as source material for those two meetings, which were to have such far-reaching effects on the polity of the Missouri Synod. J. F. Koestering, *Auswanderung*, quotes eight pages, 44—52, from a manuscript which Walther used at Altenburg. The present writer discussed the reliability of Koestering with Dr. L. Fuerbringer on August 4, 1941. Fuerbringer's opinion was that Koestering is reliable and accurate whenever he uses manuscript material; his mistakes are due to a reliance on oral tradition, which at times was faulty. Fuerbringer also stated that his mother, whose maiden name was Agnes Buenger and who came via New York with her mother at the time of the Saxon Immigration, derived much pleasure from reading Koestering's account, although she noticed several inaccuracies because of his reliance on oral tradition. His long quotation from Walther's MS. must be regarded as valuable source material. Dr. Fuerbringer thinks that Walther's MS. may be in existence, but he does not know of its present whereabouts.

11 "Erklaerung zum Protokol" in Marbach's handwriting, Fasc. VI, C. H. I.

the champion of the clerical party, formulated and defended over against Marbach, the leader of the lay party. These theses finally won the day and became the foundation stones for Missouri Synod church polity.[12]

Marbach's attitude at Altenburg was foreshadowed in the statements he made in the conference at Dresden, Perry County, in March, 1841, and in his manifesto, dated March 3, 1841, and entitled "An meine Landsleute." At the outset it should be stated, however, that Marbach was not nearly as belligerent as Vehse and certainly not as bitter and pugnacious as the redoubtable Sproede. One gets the impression that his was a more noble spirit. At the very beginning of the discussion he wants it understood that he is not entering this debate as a professional theologian. He still has very high regard for scientific theology.

> I think very highly of all science, especially of the science of theology. Far be it from me to entertain the opinion of enthusiasts who say that theology is not necessary or that it can be learned as child's play ("als koenne man sich ihrer spielend bemeistern") or that it is not a great gift of God ("keine hohe Gabe Gottes").

He would regard it as a great sin against God if he were to break into a profession into which the Lord had not placed him and which requires careful preparation and years of scientific study of a peculiar kind.[13] As a simple layman, on the basis of the doctrine of the priesthood of all believers, he insists that it is not only his privilege but also his sacred and solemn duty to investigate and criticize all doctrines and the polity of the Church. This, he says, must be done according to God's Word and the Confessions of the Lutheran Church. His one concern is to be sure in his own heart that this group of Lutherans has the right to call pastors. He will

---

[12] Walther's theses are found in Marbach's notes. This is the oldest copy extant. They have been reprinted by Koestering, *Auswanderung;* also by C. Hochstetter, *op. cit.* The English translation is found in the *Concordia Cyclopedia,* p. 15. They are officially known as the Altenburg Theses. From them Walther developed his book *Kirche und Amt,* 1851. They are the Missouri Synod's polity *in nuce.*

[13] Marbach is thoroughly convinced of Luther's teaching that every man should remain in the calling into which God has placed him. He believes in the divinity of the call to be a lawyer, a doctor of medicine, a shoemaker, a tailor, etc. No man can leave his calling without exposing himself to the wrath of God. "Ich wuerde Gottes Zorn fuerchten, wenn ich den Theologen machen wollte." He repeats this thought several times in his notes. Like the medievalists, he places theology first among the professions.

do all in his power to establish a similar certainty in the hearts of his fellow colonists. Doubt and uncertainty in this matter lies heavy on all who have emigrated, including the theologians; and he believes that the matter can be clarified by a free and full public discussion of the issues involved. He hopes that this will not be an acrimonious debate or a fight in which two opposing factions are lined up in battle array ("Ich will die Herrn Theologen nicht herausfordern, mit mir einen theologischen Zweikampf zu bestehen"). The notes indicate a feeling on the part of Marbach that the theologians are turning this discussion into a formal theological disputation. He expresses his disapproval of the manner in which Walther has formulated theological theses. He expresses the wish that the problems confronting them had not been put forth with such theological formality and finesse. His only reason for continuing the discussion at this time is his solicitude for the existence of the Church. He is in no wise opposed to the Lutheran Church. Quite the contrary. Since his renunciation of Stephanism his heart, his soul, and his tongue have been at work for the Lutheran Church. The opposing parties in this debate, he says, are not out-and-out heretics ("entschiedene Ketzer") on the one hand and simon-pure orthodoxists on the other ("die glaenzendste rechtglaeubige Theologie des Neuen Testaments auf der anderen Seite"), but rather men who see their beloved Church in peril and who would like to help her escape destruction. Both groups are equally concerned about the welfare of the Church. They differ in their attitude towards the nature of the Church's peril and the nature of the remedy. It is true, he has separated himself from his erstwhile brethren and steadfastly kept aloof from all activities of the Church but this he has done for the following five reasons: first, because, as he sees the situation, Stephanism has not been completely eradicated from the colony ("weil ich nicht sehe, dass der Stephanismus wirklich abgethan ist"); secondly, because the great public offenses have not been acknowledged and removed ("die gegebenen grossen oeffentlichen Aergernisse nicht erkannt und beseitigt sind"); thirdly, because the entire church polity of the colony rests upon an indefinite, unclear, and insecure foundation ("weil mir die ganzen hiesigen kirchlichen Verhaeltnisse auf einem unklaren, unsicheren und bedenklichen Grunde zu ruhen scheinen"). The question whether there is a properly constituted authority in their midst should be thoroughly ventilated, because they have been terribly misled and deceived once. His fourth reason for withdrawing from all church activities is the fact that it is doubtful in his mind whether their local congregation is a true Christian church ("weil es mir aus angegebenen Gruenden zweifelhaft ist, ob die hiesige Gemeinde als wahre christliche Gemeinde anzusehen sey"); and fifthly, it is doubtful in his mind whether the office of the ministry as constituted among them is to be regarded as a command and work of God ("ob das von ihr aufgerichtete Predigtamt als ein Befehl und Werk Gottes anzusehen sey").

Marbach was guilty of oversimplification in that he was bent on making the problem confronting the colony a simple moral issue. They — and here he made one of his chief mistakes, for he made no distinction between those who had been misled and those who had done the misleading — had committed a grave sin; and therefore they could not be the Church. Since they were not the Church, they could not possibly be the properly constituted authority to call a pastor. The entire crowd, leaders and followers, were all under the same condemnation. There was only one thing to do, and that was to right the great moral wrong they had been guilty of. This could be done only by a solemn collective public confession on the part of the whole company, for all shared equally in the guilt, and a return to Germany, where they belonged. Any plan which did not envisage a collective public confession and a return to Germany was for that very reason inadequate, immoral, and doomed to failure.[14] Undoubtedly Marbach did not realize it at the

---

[14] In keeping with his moral conviction Marbach wrote letters to the king of Saxony, the king's ministers, and other influential people in Saxony ("Geheimraethe," etc.) confessing his "great wrong" ("die Notorietaet der Dinge, in die ich in meiner Verkehrtheit gerathen war" — "Gott hat mich die Bedeutung seines Befehls 'Bleibe im Lande und naehre dich redlich' und 'Ein jeglicher bleibe in dem Beruf, darin er berufen ist' erkennen lassen"). (From a letter written to the king of Saxony, dated May 10, 1841.) He confessed that the emigration was a wrong per se, that it gave evidence of a lack of love for the king and his entire family and a lack of appreciation of the blessings of the king's government. He had sinned grievously, so he believed, not only against the king but also against God, inasmuch as the king had been placed over him by God and as God had placed him into his profession in Saxony. Fasc. VI contains copies of these letters in Marbach's own handwriting. Marbach and Buerger also took the next step; they sold their possessions in order to raise funds for a return to Germany. Both families decided to return together, making the journey up the Ohio over Pittsburgh, Buffalo, and New York. Buerger was a widower, his wife having died as the result of childbirth in October, 1840. He had two small children. In the spring and summer of 1841 Marbach's wife, who had strenuously opposed the emigration from the very outset and who had almost remained in Dresden

time, but his strong effort to make a moral issue out of the emigration and to make the intensity of their confession a condition of God's grace was in reality a big hangover of Stephanism itself. It was something which Stephanism had inherited from the pietistic elements in the *Saechsische Erweckungsbewegung* of the early nineteenth century.

Marbach's morality complex is evident from the way in which he conducts his part of the discussion. He has set up a group of countertheses with which he hopes to destroy the propositions that Walther has set up. He attacks the problem negatively. His first question is: "What is a false church?" He offers a threefold definition in answer. A false church, he says, is every church which is not the true, orthodox Church ("die nicht die wahre, rechtglaeubige Kirche ist"). It is every church which has been adulterated, but which has not entirely lost the foundation of the true Church, which is Jesus Christ.

> Die falsche Kirche im gewoehnlichen Sinn ist jede ver-
> faelschte Kirche, die aber doch den Grund der wahren
> Kirche, Christum, nicht ganz verloren hat, d. i., in der einige
> Christo angehoerige Schafe oder Glieder der unsichtbaren
> Kirche in Verbindung mit dem, was vom reinen Wort und
> Sakrament noch da ist, den Grund erhalten; daher der ganze
> Haufe nach der Figur Synekdoche Kirche genannt wird.

Finally, he says, a false church in the most eminent sense is a group of people who have not been called by means of the true Word to the true Christ, but by means of a false word to a false Christ. Such a group is anti-christian. It is called a church to distinguish it from a Jewish or pagan or Turkish organization, as well as from purely secular and nonreligious groups. It has the appearance of the Christian religion, but not its essence.

> Falsche Kirche im hervorragendsten Sinn — *sensu eminenti*
> — ist der Haufe derjenigen, die nicht durch wahres Wort
> zum wahren Christus, sondern durch falsches Wort zu einem
> falschen Christus unter dem Schein der Wahrheit berufen
> sind. . . . Die falsche Kirche in diesem Sinne ist die anti-
> christische Kirche. Sie wird deshalb Kirche genannt, weil

---

when the emigration got under way, was constantly urging her husband to go back to Germany, where they belonged. Her "I told you so" spirit did not contribute to his peace of mind. He wrote to a friend, a certain Mr. Brunner, with whom he had some financial dealings, that things were getting rather unpleasant from day to day ("von Tag zu Tage peinlicher"). This letter is also found in Fasc. VI.

sie einen Gegensatz bildet von Judenthum, Heidenthum und Tuerkenthum sowie von der puren Welt und allen weltlichen Gemeinschaften und weil sie den Schein des Wortes Gottes, den Schein des Berufs zu Gott und Christo und ueberhaupt den Schein des Christenthums hat.

This latter definition of a false church is the one which he applies to their colony. The conclusions which he draws from his various definitions of a false church show how completely he is caught in the idea that their problem is a moral one. To apply the word "church" to an organization that is built upon something that looks like the Word of God but is not, is not a misuse of the term, he maintains, but it is not Scriptural. God never calls such people a "church" or "His children." Since such people have a false word, a false spirit, and a false Christ in their hearts, they cannot be saved. There is no salvation in such a church. Such churches, he claims, have no God-given authority to administer the mysteries of God which have been entrusted to the Church. Until they have repented and renounced the false word and the false Christ and returned to the true Christ, they cannot call a pastor or administer the Sacraments. Until such time they are only a godless mob. Such a mob is not merely to be reformed, but to be built anew from the ground up. Until it destroys its old foundation, it is under the wrath of God, and he who wishes to save his soul must avoid contact with such a mob.

> Es ist zwar aus den angefuehrten Gruenden kein eigentlicher Missbrauch des Namens Kirche, wenn ein solcher Haufe Kirche genannt wird; aber die Redeweise des Wortes ist es nicht. Gott redet in seinem Worte nicht in einer solchen Weise von solchen Haufen, dass er damit die Glieder derselben als seine Kinder ehren und troesten wolle. . . . Dergleichen abgefallene oder irrglaeubige Kirchen haben keine Kirchengewalt. Die Gueter der Kirche sind ihnen nicht gegeben; sie koennen sie also auch nicht verwalten, solange sie nicht Busse thun, dem falschen Christus und seinem falschen Worte nicht entsagen und zu dem rechten Christus zurueckgekehrt sind. . . . Ein solcher Haufe ist nicht bloss zu reformieren, sondern von Grund aus neu zu bauen. Er steht unter dem Zorn Gottes; und wer seine Seele retten will, muss, sobald er den Geist des Haufens erkannt, ausgehen.

Walther was violently opposed to those who saw only a moral issue in their problem and who made the intensity of their own contrition a yardstick with which to measure the sincerity of other people's confession. He called such men conscience pounders ("Gewissensdraenger"). He spoke of tyranny of the conscience ("Gewissensbeherrscherei"), of making things to be sin which are not sin ("die neue Pest der Suendenmacherei"), of calling into question the grace of God which many of us believe we have received ("die Verdaechtigmachung der von vielen unter uns schon vorher gemachten wahrhaften Gnadenerfahrungen"). He spoke of a conscience whip ("Gewissensgeissel"), of people who made the grace of God depend upon the intensity of their contrition and who insisted that other people do likewise. Why should men, Walther asks, who were private secretaries of Stephan and initiated into all the secrets of Stephan, who knew what was going on — why should they make the amount of their guilt and the intensity of their confession the yardstick with which to measure the amount of guilt to be assessed against the simple, uninitiated layman? Many followed Stephan, Walther says, who had neither the ability nor the opportunity to judge. They did it in their ignorance. They were not wicked; they were misled. Would it be fair and just to hold them equally responsible with the private secretaries of Stephan? Besides, what good could come from a collective public confession? Walther sensed in Marbach's position the effects of early-nineteenth-century Pietism, the movement which laid so much stress on the intensity and depth of the acknowledgment of sin and which tried to externalize the Church. The habit of identifying the invisible Church with the visible had been the source of much confusion and much unnecessary heartache among the Pietists. Walther would have none of it.

Walther, on the other hand, took his cue from Vehse and attacked the problem from the viewpoint of sixteenth-century theology. To get a clear view, he pushed personalities and morals into the background. He even thought that their emigration might be a work of God; but whether it was or was not, it certainly was not the issue on which to lose time right now. The burning issue was whether they were a part of the Christian Church and whether as part of the Christian Church they had the right to call ministers and to be called as ministers and whether their ministerial functions were valid also in the sight of God.

To establish this, he advised that they follow Vehse back to Martin Luther and John Gerhard and to the definition of the Church which these men had learned from the Word of God.[15]   John Gerhard especially made a sharp distinction between the invisible Church, which consists solely and alone of believers and which is the true Church, the communion of saints found among all peoples and kindreds and tongues, and the visible Church, which besides the true believers also includes people who say that they believe but do not.   By means of this sixteenth-century distinction Walther was able to answer the question "Are we a part of the Church?" in the affirmative and to extricate himself from the rather uncomfortable necessity of returning to Saxony.

At this time he was above all anxious to establish from Luther's and Gerhard's writings the fact that the name "church" may be properly applied to churches which have been adulterated with false doctrine and ungodly life, and to show — of course, on the basis of Lutheran authorities of the sixteenth century — that such adulterated churches have the power to call pastors and that the ministerial acts of these pastors are valid also in the sight of God. If he could establish this fact from the writings of Luther and John Gerhard, he would effectively undermine all talk of going back to Saxony.   Theses IV—VIII supplement Vehse and therefore are really, as they existed at that moment, the heart of Walther's contribution at Altenburg.   They show the real issues between him and Marbach.

---

15 J. P. Koehler, *Geschichte der Allgemeinen Evangelisch-Lutherischen Synode von Wisconsin und andern Staaten*, p. 158. Speaking of the Old Lutheran movement both in Europe and in North America, the writer says: "The weapons of their warfare differed from those of Martin Luther. He stood on the Scriptures alone and made them the sole norm of doctrine which everybody acknowledged. He expounded the Scriptures and led people back to the source from which they could obtain spiritual strength for the battles which beset them. In the nineteenth century Luther and the Lutheran fathers supplied the weapons with which theologians fought. It was an entirely different approach ('Es ist eine ganz andere Geisteseinstellung, die auf solche Weise entsteht'). . . . Luther enjoyed a greater freedom and abandon because he worked directly with the facts of the Gospel. In the nineteenth century there was a cramping of the spirit on both sides ('Im 19. Jahrhundert waltete die Geistesenge auf beiden Seiten, die aus der Geisteserziehung der voraufgegangenen zwei Jahrhunderte herkam')." In his letter dated July 12, 1844, and reprinted in Loeber's "Der Hirtenbrief," etc., J. A. A. Grabau, a contemporary of the Saxons, makes this same complaint of them. On page 37 he writes: "Speaking generally in their criticism of my 'Hirtenbrief,' I missed the principle that the Word of God must first be used exhaustively in the defense and criticism of Christian doctrine. In fact, they used nothing but quotations from Luther's writings and no statements from the Word of God."

Thesis IV: "It is not improper to apply the name 'church' to heterodox societies, but this is in accord with the manner of speech in the Word of God itself. And it is not immaterial that this high name is granted to such societies, for from this follows: (1) That members also of such societies may be saved; for without the Church there is no salvation."

Thesis V: " (2) That the outward separation of a heterodox society from the orthodox Church is not necessarily a separation from the universal Christian Church or a relapse into heathenism and does not yet deprive that society of the name 'church.' "

Thesis VI: " (3) Even heterodox societies have church power; even among them the treasures of the Church may be validly dispensed, the ministry established, the Sacraments validly administered, and the keys of the kingdom of heaven exercised."

Thesis VII: "Even heterodox societies are not to be dissolved, but reformed."

Thesis VIII: "The orthodox Church is to be judged principally by the common, orthodox, and public confession to which the members acknowledge themselves to have been pledged and which they profess."

Walther proceeded in a very impersonal manner. As far as we know, he made no mention of the names of his opponents — Marbach, Buerger, and Wege. He did not engage in wordy harangues, like the Homeric warriors before they came to blows, to work up the necessary psychosis of aggressive complexes. Quite the contrary. The situation called for tact and deft handling of the opposition.

Unhesitatingly he acknowledges the contribution which Vehse, Fischer, and Jaeckel had made with their document of September 19, 1839. This document, he says, gave him the chief impulse to study the remnants of Stephanism that were still manifest among them and to evaluate them on the basis of Luther's writings. Without this document, he acknowledges solemnly and publicly, they probably would still be groping in the dark or wandering about in labyrinths of error, from which they have been happily extricated. For his own person he is all the more ready to acknowledge the contribution of the lay party, since at first he was extremely antagonistic to their document. Simply but quietly he built his case on the same authority which Marbach, Buerger, Vehse, Fischer, Jaeckel, and Wege had used. Just how many quotations he used from Luther and how many from Gerhard we do not know. But we may get some idea by examining a book which grew out of the Altenburg Debate, which, however, was modified by the controversy which the Saxons of Missouri had with J. A. A. Grabau, the Prussian immigrant who founded the Buffalo Synod.[16] In the book of 1851 Walther prints his revised theses. Underneath each thesis he reprints the pertinent quotations. There are one hundred thirty-three excerpts from Luther's writings, some running into several pages; sixty-five from John Gerhard ("the archtheologian and standard dogmatician of the period of orthodoxy" — *Concordia Cyclopedia,* p. 283); eighteen from Martin Chemnitz ("If Chemnitz had not come, Luther had not stood"); thirteen from Quenstedt ("bookkeeper of Lutheran orthodoxy"; he was the nephew of Gerhard); twelve from Dannhauer ("foremost Lutheran theologian of his age, 1603—1666"); nine from Calov ("the staunchest champion of strict Lutheranism"); eight from Balduin (member of the faculty at Wittenberg); five each from Baier, J. B. Carpzov, and Huelsemann. In addition, twenty-seven other writers are quoted at length from one to four times each.

---

[16] The genesis of the controversy was briefly this: On December 1, 1840, J. A. A. Grabau, who had emigrated from Prussia and settled with a part of his congregation in Buffalo, New York, in the previous year, sent a Pastoral Letter ("Hirtenbrief") to the Missourians. In this letter he explained in detail his ideal of the Lutheran Church in America. His plan envisaged power highly concentrated in the clergy. It was not so very different from Stephan's scheme. The letter was sent to Perry County and to St. Louis with a request for an opinion on the plan. Although they had no pastor at the time, the St. Louis congregation took up the letter in its meeting of February 22, 1841. The minutes show that the letter was read and that certain false viewpoints ("falsche Punkte") were discussed. However, it was decided to postpone the answer until their new pastor had assumed office. The matter dragged on for two years. Grabau was clamoring for an answer. Evidently the Missourians hated to break with Grabau, who shared their attitude to the Confessions of the Lutheran Church. A collective opinion of the Saxons was finally written by Loeber and is dated July 3, 1843. The Missourians opposed Grabau's hierarchical plans, and thus a twenty-five-year controversy began. In the course of this controversy Walther published his first book. It was an expansion of the Altenburg Theses. The draft of this treatise had been submitted to the fifth convention of the Missouri Synod at Milwaukee, Wisconsin, in 1851. After discussing it in eight sessions, the convention unanimously voted its enthusiastic approval and ordered its publication in book form. It was printed 1852, and its title was *Die Stimme unserer Kirche in der Frage von Kirche und Amt.* The abbreviated title is *Kirche und Amt* (the Church and the Ministry). Here Walther takes the same position which he took at Altenburg, April 15 and 20, 1841.

At Altenburg Walther succeeded in establishing the fact that
according to Luther and John Gerhard and other reliable Lutheran theologians they were still a part of the Church. The
Stephanistic errors still rampant among them were not sufficient
to destroy all faith. There was a sufficient remnant of the Word
of God to create faith at least in the hearts of some. Since there
were some Christians among them, the Church was represented
in their midst, they had not only the privilege but also the duty
to call ministers, and the official acts of these ministers were valid
also in the sight of God. He convinced the overwhelming majority that the immediate objective of the company must be not
destruction but a thorough reformation of doctrine and life based
upon purified doctrine and thorough reconstruction of their church
life as constituted under Stephan ("Kirchenverfassung"). Not
only the rank and file but also the theologians, including Magister
Wege and, at least temporarily, Buerger, were convinced by Walther's quotations and the remarks which he made apropos of these
quotations. Even Marbach came around to Walther's way of
thinking. He wrote a long personal confession,[17] in which he
talked only of his own personal sins and not of the sins of the
group. He spoke of his purged confession of faith ("ein gerei-
nigtes Glaubensbekenntnis"). He recognized four facts: 1. "I admit that the Church is in our midst." 2. "I give up my basic
conception as false" ("Grundirrtum"). 3. "I admit that the genuine Lord's Supper is celebrated in our midst." 4. "However, I am
not quite convinced that I ought to participate in its celebration."
Teacher Winter reported that Walther continued to make efforts
in Marbach's behalf and that Marbach seemed to be open to conviction.[18] Winter closes this part of his letter with a doxology:
"God be praised that these controversial issues have come up for
public discussion, for through this debate many a soul has been
put back on the right path" ("dadurch manche Seele wieder in
das rechte Geleis gekommen ist"). In a letter to Superintendent
Guericke, dated April 28, 1841, Loeber calls it a remarkable public

[17] Entitled "An meine deutschen Landsleute, mit denen ich unter Pastor
Stephan nach Nordamerika ausgewandert bin." Fasc. VI, C. H. I. This docu-
ment is not to be confused with one of a similar title dated March 3, 1841.
Cf. also especially Teacher Winter's letter in Rudelbach und Guerickes
Zeitschrift, II (1841), No. 3, p. 130.

[18] Letter, *op. cit.,* p. 130. "Ueber letzteren Punkt hat ihn Pastor Walther
sogleich belehrt, wobei er sich empfaenglich gezeigt haben soll."

discussion ("eine merkwuerdige oeffentliche Besprechung"). He says that many doubts have vanished and that those who had formerly been convinced were now strengthened in their conviction ("Vieler Scrupel sind geschwunden und die schon vorher ueberzeugten Herzen noch mehr bestaerkt worden").[19]

The conviction grew generally that they were a part of the invisible Christian Church (*una sancta ecclesia*), that as such they had the power to call ministers, and that ministerial acts of such properly called ministers were valid also in the sight of God. A few individuals, including Pastor E. M. Buerger, were still confused.[20] A few of the laymen were tired of strife and occupied themselves with the hard task of making a living in the backwoods of Missouri or in the frontier town of St. Louis rather than engage in theological discussions.[21] The individual congregations did not hesitate to call pastors, and a healthy church life began to develop.

Just how did the principles which Vehse and Walther derived from the writings of Luther work out in the day-to-day life of a Lutheran congregation? Was the Vehse-Walther-Luther principle, that laymen have the power by majority vote to regulate financial and spiritual matters, practicable? Did the theory of the "supremacy of the congregation" work? Nowhere is the working of this principle better revealed than in the minutes of Trinity Lutheran Church, St. Louis, one of the mother churches of the Missouri Synod. The present writer has gone over the minutes of the early years several times with a view to tracing the application of the Vehse-Walther-Luther principle. Though the shrewdness of Walther and his ability to get around difficulties, even if those difficulties were constitutional, must be taken into consideration, it can be said that by and large the principle of congregational supremacy was applied in the early years of "Old Trinity" and that it worked.

In the first meeting recorded in the book of minutes and dated December 16, 1839, we get a picture of the congregation in action. Three items were discussed and decided upon: first, to give the

---

[19] Letter to Guericke, reprinted in Rudelbach und Guerickes *Zeitschrift*, II (1841), No. 3, p. 112.

[20] Loeber's letter to Guericke, April 28, 1841, *op. cit.:* "Aber freilich noch immer steht uns eine Anzahl, darunter auch einer der Amtsbrueder (P. B.), mit fast donatistischen Grundsaetzen entgegen."

[21] Loeber's letter, *op. cit.*, p. 112.

pastor permission to use some of the congregation's wood as fuel
for his personal use; secondly, to have a new gown made for
the pastor; and, thirdly, to have one of the members, Mr. Traenkhahn, make a hymnboard. The second item occupied by far the
most time of the congregation. It was brought out in the discussion that a change had taken place in their midst and that a
different style of gown was now necessary. This was one of those
covert references to the abolition of Stephanism which one finds
every now and then in the documents of the oldest churches of
the Missouri Synod. Stephan had advocated a white surplice,
a chasuble, and other ornate vestments for the clergy. With the
passing of Stephan a return to the old type — the black, or Geneva,
gown — was thought to be more appropriate. Another fact that
was brought out in the discussion was that there were sufficient
goods remaining from the amount that had been brought over from
Europe. All that was necessary was to pay for the tailoring of
the new gown. The big question was whether in their poverty it
would be right for them to have a new gown made. Quite a
number favored the remodeling of the present gown. Finally,
after much discussion of their present economic stringency ("nach
mehreren Amendements wegen der gedraengten Umstaende"), it
was decided by majority vote to have a brand-new gown made.[22]

Very early in its history Trinity Congregation had occasion
to call a pastor. Every step which the congregation took was
apparently in agreement with Walther's principle of the supremacy
of the congregation, as is revealed in the minutes. In the meeting of January 11, 1841, it was reported that Pastor O. H. Walther
was very sick. A resolution was adopted to ask Candidate J. F.
Buenger to preach a sermon of his own making in the Sunday
afternoon service and to read a printed sermon in the Sunday
morning service. Pastor Walther died January 21, 1841. The
elders, who had been elected by majority vote of the congregation,
made all arrangements for the funeral, together with the widow.
They also resolved to recommend to the voting members that the
congregation pay all the funeral expenses. In the meeting of
January 25, 1841, the recommendation of the elders was adopted
unanimously ("Dies wurde durch einstimmigen Beschluss der
Gemeinde angenommen"). The entire expense was $27.95½; and

---

[22] Book of Minutes, Trinity Congregation, December 16, 1839.

the money, by resolution of the congregation, was to be raised by individual freewill offerings. Each elder was appointed a committee of one to receive contributions for this purpose. All money was to be paid in by the following Monday evening. It was furthermore stipulated at this meeting that Candidates of Theology Buenger and Schieferdecker were to alternate in preaching sermons of their own making in the afternoon service every other Sunday and to read a sermon out of the book of *Catechism Sermons* by Arndt in the early morning service. The sermons to be preached by the candidates of theology were, by resolution of the congregation, to be based on the Epistles of the day. In the very utmost emergency ("im allerhoechsten Nothfall") — and here their Stephanism still protrudes — Candidate Buenger should be given the authority ("es soll ihm uebertragen sein") to administer Holy Communion. As far as Baptism was concerned, the members might choose between Pfarrer Wall (an "Unierter"; he served a mixed congregation consisting of Lutherans and Reformed in the frontier town of St. Louis) and Candidate J. F. Buenger.

In the meeting of February 1, 1841, it was decided to begin the process of calling a new pastor. The elders were asked to recommend candidates for the vacancy. It seems that they expected something like that. Perhaps there had been some discussion during the period between the meetings, which, of course, was not recorded in the minutes. At any rate, the elders were ready on the spot with six candidates — three ministers: G. H. Loeber, C. F. W. Walther, and O. Fuerbringer; three candidates of theology: J. F. Buenger, G. Schieferdecker, and T. J. Brohm. It was decided that the election should take place in this wise, that every member (male communicant over twenty-five years of age) should vote for two candidates on the list. The two highest candidates should remain before the congregation until the next meeting, and then the final election should take place. Before they proceeded to the primary election, however, two voting members were elected to count the ballots. Mr. Niemann and Mr. Stephan were accorded this honor. After the formal ballot had been taken, it was revealed that Pastor C. F. W. Walther and Candidate of Theology G. Schieferdecker had received the highest number of votes ("durch die Mehrheit der Stimmen gewaehlt"). After voting that the widow of Pastor O. H. Walther should re-

ceive the full salary of her deceased husband until the new pastor
had been installed (here they followed contemporary church
custom) and after approving the minutes of that particular meeting (they always did that at the close of each meeting), the voters
adjourned the meeting.

The two candidates were before the congregation for eight
days. That gave everybody an opportunity to register his opposition. On February 8, 1841, it was decided to conduct the final
election. Mr. Kampmeier and Mr. Schmeister were elected to be
assistants to the chairman ("als Beisitzer erwaehlt"). Pastor C. F.
W. Walther received the majority of the votes; and it was decided that a document setting forth his relation to the congregation ("Vocation") should be read in the meeting, approved by
the voters, and then taken to him. Mr. Quast was elected to take
the document setting forth the conditions of the call to Pastor C.
F. W. Walther. Ten dollars were set aside as expense money for
Mr. Quast on his journey to Perry County. He was also asked
to take along ten dollars for the traveling expenses of Pastor Walther; since Walther was more or less foot-loose at the time, the
congregation had good reason to believe that he would accept
their call.

In the meeting of February 22, 1841, a letter in which Pastor
Walther thanked them for the confidence which they had placed
in him was read to the congregation. In this letter he asked them,
for reasons beyond his control, for additional time to consider the
call. His health, for one thing, did not permit him to give them
a definite answer at that time. Then there were other considerations, which he did not wish to mention at this time, but which
prevented him from giving them a definite answer. It was decided
to have patience and to await the final decision of Pastor Walther.
By March 8, 1841, some of the brethren were getting a little
restless. They argued that either a messenger or a message should
be sent to Perry County to inquire as to the decision of Pastor
C. F. W. Walther. After much discussion it was decided not to
send a message or a messenger to Pastor Walther, but to wait
until he himself should report. After resolving by majority vote
to put a fence around the grave of their deceased pastor, the
meeting adjourned.

In the meantime, as we have previously seen, Marbach started
a big squabble with his manifesto of March 3, 1841. The colony

down in Perry County was in a turmoil; meetings and conferences were held; and preparations for the great Altenburg Debate were being made. Pastor Walther, who had his fingers pretty much in the thick of things, and who was beset by Brother Sproede, *et al.*, had neither the time nor the inclination to make a definite decision.

Finally, on April 26, 1841, six days after his big victory over Marbach, Pastor Walther appeared in person before the congregation. It is a new Pastor Walther. He is sure of himself. He knows what he wants. The effects of the victory are written all over his actions. The congregation was hurriedly called together, since Pastor Walther was anxious to give them a definite statement ("eine bestimmte Erklaerung"). He told them that four factors had prevented him from giving them an immediate answer. The first was his sickness, which had lasted for a good year. The second was his feeling of unfitness for the office of the holy ministry ("das Gefuehl der Untuechtigkeit zum geistlichen Amt"). The third was a sense of unworthiness, which developed particularly during his sickness. And finally, the confusion concerning church polity, more specifically the right to call a minister and to administer the blessed Sacrament, caused him to postpone his final answer to the congregation.

Thereupon Pastor Walther declared simply but firmly that all these hindrances to the acceptance of the call had been removed ("Er erklaerte ganz offen, dass alle diese Hindernisse nun aus dem Wege geraeumt waeren"). The first hindrance was cleared away by a recovery of his health. The second difficulty was removed by his energetic search and study of the Lutheran fathers. These writers, he said, had conclusively set forth that if the men who issue a call do so according to the ordinance of God, then he who is being called should not in the least hesitate to accept the call ("Sobald von seiten der Berufer alles nach goettlicher Ordnung geschehen ist, soll derjenige, der berufen wird, durchaus sich nicht weigern, solche [*sic!*] anzunehmen"). In discussing the third factor, he very deftly made a rather indirect bid for an expression of opinion on their part, which he then used to show that his doubts in this respect were removed. This point concerned the pastor's reputation among people outside of the Church. This seems to have been his greatest trouble. The rule according to the Lutheran fathers is that one must be worthy of the minis-

9

terial office; i. e., he must be above reproach, he must not have committed an act which might make him obnoxious in the eyes of nonreligious men.

Undoubtedly the many difficulties which C. F. W. Walther had had with the government authorities of Saxony on account of his rabid Stephanism, to which we have alluded in footnote 7 of this chapter, particularly the Nagel lawsuit, the kidnaping of the Schubert children, and the fact that his release from the Braeunsdorf parish was not quite clean, were still troubling him. These were facts that might be construed as sufficient infringement of public law to disqualify a man for the Lutheran ministry. Furthermore, Walther may have known by this time that Sproede, his archenemy and thorn in the flesh, had already made plans to follow him to St. Louis in order to make life miserable for him in his new field of operations. This careful maneuver on the part of Walther was to forestall anything that Sproede might attempt. So he built up his defense shrewdly in advance by telling the congregation that if a man had committed an act that made him offensive to the unbelieving world, and if he informed the congregation of this fact or if they found out about it in some other way in advance, and if they still called him in full possession of such knowledge, then a man could accept such a call without the slightest compunctions of conscience.[23] The minutes on the third point read as follows:

---

[23] The Rev. Rud. H. C. Meyer, the present pastor of Old Trinity, maintains that there is an old, but strong tradition in the congregation that Walther's hesitation was caused by the fact that he had entered the country under an assumed name, and that he was afraid of immigration officers in the United States. This tradition probably received support from a statement in Guenther's *C. F. W. Walther*, p. 33: "Walther was to make the voyage to America on the *Amalia;* but — oh, marvelous intervention of God's providence! — when he arrived in Bremen, he was not permitted to board the *Amalia*. He tries for a place on the ship *Johann Georg*. Alas, there is no vacant space on this ship. Finally a young man offers to yield his place on the *Johann Georg* to Walther. This young man made the journey on another ship, while Walther sailed under the name of the young man." In a footnote to this paragraph Guenther makes the following remark. "Not under the name of Rector Goenner. Goenner was not made rector until 1843." While Professor Guenther's story is edifying, it is not in agreement with the documents. The passenger list of the captain of the *Johann Georg*, on file in New Orleans, a photostatic copy of which has been made for Concordia Historical Institute, plainly reveals the name of C. F. W. Walther of Braeunsdorf, aged 28 years. The infringement of public law which might have disqualified Walther from the ministry and which no doubt was troubling him during the time in which he was considering the call from Trinity Congregation, St. Louis, was that mentioned in footnote 7 of this chapter.

Der dritte Grund wegen Unwuerdigkeit: dass der Berufene zu dem geistlichen Amt tuechtig sei, dass er namentlich ein gutes Zeugnis von Aussen haben muesse oder untadelich sein, nicht gemeint seine Suende und Suendenfaelle, sondern auf die Art der Suende, namentlich besonders buergerliche Verbrechen, oder auch zweitens, wenn die Gemeinde die Suende wisse und ihnen (*sic!*) dennoch vergeben wolle, derselbe getrost und freudig sein Amt annehmen kann.

The fourth point was setttled, as far as Walther was concerned, by the results of the Altenburg Debate. He was thoroughly convinced by the writings of the Lutheran fathers that in spite of all false doctrines that had crept in during their Stephanistic days they were still a Christian Church, and no one could take from them the rights of a Christian congregation, particularly not the right to call a pastor.

The minutes are none too clear on the action which followed immediately after Walther's statement to the congregation. Evidently the secretary did not quite understand what was really going on, or he understood too well and did not wish to write too plainly about the matter. At any rate, there was some discussion on the part of the voters concerning Walther's attitude toward church polity and also concerning his personal qualifications, particularly his reputation with those outside the Church. Then followed — undoubtedly what Walther was fishing for — a very clear resolution that Pastor Walther be asked to preach his initial sermon the following Sunday and that he be allowed to make his own choice of a text for this occasion. The minutes read as follows:

Nachdem von Seiten der Gemeinde kein Anstoss im Betreff der Ueberzeugung ueber die Frage kirchlicher Verhaeltnisse des Herrn Pastors war, ebenso auch nicht ueber die Person desselben, wurde endlich dahin beschlossen, dass der Herr Pastor Walther naechsten Sonntag seine Antrittspredigt halten moechte, wobei ihm die Wahl des Textes ueberlassen wurde.

The final resolution of this eventful meeting of April 26, 1841, was to the effect that on Cantate Sunday the blessed Sacrament be celebrated for the first time since the death of their beloved pastor. Either the congregation had followed the State Church rule of observing several months of mourning in memory of their deceased pastor, or — and that seems to me to be more likely —

they had not celebrated the Lord's Supper because of their mis-givings concerning the administration of Holy Communion by a candidate of theology. As far as the minutes show, no minister had served them during this entire period.

The relationship between Walther and the congregation, a relationship which began on the evening of April 26, 1841, was not marred by the principle of the supremacy of the congregation. There were other factors which counterbalanced this principle. For one thing, the congregation readily adopted the peculiarly Lutheran principle that when a congregation calls a pastor, then that pastor is placed over them by God and must be respected as God's servant and not the servant of men. Furthermore, the pastor was accorded respect and honor because the Word which he preached was accepted as God's Word. And, finally, the con-gregation was definitely imbued with the characteristic Lutheran doctrine of the means of grace, i. e., that through the Word which the pastor preaches faith is created in hearts in which there is no faith, and faith is strengthened in hearts in which it has already been created; likewise, that through the administration of the Sacraments faith is created and strengthened. These purely Lu-theran doctrines tended to give the minister a dignity which was unique. The many arrangements concerning services which Trinity Congregation made out of deference to the pastor's health, the many financial arrangements so liberally made for the well-being of the pastor, the increasing respect which the congregation showed for the pastor's opinions and advice, which becomes evident from the minutes as the years go by — all these show that the principle of congregational supremacy did not conflict with the dignity of the ministry.

Another major project of Trinity Congregation, of which we have an extensive record in the minutes and which illustrates the working of Walther's polity as derived through Vehse from Lu-ther, is the framing of a constitution for the congregation (*Ge-meindeordnung*). In fact, this is a project par excellence for a study of Walther's polity. Here the principles enunciated and defended at Altenburg are put to the test. To what extent is the constitutional and administrative law of Trinity Congregation based on the principles that won the day at Altenburg? With this ques-tion the present writer approached the minutes of Old Trinity.

Since Trinity Church was one of the mother churches of the Missouri Synod, the procedure here becomes doubly important.[24]

In the very nature of things, the officers that were elected in 1839 and 1840 received their instructions from time to time as the need arose. The resolutions were *ad hoc* instructions, passed by majority vote of the congregation. The only standing officers were the elders and the treasurer. Three months after Pastor C. F. W. Walther had arrived, in the meeting of August 9, 1841, the congregation formally resolved to ask the pastor to gather testimonies ("Zeugnisse"; quotations from Luther and other reliable theologians of the Lutheran Church are meant) on the relationship of the elders to the congregation and to read them

---

[24] J. L. Gruber, *Erinnerungen*, 1930, pp. 7—8. "The mother church was Trinity Congregation, which was founded by the Saxons who immigrated with Martin Stephan in 1839. It was the richest and most respected congregation." (The author was writing of the time when he became teacher in Trinity's school system, September, 1862.) "Most of the old Saxons, also called Stephanites, lived within the parish and were members of the church. Popularly all Lutherans were called Saxons. People commonly spoke of the Saxon church, Saxon schools, Saxon drug stores, and Saxon mills. The name Saxon stood in good repute also with the nonreligious world. It would be very hard to find a congregation that could compare with Old Trinity in morals, in true piety, in love for their fellow men, and in zeal for the Kingdom of God." Gruber wrote this many years after he had left the Missouri Synod.

What St. Michael's Church of Philadelphia was to the congregations of the General Synod and of the General Council, that Old Trinity was to the Missouri Synod. "By special request of several brethren," as the editor informs us, the constitution of 1843 was reprinted without change in *Der Lutheraner*, VI (1850), pp. 105—106. Final quotations from the constitution in this study are made from the copy in *Der Lutheraner*. In July, 1897, Dr. A. L. Graebner, then professor of church history at Concordia Seminary, St. Louis, and editor of the *Theological Quarterly*, translated the constitution of Old Trinity Church and published it in the *Theological Quarterly*, I (1897), pp. 326—335, under the heading "Constitution and By-Laws of a Lutheran Congregation." Dr. Graebner's translation was published in pamphlet form by Concordia Publishing House and was commonly used as a model by all Missouri Synod congregations who wished to revise their old constitutions or get out new ones in the English language. As late as 1917 graduates of Concordia Seminary, St. Louis, were advised to use this model whenever they were confronted with constitutional problems in their future congregations. The present writer used this model in organizing and incorporating four Missouri Synod congregations in the State of Minnesota, and these congregations are still operating under that constitution. Every congregation which desires to become a member of the Missouri Synod must submit its constitution to a Constitution Committee of Synod. Such a constitution is judged largely on the basis of Old Trinity's constitution. C. O. Kraushaar, *Verfassungsformen der lutherischen Kirche Amerikas*, p. 139, refers to the remarkable unanimity that exists in the constitutions of the various congregations of the Missouri Synod. Incidentally, he reprints the constitution of Old Trinity in his *Verfassungsformen*, pp. 125—129.

to the congregation four weeks hence. This manner of making constitutional law was stereotype with the congregation. Whenever a constitutional problem presented itself, the first thing which the congregation did was to instruct the pastor to cull quotations from Luther's and Gerhard's writings on the problem confronting them and then to make their law in conformity with these quotations. In the meeting of September 13, 1841, the secretary reported that the congregation had decided in its last meeting that the pastor in co-operation with all the elders was to work out an "Instruction" for the elders ("eine Instruction der Gemeindevorsteher"). Thereupon the whole problem was discussed. From the discussion it became evident that many difficulties were involved in the relationship of the elders to the congregation. In fact, the fundamental question of congregational supremacy was involved in this relationship. There was grave danger of usurpation of authority. Since this relationship was such a highly important matter, it was decided to postpone the election of elders until after the "Instruction" had been read and discussed in the meeting three weeks hence.

On October 4, 1841, the "Instruction" was read and adopted after the following amendments had been offered from the floor: (1) Any member of the church board ("Kirchenrath") who ceases to be a blessing to the congregation and becomes an offense may be removed by vote of the congregation at any time. (2) The activity of the church council shall in no wise deprive an individual church member of the rights and privileges guaranteed to him by the priesthood of all believers. (3) Members of the church council must observe the utmost secrecy concerning all private matters that are discussed in the meetings of the council. (4) At every election to church office this "Instruction" shall be read to the voters. In the meeting of November 8, 1841, the "Instruction" was changed to the effect that the name "Kirchenrath" was stricken, because it was offensive to some ("weil er einigen anstoessig gewesen ist"). *Gemeindevorstand* was substituted. In the meeting of January 24, 1842, it was decided that the four elders were to change off in presiding over the meetings of the voters. In the meeting of February 28, 1842, someone suggested that the congregation follow the constitution of Zion Church in Baltimore in appointing a committee to nominate suitable candidates for the election of elders. This suggestion was flatly re-

jected, because the voters wished to retain full freedom in electing their elders ("sondern dass die Gemeinde die freieste Wahl
behaelt").

Subsequent minutes show that the congregation watched over
its officers with an eagle eye and held them to strict accountability.
During the discussion of plans for a new church, April 11, 1842,
several elders were absent. They were asked to give a reason
for their absence. "Vorsteher" Goenner, who was one of them, was
offended about some action of the congregation. Immediately, in
the meeting of May 10, 1842, a resolution was passed to extend
a written invitation to Vorsteher Goenner to appear before the
congregation and give an account of his stewardship ("damit
Ruecksprache mit ihm ueber die Verwaltung seines Vorsteher-
amtes in jetziger Lage der Dinge genommen werden koenne"). In
the same meeting "Vorsteher" Hoffmann, who also seems to have
been out of sorts, asked to be relieved of his office. His request
was promptly granted. Two days later, in a meeting on May 12,
1842, Goenner promised solemnly that he would not willfully absent himself from any future meetings of the congregation and
that he would be willing to serve the congregation as faithfully
as his health would permit. However, if the congregation was
of the opinion that his services were inadequate in the present
situation ("in jetziger Lage der Dinge"), he would be satisfied
if they declared the office vacant and elected a new elder. After
discussing his case, the congregation voted that he remain in office.
In the meeting of August 8, 1842, it was decided that the secretary write up a formal release for the former elder Herr Hoffmann.
It seems that the elders were out of sorts because they failed to
realize that their duties and powers were largely administrative
and not discretionary.[25] The displeasure of Vorsteher Goenner

---

[25] Unfortunately, the "Instruction," called *Gemeindevorsteherordnung*
after November 8, 1841, was not incorporated in the book of minutes. It was
recorded in some other book, which is not available at present. However,
in 1848 Immanuel Congregation was organized as a part of Trinity Congregation, and the *Vorsteherordnung* of this congregation has come down to us.
This *Ordnung* has been reprinted by Kraushaar, *op. cit.*, pp. 132—135. It contains the amendments verbatim that were adopted in the meetings of Trinity
Congregation. It is probably an exact copy of the Trinity *Gemeindevorsteherordnung*. While this *Ordnung* gives the elders a certain amount of discretionary power, it does insist that most of these powers are administrative.
In all cases the elders are responsible to the voting members of the congregation. They dare usurp no rights which belong to the individual Christian
by virtue of the priesthood of all believers. The last section of paragraph 12

manifested itself immediately after the election of a special building committee for the erection of a church.   Neither Hoffmann
nor Goenner were elected to this committee.   This may have been
the cause of their ill humor.   But whatever the cause, the congregation held them strictly accountable for every move they made.

It is seldom that a constitution for a church organization has
been adopted with so much care and such endless discussion as
the constitution of Trinity Congregation, St. Louis.   The first impetus to the adoption of a constitution (*Gemeindeordnung*) was
given by Pastor Walther in the meeting of February 28, 1842.   The
purchase and tenure of the real estate on which a new church
was to be erected by the congregation made the adoption of a
constitution that could be recorded in the courthouse ("ein ge-
richtlich beglaubigtes Dokument") necessary.   Walther had prepared a preliminary draft of such a document.   After it had been
read, Walther admonished the voters to study it with the utmost
care ("reifliche Ueberlegung wurde vom Herrn Pastor anemp-
fohlen").   More than a year later, July 3, 1843, they were still discussing the implications in signing this constitution.   The constitution or parts of it came up for discussion in no fewer than
thirty-one meetings.   On March 1, 1843, Pastor Walther read a
long quotation from Vol. X of Luther's works, "Von der deutschen Messe," and proved conclusively that Luther was not opposed to a written constitution for any congregation.   March 14,
1842, a strong plea for purity of doctrine and a warning against
unionism, written by Candidate of Theology Goenner, was read to
the voters.   Every effort, he said in this document, ought to be
made to build a church in which the pure doctrine of the Lutheran
Church was safeguarded for posterity.

March 18, 1842, the name "Trinity," suggested by Walther, be-

---

of the Immanuel *Gemeindevorsteherordnung* reads, according to Kraushaar,
p. 134: "The board of elders has authority to make decisions and rules
'Anordnungen' only when the congregation has given them specific authority."
In the constitution of the congregation 'Gemeindeordnung', adopted in 1843,
paragraph 11 shows that their powers were largely administrative.   It reads:
"The elders 'Gemeindevorsteher' at any time in office shall have no authority
beyond that which has been conferred upon them by the congregation, and
whatever power may have been delegated to them shall be at all times liable
to change or recision by the congregation."   Paragraph 10 of the constitution
of Old Trinity also limits the powers of the board of elders, particularly in
the calling of a minister.   This paragraph reads: "The right of choosing and
calling ministers and teachers and of electing all other officers shall ever be
vested in the congregation and shall never be delegated to an individual
or to a minor body within the congregation."

cause it was emblematic of doctrine and because it would not give them that are without occasion to make witty remarks, was adopted by the congregation. March 21, 1842, arrangements were begun to purchase a seal for the congregation with the name "Trinity." The congregation passed a resolution that a design be submitted to the voters before the seal were adopted. April 4, 1842, new instructions regarding the seal were given to the committee. April 11, 1842, the committee reported that a seal with nothing more than the name of the congregation would cost $15 and one with an engraved design $25. Because of their poverty the voters thought they ought to purchase the simpler seal. However, if someone were willing to donate the difference, they would accept such a donation without opposition ("die Gemeinde hat nichts degegen"). April 14, 1842, Mr. Motz reported that sufficient money had been donated to purchase the more elaborate seal, and it was so ordered after considerable discussion. May 30, 1842, Pastor Walther read quotations from Luther's writings which dealt with the subject of lay elders ("das Amt der Laienvorsteher"). June 1, 1842, Walther read more testimonies from reliable Lutheran theologians concerning the office of elders. After considerable discussion it was decided that if anyone wished to become a member of Trinity Congregation, he should be advised to see the pastor, so that the pastor could examine him regarding his knowledge of Christian doctrine. Thereupon he should be sent to one of the elders, and the elder should inquire among the people ("welcher bei der Gemeinde nachzufragen hat") whether the man should be received as a member.

June 3, 1842, the *Gemeindevorstandsordnung* was taken up for revision and incorporation into the new constitution. Paragraph 14 was changed to read: "that whenever the health of an elder becomes precarious, he shall be relieved of the part duties of the treasury which he has been exercising heretofore." June 6, 1842, Vorsteher Quast submitted a writing in which he expressed his misgivings regarding the proposed changes in the *Aeltestenordnung*. It was read and discussed. June 8, 1842, Mr. Roemer read a paper entitled "Suggestions for the Election of Elders" ("Unmassgebliche Vorschlaege zur Beachtung bei etwaiger Anstellung der Vorsteherwahl"). It was read and discussed. In this meeting it was also decided to elect six elders, as heretofore, but to divide them into two groups. One group of three should be called "Aelteste," and another group of three should be called "Diaconen." Furthermore, it was stipulated that if a man was not able to take care of physical or financial matters ("aeusserliche Angelegenheiten"), he should not for that reason be declared ineligible for the office of elder. Paragraphs 2, 3, 4, 5, and 6 were retained from the old *Vorsteherordnung*.

June 13, 1842, two letters from Pastor Grabau in Buffalo, New York, regarding constitutional matters ("Aussprache ueber Kirchenverfassung") were read and discussed. June 15, 1842, the voters continued to discuss the proposed new constitution. The rules for the elders still occupied the attention of the voters. It was decided that an elder who is absent from any meeting of the congregation must excuse himself at once ("sogleich") or at the next meeting. Furthermore, it was decided that the congregation has the right to dismiss an elder at once if the members are convinced that he is not administering his office in the proper manner. Paragraphs 10, 11, 12, 13, 14, 15, 16, 18, 19, and 20 were declared adopted without change. Paragraph 21 was to read: "No man under twenty-five years of age is eligible for the office of elder." Furthermore, it was decided that young men who had reached their majority must announce their intention to become voting members to the congregation, even though their fathers were members of the congregation. June 20, 1842, the pastor delivered a heart-searching address concerning the importance of the office of elder. June 27, 1842, a copy of the constitution of the congregation that was to be recorded in the courthouse was read. July 5, 1842, the constitution (*Gemeindeordnung*) was read and discussed paragraph by paragraph. Paragraphs 1 and 2 were adopted without change. Paragraph 3 was changed, but the changes were not yet formally adopted. Paragraph 3 was to be changed so that two sections should be made out of one. The first should contain a declaration of adherence to the Catechism of Luther, and the second a declaration of adherence to all the Symbolical Books of the Lutheran Church. Sections c and d of paragraph 3 should remain unaltered.[26]

---

[26] Paragraph 3 was given its final wording, according to a report in *Der Lutheraner,* VI (1850), p. 105. The wording was: "This congregation accepts and acknowledges all the canonical books of the Old and New Testaments as the inspired Word of God, and all the Symbolical Books of the Evangelical Lutheran Church, contained in the Book of Concord, as a true and sound exhibition of Christian doctrine taken from, and in full agreement with, the Holy Scriptures; and in this congregation all doctrine shall be examined ("geprueft") and judged on the basis of these books, and all doctrinal disputes shall be adjudicated according to this norm. No doctrine

July 12, 1842, quotations from Luther's *Church Postil* were read by the pastor to show that the congregation ought to make arrangements for a poor fund (*Armenkasse*). Toward the end of the meeting the pastor was asked to work out a constitution for a poor fund (*Armenkasseordnung*). July 18, 1842, the constitution for the poor fund which the pastor had been commissioned to write was read and discussed. Several changes were made from the floor, and then the entire constitution was adopted. August 1, 1842, it was resolved that Pastor Walther read the testimonies in Vehse's book which refer to the rights of a congregation. August 3, 1842, it was decided to continue to hear the testimonies which Dr. Vehse had collected in his book regarding the relationship between pastor and congregation. August 10, 1842, the reading of the testimonies which Dr. Vehse had collected was completed; and fifteen paragraphs which Pastor Walther had composed and which set forth the relationship of the pastor to the congregation were read. Thereupon quotations from the Bible, from the Symbolical Books of the Lutheran Church, and from reliable theologians of the Lutheran Church were read. August 15, 1842, more testimonies concerning the office of the holy ministry were read. September 15, 1842, the proposed new constitution was read, beginning with paragraph 3. In the meeting of September 19, 1842, an addition was made to paragraph 4 of the proposed new constitution, which would sharpen its confessional character. In addition to this change another statement should be added as section 6 of paragraph 4, which would state that every member must be familiar with the Augsburg Confession in addition to Luther's Small Catechism. In this meeting it was also decided that much more ceremony should accompany the reception of a voting member into the congregation. One member registered his misgivings about the increase in ceremony. It was then decided to postpone adoption of the change until the member who was troubled with misgivings could think the matter over in the privacy of his own home. It was furthermore decided that every man who had reached the age of twenty-five years and who had been a member for at least one year should be eligible for office.

---

shall be taught or tolerated which is at variance with these Symbols of the Evangelical Lutheran Church, viz., 1. the three ecumenical creeds; 2. the Unaltered Augsburg Confession; 3. the Apology of the same; 4. the Smalcald Articles; 5. Luther's Large Catechism; 6. Luther's Small Catechism; 7. the Formula of Concord; 8. the Visitation Articles."

In the meeting of September 22, 1842, it was decided not to receive members into the congregation in the public service, with all baptized members present, but rather in the voters' meeting, where they should be duly examined before they signed the constitution in the presence of all voters. The reason given for the relinquishment of the idea of receiving members in the public service is significant. It was stated that such ceremony might create the bad impression that this Church was the only true Church ("um nicht den boesen Schein zu geben, als ob unsere Gemeinschaft die alleinige rechte sei"). In this meeting it was also decided to add the Saxon "Christliche Visitationsartikel" to the list of Symbolical Books of the Lutheran Church in the confessional paragraph. Paragraphs 8 and 9 were adopted without change. October 17, 1842, the proposed new constitution was again taken up for consideration. Paragraph 10 was adopted without change and as finally adopted reads as follows:

> The right of choosing and calling ministers and schoolteachers and of electing all other officers of the congregation shall ever be vested in the congregation in its totality (in ihrer Gesamtheit) and shall never be delegated to an individual or to a minor body or circle within the congregation.

Paragraph 12 was adopted without alterations. In its final wording it reads as follows:

> All property of the congregation shall be entrusted to regularly elected trustees, who are to administer it as a trust in the name of the congregation. The trustees are to execute contracts, make payments, give receipts, sign documents, appear before court, in short, do all things which the congregation as the owner would have to do, but with the understanding that they are not the owners and that they are not permitted to do with the property as they please but can act only according to regularly passed resolutions and formally given commissions of the congregation. Whatever the trustees do by resolution and command of the congregation relieves them from all personal financial obligation. However, if the trustees act without resolution or command of the congregation, they are personally responsible to the congregation for losses incurred.

In the meeting of January 23, 1843, it was decided to insert a paragraph into the constitution which would make it obligatory for all young unmarried men and women to attend a review class in Lutheran doctrines conducted by the pastor as part of the public services ("Christenlehre" — "Catechismusexamina"). In the meeting of February 6, 1846, the paragraph concerning the review of Christian doctrine was given its final wording as follows: "All members of the congregation who have not reached their majority are obligated to attend special Catechism review classes ("Catechismusexamina"), which are to be arranged for them in the church." In this meeting the final wording was given to a paragraph regarding hymnbooks and books of forms (*Agende*) to be used in the public services:

> In the public services only purely Lutheran hymns ("rein-lutherische Lieder") and in all administrative acts of the pastor only purely Lutheran forms are to be used. In the school, in addition to the Scriptures and Luther's Small Catechism, only purely Lutheran books shall be introduced. Parents who are members of the congregation are obligated ("sind gehalten") to send their children to the Christian day school or to make the necessary provisions for their instruction in Christian doctrine.

The manner in which members were to be received was definitely fixed in this meeting as follows:

> All who wish to become members must announce such intention to the pastor of the congregation, in order that he may examine them with respect to their Christian knowledge. Thereupon they are to present a formal application for membership to one of the elders. He, in turn, is to present this application to the congregation. If the congregation finds no objection to the application, then he who wishes to be a member, whether male or female, must sign the constitution of the congregation. If the proposed member is a male and has reached his majority, he must do so in the voters' meeting; if female, in the pastor's study in the presence of one of the elders.

The following addition was made to paragraph 13: "Sufficient causes for the removal of a pastor or a schoolteacher are: continued adherence to false doctrine, offensive conduct, and intentional carelessness in the administration of his official duties." In the meeting of February 27, 1843, it was decided to change paragraph 4 in this way, that the words "which are in accordance with the Word of God" should read, "which are not contrary to the Word of God." In the meeting of March 6, 1843, the following paragraphs of the constitution were declared unalterable and nonrepealable: 2, 3, 4, 6a, 7, 8, 9, 10, 11, 13, 14, and 19.

Paragraph 2 contains the name of the congregation; paragraph 3 is the confessional paragraph; paragraph 4 states conditions of membership in the congregation; paragraph 6, section a, stresses the duty of the members to contribute to the maintenance of church and school; paragraph 7 treats of Christian admonition according to Matthew 18, and, if necessary, expulsion; paragraph 8 says that only pastors who subscribe to the Symbolical Books of the Lutheran Church can be called as pastors of the congregation; paragraph 9 treats of the supremacy of the congregation and the delegation of powers to administrative officers; paragraph 10 reserves the right to call pastors and schoolteachers and to elect officers to the congregation; no delegation of powers is permissible. Paragraph 11 limits the powers of the elders. Paragraph 12 empowers the elders to represent the congregation as trustees. For every action of the trustees there must be a resolution of the congregation. Paragraph 13 describes conditions under which pastors, teachers, and officers may be removed from office. Paragraph 14 states that only the German language shall be used in the public services of the congregation, and paragraph 19 stipulates that only purely Lutheran hymns and forms and schoolbooks may be used in the congregation.

Pastor Walther read testimonies concerning the Sabbath. These testimonies showed that the Old Testament Sabbath had been abrogated and that the New Testament Christians had chosen Sunday for their day of worship in their own free will ("aus christlicher Freiheit"). March 20, 1843, the language paragraph, paragraph 14, was declared unalterable and nonrepealable; also, that all the Symbolical Books of the Lutheran Church should be named in the third paragraph. A resolution was passed which stated that announcement should be made in the next Sunday's service to the effect that on Monday evening all voting members should assemble in the church for the purpose of signing the new constitution. Mr. Schuricht announced that he would make a special copy of the constitution for this purpose. It was furthermore resolved that all members who were troubled with scruples about signing the constitution were to see the pastor or one of the elders. It was furthermore resolved that those members who felt that they could not sign the constitution should be given one month's time to think the matter over. Every member was given the privilege of making a copy of the constitution.

The meeting of March 27, 1843, was opened with special solemnity. The pastor was present and offered a special prayer and then delivered a prepared address. In this address he first reviewed the history of the congregation during the past four years, praising the loving care and grace of God. Then he discussed the following four points concerning the signing of the new constitution: 1. It is God's earnest will that a Christian congregation have a constitution ("ihre Ordnung"). 2. That God has given his children freedom of action in the framing of a constitution. They may arrange such a constitution according to the conditions as they see them; however, they must make no stipulation which is contrary to the pure Word of God ("nichts wider sein geoffenbartes Wort"). 3. In adopting a constitution we have the example of the Church throughout the ages. 4. A constitution is particularly necessary in America, since the Government makes no provision for the maintenance of the Church ("wo die Obrigkeit sich der Kirche nicht annehme").

Thereupon the constitution was read in its entirety before the assembled congregation. Then those who were present began to sign the constitution. An unexpected debate developed concerning the unalterability of paragraph 14. This stopped all further signing of the constitution for this meeting. Paragraph 14 read that only the German language should be used in the church services. Walther and the majority of the congregation wanted this paragraph to be unalterable and nonrepealable. Some members had their misgivings about the unalterability of this paragraph. The problem was solved temporarily in the next meeting, April 3, 1843, when an addition was made to paragraph 21 stating that the congregation regarded their church as an institution for German Lutherans to maintain divine services as they had had them ("weil wir es fuer eine Stiftung fuer deutsche Lutheraner zur Erhaltung ihres Gottesdienstes ansehen"). Evidently they connected orthodoxy with language, which was done repeatedly in the Missouri Synod, a habit which stemmed from C. F. W. Walther in his youth.[27] In the meeting of April 10, 1843, it was de-

---

27 Cf. Walther's letter of January 2, 1845, to Sihler, *Walthers Briefe,* I, p. 14: "I do not suppose that it is necessary for me to mention that we are doing all in our power to maintain the German language, in order to keep out the wicked leaven which, together with the English language, threatens the pure doctrine and polity of our Church (das wir alle mit dem groessten Ernste darauf denken, alles zu tun, um hier die deutsche Sprache zu erhalten

cided that the recording secretary compose a special closing paragraph to the constitution, in which he is to list all the property of Trinity Congregation. This list of property is to be one of the unalterable and nonrepealable paragraphs and is to be handed down to descendants as a testament ("testamentarisch verschrieben"). They were extremely concerned about their posterity at all times. The language problem kicked up dust again in the meeting of April 17, 1843. An addition was made to paragraph 21 to this effect: "The unalterability and nonrepealability of paragraph 14 should not be regarded as a command of God — but as an intention of the congregation to regard this congregation with all its movable and immovable property as an institution for German Lutherans to keep our divine services pure in the German language and our German school for all times to come ("weil wir die Evangelisch-Lutherische Dreieinigkeitskirche allhie mit allen ihren beweglichen und unbeweglichen Guetern als eine Stiftung fur die deutschen Lutheraner zur Erhaltung ihres reinen Gottesdienstes in der deutschen Sprache und ihrer deutschen Schule ansehen und allezeit angesehen haben wollen").

In this meeting Mr. Roemer made the formal suggestion that a paragraph be inserted in the constitution to the effect that no member of a secret society, such as Freemasons, be permitted to become and remain a member of Trinity Congregation. As far as can be ascertained, this was the first time that the question of lodge membership ever came up for discussion in the mother church of the Missouri Synod. Mr. Roemer, a layman, seems to have brought the matter up on his own initiative. The idea seemed to be his, not Walther's. It was decided to take this matter up at the next meeting. The suggestion was definitely codified in the meeting of April 24, 1843, and thus became a model "lodge paragraph" for Missouri Synod congregations. It read: "No member of a secret society, such as Freemasons, etc., shall be accepted as a member of this congregation, because it is contrary to the Word of God, which says: 'That which ye have spoken in the ear in the closets shall be proclaimed upon the housetops'

---

und den boesen Sauerteig abzuweisen, der sich mit der englischen Sprache hier so leicht der reinen Lehre und Verfassung unserer Kirche beimischt, bedarf wohl keiner Erwaehnung)." Sihler, *Lebenslauf* von ihm selber beschrieben, Vol. II, p. 35, claims that he took no narrow view of the language question, although he was strong for the maintenance of the German language.

(Luke 12:3), and: 'For everyone that doeth evil hateth the light, neither cometh to the light, lest his deeds should be reproved' (John 3:20)." For some strange reason this paragraph was not published when the constitution was reprinted in *Der Lutheraner,* VI (1850), pp. 105—106. Dr. A. L. Graebner has abbreviated the paragraph and inserted in it paragraph 3, section g: "No one can be or remain a member of this congregation, or hold office in the same, or enjoy and exercise the rights and privileges of a member, but such as [then follow a, b, c, d, e, and f] g: are not members of any ungodly society." (*Theological Quarterly,* I [1897], p. 327.)

In the meeting of April 24, 1843, the knotty problem of signing the constitution came up again. This matter consumed as much time as any other single problem in the constitution, possibly more. It was resolved that communicants who had not reached their majority should not sign the constitution, at least not until the congregation had arrived at a greater degree of clarity in the matter. All members were given four weeks' time, by resolution, in which to make up their minds whether to sign or not to sign the constitution. On May 1, 1843, the members continued to sign the constitution. The question of signing the constitution on the part of those who had not reached their majority came up again for much discussion. This time it was definitely decided that no one who had not reached his majority should be permitted to sign the constitution.

The troublesome paragraph 14, concerning the exclusive use of the German language in the public services, received much attention. After much discussion some slight changes were made in paragraph 21, which concerned the unalterability and nonrepealability of certain paragraphs. At first it was again decided to state the reason for the unalterability and nonrepealability of paragraph 14 in paragraph 21; but then after much discussion the paragraph was permitted to stand as originally adopted. The names of the men who spoke in the debate on the language paragraph are not mentioned. We do know, however, that the idea came originally from Walther himself. He proposed it in connection with the first plans for a new church. Mr. Schuricht, the watchdog of proper procedure, probably opposed the insertion of this paragraph into the constitution. The fact that certain men argued for the insertion of the paragraph on the basis of God's Word and that this basis for the insertion was strenuously opposed

10

points to Schuricht. He was at times not opposed to insertions into the constitution, but he was unalterably opposed to the reasons for insertions as they were sometimes given.

In the meeting of May 8, 1843, it was decided to have a special meeting the following Sunday afternoon for the purpose of granting an opportunity to sign the constitution to those members whose employment kept them from attending weekday meetings. It was furthermore resolved to take up paragraph 6 in the next meeting. Paragraph 6 regulated the financial contributions which members were obligated to pay for the maintenance of church and school. Only poverty excused a member from that obligation, but such poverty had to be declared in the voters' meeting.

In the meeting of May 15, 1843, the process of signing the constitution was suddenly interrupted when one member expressed grave scruples about the propriety of signing the constitution at all. His misgivings were discussed at great length, but the congregation could come to no definite conclusions. In the meeting of June 6, 1843, there was more discussion about signing the constitution. The vexatious problem of what to do with women who had reached their majority and with the young men who had not, came up for lengthy consideration. Finally it was decided to change paragraph 20 to read: "Only male members who have reached their majority shall sign the constitution. Women who have reached their majority shall declare that they belong to the congregation. Their names shall be enrolled in the lists of the congregation's members." Equally vexatious was the problem of what to do with those members who had reached their majority but by reason of some quirk of conscience refused to sign the constitution. This question was given much time in the deliberations. Finally it was decided by majority vote that all members who had not signed the constitution should receive a written invitation to appear one week from the following Thursday in order to give their reasons for not signing the constitution.

The greater part of the meeting of June 15, 1843, was devoted to the old knotty problem of signing the constitution. Mr. Augustin appeared and gave as his reason for not signing that he was not sufficiently acquainted with the constitution. His explanation was accepted with the admonition that he familiarize himself with the constitution as quickly as possible. Mr. Krauss appeared and gave some explanation for his refusal. The recording secretary did not record his explanation but merely stated that the congregation was satisfied with it.   There were lengthy discussions with Mr. Wirth about signing the constitution, but no conclusions could be reached at this meeting.   In order to satisfy some conscientious objectors, it was decided to insert a paragraph into the constitution which would read: "Whoever severs his connection with the congregation has no further financial obligations to the congregation."   June 19, 1843, Mr. Wirth asked for more time to consider the signing of the constitution.   It was decided to grant him enough time that he might become clear in his own mind whether it were right for him to sign the constitution or not.

Finally, on July 3, 1843, a definite policy regarding nonsigners was adopted.   Walther was probably beginning to notice that certain members were frittering time away and using their "consciences" as shields for their refusal to sign.   He used a trick that promised to be effective.   All who did not sign for conscience' sake should be declared weak brethren ("schwach in der Erkenntnis").   Of course, no one who amounted to anything or who thought that he amounted to anything in the congregation would care to be declared a "weak brother."   The full resolution read as follows: "The members who have not signed the constitution shall be regarded as members in good standing ("als voellige Gemeindeglieder") so long as their refusal must be regarded as a weakness of Christian knowledge ("Schwachheit in der Erkenntnis") and on the condition that they declare publicly before the congregation that they will abide by all other provisions of this constitution.   Furthermore, they must promise to strive to improve their Christian knowledge in order that eventually they may see their way clear to sign.   If they refuse to make such a solemn declaration, they shall not be regarded as members."

This seems to have solved the problem.   Saxons with hundreds of years of Lutheran blood in their veins just hated to appear as weak brethren.   It is true, the matter came up again in the meeting of July 10, 1843; but no further resolution was passed, and no new conclusions were recorded.   Mr. Krauss, who was a stubborn holdout, declared his willingness to sign July 17, 1843.   In this same meeting some members who had signed several months before were beginning to lose faith in the "weak brethren" principle.   They were ready to use force on the obstreperous conscientious objectors.   However, the opinion of the more temperate prevailed; and it was decided to give those who had not signed more time. Two impatient hotbloods voted against this resolution. It was decided to hear their objections to the motion in the next meeting. Thus the device of a cooling-off period was introduced at a time when things looked ominous. "For the present," the minutes of this meeting read, "the congregation does not wish to create the impression that anyone's conscience should be pressed beyond Christian limits." A twentieth-century reader of the minutes gets the impression that most of the signers had the patience of Job with the nonsigners and that time was a commodity that existed in great quantities. In the meeting of July 21, 1843, Mr. Purfuerst, perhaps the most stubborn holdout of them all, sent a written statement to the congregation, in which he stated the reasons for his refusal to sign. A long discussion ensued. The letter was taken up again in the meeting of July 24, 1843; but no definite conclusions could be reached, nor was any resolution passed in regard to it. The "weak brethren" principle was the final device used. Nothing more about signing the constitution is recorded in the minutes of the congregation.

Looking over the entire process of adoption of the constitution and examining the constitution itself in its entirety, the present writer could not escape the impression that genuinely democratic methods were used on the part of the congregation and that the constitution safeguarded the principle of congregational supremacy at every turn. It is true, the authoritarian principle was introduced freely, in that the pastor was asked repeatedly "to gather quotations from Luther and other reliable theologians of the Lutheran Church" and that these quotations of Luther at times determined the wording of some part of the constitution. On the other hand, the democratic processes were in evidence in that an abundance of time was given to discussion. If there was any "railroading" or "boss rule," the evidence of it was quite cleverly concealed. In estimating the almost morbid concern of the congregation to safeguard the principle of congregational supremacy the present writer wishes to point to three factors: First, the makers of the constitution had been subjected to priest rule in its most offensive form for half a dozen years in their early adult life. That they should act like burnt children does not surprise us. Secondly, the baker Sproede had followed Walther from Perry County to St. Louis and continued his feud with unabated fury, accusing Walther of priest rule in endless communications to the congregation and in paid insertions in *Der Anzeiger des Westens*. Sproede's energy in stirring up trouble for Walther in the congregation was prodigious. That Walther would take every step cautiously and with one eye on Sproede was to be expected. Finally, the liberal Germans, whom Walther calls "deutsche Demagogen," were beating their tom-toms in *Der Anzeiger des Westens* and in *Der Anti-Pfaff* against every form of priest rule. That the writings of these men restrained Walther and made him exceedingly cautious is evident from a letter which he wrote to W. Sihler, January 2, 1845.[28]

Thus far we have studied the application of the principle of congregational supremacy to the calling of a pastor and to the adoption of a constitution. Just how did the principle work out in more mundane matters, those that were purely financial or economic? Did the principle derived from Luther's writings and defended by Walther at Altenburg work in such affairs? The present writer selected the building of a new church as a study of the working out of this principle in the more secular affairs of the congregation. The stresses and strains of church building reveal the temper of a congregation and show what spirit prevails. The many financial matters involved in church building and the vexatious problem of co-operation sometimes move a congregation to ease up on principles that are easily applied in fair weather.

When the Saxons first came to St. Louis, the basement of the Episcopalian Christ Church Cathedral was turned over to them for services at a certain time of the day.[29] This arrangement

---

28 L. Fuerbringer, *Walthers Briefe*, Vol. I, p. 11. Sihler had advised the organization of a Synod. Walther discusses the possibilities of a synod and writes, among other things, these words: "Doch muss ich das bemerken, dass der ganze Westen von deutschen Demagogen erfuellt ist, die alles aufbieten, jede Art eines Synodalverbandes verhasst zu machen; selbst Gutgesinnte bleiben hiervon nicht ganz unberuehrt; es herrscht daher im ganzen eine gewisse Scheu vor dergleichen Anstalten; man fuerchtet Priesterherrschaft."

29 In response to their request for the use of Christ Church, Bishop Jackson Kemper, missionary bishop of the Northwest (Missouri and Indiana), read the following notice to his congregation (March, 1839): "A body of Lutherans, having been persecuted by the Saxon government because they believed it their duty to adhere to the doctrines inculcated by their great leader and contained in the Augsburg Confession of Faith, have arrived here with the intention of settling in this or one of the neighboring States; and having been deprived of the privilege of public worship for three months, they have earnestly and most respectfully requested the use of our church that they may again unite in all the ordinances of our holy religion. I have

worked well during the years 1839 and 1840. But as the congregation grew and more and more services became necessary, certain things happened which showed the inadequacy of this arrangement. Furthermore, the Episcopalians were getting tired of the arrangement, since it inconvenienced them not a little. They therefore definitely refused to let the Saxons have Christ Church Cathedral after January 1, 1842. The first step which the Saxon congregation took to meet the situation was an appeal to the German Protestant Church for permission to use their church. At first the German Protestants were willing; and in the meeting of January 10, 1842, it was announced that the German Protestant Congregation would permit the Saxons to use their church on three successive Sundays in the afternoon at 2 o'clock. After that the congregation hoped to use the basement of Christ Church Cathedral again.

As early as November 16, 1840, it had been decided that all current expenses of the congregation should be met by definite subscriptions to be made by the individual members at regular intervals. The freewill offerings taken up at the church door after each service should be set aside for a church building fund or a cemetery fund, whichever need would be the first to become urgent as time went on. The immediate impetus to erect a church building was given by the impatience of the Christ Church vestry and by the hesitation of the German Protestant Church, particularly of its pastor, the Rev. Mr. G. Wall, to grant the Saxons permission to use their new church building.

Early in January a special committee, charged with the duty of finding a suitable building site, made a preliminary report. In order to give the voters sufficient time to think over the suggestions of the committee, the resolution was passed to postpone the consideration of the report for eight days.[30] Evidently the composition and work of this committee was not satisfactory, for eight days later a new committee, consisting of Messrs. Querl, Funk,

---

therefore, with the entire approbation of the vestry, granted the use of our church for this day from 2 P. M. until sunset to a denomination whose early members were highly esteemed by the English Reformers, and with whom our glorious martyrs, Cranmer, Ridley, and others, had much early intercourse." The basement of the church was occupied for three years (1839 to December 4, 1842). Cf. Scharf, J. T., *History of Saint Louis and County*, II, p. 1735. Also Schneider, *The German Church on the American Frontier*, p. 103.

[30] Minutes, January 10, 1842.

Hoehn, Schmeister, and Quast, was elected. The task of this committee was to investigate two building sites, one on Seventh Street
and the other on Thirteenth Street, and to present their opinion
about the relative merits of both sites. The one on Seventh Street
was offered for sale at $20 per front foot, and that on Thirteenth
for $15 per front foot. In this meeting it was also resolved, rather
prematurely, as subsequent events proved, to thank the German
Protestant Congregation in writing for the use of their church on
three successive Sundays.[31]

For reasons that were not recorded in the minutes both sites
were declared unsuitable, and a resolution was passed to postpone
the purchase of a building site. This did not mean that the purchase should be postponed indefinitely. In fact the matter of a
building site was becoming of greater concern to the voting members at each successive meeting. This is evident from the discussion of the necessity of electing a new committee. It was
stated that the new committee must be elected and must consist
of men who were thoroughly acquainted with the city of St. Louis.
The following men, some of whom had been on the second site
committee, were now elected by the voters to the third site com-

---

[31] Minutes, January 17, 1842. In the meeting of January 10, 1842, the report
was made that the German Protestant Congregation would grant them permission to use their church for three Sundays. But in some way or other
the Saxons were hindered from using the German Protestant Church. C. E.
Schneider, *op. cit.*, pp. 105—106, published two letters; one is written by Mr. G.
Wall, the pastor of the German Protestant Church, and is addressed to T. H.
Gallaudet, the executive secretary of the Looking Upward, Press Onward
Society, and is dated May 11, 1840. In this letter Pastor Wall complains
bitterly about the Saxons. "They hope to get our church for their services
when it is finished; and many of our congregation are inclined and regard
it as their duty to open it for them, although I can never consent, because
the Stephanists only would — as they already did — bring into our congregation disharmony." The other letter was written by Pastor L. Nollau, also
active among the German Protestants in St. Louis, to the Barmen Mission
Society and is dated November 19, 1840. It contains the same complaint,
but adds that the Stephanists offered to contribute money toward the erection
of the German Protestant Church in order that they might have a legal claim
to its use. After the officials of the German Protestant Church turned down
the offer, the Stephanists appealed to the whole congregation ("Sie appellierten
an die Gemeinde in fast unverschaemten Ausdruecken"). Brother Wall
threatened to resign at once ("augenblicklich") if the Stephanists wer permitted to use the church. Undoubtedly Pastor Wall succeeded in keeping
the Stephanists out of his church, for in the meeting of Trinity Congregation
on March 21, 1842, a letter from the German Protestant Congregation was
read. In this letter the German Protestants refused to grant the Saxons the
use of their church. At the same time they accused several members of
Trinity Congregation of ulterior motives ("eigennuetzige Absichten") in their
efforts to secure the use of the church.

mittee: Schmeister, Schmidt, Jung, Querl, Hoehn, Stephan, Haenschen, and Faulstich. The question of the price of the lots came up again. In the heat of the discussion one good pillar of the congregation, who was evidently a little emotional, exclaimed, "That's too damn much money!" ("Das ist verdammt viel Geld!"). A discussion of the impropriety of this remark ensued; the brother was duly admonished, and he asked to be pardoned. There was no more talk about building sites at that meeting.[32]

The new committee set to work. Within twenty-one days they had canvassed the situation to such an extent that they were able to make a report. They had found what they believed to be a more adequate site down nearer the Mississippi River and closer to the heart of the city. It was between Third and Fourth and faced Lombard Street. The width was fifty feet, and the length was sixty feet. The committee had evidence that it could be bought for $1,000. The committee members were instructed to make further investigations and, if necessary, to make an offer to the owner.[33]

In the meantime the Episcopalians were pressing the Saxons to get out.[34] Within two days the site committee reported on the details of the proposed purchase. The site between Third and Fourth Streets could not be purchased for a cent less than $1,000. Six hundred dollars must constitute the first payment. Eight per cent interest must be paid on the remaining $400 for the first six months and ten per cent thereafter. It was unanimously decided to buy this site, since all were convinced that they could not find a more suitable site at less cost anywhere. A subcommittee of the site committee was elected to determine in whose name the deed to the property should be entered in the legal records.[35]

---

[32] Minutes, January 24, 1842.

[33] Minutes, February 14, 1842.

[34] Minutes, February 14, 1842. It was decided to pay the janitor of Christ Church a honorarium of $4.00 for his faithful services during the Christmas holidays. In this meeting they also received a notice from Mr. Peake of the Christ Church vestry to the effect that they could not use Christ Church for their services any longer. They decided to write a letter to the entire vestry, begging for just a little longer time ("noch um eine kleine Frist").

[35] Minutes, February 16, 1842. Mr. Warren, whom they had engaged for the sum of $2.00 to translate their petition to the vestry of Christ Church into the English language, could not finish his task as rapidly as they had hoped. So the report was made that their request for an extension of time

Since things were now beginning to look as though they would have a church building of their own before very long, C. F. W. Walther made a special suggestion, one of the very few that came from the pastor during the entire time that the building was under consideration. He suggested that in the church which they were about to build only the German language should be used for divine worship. The suggestion was adopted by unanimous vote.[36]

Financial problems were beginning to come to the fore the moment the voters decided to buy the downtown church site. The suggestion that every member be asked to make a pledge for the new church building came from Mr. Schuricht. In a rather lengthy discussion he suggested that every member not only state the exact amount he would contribute but also the day on which he would pay the pledge. His suggestion was accepted by the voters, with a special note of warning that the officers of the congregation should not permit strangers to get a special claim to the property of the church through a pledge ("dass kein Fremder durch solche Unterschrift ein Recht an die Kirche bekomme"). Undoubtedly this warning was connected in some way with their scheme to get possession of some rights in the new church of the German Protestant Church.[37]

The wording of the deed caused the voters no little amount of trouble. Their chief concern was caused by the fact that the deed was made out in English, and they understood no English. Finally they decided that the deed be examined by Justice of the Peace Kretzschmar, since there was no reason to doubt his ability, honesty,

---

could not reach the vestry of Christ Church. For that reason another attempt was made to secure the use of the new church of the German Protestant Congregation. It was announced that the service for the following Sunday would have to be conducted in their own schoolroom.

[36] Minutes, February 21, 1842. "Der Vortrag des Herrn Pastor, dass in der zu erbauenden Kirche allein in der deutschen Sprache Gottesdienst gehalten werden moechte, wurde einstimmig angenommen. Und es soll dies ein Paragraph jenes Dokuments sein." The caution with which the congregation proceeded is evident from the fact that the petition to the German Protestant Church was read and approved ("genehmigt") by all the members. All letters and petitions that went out in the name of the congregation, even those composed by Walther, had to be read to the plenary session of the voters and approved by them.

[37] Minutes, February 21, 1842. Five trustees were elected in this meeting, and the resolution was passed that the deed should be translated into German and read to the congregation. Cf. Footnote No. 31 for the attempt of the Saxons to get an interest in the German Protestant Church.

and good will. The deed was to be translated and read in the meeting of the following evening. If, however, a German translation of the deed could not be made by that time, the trustees should examine the deed carefully, close the deal, and make the payment.[38]

The name of the new church came in for much attention in the meeting of March 1, 1842. Hitherto they had called themselves The Lutheran Congregation of the Unaltered Augsburg Confession. Popularly they were known as Stephanists. In this discussion Pastor Walther, who according to the minutes had very little if anything to say about the name, suggested that the new church now under consideration should have a name which would express some Christian doctrine ("Bekenntnis") and that it should not lend itself to jocular remarks on the part of the unbelieving world ("dass er nicht sogleich den Spott der Welt errege").

The first official remarks about plans for the new church were not made until March 14, 1842. Even the secretary seems to indicate an awareness of the unusual deliberativeness of the congregation. He writes, "A beginning was made of the discussions concerning the church building" ("Es wurde angefangen, ueber den Kirchbau zu reden"). Preliminary plans and bids were to be sought, and further discussion of these matters should be carried on in the next meeting.

Finally on March 18, 1842, the congregation resolved to build. According to the decision of this day the size of the building was to be fifty feet by fifty-five feet, with the entrance from the main street, which was Lombard Street. Furthermore, a collection ("Collecte" — what they really meant was a campaign for cash and pledges) was to be inaugurated, in which every member of the congregation was to visit one of the elders and announce the exact amount he wished to pledge and when he would pay his pledge. Opportunity was to be given each member to state whether he wished to pay at once or after six months. All pledges should be in the hands of the elders by the following Thursday.[39]

---

[38] Minutes, February 28, 1842. Subsequent minutes (March 1, 1842) show that the deed was translated into the German language, that it was read before the voters' assembly, and that no objections were raised against its wording.

[39] The minutes of March 18 also show that the vestry of Christ Church had relented and decided to let them have the basement of their church a little while longer. However, the Saxons were restricted to the afternoon in their use of Christ Church. This was praised as a great favor ("als eine grosse Wohlthat"). It was resolved to insert a special announcement in the

The meetings which followed March 18 were given over to discussion of the plans for the new church. Details of the plan were adopted, only to be changed in the following meeting or to be maintained over against violent opposition. Decentralized government seems to have had full play. On March 21 it was decided to build a full basement under the church, and the full basement should be used to house the Christian day school of the congregation. On March 24 it was decided to rescind the motion concerning the size of the church adopted on March 18 and to follow Mr. Schmeister's plan instead. Mr. Schmeister's plan called for a church size fifty feet by fifty-nine and one half feet, and twenty-two feet high in the studs ("im Lichten"). Messrs. Motz and Niemann were commissioned to make inquiry concerning a loan that a certain man had offered to make them. On March 31 Motz and Niemann reported that the man who had offered to make the loan was willing to lend them $1,400 in that year and as much as would be needed for next year. However, he would lend them what they needed only for three and a half years. Thereupon Mr. Purfuerst made the suggestion that a builder be consulted to determine how much the congregation would need and whether the builder would have to have cash or whether he would arrange for terms. This suggestion was adopted.

Interesting in the light of subsequent history was a proposition discussed in the meeting of March 31, namely, the collection of funds from outsiders ("Fremden"). Some voters had their misgivings. Not that it was improper. At that time no one, not even Walther, seemed to have any misgivings about the propriety of such procedure. The thing that caused them concern was that the outsiders who contributed might in some way acquire some right or title to their property. Finally it was decided to collect from outsiders, but to exercise the utmost discretion. For the first it would be wise to collect from Lutherans in the East ("im Osten" — undoubtedly from General Synod congregations) and to postpone collecting from outsiders in St. Louis until building operations had begun. Later on, April 25, Mr. Scheel was commissioned to get information from their oracle, Justice of Peace Kretzschmar, on the question whether they could make a collection from house to house for their new church without getting special authorization from the

---

St. Louis German daily stating that henceforth the services would again be conducted in the Episcopalian Church. This meeting was significant also in this, that the name "Trinity" was adopted for the new church.

city government ("ohne gerichtliche Beglaubigung"). The actual house-to-house collection among the Christian men and women of St. Louis who did not belong to Trinity Church was not begun until the Monday following August 3, 1842. None other than Pastor Walther drew up a petition for this collection. Volunteers came forward in the meeting of August 8 and announced their readiness to collect for the new church. The collection was to begin on Wednesday, August 9, and continue till Tuesday, August 15. The minutes give the impression that they were making a "drive" for funds among the non-Lutherans. On August 18 additional collectors were chosen to collect among the Christian men and women of St. Louis. Finally, on August 22 another set of collectors was elected for the same purpose.

By April 25 the voters were far enough along with the discussion of the plans for the new church that Mr. Walther (not Pastor Walther, but a layman with the same name, who was popularly known as "Hutmacher Walther") could be commissioned by vote of the congregation to insert an announcement in the newspapers, both German and English, inviting contractors to put in their bids on the new church. All bids were to be in hand by the following Monday.

The building committee seems to have had very few discretionary powers. Even the matter of opening the bids was retained for a plenary session of all the voters on May 6. Thirteen contractors submitted their bids. The two lowest bids were Mack (or Maah), whose bid was $4,000, and Sellar and Company, whose bid was $4,200. The resolution was passed to carry on further negotiations with these two lowest bidders.

Three days later the plans were again submitted to the congregation in solemn assembly.[40] All reiterated their vote in favor of the plans except one man, who feared the great debt load. In consideration of the fact that the members of Trinity Congregation were mostly *Unbemittelte* and that they had never been conditioned to contribute toward the maintenance of the church during their younger days in Germany, their readiness to assume a debt of over $4,000 is astonishing.

Although the contract was awarded to Sellar and Company by

---

[40] Minutes, May 9, 1842. "Nochmalige ernste Anfrage an die Gemeinde, ob der Kirchbau nach dem gefertigten Plane vorgenommen werden solle."

unanimous vote,[41] major changes in the plans were made by vote of the members after the contract had been awarded. The row of pillars running parallel to the north and the south wall were not to extend to the ceiling but only to the bottom of the balcony ("Chor"). A hole was placed in the ceiling for acoustical purposes.[42] The size of the building was changed from fifty feet by fifty-five feet to forty-seven and one half feet by fifty-two feet in order to provide more space between the "Steinpflaster" ("pavement" [sic!]) and the church for people to assemble as they entered the church.[43] The basement was dug deeper than originally planned.[44] The foundation was strengthened by a special process.[45] Specially large stones were placed as footing underneath the pillars.[46] The balcony ("Emporkirche") was placed lower by majority vote.[47] Two weeks later the voters reversed themselves and decided to place the balcony as originally planned.[48] The original plan to build a specially high platform on which the altar was to rest was changed so that the base of the altar would be only one step higher than the floor of the nave.[49]

There is an ominous tone about the resolution of the voters concerning the cornerstone-laying festivities. On May 30 the motion was carried to lay the cornerstone the following Sunday. It was decided, however, not to have the cornerstone laying at the building, but in the basement of Christ Church, because "there might be some disturbances on the part of enemies of the church." [50]

---

[41] Minutes, May 9, 1842. Motion was repeated in the meeting of May 17, 1842.

[42] Minutes, May 9, 1842. "Schalloch in der Decke."

[43] Minutes, May 18, 1842. By a majority vote ("Mehrzahl der Stimmen").

[44] Minutes, June 6, 1842. No reason given in the minutes. ("If the committee found that it was necessary.")

[45] Minutes, June 10, 1842. This process was recommended by the builder.

[46] Minutes, June 15, 1842.

[47] Minutes, June 27, 1842. This was necessary; so it was stated from the floor, because the seats placed on the floor in the rear of the balcony were to be higher than those placed on the same floor in front to enable the members who were seated in back pews to see the pastor ("eine hoehere Steigerung der Sitze auf der Emporkirche").

[48] Minutes, July 11, 1842. The people in favor of the original higher balcony said the lower balcony would be out of proportion with the height of the pulpit. Their argument carried the day.

[49] Minutes, September 26, 1842.

[50] Minutes, May 30, 1842. The antireligious bitterness and intemperance reached its high mark in the notorious *Anti-Pfaff,* a "rude and turbulent journal" founded by the watchmaker Koch in April, 1842. Koch, a born

The readiness with which members and nonmembers offered loans to the congregation indicates that the general public was beginning to have confidence in the polity of the young organization. We have already noted that the owner of the site was willing to trust them with $400. Messrs. Motz and Niemann, as was previously pointed out, reported that a certain man (no name mentioned) was willing to lend them $1,400 in that year and as much thereafter as they would need.[51] Mr. Krenning came forward with an offer to lend $300; [52] the widow of the former pastor, O. H. Walther, offered $100; [53] Mr. Landgraf, $5.00; [54] Mr. Feroes, $1,000; [55] Mr. Christoph Pfahl, $150.[56]

Under the management of a committee consisting entirely of laymen [57] the erection of the new church progressed normally. No member of the congregation who was not a member of the building committee had a right to issue any orders to the contractor or talk to him about the building. Any member who saw, or thought he saw, something objectionable in connection with the building was obligated to inform the building committee.[58] If anyone of the committee would accept employment from Sellar and Company, he had to get off the committee at once, and a new man was to be elected in his stead immediately.[59] By August 8 arrangement could be made for a raising bee.[60] August 23 the church was under roof, and provisions were made to insure it

---

agitator, loved to berate Walther and his followers with the opprobrious term of "Stephanists." Cf. Schneider, *op. cit.*, pp. 125—128. In *Der Lutheraner*, I (1844), p. 12, Walther published a sharp rejoinder, in which he exhorted Koch to read the Augsburg Confession and Luther's Large Catechism that he might learn the Lutheran view of the Sabbath. Koch had expressed fear that Walther would rob the American people of their freedom by his attitude toward the Sabbath.

[51] Minutes, March 31, 1842.   [54] *Ibid.*

[52] Minutes, May 12, 1842.   [55] Minutes, June 6, 1842.

[53] *Ibid.*   [56] Minutes, July 25, 1842.

[57] Minutes, May 12, 1842. A permanent building committee was elected, consisting of the following: Jung, Querl, Faulstich, Stephan, Fischer, Purfuerst, Geistler, Grest (Quast?), Traenkhahn, Tirmenstein, Kampmeier, Krenning, and Buenger.

[58] *Ibid.*

[59] *Ibid.*

[60] Minutes, August 8, 1842. The resolution was passed to give a little something to every man who would help at the raising bee ("eine Gratification fuer alle Arbeiter, die beim Heben der Kirche helfen").

against fire.[61] As the church neared completion, the women were given permission to collect funds for the new altar and pulpit.[62] On October 10 the plans for an altar and pulpit were submitted by Mr. Traenkhahn, a cabinetmaker of high reputation and a member of the congregation. Two men voted against the plans.[63]

The day was fast approaching when the new church could be dedicated; so on November 24 the resolution was passed to dedicate the new church on the Second Sunday in Advent, which was December 4 in that year. All the details of the dedicatory service were decided by majority vote in a plenary session of the congregation. A hymn sheet was to be printed.[64] It was resolved to have four large candles burn on the altar throughout the service on dedication day.[65] In a supplemental resolution it was decided to restrict the burning of four candles to the morning service. A special announcement was to be inserted in the *Anzeiger des Westens,* a German daily, to the effect that all services were now being conducted in their own church. It was resolved to have dedicatory services on two successive days provided the pastors of Perry County and Illinois could come. All communicants were to place themselves as close to the altar as possible when they took their seats for the dedicatory services.[66] All ecclesiastical acts ("kirchliche Handlungen"), such as baptism, Lord's Supper, marriage, were to be performed during the dedicatory services. The pastor was given permission to make the necessary assignments to

[61] Minutes, August 23, 1842. A committee of three was instructed to carry on investigations of fire insurance companies in St. Louis ("Feuersecurenz Compagnie"). On August 25 the decision was made to insure with the St. Louis Fire Insurance Company for $3,000. Some of the voters were in favor of insuring for $4,500, but the members advocating the lower sum prevailed. September 5 the resolution was repeated to insure for $3,000.

[62] Minutes, August 10, 1842, indicate that there was marked difference of opinion on the advisability of having the women raise funds. Finally the voters decided that such action need not give offense ("nicht nothwendig zu Aergernissen fuehrt").

[63] Minutes, October 10, 1842. Mr. Traenkhahn was appointed to manage the construction of the altar and pulpit. All volunteer workers were placed under his supervision. The labor required to complete the altar was greater than the members expected. On December 5 it was decided to ask the volunteer workers whether they would be satisfied with six bits ("ob sie mit 6 bit [*sic!*] zufrieden sein wollen").

[64] Minutes, November 24, 1842. Mr. Wichmann was elected to receive subscriptions for the hymn sheet.

[65] *Ibid.*

[66] Minutes, November 30, 1842.

the various visiting pastors. A letter of thanks was to be sent to the vestry of Christ Church.[67]

The principle of decentralized government championed by Vehse and Marbach and adopted by Walther was upheld beyond a doubt in all operations connected with the building of the mother church of the Missouri Synod. A thousand and one things had to be decided, some of them exceedingly weighty and of great consequence, others insignificant and of little or no importance. In each instance, however, the voters safeguarded the principle of congregational supremacy and made it work. Matters which normally would have been referred to the building committee were decided in the meeting of all the voters. There was a morbid fear of delegating powers to an individual or to a committee. This morbid fear had its origin in their untoward experience with Stephan. Many of these men had lost large sums of money by delegating power over their private possessions to the committee which administered the "Commun-Casse," specifically to Stephan. They would not be caught a second time in carelessly delegating power. For every such delegation, in the rare cases in which they made use of this administrative device, they insisted upon a specific resolution limiting the delegation to specific persons and to a specific act. The congregation could not have been more cautious.

The cumbersomeness of "pure democracy" is evident in the story of this building project. Sixty-seven plenary sessions of the voters were necessary for the building of the church. Frequently the voters met in three full-length sessions in one week. The simple life in the isolation of the frontier made the frequent meetings possible.[68] Means of transportation were limited to human

---

[67] Minutes, November 14, 1842.

[68] It must be remembered that the number of amusements for them was definitely limited. They had no moving pictures. Theatrical presentations in the German language, although quite plentiful, were regarded as sinful. (J. L. Gruber, *op. cit.*, p. 3, writing of the time when he was teacher of a branch school of Trinity Church, September, 1862, to March, 1875, says: "In a German theater a regularly engaged troupe of German actors and actresses gave German plays every evening. They preferred the classical German plays. Traveling artists of high rank assisted the local troupe in so-called guest performances.") The chief amusements which the Saxons found were in beer gardens. Gruber, *op. cit.*, p. 4, writes: "In the German sections of the city there was a veritable swarm of saloons and beer gardens. At round tables this 'race of poets and thinkers' drank beer, played cards, and discussed the news of the day." ("In den deutschen Vierteln wimmelte

legs. Artificial lighting was rather inadequate for reading. So the attendance at endless meetings offered an outlet for their energy and took the place now occupied by modern amusements.

There is not the slightest indication that boss rule controlled the plenary sessions of the voters or the meetings of the building committee. In fact it is difficult to select one man and say that he stood out over his fellows as the leader. If Pastor Walther exercised undue influence, there is no evidence to that effect extant. He was not a member of the building committee. Up until August 22, 1842, he did not attend the business meetings of the congregation. His absence was caused by the scruples which some members entertained.[69] The fear of priest rule had taken deep root in the hearts of many. They were exceedingly jealous about "die Rechte der Gemeinde." Even while their new church was under construction and many things had to be decided, time was taken to discuss and clarify "the relationship of the rights of the congregation to the rights of the pastor."[70] The anticlerical party was still strong in Trinity and watched with the eye of an eagle for any infringement of congregational and personal rights. At times the insistence on individual rights in the congregation led to ludicrous scenes.[71]

---

es foermlich von Bier-saloons und Biergaerten. Hier sass an runden Bier-tischen, besonders abends und Sonntags, 'das Volk der Dichter und Denker,' spielte Karten oder besprach die Tagesneuigkeiten.") It should be noted, however, that Walther and the majority of his voting members took a firm stand against excessive drinking. The minutes of Trinity Congregation give ample testimony to an exceedingly firm stand over against excessive drinking.

[69] Minutes, August 22, 1842. "Resolved that we make no decision concerning the appearance or nonappearance of the pastor in the voters' meeting on account of the scruples of one of our members." ("Beschlossen, dass eine Entscheidung ueber das Erscheinen oder nicht Erscheinen des Herrn Pastors in der Versammelung wegen eines Scrupels eines Gemeindegliedes noch aufgeschoben werde.") Apparently the congregation could not come to a clear decision on the matter. The matter was taken up again the next night, and the resolution was passed "not to enter anything in the minutes about the appearance of the pastor." ("Beschlossen, dass ueber das Erscheinen des Herrn Pastors in der Versammelung nichts protocolliert werde.")

[70] Minutes, July 25, 1842. This relationship was discussed on the basis of Dr. Vehse's book. The minutes of August 1, 1842, contain the following significant motion: "Resolved that the pastor read only the testimonies of Dr. Vehse on the rights of the congregation." ("Beschlossen, dass der Herr Pastor nur die gesammelten Zeugnisse von Herrn Dr. Vehse ueber die Rechte der Gemeinde vorlesen soll.") The pertinent passages of Vehse's book were read again in the meeting of August 3, 1842. On August 5, 1842, more passages of Vehse's book were read. Vehse affected the thinking of the Saxons on constitutional matters three years after his return to Germany.

[71] Minutes, November 21, 1843. A big controversy raged about the

11

The same processes of decentralized government that were so noticeable in the erection of a new church are just as conspicuous in the founding of *Der Lutheraner*,[72] in the publication of a new hymnbook,[73] and in joining the Missouri Synod.[74]   In fine, the principles which Vehse and Marbach had gathered from the writings of Luther, and which Walther adopted, were beginning to determine the routine of the congregation.

lighting of the new church.   Mr. Putzer had sent in a written complaint. His individual rights had been infringed upon by Mr. Fischer, the man who had been elected to take care of the church building ("Bauvorsteher"). The congregation had tried candles, then sperm oil, and finally they were considering gas for lighting purposes.   Mr. Putzer brought his own private candle and nailed it to the pew, causing a considerable mess on the floor from the drippings of his candles.   "Der Herr Bauvorsteher" Fischer forbade Putzer to nail his candle to the pew and to mess up the floor.   He defended his action before the voters, and a resolution was solemnly passed after much discussion "that every member shall be permitted to bring his own candle to church, but that he shall not be permitted to nail it to his pew, nor shall he be permitted to mess up the church (die Kirche beschmutzen)." The episode reveals the democratic process of compromise.   Fischer did not get his way completely, and neither did Putzer.   Putzer evidently was pouty and stayed away from the meeting, a device of protest that was frequently used by members of Trinity.   The resolution was passed to send him a written invitation, so that he might appear in the next meeting and present his side of the story.   There is no reference to his complaint in subsequent minutes.   His name appears again in the minutes of January 8, 1844, when he asked for three dollars support out of the *Armenkasse*.   He was granted three dollars because of his poverty ("in seiner Duerftigkeit").

[72] The founding of *Der Lutheraner* was of far-reaching consequences for Lutheranism in America.   Walther suggested it for the first time in a meeting on June 3, 1844.   There was a long discussion of his proposals.   The plan and tendency of the journal was thoroughly ventilated.   August 12, 1844, it was decided to pay any deficiency that might occur in the publication of the first number from the treasury of the congregation.   If necessary a free-will offering was to be taken up to insure the publication of the second number. All details of the journal were approved by the laymen.

[73] The publication of the new hymnal was a $10,000 job.   Cf. the *Geschichte der Evangelisch-Lutherischen Gemeinde ungeaenderter Augsburgischer Confession zu St. Louis, Mo.*, von der Grundsteinlegung der Dreieinigkeits-Kirche (an der Lombard-Strasse) an bis zur Grundsteinlegung der Immanuels-Kirche den 30. Juli, 1847.   This was MS. history that was inserted in the cornerstone of the second church built, on Eleventh and Franklin, in St. Louis.   The account is a little expansive.   "Der Druck mit Stereotypen, welches in New York besorgt worden ist, kostete inclus. des Einbandes circa $10,000."   The congregation decided on the number of pages, the method of raising the money, the retail price of the individual hymnbook, the kind of binding, the number of bound and the number of unbound copies in the first edition, the place of publication (New York), place of deposit for the stereotype plates, the number of lines on each page, the size of type. These items were decided in plenary sessions of the congregation over a period from November 10, 1845, to January 27, 1847.   Nine meetings of the congregation were devoted to this project.   Incidentally, the pastor was elected on the hymnbook committee, together with six laymen.

[74] The organization of the Missouri Synod will be discussed in the next chapter of the present study.   There was endless discussion about the proposed synod all through 1846 and down to April, 1847.

CHAPTER SIX

CRYSTALLIZATION OF GOVERNMENTAL FORMS
THE ORGANIZATION OF THE MISSOURI SYNOD

VARIOUS FACTORS in the fourth decade of the nineteenth century contributed to the necessity of forming a Lutheran synod which would serve the German immigrants on the American frontier. The Lutheran General Synod, at the time by far the largest and most influential body of Lutherans on American soil, organized in 1820, suffered from an Eastern orientation and was overwhelmingly committed to the use of the English language. Furthermore, the internecine struggle raging within this body between the advocates of "New Measurism" and the champions of an emerging conservatism ever since 1835 [1] made the immigrant who had left a Church behind that was steadily becoming more conservative in its Lutheranism [2] rather hesitant about joining any organization

---

[1] A. R. Wentz, *The Lutheran Church in American History*, pp. 198—204. — Karl Kretzmann, *The Atlantic District of the Evangelical Lutheran Synod of Missouri, Ohio, and Other States, and Its Antecedents*, pp. 14—15. — Neve-Allbeck, *History of the Lutheran Church in America*, pp. 86—88.

[2] In Chapter II, p. 25, of the present work there is a reference to the fact that conservatism was steadily gaining ground among Lutherans of Germany. C. F. W. Walther, who was bitterly opposed to rationalism whenever and wherever he found it, wrote of the great gains which conservatism was making among Lutherans of Germany. This statement is found in a report of his trip to Germany in 1851, *Der Lutheraner*, Vols. VII and VIII (1851—1852). Rather striking proof that conditions were improving in Saxony from the viewpoint of the conservative Lutheran is to be found in the "Vermeldungsbuch" (book of announcements) which Pastor G. H. Loeber used in Eichenberg and Bibra, beginning with the First Sunday in Advent, 1835. This book is now a part of the archives of the Lutheran church in Altenburg, Missouri. On New Year's Day, 1836, Pastor G. H. Loeber read a long announcement to his congregation. He called it a *Consistorialverordnung*, which was directed to all the churches of Saxony. It was also incorporated in Book XI of the current *Gesetzsammelung* of Altenburg, according to Pastor G. H. Loeber's announcement. This new order of the consistory increased the amount of instruction preparatory to confirmation. From now on every child was to receive two hours of instruction every week in Luther's Small Catechism, beginning with the week of the First Sunday after Trinity and lasting to Palm Sunday — roughly speaking, about ten months out of the year. Furthermore, the old Lutheran custom of re-instructing confirmed, both old and young, in the fundamental doctrines of Christianity as contained in Martin Luther's Catechism was to be revived. According to the new law boys and girls were to attend these "refresher" classes on Sunday afternoon up to their eighteenth

connected with the General Synod or adhering to the doctrines and polity of that synod. The fact that the leaders of the General Synod were becoming more pronounced in their Puritanism made many immigrants look with suspicion on their Lutheranism.[3] The all-out battle for the loyalty and support of the German immigrant waged by a virile Church of the frontier, the Methodists, bade the forces of German Lutheran conservatism to close their ranks.[4] And finally the very nature of a lonesome frontier life — the physical isolation — suggested the need of perfecting an organization in which kindred spirits could discuss their common problems sympathetically and carry out joint action energetically.

The difficulties which followed the removal of Stephan naturally drove the pastors who had immigrated together into a closer union. In a letter written to Dr. W. Sihler, dated January 2, 1845, Walther describes their oneness in faith and confession and the efforts which they were making to maintain this concord in spite of the absence of every form of an organization. He writes of their "most intimate friendship," of "their constant exchange of letters in which they tell each other of their experiences and in which they comfort, advise, admonish, and exhort one another."[5]

---

year. The law said that older people were to be present and to follow the instruction. Furthermore, fathers were to accompany the sponsors who brought their newborn babes to the baptismal font. The law said that if fathers did not present themselves at the baptism of their children, they would be subject to fine. Loeber calls the custom which was to receive new emphasis according to the new order of the consistory a "good old Christian custom."

[3] The experience of Sihler and Wyneken is significant. They were not Saxons, but were sent by mission-minded Lutherans to attend to the spiritual needs of German-Americans. Shortly after their arrival in America they joined synods connected with the General Synod. Hardly had they got acquainted with their new synodical surroundings, when both of them took immediate steps to leave their respective synods. Sihler, *Lebenslauf*, II, p. 46.

[4] The early numbers of *Der Lutheraner* are studded with polemical articles against Methodists and Methodism. The following references or to longer articles only: I (1844), p. 11; I, pp. 59—60; I (1845), p. 68; I, pp. 79—81; II (1845), pp. 23—24; II, pp. 25—26; II (1846), pp. 49—60; II, pp. 82—83; II, pp. 69—72. The whole issue is devoted to the Methodists. II, pp. 73—74; II, pp. 85—88. Over three quarters of the issue are devoted to Methodism. III (1846), pp. 11—12; III (1847), pp. 117—118; III, pp. 126—128; III, pp. 137—139. Dr. W. Sihler wrote a pamphlet on Methodism, of which 12,000 copies were sold. It was translated into English, Norwegian, and Swedish. *Lebenslauf*, II, p. 22.

[5] *Walthers Briefe*, I, p. 11. "Es besteht unter uns ein Verhaeltnis der innigsten Freundschaft; auch stehen die Gemeinden, die durch mit uns Ausgewanderte entstanden sind, in lebendigem bruederlichen Verkehr. . . . Dabei unterhalten wir einen steten Briefwechsel, worin wir uns unsere Erfahrung mitteilen, uns gegenseitig beraten, ermahnen, troesten, strafen und ermuntern."

Their chief objective was to strengthen one another in Lutheran faith and polity. As a consequence of their experience with Stephan and Stephanism they had become extremely skeptical and critical of their own judgments. Harassed by doubts, the members of this "correspondence synod" turned to Martin Luther as their chief authority.[6] All doctrines and polity received a thorough going over and purging on the basis of the Reformer's writings. Walther states that their ultimate aim was to introduce uniform church government in all congregations served by them according to the pattern set by Luther.

Being *Amtsbrueder,* they were accused as a group and obliged to defend themselves as a group. Though the Altenburg Debate had removed doubts and unbelief from the hearts of some, it did not wipe out the memory of heavy financial and social losses endured by many of the faithful in connection with the immigration. The *Amtsbrueder* had to defend themselves collectively against many a bitter accusation, and the waging of this common defense made for solidarity. From the very outset the *Korpsgeist* which has been the object of so much comment was prevalent among the Missourians. In the very first controversy *ad extra*, the controversy with the Prussian Pastor Grabau of Buffalo, New York, this solidarity is in evidence.[7] The common defense was a factor

---

[6] *Walthers Briefe,* I, p. 11. Walther to Sihler: "Durch die Entdeckung der Stephanschen Taeuschung sind wir in die Schriften Luthers getrieben worden; diese haben wir nun alle neben Gottes Wort fast ausschliesslich studiert und glauben durch Leitung des Heiligen Geistes vermittelst dieses unvergleichlichen Nachlasses nun erst zu rechter Klarheit gekommen zu sein."

[7] Grabau had sent the Saxons his "Hirtenbrief" on December 1, 1840, with a request for an opinion. Some of Grabau's concepts of church government and the ministry were identical with those of the discredited Stephan. The Saxons recognized the similarity between Grabau and their fallen idol at once. Even the laymen who received the document shortly after the death of their beloved Pastor O. H. Walther discussed the principles of Grabau in the voters' meeting of Trinity Congregation, St. Louis, though they were without a pastor at the time. But because Grabau stood shoulder to shoulder with them in his attitude toward the Lutheran Confessions, and because he had suffered so much from the Prussian government on account of his opposition to the Prussian Union, they were reluctant to tell him straight out that his views on church government were hierarchical. Therefore they waited with their answer until July 3, 1843. Only after Grabau had prodded them repeatedly, did they come out with their opinion, and then most unwillingly. In transmitting their answer, Loeber, who wrote in the name of the group, told Grabau that they had gone over his document in a number of meetings and that now (on July 3, 1843) they had co-operated with all earnestness to get their answer into final form. In his letter Loeber refers to their group as "Missouri pastors." The whole correspondence, beginning with Pastor Grabau's "Hirtenbrief" of December 1, 1840, was published by the Missourians in 1849, under the follow-

which gradually drove the ministers of Missouri and their congregations into a more perfect union.

But a common offense also played a role in establishing unusual solidarity. The Saxons came with high ideals of planting a soundly Lutheran Church on American soil. The college built in the hot summer of 1839, six months after the purchase of the so-called Brazeau Bottoms in Perry County, was the first aggressive action of the virile immigrant Church. This institution had a unifying influence. It contributed to the formation of the Missouri Synod. Though small and at times on the verge of collapse, the college gave the congregations and the pastors a common objective.[8] That the growth of a Church is dependent, under God, upon the type of minister which the Church itself educates and trains was a principle derived from the Lutheran doctrine of the means of grace and tenaciously defended by every Saxon pastor. Both pastors and laymen were keenly alive to their duty of training future ministers.[9] The minutes of Trinity Congregation, St. Louis, give ample evidence of the laymen's intense interest in maintaining the college. As a matter of fact, during the first eight years of its existence Concordia Seminary was largely financed by Trinity Con-

---

ing title: *Der Hirtenbrief des Herrn Pastor Grabau zu Buffalo nebst den zwischen ihm und mehreren lutherischen Pastoren in Missouri gewechselten Schriften.* Der Oeffentlichkeit uebergeben als eine Protestation gegen Geltendmachung hierarchischer Grundsaetze innerhalb der lutherischen Kirche.

8. In an article on the proper call of a pastor ("Von ordentlicher Berufung zum Predigtamt") Pastor Th. Brohm, then of New York City, wrote in *Der Lutheraner,* I, April 5, 1845: "In order that there be no dearth of qualified Lutheran pastors, Lutheran congregations are in duty bound to maintain institutions for the proper training of such men." Pastor Loeber reports on the present state of the college in *Der Lutheraner,* I (1845), pp. 93—94. He sees eye to eye with Brohm on the duty of the congregations to educate their own pastors, and his report is an effort to rally the congregations around a common cause.

9 Although H. M. Muhlenberg did much for the American Lutheran Church of the eighteenth century, and though he rightly bears the title of "Patriarch of the American Lutheran Church," it cannot be denied that he fumbled with various plans for the education and training of an indigenous ministry. For a while the future Lutheran ministers were trained in a department of Pennsylvania University. Others were trained at Franklin College, Lancaster, Pennsylvania, under a partly Reformed and partly Lutheran faculty. Many were trained at the Presbyterian school at Princeton, New Jersey. The effects of Muhlenberg's failure to persuade the American Lutheran Church of the eighteenth century to educate its own ministers is distinctly visible in the Lutheran General Synod of the nineteenth century. See Neve-Allbeck, *op. cit.,* pp. 66—70. The Missouri Synod, cut off from European connections, trained its own ministry from the very beginning and thus established a solidarity that is unique in the annals of American Protestantism.

gregation. At times the minutes of the congregation sound like the minutes of the Board of Control.[10] The college tended to tie the pastors and the congregations together.[11]

---

[10] The following dates are references to the minutes of Trinity Church which deal with questions pertaining to the college: 5/20/43: A letter from Mr. Ahner in Perry County was read, in which he spoke of the great blessings of the Gospel and of the education of the future ministers of the Church. A long discussion followed, which centered on the college — its necessity and it possibilities. 6/19/43: A meeting was announced for the following Thursday. The purpose of this meeting was to discuss the problems of the college. Pastors Loeber, Gruber, Fuerbringer, and Schieferdecker were to be invited to take part in the discussions. 6/22/43: A long discussion concerning the college. Points of emphasis were the great necessity of the college and the advisability of moving it from Perry County to St. Louis. The upshot of the discussion in this meeting was that the college was to be an institution of the congregations in St. Louis and Perry County "in order that it may have a greater degree of solidity" ("damit es dadurch mehr Festigkeit erlange"). Other Lutheran congregations (presumably those in Illinois, which were in close relationship with the Missouri pastors) were to be asked to contribute toward the maintenance of the college. A subscription list was to be started among the members of Trinity Congregation for the college. The list should be completed by the following Monday. 6/26/43: The college was the main topic. Resolved, that the entire congregation regard the college as absolutely necessary, that a college be founded (Evidently the first college, founded in the fall of 1839, had either collapsed or was about to collapse) in which those sciences be taught which are necessary for the proper training of pastors and school teachers in the Lutheran Church. ("Beschlossen, die ganze Gemeinde haelt es fuer nothwendig, dass ein College errichtet werde, auf welchem diejenigen Wissenschaften, die zur Bildung von luth. Predigern und Schullehrern noethig sind, und namentlich die alten Sprachen gelehrt werden.") Special emphasis was to be placed upon the ancient languages. The college was to be erected in Perry County. This arrangement, as to location, should be regarded as temporary only. The congregation would contribute $7.00 every month for the maintenance of the college. These amounts were to be raised by voluntary subscriptions. Instruction was to begin as soon as possible. 6/29/43: The congregation resolved to contribute $5.00 a month toward the salary of one college teacher. It should be remembered that this was almost one fourth of the salary which they were then paying their pastor (The pastor's salary was $21.75 a month). Payments to the college were to begin with July 1, 1843. 7/10/43: A letter written by Pastor Loeber from Perry County was read to the congregation. Pastor Loeber thanked the congregation for their help in defraying his traveling expenses to the college meeting.

9/4/43: Two letters from Pastor Loeber regarding the college were read to the voters. The Perry County brethren were ready to receive Candidate Goenner as rector (principal teacher) of the college. A very important question arose involving the doctrine of the call. From the very outset the Missourians had laid great stress on the activity of the local congregation in calling pastors. On the basis of the priesthood of all believers the right to exercise the functions of the priesthood inheres potentially in every Christian. He relinquishes this right temporarily and transfers it when he joins other Christians in calling a man to perform the services of a pastor publicly. (See Walther, *Kirche und Amt,* fourth edition, 1894, originally published 1852.) On pages 245—341 the author sets forth the Missouri Synod's doctrine of the transfer of the public ministerial functions from the laity to the individual pastor. See also Engelder-Dallmann-Dau, *Walther and the Church,* pp. 74—78. See also Walther's *Pastoraltheologie,* pp. 23—62. In the meeting of 9/4/43 the question arose: "Who shall call Rector Goenner? Shall Trinity of St. Louis call him?" Some said, If we do, we are under obligation to pay his entire salary. Shall the congregation in Altenburg call him? They were financially unable to do so. Shall individuals call him? There was a lack of clarity on the whole issue. There was definite disagreement ("Misshelligkeit" the secretary calls it). 9/7/43: It was decided that the college should become a private matter, that is, that a special organization should be formed apart from the congregation, and that this organization should take care of all matters pertaining to the college. Pastor Walther was asked to prepare a form for the calling of Rector Goenner. A meeting of all interested in the forming of a college society was called for the following Tuesday at 7:45 in the evening. The present writer has not been able to get hold of any minutes of the society for the college. Whether such a society was organized or not is difficult to determine. On the 18th of March, 1844, matters pertaining to the college were discussed by the voters and recorded in the minutes. There was a letter from Rector Goenner. His *Vocation*, signed by the brethren in Perry County, was mentioned and apparently approved by the congregation. A resolution was passed which made the college the business of the congregation again: "Beschlossen, dass das College von nun an eine Gemeindesache seyn soll, jedoch nur von freiwilligen Beitraegen unterstuetzt werden." Evidently the plan to have a separate society for the maintenance and promotion of the college, tried from September 7, 1843, to March 18, 1844, failed. During this period, in which they were trying to find a solution to the question of the professor's call, very little was done in a practical way for the promotion of the college. The new solution was to put the contributions for the college on a voluntary basis. The principle that the education and training of the future pastors was the duty of the congregation was upheld. The great interest of Trinity Congregation in the college continued unabated.

6/24/44: Mr. Bischoff was authorized by the congregation to buy a pair of trousers, some English books, and some Latin classics for Student Martin Guenther. 9/9/44: Mr. Wichmann inquired about the condition of the college in Perry County. C. F. W. Walther, who had recently visited the college, tendered a report. He found the college in better condition than he had expected. Instruction in the ancient languages was particularly efficient. A resolution was passed encouraging the students to send essays (*Abhandlungen*) in the German language to the congregation. 10/14/44: Rector Goenner was to receive two barrels of flour as a special remuneration for the board which he gave to two students from St. Louis. 12/9/44: The students of the college were to receive a Christmas gift of $10 from the treasury of the congregation. 2/10/45: An essay ("eine schriftliche Ausarbeitung") written by Student Julius Biltz was read to the congregation by Pastor Walther. The college student Guenther was to receive a new suit by resolution of the congregation. Rector Goenner should be asked to inform the congregation about the needs of the individual students. ("Rector Goenner soll gebeten werden, es der Gemeinde anzuzeigen, wenn ein Schueler etwas beduerftig ist.") 4/14/45: Pastor Brohm's congregation in New York sent $19 to the treasurer of Trinity Congregation for the college. Pastor Brohm asked for exact information about the college. 5/14/45: An essay on the value of church history ("ueber den Nutzen der Kirchengeschichte") written by Student Mueller was read by Pastor Walther to the assembled voters. Mr. Doederlein was authorized by the congregation to buy such books as were necessary for the college. 8/11/45: A letter from Mr. Boehlau, whose home was in Wittenberg, Perry County, was read. The letter concerned the college. A bedstead was to be bought for the college at a cost of $1.00. Rector Goenner was to receive a special gratuity of $2.00 for boarding two college students. After the initial two dollars had been paid, the congregation agreed to pay $2.00 monthly for this service. Pastor Loeber was to receive a special gift of $10 for his many services and sacrifices in behalf of the college. The congregation wished to express its gratitude by means of this gift. A financial report on the congregation's college treasury was given to the voters. The report covered six months. Income, $81.22¾; disbursements, $58.60. 10/13/45: The financial report of the college treasury covering the last month showed an income of $8.63¾. 12/8/45: The financial report for the previous month showed an income of the college treasury of the congregation amounting to $12.43. This was a relatively large sum when compared with Pastor Walther's salary, which in that month was still $21.75. 2/9/46: The financial report of the college treasury showed an income of $16.65 and disbursements of $7.00. 6/2/46: Since a new student by the name of Kitz had been added to the student group, Rector Goenner was to receive $10 a month. 5/18/46: The two college students Metz and Guenther were to receive cash from Mr. Bischoff in order to purchase certain necessities. 6/8/46: The financial report of the college treasury showed an income for the previous month of $12.30. 8/10/46: Income for the college, $11.85. 8/29/46: Pastors Loeber and Keyl were asked to serve on the faculty as heretofore. 9/14/46: A letter from the Perry County congregations concerning the college was read and discussed, but no resolutions were formulated. The treasury report for the month showed an income of $10.67½. 9/21/46: The members of the church engaged in a long discussion pertaining to the college. Major repairs of the building were necessary. The necessary building material for these repairs should be paid by Trinity Congregation. The necessary funds were to be borrowed from the cemetery fund. 9/29/46: Thirty dollars were set aside for repairs and enlargement of the college. An assistant professor was to be engaged. The call extended to the assistant should be a temporary one. 10/12/46: Income for the month in the college treasury was $23.82½. 10/26/46: Pastor Walther's letter written in the name of Trinity Congregation to the brethren in Perry County concerning the repairs on, and the enlargement of, the college building was read and approved by the voters. The semi-annual report showed an income in the college treasury of $110.79 and disbursements of $107.90. 11/23/46: A box of books for the college had arrived from Germany. The freight was to be paid out of the college treasury. Since the shipment contained schoolbooks, Mr. Tschirpe was to petition the Government for a cancellation of the import duties. Mr. Fischer made a formal suggestion that the entire income from the cemetery be used to support the college. No resolution was passed. 12/15/46: The resolution was passed that any profit accruing from the cemetery transactions should forever be used for the education of the servants of the Church ("Beschlossen, dass der Ueberschuss des Ertrags vom Kirchhof fuer immer allein zu Zwecken der Erziehung von Dienern der luth. Kirche verwendet werden soll").

2/8/47: A motion was carried to purchase a coat for Student Mueller. The purchase was to be made out of the congregation's college treasury. 2/22/47: A report was submitted on the collection for the repairs on, and the extension of, the college building. Thirty dollars had been collected, and six dollars were added to the original grant of thirty dollars. 3/15/47: The income of the college treasury for the previous month was $16.67½. 4/8/47: Pastor Loeber was to receive $20 as a special gratuity for his services to the college. 4/19/47: The delegate to the convention of the Missouri Synod in Chicago, Illinois, was to inform the convention of the attitude of Trinity Congregation toward the college if the opportunity should present itself. 5/10/47: The semiannual report of the treasurer showed an income of $130.42 for the college. 6/14/47: The treasurer's report showed an income of $21.47½ for the college. 7/12/47: The treasurer's report showed an income of $21.62½ for the college during the previous month. 8/9/47: Income in the college treasury during the past month, $22.75. 8/12/47: The English books recommended for the college by Pastor Walther and Mr. Nitschke were to be purchased. Pastor Walther submitted a report on the action of the synodical convention concerning the college. He asked the congregation whether it would be willing to give the college to Synod. A long discussion followed. Finally the resolution was passed to give the college to Synod provided it be moved to St. Louis. 12/27/47: Pastor Walther read a letter containing all the themes and titles of essays written by the students of the college. Several of the essays were read to the congregation.

In the summer of 1844 a project was launched that was destined to be a most powerful instrument in the formation of the new conservative body. On June 3 of that year Pastor Walther suggested to the voting members of Trinity Congregation a plan for the publication of a *Zeitschrift*. Much time was spent in discussing the projected journal. Enthusiasm ran high. In the meeting of August 12, 1844, members offered to take two subscriptions. In order to insure publication, the congregation as a whole voted to grant the magazine its financial support.

The first number, published September 7, 1844, contained the program of the editor. An aggressively militant spirit fills the thirty-three-year-old leader. After stating in the opening article that no Church was more completely cut off from its coreligionists than the Lutherans of the Augsburg Confession on the western fringe of our land, he proceeds to show how this journal would develop a Lutheran consciousness and solidarity in the isolated brethren of the frontier. Its columns would make readers familiar with the doctrines, the treasures, and the history of the Lutheran Church. Error would be attacked whenever and wherever found, whether among the sects or among pseudo-Lutherans. The energetic editor promised to furnish proof that the Lutheran Church is the ancient true Church of Christ on earth.[12] As might have been expected, Walther adduces "Testimonies from Luther" immediately after his introductory article.

What was the significance of *Der Lutheraner* in the formation of the Missouri Synod? What bearing did this journal have on the polity of the future synod? It was a channel through which Luther's concepts of church government and of doctrine generally flowed incessantly to the Lutheran laity of the American frontier, and it was a means of publicity whereby the Saxon pastors placed what they believed to be a true picture of themselves, their doctrine and polity, before the Lutheran Church of America at a time when rationalism was definitely on the decline in Germany and when members of the General Synod, trailing about twenty years behind the Lutherans in Germany, were embracing this movement so foreign to genuine Lutheranism. Strange as it may

---

[11] *Der Lutheraner,* I (1845), pp. 93—94. Pastor Loeber's report on the current state of the college.

[12] *Der Lutheraner,* I (1844), p. 1: "Vorbemerkungen ueber Ursache, Zweck und Inhalt des Blattes."

seem, in view of their absolute rejection of rationalism, Walther and his companions were much more abreast of leading contemporary Lutheran thought in Germany than the leading spokesmen of the General Synod. The parade had long passed the spot where the leaders of a denatured Lutheranism were standing. The men and women among whom Walther and his associates were working had but recently left Germany; some had been in this country only six months, others a year, others two years. The sound of his trumpet was strikingly familiar to ears that had but recently listened to the clarion calls for Lutheran loyalty to Claus Harms in Hannover, of Vilmar in Hesse, of Loehe and Harless in Bavaria, of Rudelbach, Guericke, and Ahlfeld in Saxony, and of the many lesser lights that were espousing the cause of conservative Lutheranism all over Germany. Four months after the first issue of *Der Lutheraner* had left the presses of Weber and Olshausen in St. Louis, Pastor Walther could read to the assembled voters of Trinity Congregation in St. Louis "very important letters from Pastor Brohm in New York, Pastor Ernst in Ohio, Dr. Sihler in Pomeroy, Ohio, Professor Schmidt in Pittsburgh, Pastor Barthels in Zanesville, Ohio, and Pastor Meissner in Brownstown, Indiana."[13] These letters glowed with sympathy for the cause which *Der Lutheraner* represented. Dr. Sihler's heart leaped for joy when the first number of Walther's publication came into his hands.[14] Wyneken, then pastor in Fort Wayne, Indiana, cried out after perusing the first number, "Thank God, there are still real Lutherans in America!"[15] Pastor Ernst in Marysville, Ohio, having seen the first number, wrote to Pfarrer Loehe in Neuendettelsau, Bavaria: "No doubt great things may be expected from Pastor Walther."[16] As far as the organization of a new synod was concerned, Pastor Sihler's letter of December 11, 1844, was most significant.[17] This letter contained vital questions pertaining to church life on the Mississippi. Question Five was:

---

[13] Minutes of Trinity Congregation, January 13, 1845: "Sehr wichtige Briefe von Herrn Pastor Brohm aus New York; von Herrn Pastor Ernst aus Ohio; von Herrn Doktor Sihler aus Pomeroy, Ohio; von Herrn Professor Schmidt aus Pittsburg; von Herrn Pastor Barthels aus Zanesville, Ohio; und Herrn Pastor Meissner aus Brownstown, Indiana, wurden vom Herrn Pastor vorgelesen."

[14] *Lebenslauf*, II, pp. 39—40.

[15] Neve-Allbeck, *op. cit.*, p. 185.

[16] *Ebenezer*, p. 49.

[17] In his reply, dated January 2, 1845, Walther quotes at length from Sihler's letter. See *Walthers Briefe*, I, pp. 6—15.

"With whom do the Saxon pastors form a synod?" Question Six was: "Would it not be possible for them to form a synod together with us?" Walther's reply to these questions shows that he is enthusiastically in favor of organizing a new synod, although he realizes certain difficulties. The first and perhaps foremost difficulty is that public opinion, guided by certain German liberals, would be definitely set against any form of synodical organization. They would denounce it as a device of priest rule. Secondly, the immigrant congregations, acting like burnt children, would fear anything that might remind them of hierarchical institutions. Therefore he writes: "The West is full of German demagogues who leave no stone unturned in their efforts to create suspicion and to make every form of synodical organization appear dangerous. Even well-meaning people will be affected by their activity. There is a general fear and timidity over against such an institution; people fear priest rule. Furthermore, our immigrant congregations view with alarm every institution that even faintly resembles a hierarchy, because of their terrible experience with Stephan." [18]

There is an interesting letter extant which Walther wrote to Pastor Ernst of Marysville, Ohio. As already stated, Pastor Ernst had written to the editor of *Der Lutheraner*, sometime late in November or early in December, 1844. This letter was read in the voters' meeting of Trinity Congregation on January 13, 1845. Ernst wrote again under date of August 6, 1845. In this second letter he proposes that a synod upholding pure Lutheranism be organized, first in the State of Ohio. To Pastor Ernst's letter of August 6 Walther replies on August 21, 1845. The editor of *Der Lutheraner* is wholeheartedly in favor of Pastor Ernst's plan for a new synod. He is pleased to inform the Ohio pastor that the fear and anxiety regarding synods is declining daily in the St. Louis area. In fact, the desire for an organic union of all truly Lutheran pastors and all truly Lutheran congregations is gaining ground steadily. Thereupon Walther — and this is what makes this letter so very im-

---

[18] *Walthers Briefe*, I, pp. 11—12. "Doch muss ich das bemerken, dass der ganze Westen von deutschen Demagogen erfuellt ist, die alles aufbieten, jede Art eines Synodalverbandes verhasst zu machen; selbst Gutgesinnte bleiben hiervon nicht ganz unberuehrt; es herrscht daher im ganzen eine gewisse Scheu vor dergleichen Anstalten; man fuerchtet Priesterherrschaft. Dazu kommt noch, dass gerade unsere ausgewanderten Gemeinden alles mit einer gewissen Bangigkeit betrachten, was im entferntesten eine Hierarchie befuerchten laesst, da sie unter Stephan's Tyrannei so entsetzlich gelitten haben."

portant — establishes six characteristics of a synod that he would regard as ideal: 1. The constitution of the synod must be based upon the confessional writings of the Lutheran Church, including, if possible, the Saxon Visitation Articles. 2. The constitution of the synod must obligate all members of synod to ban all syncretistic activity from their midst. 3. The chief objective of the synod should be to conserve, promote, and watch over the unity and purity of Lutheran doctrine. 4. The synod should not be a court with power and authority to execute laws, but rather a consultative body, to which perplexed and helpless congregations might take refuge and seek counsel; the member congregations' right of calling a pastor must be safeguarded against any and every attempt at highhanded officiousness. 5. Lay delegates should have the same right of suffrage as the clergy, but a clergyman should be chairman at the meetings. 6. Every member congregation should have the right to pass judgment on the decisions and resolutions of the synod.[19]

Walther's reason for communicating his conception of an ideal synod to Pastor Ernst at this time was undoubtedly the fact that the "Eastern" pastors were about to have a meeting in which a preliminary draft of the constitution for a new synod was to be discussed. This meeting was the first one of a series of meetings which eventually culminated in the organization of the Missouri Synod.

The meeting was held in Cleveland, Ohio, September 13 to 18, 1845. Some of the more prominent men present were Pastor W. Sih-

---

[19] *Walthers Briefe*, I, pp. 15—19. "Meine Wuensche betreffs dieser Angelegenheit gehen hauptsaechlich dahin, 1. dass die Synode sich naechst dem Worte Gottes auf die saemtlichen Symbole unserer Kirche, wo moeglich (?), mit Einschluss der saechsischen Visitationsartikel, konstituiere, ohne dass ich jedoch auf das letztere herrliche, buendige Bekenntnis unbedingt dringen wollte. Ich wuensche zweitens, dass nach der Konstitution alles synkretistische Wirken von seiten der Synodalen durch einen besonderen Paragraphen abgeschnitten und ausgeschlossen wuerde; 3. dass die Hauptwirksamkeit der Synode auf Erhaltung und Foerderung und Bewachung der Einheit und Reinheit der lutherischen Lehre gerichtet werden moechte; 4. dass die Synode nicht sowohl als ein machthabender Gerichtshof dastuende als vielmehr als ein beratender Koerper, zu welchem eine ratlose Gemeinde ihre Zuflucht nehmen koennte; besonders muesste sie sich von allen Eingriffen in das Berufungsrecht der Gemeinde fernhalten. Fuenftens wuensche ich, dass die abgeordneten Laien, ja ein jeder, der in den Verband gehoert, Sitz und Stimme in der Synode habe wie die Prediger, aus denen jedoch stets der Vorsitzende zu erwaehlen waere. (Vergl. Apost. 15, 23.) Endlich meine ich, dass in keiner Sache, die von der Synode entschieden wuerde, die Appellation an die Entscheidung und Abstimmung saemtlicher verbundenen Gemeinden Mann fuer Mann benommen waere."

ler, Ph. D., then of Fort Wayne, Indiana; Pastor Adam Ernst of Marysville, Ohio; Pastor C. A. T. Selle, then of Columbiana County, Ohio; Pastor F. Lochner of Toledo, Ohio; Pastor F. C. D. Wyneken, lately of Fort Wayne, but now of Baltimore, Maryland; and Pastor George Burger of Willshire, Van Wert County, Ohio.[20] The chief purpose of this and the subsequent preliminary conferences was to draft a constitution for a synod whose doctrine and polity would be taken from the Word of God and the Confessional Writings of the Evangelical Lutheran Church. The men sent over by Loehe and

---

[20] Walther and the Saxons were invited, but the editor of *Der Lutheraner* could not be present. In his letter to Pastor Ernst dated August 21, 1845, and already referred to, he merely states that it is impossible for him to be present at the Cleveland meeting. The minutes of Trinity Congregation, St. Louis, indicate that Walther's health was rather precarious at the time. The congregation excused him from all ministerial duties for a period of two weeks because of sickness. ("Herr Pastor Walther ist seiner Kraenklichkeit wegen 14 Tage lang von allen Amtsverrichtungen dispensiert worden.") For references concerning the Cleveland meeting cf. Walther's letter to Ernst dated August 21, 1845, reprinted in *Walthers Briefe*, I, pp. 15—19; *Erster Synodal-Bericht der deutschen Ev. Luth. Synode von Missouri, Ohio und anderen Staaten*, 1847, p. 3. *Der Lutheraner*, II (1846), p. 42, is very important as a source for the Cleveland meeting, since it cites the reasons for the severance of relations between the "Eastern" pastors and the Ohio Synod. It contains a report of the Ohio Synod's syncretistic attitude. The fact that the Ohio Synod had introduced the same form for the distribution of the Lord's Supper which the syncretistic State Church of Prussia and the organization composed of Lutherans and Reformed in the United States were using, was especially offensive to the men at the Cleveland meeting. Instead of using the old Lutheran form: "This is the true body of our Lord Jesus Christ," etc., the Ohio Synod had introduced the Prussian form: "Christ says, This is My body," thus leaving the doctrine of the real presence in suspense. For the confessional position of the Ohio Synod cf. a reprint of the Ohio Synod's *Lutheran Standard* in *Der Lutheraner* of February 9, 1847 (III, p. 69). Cf. also Pastor Keyl's article in *Der Lutheraner*, I, p. 47: "Ueber die Abschaffung der unlutherischen Ausspendungsformel beim hl. Abendmahle: Christus spricht, etc." This article was caused by Sihler's petition to the Ohio Synod. A report on this petition is given in *Der Lutheraner*, I (1844), p. 9. Sihler was trying to introduce Lutheran doctrine and polity into the Ohio Synod. His petition was disregarded, and this resulted in his *Austrittserklaerung*, which came on the last day of the Cleveland meeting, September 18, 1845. Another source of information on the Cleveland meeting is to be found in the archives of Pastor F. Lochner. He left some autobiographical notes which have been printed in the *Concordia Historical Institute Quarterly*, VII, No. 3 (October, 1934). The article is headed "F. Lochner, Report on His First Contacts with the Saxons." Lochner wrote these notes in his old age, but he based them in part on a letter which he had written to Loehe shortly after the meeting. Cf. *Kirchliche Mittheilungen*, 1845, 9, 10. For Sihler's attitude on church government see the article which Sihler wrote in the winter of 1845 and which was published in *Lutherische Kirchenzeitung*, 1845, reprinted in *Der Lutheraner*, II (1845), pp. 29—30. The article was headed: "What Are the Leading Principles for the Establishment of Orthodox Synods of the Lutheran Church in This Country?"

other conservative leaders were yearning for such a synod on
American soil.

Neither the autobiography of Sihler nor the correspondence of
Walther nor the minutes of Trinity Congregation, St. Louis, nor the
Synodal-Bericht of 1847 tells us anything about the results in the
way of constitution making at the Cleveland meeting. A kind of
rough draft of a constitution was made in Cleveland, but for some
reason or other it did not survive the second preliminary meeting.*
Sihler claimed that the "Eastern" brethren were inexperienced in
the making of constitutions and that in theological learning they
were mere babes in the woods compared with Walther and the
Saxons.[21] It may be that the results of the Cleveland conference
were rather meager and that this meagerness was due to their in-

---

* EDITOR'S NOTE. — *In Quellen und Dokumente* (Wartburg Publishing
House, Chicago, Ill. No date of publication given), p. 47, reference is made,
in connection with the Cleveland meeting, to a synodical constitution ("dem
Entwurfe nach schon vorhanden"), which was discussed at that time (September, 1845). A little later in the same chapter the statement is made:
"Sogleich nach der Konstituierung der neuen Synode (also im September
dieses Jahres — 1845?) reisten unsere Freunde Dr. Sihler und Ernst nach
St. Louis zu den letztgenannten Sachsen, etc." These statements are not clear,
but they do seem to indicate that some sort of draft of a synodical constitution
was, if not actually adopted, discussed at Cleveland.

However, no such draft is available in spite of careful search. It may be
that we have a reflection of what was discussed at Cleveland in a series of
articles which Dr. Sihler published shortly after the Cleveland meeting in
Lutherische Kirchenzeitung, edited at Pittsburgh by the Rev. F. Schmidt of the
Ohio Synod. C. F. W. Walther reprinted several installments of this series in
Der Lutheraner, Vol. II.

In these articles Sihler enters upon a detailed presentation of the problem
of establishing a synodical organization in a country in which the Church is
free from any rule or supervision on the part of the State, and he shows
how impossible it would be to transplant to American soil the organization
of the Church as these men had seen it in their European homeland. Then
he sets forth his own views as to the proper manner in which a synod should
be constituted.

According to Sihler a synod should not merely be advisory, but it should
be a body, or corporation, which would in the name of the Church, i. e., the
whole number of the adult and confirmed members, direct, watch over, and
administer the Church. The synod should not be simply a ministerium,
composed of members of the clergy only, but worthy members of the laity
would be elected by their congregations to synodical membership. These
laymen, together with the clergymen, would constitute the synod. This synod
would then regulate, direct, and administer all matters pertaining to the
doctrine, life, worship, and discipline of the Church. To quote Sihler:
"All means, therefore, which would in any way preserve and further the
Church according to its essence and purpose, the synod, according to its
ability, would have to inaugurate energetically and watch over its harmonious
and active co-operation." This conception of a synod and its jurisdiction
was radically different from that held by Walther in St. Louis. — W. G. P.

[21] Sihler, *Lebenslauf*, II, p. 72.

experience and lack of theological training. Neither Sihler nor Ernst nor Burger nor Lochner had anything like the technical theological training which Walther and his associates had received.[22] Furthermore, these men had just stepped out of synods, or were in the act of stepping out of synods, which they believed to be guilty of un-Lutheran polity. They knew what they did not want, but they may not yet have known what they wanted, particularly since most of them had been in this country but a very short time.

The second in the series of preliminary conferences was conducted in St. Louis. During the day, meetings of the pastors were conducted in Pastor Walther's study. In the evening plenary sessions were held together with the voting members of Trinity Congregation. According to the minutes of Trinity Congregation the first plenary meeting was conducted on May 18, 1846. Sihler, Loeber, Gruber, Keyl, Lochner, Fuerbringer, and Schieferdecker were present, together with the pastors and voting members of Trinity Congregation. Plenary sessions in which the voting members of Trinity Congregation were present, together with the visiting pastors, took place on the 18th, the 22d, and the 25th of May. Sihler, who makes much more of the St. Louis conference than he does of the Cleveland gathering, speaks of a week of meetings at St. Louis.[23] Strange as it may seem, the *Synodal-Bericht* of the first convention of the Missouri Synod in Chicago has not a word to say about the St. Louis conference. *Der Lutheraner*, III (1846), p. 1, which pre-

---

[22] Sihler had studied philosophy and geography at Berlin University. After he had given up the career of a soldier, he had become an educator. He was more or less of an autodidact in theology. At the time of the Cleveland conference he had completed about eighteen months in the ministry. Adam Ernst, a native of Bohemia, had been a cobbler's apprentice in Germany. He had received a short course from Loehe lasting about one year. George Burger was a native of Noerdlingen and had received the same short course. Lochner, the son of a copperplate printer, was an engraver by trade. Upon the special request of his parents he had entered the theological training school which Pastor Loehe conducted in addition to his work as pastor of a large congregation in Franconia. At the time of the Cleveland conference he was not quite twenty-three years old, and his experience in the ministry covered the months of June, July, and August, 1845. Cf. his autobiography, printed in the *Concordia Historical Institute Quarterly*, VI, No. 4 (January, 1934), pp. 110—117. For the information on Ernst and Burger I am indebted to an article in *C. H. I. Quarterly*, XII, No. 2 (July, 1939), pp. 57—64, entitled: "The Loehe Missioners Outside of Michigan." In his report on his first contacts with the Saxons published in *C. H. I. Quarterly*, VII, No. 3 (October, 1934), pp. 77—81, Lochner tells of the Saxons' distrust of the Loehe men, particularly because the majority of them had had no university training.

[23] Sihler, *Lebenslauf*, II, pp. 52—58.

sents the first draft of the constitution, with annotations by the editor, says nothing at all about the St. Louis conference. Why this conference receives no mention in *Der Lutheraner* or in the first *Synodal-Bericht* is difficult to explain, particularly since the tangible results were greater and far more decisive in St. Louis than at Cleveland. The reason may be that in point of time the St. Louis gathering occurred only a month before the Fort Wayne conference and that it was regarded merely as an informal preliminary conference to the more formal constitutional convention on the Maumee. However, the significant facts about the informal gathering at St. Louis are these: The wording was fixed in the midst of a congregation that was intensely jealous of its congregational rights. This fact made a deep impression on the "Eastern" men, especially on Sihler and Lochner. The "Eastern" men for the first time saw Walther and the Western men face to face. The "Eastern" men were won over to a form of church government in which the laymen played an important role. The wavering souls in Trinity Congregation were won over for the project; and Trinity Congregation, St. Louis, became the leading congregation of the Missouri Synod and remained so for over half a century. The contribution of the St. Louis laymen dare not be overlooked. What were these contributions? Trinity Congregation was surrounded by liberal Germans.[24]   That Walther feared the opinion and activity of these men is clearly evident from his letter to Sihler.[25] Furthermore, Trinity had passed through a long and terrible struggle. Even now there was a group within the congregation that could not forget Walther's erstwhile *Amtsbruederlichkeit* with Martin Stephan.[26] In

---

[24] The press exercised great influence on the thinking of the people. Since there were no telegraphic reports, local news was played up, and editorials claimed the attention of the readers. St. Louis had two dailies published in the German language. The editors were usually German university-trained liberals. Anticlerical statements were common. Clergymen were portrayed as men who were bent on curtailing the liberty of the people. Cf. Gruber, *op. cit.* Cf. also the files of the *Anti-Pfaff.* This was an anticlerical publication that made scurrilous attacks also on Pastor Walther.

[25] *Walthers Briefe,* I, p. 11.

[26] That Walther suffered intensely from his former connection with Martin Stephan is evident from a reply which he made to Pastor Nollau of the Evangelical church in the Gravois settlement near St. Louis. Nollau wrote a pamphlet and entitled it *A Word for the Good Cause of Union.* In this pamphlet he made a personal attack on Pastor Walther. In fact, he went out of his way to remind his readers of Walther's connection with Stephan. Walther wrote a series of articles in reply. The first one was

this section of the congregation we must look for the origin of that anxious concern for congregational rights. If there was anything these men hated from the depth of their souls, it was priest rule. Making a virtue of necessity, Walther was extremely careful about every detail of congregational power. But in spite of Walther's most strenuous and painstaking efforts to safeguard the independence of the local congregation,[27] there was a group within the congregation that was not satisfied. The constitutional stipulation that the voting strength of the clerics must never exceed the voting strength of the laymen had its origin in this group. In the meeting of May 18, 1846, the constitutional provision was made from the floor, not by Walther, but by a layman, that if a congregation should send two pastors, only one of them should have the right to vote in any one session.[28] This provision of *Stimmengleichheit* was definitely established in the meeting of June 2, 1846.[29]

Another constitutional provision that came from the floor of the voters' meeting in Trinity concerned the right of nomination for the ministry in those congregations which were temporarily without a pastor. The provision as adopted in the meeting of the congregation on June 8, 1846, reads: "Synod shall have the right to nominate candidates for the ministry of those congregations that are without a pastor." [30]

Another constitutional provision in the Missouri Synod's constitution that came from the laity of Trinity Congregation refers to the judicial function of Synod. Walther and the pastors who worked with him on the constitution had inserted a provision that Synod

published in *Der Lutheraner*, I (1845), p. 20. It is very evident from Walther's reply that he felt the sting of Nollau's attack most keenly. At times Walther becomes devastatingly bitter in his reply to Nollau.

27 In the meeting of May 11, 1846, Walther addressed the congregation on the necessity and blessing of a synodical organization, which would, however, in no wise infringe upon the rights and privileges of the congregation ("Herr Pastor Walther trug der Gemeinde vor, wie nothwendig und heilsam es sei, wenn eine Synodalverbindung der rechtglaeubigen Prediger und Gemeinden in den Vereinigten Staaten entstehe, jedoch ohne Schmaelerung der Gemeinderechte").

28 Minutes of Trinity Congregation, May 18, 1846.

29 Minutes, June 2, 1846: "Beschlossen, dass der Paragraph in welchem von der Stimmengleichheit die Rede ist, so stehen bleiben soll."

30 Minutes, June 8, 1846: "Indem die Synode denselben Candidaten fuer das vacante Pfarramt vorschlaegt." Synod shall have no right to appoint ministers to vacant congregations, but may merely suggest candidates. To the local congregation must be reserved the right to vote on these candidates.

was to act as referee in disputes between two or more parties. Thus, if a dispute arose between a pastor and his congregation or between two pastors, Synod should hear the case and then render a decision. To this the laymen of Trinity added, "Provided that all parties concerned have requested Synod to function in such capacity in their case." [31]

The result of the May meeting in St. Louis was a complete draft of a constitution which safeguarded the rights of the congregation and at the same time was workable. Walther's five years' experience on American soil with a congregation that suffered from morbid fear of priest rule, and the influence of a certain group in that congregation, left their marks on the constitution. From past experience Walther knew that the voters of Trinity would not tolerate another priest rule.[32] In a certain sense one may call the constitution of the Missouri Synod the result of a seven-year battle for congregational rights. The contribution of Walther's enemies should not be overlooked.[33] Had it not been for Walther's opponents, the principle of congregational rights would not have bulked so large or been worded so precisely in Missouri's constitution.

---

[31] Minutes, June 8, 1846: "Wenn die Synode um dieselbe (nemlich schiedsrichterliche Handlung) von allen, die es betrifft, angegangen wird."

[32] Sihler, *Lebenslauf*, II, p. 72. Sihler makes the assertion that Walther drafted the first constitution of the Missouri Synod. The minutes of Trinity Congregation, June 18, 1846, say that the complete draft of a synodical constitution as worked out by the local pastors was read to the voters in the presence of the visiting pastors. "Der Entwurf zu einer Synodalverbindung, welche von den saemtlichen hiesigen Pastoren ausgearbeitet worden war, wurde in Gegenwart der fremden Herrn Pastoren Sihler, Loeber, Gruber, Keyl, Ernst, Lochner, Fuerbringer und Schieferdecker der Gemeinde vorgelesen." The question arises: What is meant by "saemtliche hiesige Pastoren"? Since Fuerbringer, who was then pastor over in Venedy, Illinois, is listed with the "fremde Pastoren," I am inclined to believe that the secretary meant Walther and Buenger. On the other hand, we have Pastor Lochner's statement in *Concordia Historical Institute Quarterly*, VII, No. 2 (July, 1934), p. 48: "I had occasion to see what an important part Ottomar Fuerbringer had in this work [namely, of making a constitution] and in general in the organization of Synod." Lochner was present at the meeting, and he was a brother-in-law of Walther. Speaking of the conference in St. Louis, Lochner writes in his autobiography, printed in *C. H. I. Quarterly*, VI, No. 4 (January, 1934), p. 112: "The result of this convention was the joint draft of a Lutheran synodical constitution founded on the idea of a free church and the principle of congregational rights. Upon the basis of this draft later on, in the spring of 1847, the Evangelical Lutheran Synod of Missouri, Ohio, and Other States was organized."

[33] *Der Lutheraner*, I (1845), p. 20. Walther confesses that his enemies helped him more than his friends: "Wir bezeugen, dass uns daher unsere bittersten Feinde mehr genutzt haben als unsere mit der Liebe alles zudeckenden Freunde."

The formal meeting to bring all discussion regarding the constitution to a successful conclusion was held in Fort Wayne, Indiana. According to the minutes of Trinity Congregation, St. Louis, June 18, 1846, the conference was to begin on the second day of July, 1846. The good will of Trinity is evidenced by the fact that the congregation voted to grant Pastor Walther permission to attend the meeting and $50 for his traveling expenses to Fort Wayne and return.[34]

A report on the constitutional convention in Fort Wayne was given to the voters of Trinity Congregation by Pastor Walther in the meeting of July 27, 1846. In Vol. III (1846), No. 1, of *Der Lutheraner* an extensive report is given, together with the entire constitution as adopted in Fort Wayne. Dr. Sihler gives his account of the Fort Wayne conference in *Lebenslauf*, II, pp. 71—74. There are some scattered references to the Fort Wayne gathering in a letter from Walther to his brother-in-law, Lochner, in Toledo, dated August 20, 1846, *Walthers Briefe*, I, pp. 25—30. Pfarrer Loehe of Neuendettelsau, Bavaria, published the entire draft and made some annotations in his *Mittheilungen*. Chr. Hochstetter, *op. cit.*, pp. 154 to 159, bases his report of the Fort Wayne convention on the article in *Der Lutheraner* and on Pfarrer Loehe's *Mittheilungen*. He calls attention to the fact that at the time Loehe was completely satisfied with the constitutional provisions regarding the sovereignty of the congregation and that he expressed his delight concerning the fact that his *Sendlinge* had made common cause with the Saxons.

Walther's report in *Der Lutheraner* reveals an optimistic spirit and high expectations. Men who stand for genuine Lutheranism, Walther writes, are increasing in numbers. There is no doubt about it, God is visiting His people. The rubbish of man-made doctrines under which the Lutheran Church of America has been buried these past years will be removed. There is a growing interest in, and an increasing loyalty to, the historic Confessional Writings of the Lutheran Church. Interest in doctrinal discussion, heretofore at low ebb, is on the increase. Luther's writings, long permitted to lie undisturbed with the burden of dust on their covers, are being

---

[34] Minutes, June 18, 1846: "Beschlossen, dass der Herr Pastor Walther zu der auf den zweiten Juli festgestellten Predigerkonferenz im Osten mit Zustimmung der Gemeinde reisen kann." "Beschlossen, die Gemeinde will die Reisekosten des Herrn Pastors tragen. Es sollen ihm dazu $50.00 aus der Kommunkasse gereicht werden, im Fall ihm so viel noetig ist."

taken up and studied. A great battle has broken out, and a great sifting is taking place. Evidently we are standing at the portals of most far-reaching events.

Thereupon he offers details about the meeting at Fort Wayne. Sixteen pastors were present. The Saxons were represented by Loeber and Walther from the Mississippi and Brohm from New York City; Sihler, Husmann, and Jaebker were from Indiana; Burger, Detzer, Ernst, Knape, Schmidt, Schneider, and Trautmann were from Ohio; Craemer and Hattstaedt were from Michigan; and Selle, who had accepted a call from Columbiana County, Ohio, to Chicago in the late fall of 1845, was from Illinois. All were agreed that the Confessional Writings of the Lutheran Church should not merely be mentioned incidentally and then forgotten, but that they should be a power that would effectively give shape to the constitution and direction to all ways of doing things.[35]

What were some of the more important provisions of the Fort Wayne constitution regarding church government? The synod shall consist of pastors and representatives of parishes.[36] Giving the laity equality with the clergy was something new in the American Lutheran Church. Only the clergy had the right to vote in the old established Eastern synods. These organizations rightly called themselves *ministeria*. If not composed entirely of ministers, they were organizations that were at least dominated by ministers.[37]

---

[35] *Der Lutheraner*, III (1846), p. 2: ". . . eine ordnende und gestaltende Kraft auf die ganze Verfassung und auf die gesamte Handlungsweise der Kirche ausuebt." The general complaint against those Lutheran bodies which still mentioned the historic Lutheran Confessions was that they did mere lip service to these documents.

[36] Chapter III, paragraph 1, of the constitution as reported in *Der Lutheraner*, III (1846), p. 3, reads: "Bestandtheile des Synodalpersonals sind: die Diener der Kirche und die Deputierten der Pfarrgemeinden, von denen jede einen derselben zu waehlen das Recht hat." In a footnote Walther explains what a *Pfarrgemeinde* is. It is either a single congregation or the sum of several congregations which a pastor serves. If a pastor serves three or four different congregations, these three or four congregations taken together shall have the right to send one delegate.

[37] The constitution of the Pennsylvania Ministerium of 1748, as reported in Chr. O. Kraushaar, *op. cit.*, pp. 224—232. "Only pastors have the right to make motions and pass resolutions." ("In allen Angelegenheiten liegt die Beschlussfassung ausschliesslich bei den Gliedern des Ministeriums.") This provision was in force until 1792. In 1792 the constitution was revised. The revised constitution is reprinted in Kraushaar, *op. cit.*, pp. 245—252. This revision gave the laity permission to attend the synods of the Pennsylvania Ministerium, and even to vote. However, in the main transactions of the Ministerium the lay delegates had no right of suffrage. The idea of a synod as an association of congregations and their pastors with a balance between

A corollary to the above was the Missouri Synod's provision: Every congregation shall have the right to send one pastor and one lay delegate. This latter provision came from the voting members of Trinity Congregation, St. Louis, as we have noted above. It was the result of their experience with Stephan; and it was introduced to maintain the balance of power between the clergy and the laity. Had the founding fathers imbibed the American spirit of democracy, they would have insisted that human beings be the basis of representation. They would have counted the number of heads and arranged for one representative for every given number of communicants or voting members. But their representative arrangement was not the product of American political thought, nor was it congregationalism after the fashion of the Congregational or Baptist churches in America.[38] The polity of the Missouri Synod was

---

the voting strength of the clergy and that of the laity was far from the minds of the Pennsylvania Ministerium. The revised constitution remained in force until 1841. In this year there were only minor revisions. Kraushaar presents these on p. 254. The position of the laity was not changed in the least. The constitution of the New York Ministerium, founded in 1794, followed the older synod of Pennsylvania, although there was more participation on the part of the laity in New York than in Pennsylvania. However, there was no thought of a balance of voting strength between clergy and laity until the revision of 1883. In 1874 old St. Matthew's of New York, having imbibed some of the Missouri spirit, insisted upon congregational representation after the fashion of the Missouri Synod. They were particularly firm in their insistence upon the principle of congregational supremacy. When this principle was denied them, St. Matthew's left the New York Ministerium and joined the Missouri Synod. For ten years the question of congregational supremacy agitated the New York Ministerium. In the revision of 1883 the principle of congregational supremacy was recognized. See Kraushaar, pp. 268—270.

[38] Congregational churches hold to the autonomy of the local church and its independence of all ecclesiastical control. Cf. the article by Williston Walker, late professor of church history at Yale University, in the *Encyclopedia Americana*, Vol. 7, pp. 501—504. The polity of the Baptists is much like that of the Congregational churches, except that the individualism of each Christian is emphasized even more. The article by Henry Clay Vedder, professor emeritus of church history at Crozer Theological Seminary, in *Encyclopedia Americana*, Vol. 3, pp. 219—255. When the General Council was organized in 1866, the idea of numeric or proportional representation was expressed thus in the constitution, I, b: "The proportion of representation shall be based on the number of members in the respective synods entitled to admission to the Lord's Supper." *Documentary History of the General Council*, pp. 136—138. Also H. E. Jacobs, *History of the Evangelical Lutheran Church in the United States*, p. 474. Kraushaar prints the constitution of the General Council on pp. 456—476. The Augustana Synod has a somewhat modified numerical representation. An equal number of pastors and lay delegates are elected by the congregations, one pastor and one lay delegate for every 1,500 communicant members or fraction thereof. Cf. Neve-Allbeck, *op. cit.*, p. 319.

something apart from anything then known in America. It was the result of a catastrophic experience in their own midst.

This anxious preoccupation with the balance of power between clergy and laity is also noticeable in the definition of a parish which the Fort Wayne Conference inserted in the constitution at the insistence of Trinity Congregation, St. Louis. This official definition declares that one pastor may serve one, two, three, four, or more congregations; but for purposes of representation all congregations served by one pastor shall be regarded as one parish and shall be entitled to one lay representative only. On the other hand, pastors who are serving congregations that employ two or more clergymen cannot both vote. The congregation must designate which pastor is to do the voting in a given session. They may both attend the sessions, but only one may vote. One may vote in the morning session, and the other in the afternoon, provided they have previously indicated that this will be their procedure.

The balance-of-power theory, which had literally gripped the St. Louis laymen and had caused them to oppose Walther at various times, also dictated the device of advisory membership. Pastors who could not persuade their congregations to join the Synod could come in as advisory members. They thus acquired the right to speak on the floor of the convention, but not the right of suffrage. Professors at the seminary and the college were also regarded as advisory members.

There was a peculiar provision pertaining to the officers of Synod. These were to be elected for three years; and the President, Vice-President, and Secretary had to be clergymen, while the treasurer might be a layman.[39]

A certain amount of power was taken away from the laity by the provision of chapter III, paragraph 8, which stated that all matters of doctrine and conscience were to be decided by the Word of God.[40] If pastors could show that certain questions were matters

---

[39] At the convention in Chicago, April 24—May 6, 1847, the Synod elected temporary officers in the first session, Monday, April 26. Dr. Sihler, a clergyman, was elected Treasurer. During that same convention, in the session of Thursday, May 6, permanent officers were elected. Perhaps to satisfy the St. Louis balance-of-power group, F. W. Barthel, a layman from St. Louis, was elected permanent Treasurer. Ever since then a layman has been Treasurer of the Missouri Synod. The tradition has generally been extended to the District treasurers.

[40] Chapter II, paragraph 8: "Sachen der Lehre und des Gewissens werden allein durch Gottes Wort entschieden; alle andern Entscheidungen geschehen nach Stimmenmehrheit; bei Gleichheit der Stimmen entscheidet der Praeses."

of doctrine or conscience, no vote could be taken, nor could any power be exercised. All other decisions were to be made by majority vote; in case of a tie the President was authorized to cast the deciding vote.

The chief condition of membership, according to the Fort Wayne constitution, was the acceptance of the Bible as the inspired Word of God and all the Confessional Writings of the Lutheran Church as a pure and unadulterated interpretation and exposition of the divine Word.

Chapter II, paragraph 3 (the section on conditions of membership) forbade all syncretistic activity on the part of the pastor and the congregation. Syncretistic activity was definitely defined as serving mixed congregations (i. e., congregations consisting of Lutherans and Reformed) or taking part in a heterodox service or a heterodox celebration of the Sacraments or supporting a tract or mission society with a mixed membership (i. e., Lutherans and non-Lutherans).[41]

The constitution also insisted on purely Lutheran forms of worship, hymnbooks, Catechisms, and readers in the parish schools. If a pastor cannot immediately prevail with his protest against heterodox hymnbooks, he must use them only under protest; and during the time that he is thus using them he must make earnest and sincere attempts to introduce orthodox forms.[42]

A provision in the Fort Wayne constitution which strengthened the position of the minister in the congregation pertained to tenure of office. Almost all Lutheran synods at the time still had the un-Lutheran method of extending calls that were limited with respect to time. Some could be canceled on sixty days' notice (*auf Kuen-*

---

[41] Chapter II, paragraph 3: "Bedingungen, unter welchen der Anschluss an die Synode stattfinden und die Gemeinschaft mit derselben fortdauern kann: Lossagung von aller Kirchen- und Glaubensmengerei, als da ist: das Bedienen gemischter Gemeinden als solcher von seiten der Diener der Kirche; Teilnahme an dem Gottesdienst und den Sakramentshandlungen falschglaeubiger und gemischter Gemeinden, Teilnahme an allem falschglaeubigen Traktat- und Missionswesen usw."

[42] Chapter II, paragraph 4: "Alleiniger Gebrauch reiner Kirchen- und Schulbuecher (Agenden, Gesangbuecher, Katechismen, Lesebuecher, usw.). Wenn es in Gemeinden nicht tunlich ist, vorhandene irrglaeubige Gesangbuecher und dergl. ohne weiteres mit rechtglaeubigen zu vertauschen, so kann der Prediger einer solchen Gemeinde nur unter der Bedingung Glied der Synode werden, wenn er das irrglaeubige Gesangbuch usw. mit oeffentlichem Protest zu gebrauchen und allen Ernstes auf Einfuehrung eines rechtglaeubigen hinwirken zu wollen verspricht."

digung); that is to say: either the pastor, if he found something better, or the congregation, if it found a man who it thought would serve the congregation better or cheaper, could cancel the contract. This arrangement had been the subject of much discussion. Both the "Western" and the "Eastern" brethren were agreed that the time limit on a call extended to a pastor detracted from his dignity and that it should be eliminated.[43] A paragraph was inserted in the chapter on the condition of membership which read: "A regular, not a temporary, call must be extended to the pastor. A regular election of the lay delegate by the congregation must take place. Both pastor and lay delegate must be blameless and of good reputation." [44]

A system of visitation and supervision provided for in the constitution of 1846 shows how widely the principle of congregational supremacy as advocated by the Missourians differed from the congregationalism established in the Congregational and Baptist societies of America. Power to execute the Missouri system was concentrated in the President. According to a definite set of regulations the President is to visit every congregation belonging to Synod at least once every three years. He is to supervise the doctrine and life of the pastors and parish schoolteachers as well as the public

---

[43] Th. J. Brohm, who had accepted a call from Altenburg, Missouri, to New York City, wrote a strong denunciation of the time limit in a series of articles in *Der Lutheraner*, I (1845), pp. 61—63 and 65—66. The time limit, Pastor Brohm claims, is contrary to the doctrine of the divine call ("streitet schnurstracks wider die Lehre von der Goettlichkeit eines ordentlichen Berufs"). It is contrary to the law of love. Above all, it undermines the obedience which hearers owe their pastors. ("Der temporaere Beruf streitet wider den Gehorsam der Zuhoerer gegen ihren Lehrer und Seelsorger.") Those who think that the Missouri Synod's principle of congregational supremacy means that the congregation may do as it pleases should read this section of Brohm's article. Pastor Wyneken was still stronger in his denunciation of the temporary call. In his "Aufruf an die lutherische Kirche Deutschlands zur Unterstuetzung der Glaubensbrueder in Nordamerika," published in Dr. G. Ch. Adolph Harless' *Zeitschrift fuer Protestantismus und Kirche*, Vol. V (1843), pp. 124—170, Wyneken writes: "Nothing is more depressing than the sight of these so-called preachers and the manner in which congregations saddle themselves with these tramps. They are hired like cowhands, and oftentimes they are the most notorious characters and tricky deceivers." ("Nichts gibt ein betruebenderes Zeugnis von dem elenden Zustand der Gemeinden, als wenn man diese 'Prediger' sieht und die Art und Weise, wie die Gemeinden sie sich aufladen. Sie werden gedungen wie Viehhirten und sind oft die allergreulichsten Subjekte oder feine Betrueger.")

[44] In chapter II, which deals with conditions of membership, paragraph 5 reads: "Ordentlicher (nicht zeitweiliger) Beruf der Prediger und ordentliche Wahl der Deputierten durch die Gemeinden, sowie Unbescholtenheit des Wandels der Prediger und der Deputierten."

administration of their office. If a pastor after repeated admonitions refuses to desist from proclaiming false doctrine, or if he clings to an immoral way of living, the President must report the facts to the assembled Synod, which in turn must make a last concerted effort to win the sinner from the error of his way. If the Synod is unsuccessful, the pastor in question must be expelled from membership in Synod, and — here the Missouri system differs from that of other Lutheran synods in America [45] — his congregation must deal with him on the basis of Matt. 18: 17—20 and, if necessary, excommunicate him. The right to depose a pastor from office remains definitely in the hands of the congregation.

In addition to the supervision and control which the President is to exercise over the pastors and teachers of parish schools the constitution provides for a rather rigid control over the congregations. The President is to visit every congregation at least once during each term of office. In the course of this visit he is to examine the spiritual condition of the congregation. Is the congregation using an orthodox form of worship in its public services? Are the hymnbooks in agreement with the Confessional Writings of the Lutheran Church? Is there anything in the schoolbooks that offends against the Word of God? Are all the provisions in the constitution of the congregation in agreement with Lutheran doctrine? Are all the children properly baptized? Are all children of confirmation age confirmed? Is the Bible and devotional literature read in the homes? The President is also empowered by the constitution to ask the officers of the congregation for a meeting of the voting members. In this meeting the relationship between pastor and congregation is to be thoroughly reviewed. A complete report on the findings of each visitation is to be rendered to the assembled Synod.[46]

---

[45] See Constitution of the Missouri Synod, Art. XIII.

[46] Chapter VI of the constitution lists the rights and duties of the officers. Paragraph 7 of this chapter reads: "Der Praeses hat allen Fleiss anzuwenden, waehrend seiner dreijaehrigen Amtsverwaltung jedes Kirchspiel des Synodalbezirks wenigstens einmal zu besuchen, worueber er bei der jaehrlichen Synodalversammlung seinen Bericht erstattet." Chapter V of the 1846 constitution sets up the rules for the execution of Synod's business. Paragraph 7 of this chapter reads as follows: "Die Synode fordert von dem Praeses Bericht von den Ergebnissen seiner nach Instruktion im vergangenen Jahre gemachten Besuchsreisen, um Lehre, Leben und Amtsfuehrung der Prediger und Schullehrer zu beaufsichtigen. Sollte hierbei der Fall eintreten, dass der Praeses einen Prediger bei der Synode anzeigte, welcher selbst nach mehrmaliger Ermahnung des Praeses, der betreffenden Gemeinde und des Ministerii in

This provision inaugurating and safeguarding synodical supervision (*Lehrzucht, Synodalzucht*) was a powerful device. Very few realized the power that was given to the President in these paragraphs. Since Walther and his Saxon associates took every occasion to emphasize the tenet that the Synod was an advisory body only, the full force of the supervisory powers of Synod was not always so keenly felt; or, if felt, the feeling was soon benumbed by repeated testimony as to the advisory character of Synod.[47] As a matter of fact, through this arrangement Synod could exercise, and did exercise, control over the lives of all its pastors and

---

falscher Lehre oder aergerlichem Wandel beharrte, so macht die Synode in ihrer Gesamtheit den letzten Versuch, den Angezeigten von dem Irrtum seines Weges zu bekehren. Hoert der also Bestrafte nun auch die Synode nicht, so wird er von derselben ausgeschlossen, und die Gemeinde desselben hat an ihm Christi Befehl, Matth. 18, 17: "Hoeret er die Gemeinde nicht, so halte ihn als einen Heiden und Zoellner," auszufuehren. Auch hat der Praeses ueber den kirchlichen Zustand der besuchten Gemeinde Bericht zu erstatten, unter anderem, ob er in derselben Gemeinde- oder Kirchenordnungen, Buecher fuer Kirche und Schule und dergl. vorgefunden habe, deren Inhalt mit dem Bekenntniss der reinen Lehre in Widerspruch steht. Es ist dem Praeses waehrend seines Aufenthaltes unter den besuchten Gemeinden gestattet, durch den Vorstand der letzteren eine Gemeindeversammlung zusammenzuberufen." In the first convention of the Missouri Synod in the following year a set of rules consisting of thirteen paragraphs was adopted. The regulations were called: "Instruction for the President of the German Evangelical Lutheran Synod of Missouri, Ohio, and Other States concerning supervisory visits." *Synodal-Bericht*, 1847, pp. 13—14. These rules follow the constitution quite closely. The rules take care of details not mentioned in the constitution. For example, the President is to announce his coming to the pastor concerned. However, if the President sees fit, he may come unannounced. He must hear the pastor preach at least once during his visit. This sermon must be preached before the assembled congregation. The President is to observe the liturgical activity of the pastor in the service. The President should try to ascertain whether church discipline (*Kirchenzucht*) is being exercised. In his reports to Synod he is not to reveal anything that might unnecessarily harm the pastor whom he has visited.

[47] The presidential address delivered by Pastor Walther at the second convention of Synod in St. Louis, June 21, 1848, and published in *Synodal-Bericht*, 1848, pp. 30—38, is a highly effective attempt to promote adherence to the purely advisory character of Synod. On page 31 the President says: "According to our constitution we have only the power to advise; we have only the power of the Word, only the power to persuade. We may not issue decrees, establish rules, make laws, sit in judgment concerning any matters that we might wish to impose on our congregations, demanding that they must absolutely submit to our impositions. According to our constitution our Synod is not a sort of consistory, certainly not the highest ecclesiastical court. Quite the contrary. Our constitution grants to our congregations in all matters full liberty, nothing excepted but the Word of God, faith, and love. Constitutionally our Synod is not above our congregations, but in them, for the purpose of giving them assistance." It should be noted that this address was given in the presence of his home congregation. Men who had been consistently upholding congregational rights were sitting in the audience.

teachers and over all the doctrine taught in the member churches. It is no exaggeration to say that this provision made it possible for an energetic President of Synod to determine what should be taught, how it should be taught, and who should do the teaching. Given the other provision of the constitution that all matters of doctrine and faith are to be decided by the Word of God and not by majority vote, the President of Synod could exercise influence over doctrine and life of both pastor and congregation altogether out of keeping with the commonly accepted concept of a strictly independent local congregation.

An energetic and strong-willed President could within the framework of these supervisory powers shape the policies of the local congregation in spite of all talk of congregational supremacy. Strictly speaking, there is a logical antithesis between the supervisory powers given to the President of Synod in the constitution of 1846 and the principle of congregational supremacy so tenaciously defended by a group led particularly by certain members of Trinity Congregation, St. Louis. Any congregation that is willing to submit to the supervision and control provided for in this section of the constitution is yielding its independence in exchange for the spiritual blessings which, presumably, would accrue to it from such synodical supervision.

As a matter of fact, both congregations and pastors did submit to rather rigid supervision. Dr. William Sihler, pastor of St. Paul's in Fort Wayne and the first permanent Vice-President of the Missouri Synod, gives a detailed report in his *Lebenslauf,* II, pp. 112—116, of the manner in which he conducted these supervisory visitations. Being thoroughly convinced of the value of this institution, he tells us, he questioned congregations and pastors in great detail. His questions, so he informs us, centered on such things as family devotions (*Hausgottesdienst*), church attendance, school attendance, announcement for Communion (*Beichtanmeldung*), moral conditions in the congregation, separatistic movements, private conventicles (*Konventikelwesen*), reading of *Der Lutheraner,* and the administration of his office by the pastor (*Amtsfuehrung des Pastors*). The pastor who was being visited was asked to supply the supervising President, or in this case his substitute, with a sheaf of sermon MSS., preferably of those recently preached. In the privacy of the pastor's study Sihler would inquire into many details of the local pastor's administration which could not be discussed in the open meeting of the congregation ("eine bruederliche, vertrauliche Ruecksprache").[48]

The supervision which was exercised over pastors already in office did not mean that Synod was little concerned about the men who asked to be admitted as pastors. Quite the contrary is true. The constitution of 1846 provided that men who were not known or who could not present sufficient evidence concerning their doctrine and conduct could not become members of the body.[49] Furthermore, one of the chief functions of the Synod, as the framers of the constitution saw it, was the education and training of its own ministry.[50] The importance of a home-grown and home-trained ministry was ever before the constitution makers. In this matter Walther and the Saxons were ahead of Muhlenberg and the theologians of the Atlantic fringe. There never was a time when the Missouri Synod did not have its own system of institutions for the training of an indigenous ministry. The importance of this fact as a means of control should not be overlooked. Through its own educational institutions Synod determined the type of minister that would serve the member churches. The unusual uniformity among Missouri Synod clergymen, so often noticed by non-Missourians, has its origin in the educational system of the Synod. The power of this control device was enhanced when the office of the Presidency and the position of chief theological professor were combined in one forceful and overpowering leader.[51] A standing board of examiners, consisting of two men

---

[48] In his *Lebenslauf* Sihler gives the impression that every effort was made not to hurt the pastor who was being visited. The present writer visited Fort Wayne in June, 1941, and one responsible elderly churchman who knew Sihler gave him the impression that Sihler's efforts to refrain from hurting were none too strong. He seems to have been particularly outspoken when he visited the schools. The teacher's work was bitterly criticized in the presence of the children. Everybody in his congregation and many people in the Missouri Synod knew that he was a former Prussian army officer, and that fact probably contributed somewhat to the apocryphal accounts of his sternness.

[49] Chapter II, paragraph 8, read: "Unbekannte koennen nicht als Glieder der Synode eintreten, es sei denn, dass sie sich, was Lehre und Leben betrifft, gehoerig legitimieren koennen."

[50] Chapter I of the constitution gives the reasons for organizing a synod; and paragraph 6 mentions the erection and maintenance of a seminary for the education of ministers as one reason.

[51] C. F. W. Walther, the chief theological professor of the Missouri Synod from the day of its inception until the day of his death in May, 1887, was President of the Synod from 1847 to 1850 and again from 1864 to 1878.

reputed as expert theologians and the President of Synod, was to supervise an oral and written examination to which everyone, even those who laid claim to a complete theological education ("eine voellige theologische Ausbildung") according to the pattern of a German university, had to submit. The control of the pastors in the Synod was as complete as the constitution could make it.

We have already touched upon the control which Synod exercised over its congregations by means of presidential supervision. An additional control should not be overlooked. It lay in the method in which Synod dealt with congregations that were without a pastor and appealed to Synod to supply them with one. The President was to gather all available information regarding the congregation and then suggest suitable men for the congregation. However, if the congregation was a "mixed" congregation, that is, if it consisted of Lutherans and Reformed — and there were many such in the forties and fifties of the nineteenth century [52] — then the President was not to reject them offhand but to inform them with all candor and yet with all charity that they would be granted a pastor if they submitted to the authority of God's Word as the Lutheran Church does; if they would adhere to and confess that doctrine, especially as it concerns the doctrine of the blessed Sacrament and the Office of the Keys, and condemn every contrary doctrine as unscriptural; and if they would declare that by their participation of the Holy Supper in a Lutheran service they enter into communion with the Lutheran Church and cease being Reformed or whatever they were before.[53]

---

[52] Cf. Wyneken's "Aufruf an die lutherische Kirche Deutschlands," in Harless' *Zeitschrift fuer Protestantismus und Kirche*, Vol. V, p. 155. Kraushaar, *Verfassungsformen*, p. 8.

[53] The constitution reveals that every attempt was made to keep discordant elements out of the Synod. The founding fathers wanted unity on the basis of Lutheran doctrine above everything else. In paragraph 2 of chapter I they gave as a reason for the founding of Synod the establishment and preservation of unity on the basis of the Lutheran Confessions ("Erhaltung und Foerderung der Einheit des reinen Bekenntnisses und gemeinsamer Abwehr des separatistischen und sektiererischen Unwesens"). The position of Synod on mixed congregations was made specific in chapter V, paragraph 12: "Falls predigerlose lutherische Gemeinden die Synode um Prediger angehen, so hat dieselbe ernstliche Sorge zu tragen, dass erstere so bald als moeglich mit treuen Hirten versorgt werden, indem die Synode diesen Gemeinden Kandidaten fuer das vakante Pfarramt vorschlaegt. Sollte jedoch die bittstellende Gemeinde eine bis dahin gemischte, d. i., aus Lutheranern, Reformirten und sogenannten Evangelischen oder Unirten bestehende sein, so wird

Another control device was a codified attitude on the part of the Synod concerning the question of uniform liturgy. While the framers of the constitution remained faithful to Article VII of the Unaltered Augsburg Confession in that their demand for uniformity was not absolute, they did insist rather vigorously that the member congregations leave no stone unturned in their efforts to introduce uniform ceremonies. The constitution even goes so far as to claim that uniformity in liturgy, especially if this liturgy is increased and developed according to Lutheran standards, will be helpful in purifying the American Lutheran Church of its Reformed excrescences.[54]

Such, then, were the provisions of the constitution as adopted in Fort Wayne during the first two weeks of July, 1846. On the one hand, there was a deep regard for the rights of the local congregation. On the other, there were sufficient provisions for the concentration of power to insure efficient administration. Was the constitution satisfactory? Not entirely. At least not to the

---

sie zwar mit ihrem Gesuch nicht ohne weiteres zurueckgewiesen, doch erfordert es die Ehre Gottes, die christliche Aufrichtigkeit und Lauterkeit und die wahre Liebe des Naechsten, dass eine solche Gemeinde nur unter folgenden Bedingungen von einem Prediger der Synode bedient werden kann: a. wenn sie erklaert, sich dem Worte Gottes, wie allein die lutherische Kirche tut, unbedingt unterwerfen zu wollen; b. wenn sie sich demzufolge nach vorhergegangener Belehrung zu der allein schriftgetreuen Lehre der evangelisch-lutherischen Kirche, namentlich von den heiligen Sacramenten und dem Amt der Schluessel, bekennet und die Gegenlehre als schriftwidrig verwirft; c. wenn die vormals Nichtlutherischen der Erklaerung beipflichten, dass sie durch das Empfangen des heiligen Abendmahls aus der Hand eines Dieners der lutherischen Kirche oeffentlich in die Gemeinschaft der lutherischen Kirche eintreten und hiermit aufhoeren, Reformirte, sogenannte Evangelische oder Unirte und dergleichen zu sein."

54 The fact that a wave of revivalism and "New Measurism" was sweeping the land in the years 1830—1850 had a damaging effect on all liturgy. Revivalism is essentially antiliturgical. Fixed forms of worship were regarded as unspiritual. The leaders of the Lutheran General Synod were particularly affected by revivalism. Chapter V, paragraph 14, of the Fort Wayne constitution should be read in the light of these facts: "Zwar haelt die Synode dafuer, dass dem siebenten Artikel der Augsburgischen Konfession gemaess Gleichfoermigkeit der Zeremonien zu wahrer Einigkeit der christlichen Kirche nicht noetig sei, doch erscheint ihr andrerseits eine solche Gleichfoermigkeit heilsam und zweckmaessig, und zwar aus folgenden Gruenden: a. weil durch eine gaenzliche Verschiedenheit in den aeusserlichen Zeremonien die Schwachen an der Lehreinigkeit der Kirche leicht irre werden; b. weil die Kirche in Abschaffung bereits bewaehrter Braeuche und Weisen den Schein der Neuerungssucht und Leichtfertigkeit vermeiden soll. Uebrigens achtet die Synode dies auch fuer noetig zur Reinigung der amerikanisch-lutherischen Kirche, dass der Leerheit und Duerftigkeit in dem Aeusserlichen des Gottesdienstes entgegengearbeitet werde, die durch das Eindringen des falschen reformirten Geistes hier herrschend geworden ist."

anticlerical group in Trinity Congregation, St. Louis, who still remembered the great financial losses and the grief which they had
suffered when ecclesiastical power was vested in the clergy. Before the first meeting of the proposed Synod of Missouri, Ohio,
and Other States was held in Chicago, Illinois, April, 1847, these
hypersensitive brethren went over the constitution once more
with a fine toothcomb in the meetings of their congregation.
Finally they prepared what they thought was an airtight paragraph safeguarding the supremacy of the congregation against
any and all possible clerical encroachments. In the wording
adopted at Chicago this paragraph read: "Since Synod in its
relation to the government of the individual congregation is merely
an advisory body, the resolutions of Synod are to have no binding
effect on the individual congregation until a congregation has examined them in a formal meeting of its own and adopted them as its
own. If a congregation considers a resolution of Synod contrary
to the Word of God or unsuited to its conditions, it shall have the
right to reject such resolution." [55]

---

[55] In the original the resolution read: "Beschlossen: Als Zusatz zur
Konstitution soll den betreffenden Gemeinden zur Bestaetigung oder resp.
Zurueckweisung folgendes vorgelegt werden: Da die Synode in betreff der
Selbstregierung der einzelnen Gemeinden nur ein beratender Koerper ist,
so hat kein Beschluss der erstern, wenn selbiger der einzelnen Gemeinde
etwas auferlegt, fuer letztere bindende Kraft.   Verbindlichkeit kann ein
solcher Synodalbeschluss erst dann haben, wenn ihn die einzelne Gemeinde
geprueft und durch einen foermlichen Gemeindebeschluss freiwillig angenommen und bestaetigt hat. Findet eine Gemeinde den Beschluss nicht dem
Worte Gottes gemaess oder fuer ihre Verhaeltnisse ungeeignet, so hat sie das
Recht, den Beschluss zu verwerfen." *Synodal-Bericht,* 1847, p. 7. The adoption
of this paragraph in the meeting of 1847 did not mean that it was now a part
of the constitution. The congregations had to vote on this paragraph in their
separate meetings. *Synodal-Bericht,* 1848, p. 62, reports that several pastors
had forgotten to submit this change in the constitution to their congregations.
The Secretary was instructed to write every pastor who had not submitted
the change to his congregation and to ask him for an answer within six weeks.
It is highly significant that Mr. F. W. Barthel, a lay delegate from St. Louis,
flayed the negligence of such pastors. He suggested that hereafter a congregation which did not vote against a proposed amendment or did not vote at all
should be regarded as one that had voted for it. In *Synodal-Bericht,* 1849,
second edition, p. 83, the Secretary reports that most of the congregations
had neglected to vote on the St. Louis amendment. *Synodal-Bericht,* 1850,
p. 126, second edition, reports that the amendment had not gained the support
of every congregation and therefore must be considered lost. However, in
1854 the constitution of the Missouri Synod was revised. This revision, which
contains the paragraph submitted by the St. Louis laymen, was adopted and
received the approval of all the congregations. Since the amendment was
in keeping with the constitution, and since it was honored by the administration,
one can safely say that it was a part of the Synod's constitution from the first
meeting in Chicago. For a twentieth-century interpretation of this paragraph
compare the *Lutheran Witness,* LII, p. 163, or *Der Lutheraner,* LXXXIX
(1933), p. 146. Cf. also *Synodical Proceedings,* 1932, p. 162.

When the report on the constitution came to Pfarrer Loehe of Neuendettelsau, Bavaria — the man who had prepared and sent so many young conservative men into the service of the North American Lutheran Church — he remarked: "The entire report gives the impression of something that is compact and complete. . . . It is too bad that the synod has not yet grown more mature in its attitudes on constitutional matters. However, it cannot be denied that this constitution, compared with all other constitutions of Protestant organizations in North America that have come to my attention, is by far the most serviceable and the best." [56]

What was there about this constitution that was different from the constitutions of other Lutheran bodies then existing in the United States? In the first place, it had a different history. It was the first constitution of a Lutheran synod on American soil in the making of which laymen had a direct hand. Even at that late date the Lutheran churches of the various principalities of Germany and of the various States of America were *Pastorenkirchen*, that is, clergy-managed and clergy-controlled churches. The laymen were silent partners of the company. While Luther and the framers of *Kirchenordnungen* in the sixteenth century recognized and assigned a certain role to the common people ("das gemeine Volk") in the government of the Church, the constitutional forms of the Lutheran Church in the various German states and principalities of the seventeenth and eighteenth centuries tended to take on the color and shape of a police-state whose power — in part absolute — rested on the purely physical strength of the state governments. In the *Kultusministerium* of the nineteenth century there was a complete knotting up of political and spiritual powers. The part that laymen played in the government of the local congregations and in the provincial churches of Germany was, as we have seen in the chapter on the Saxon Church in this present study, pitifully small and insignificant.

Since the American Lutheran Church of the eighteenth century

---

[56] *Kirchliche Mittheilungen aus und ueber Nordamerika*, 1848, also quoted in Kraushaar, *Verfassungsformen*, p. 243: "Der ganze Synodalbericht gibt den Eindruck von etwas Festem und Fertigem. . . . Zu bedauern ist freilich, dass die Synode noch nicht zu besseren Ansichten ruecksichtlich der Verfassung gereift ist; aber das ist doch auch wieder nicht zu verkennen, dass ihre Synodalkonstitution im Vergleich mit allen uns bekannt gewordenen protestantischen Synodalkonstitutionen Nordamerikas bei weitem das Meiste und das Beste liefert."

was tied very closely to her mother in Europe, the constitutional development noticeable in the European mother are evident in the American daughter. The "mother of all American Lutheran synods," the Pennsylvania Ministerium, organized in 1748, was largely what its name implied, an organization of ministers, a continuation and solidification of the more or less loosely and irregularly conducted pastoral conferences of the previous decade. The laymen present were on hand merely to bring complaints or to ask for services.[57] In the constitution of the Missouri Synod, on the

---

[57] Kraushaar, *Verfassungsformen*, pp. 224—229, presents the minutes of the first meeting. The following items are relevant to the present study: Only ministers make motions and vote on them. In the contract ("Revers") which Pennsylvania ministers made with their congregations, they promised solemnly "not to undertake anything of importance without first consulting the Reverend College of Ministers and obtaining their approval and to act according to their advice and instruction." On pp. 231—232 Kraushaar prints the contract of John Nik. Kurtz with the congregation of Tulpehocken, dated August 13, 1748. According to paragraph 5 of this contract the contracting pastor agrees not to undertake anything of importance in his congregation without the consent of the Reverend College of Ministers ("nichts Wichtiges weder allein noch mit dem Kirchenrath [the officers of the local congregation] vorzunehmen, ohne solches vorher mit dem Rev.'d Collegio Pastorum communiciret und ihr Gutachten darueber vernommen zu haben, auch in dem guten Rath und Anweisung derselben zu beruhen." Paragraph 6 of this contract reads: ". . . auf Erfordern bei dem Rev.'d Collegio Pastorum muendliche oder schriftliche Rechenschaft von meiner Amtsfuehrung zu thun." According to the constitution of the Pennsylvania Ministerium of 1781 only ministers are members. See Kraushaar, *Verfassungsformen*, pp. 233—244; *Documentary History of the Evangelical Lutheran Ministerium of Pennsylvania and Other States*, p. 165. Candidates are admitted to ordination only after majority vote of the pastors. Only men who have served an apprenticeship under an American Lutheran pastor or who have been trained for the ministry in a European institution, e. g., Halle, may be admitted to examinations. The apprenticeship is standardized. The Ministerium removes from office a pastor who has made himself unworthy of continued service. While the revised constitution of 1792, which was changed in a few minor details in 1842, admitted laymen to the meetings of the Ministerium as voters, it did not permit them to vote in the most important matters. The laymen had nothing to say in matters pertaining to the office of the ministry, orthodoxy, reception of new members, expulsion of members who had given grave offense, and other important matters ("und andere aehnliche Faelle"). In other words, they were given the right to vote, but nothing to vote on. When the Missouri Synod was organized, the Pennsylvania Ministerium was still a *Pastorensynode* and nothing else. This fact was evident even in such comparatively insignificant matters as the hospitality which entertaining congregations were obliged to show members when the organization met in their midst. While the entertaining congregation had to provide shelter and food for pastors and their horses, they did not have to provide this service for any laymen that were present. See Kraushaar, *op. cit.*, pp. 245—252.

What has been said of the preponderance of clerical authority in the Pennsylvania Ministerium can be repeated with slight variations for the New York Ministerium. The New York Ministerium was the oldest daughter of the Pennsylvania Ministerium and naturally followed in her mother's

other hand, the balance of power between laymen and pastors was the most carefully guarded provision in the entire document. This provision must be credited in large part to the energetic participation in constitution making on the part of the laymen of St. Louis.

A second characteristic of the Missouri Synod's constitution was that it placed definite limitations on the powers of both the clergy and the laymen. Not since the sixteenth century, and never on American soil, had a body of men so completely and so sincerely subscribed to the Unaltered Augsburg Confession and its Apology, the Smalcald Articles, the Catechisms of Luther, and the Formula of Concord. They regarded these instruments as clear and true expositions of the meaning of the inspired Word of God, and they declared their readiness to abide by the decisions of the Lutheran Confessional Writings. Only such doctrines could be taught, and only such policies could be carried out, as in no wise conflicted with the Lutheran teachings of the sixteenth century. The respect which these men had for any opinion of Luther is indescribable. Where Luther had spoken, the case was settled.[58]

A factor not to be overlooked in an interpretation of the Missouri Synod's constitution is that it was formulated by men who had cut off all connections with the European Church. While still in Germany, the men who later took the lead in framing the constitution had been in bitter conflict with the constituted authorities. Repeated lawsuits and certain types of chicanery practiced by church officials had made them bitter. Walther especially could

---

footsteps. It should be said, however, that the New York Ministerium moved in the direction of lay participation in government at a slightly accelerated rate of speed. The New York Ministerium adopted its first constitution in 1794. In the constitution of 1816, which was in force with only slight alterations until 1870, the voting power of laymen was definitely limited. Kraushaar reprints the constitution of 1794 on pp. 259—262. The revised constitution of 1816 is found on pp. 262—266.

[58] While the constitution of the Pennsylvania Ministerium as adopted in 1781 mentions the Synodical Writings of the Lutheran Church in the paragraphs which concern the proper procedure in removing a pastor from office (see Kraushaar, *op. cit.*, p. 146), the revision of 1792, which was not revised until 1841, and then only slightly, has deleted all reference to the Symbolical Books of the Lutheran Church. Cf. Kraushaar, *op. cit.*, pp. 245—254. The constitution of the New York Ministerium, dated 1816 (slightly revised in 1836), contained no reference whatever to the Lutheran Confessions. Cf. Kraushaar, *op. cit.*, pp. 262—266. The constitution of the General Synod as adopted for all district synods in 1829 followed the 1792 constitution of the Pennsylvania Ministerium and omitted all obligations to abide by the Confessional Writings of the Lutheran Church. For this constitution cf. Kraushaar, *op. cit.*, pp. 295—307.

not think of re-establishing relationship with ecclesiastical official-
dom in Saxony.   Nor would he take kindly to any device or help
that might come from his former tormentors.[59]   He had cast his lot
completely with the American frontiersmen.   With his back turned
on Germany, he set his face resolutely to the problems of the Lutheran Church on the American frontier.   The severance of all
connections with Germany made him more independent and more
realistic in his attempts to solve constitutional problems of the
American Lutheran Church.   The question what the contemporary
theologians of Germany might say apparently never bothered him.
In this respect he differed from Muhlenberg.[60]

Though the constitution made the congregation the possessor
of all church power and the highest tribunal, it did safeguard the
ministry in various ways.   The tenure of office was made permanent.   No calls to pastors providing for a time limit were tolerated
in the Missouri Synod.[61]   The doctrine of the divinity of the call,

---

[59] In 1855 the University of Goettingen, the alma mater of Walther's friend
F. C. D. Wyneken, offered Walther an honorary doctor's degree in theology.
Walther declined politely but firmly.   In 1878 Capital University of Columbus,
Ohio, offered him the same degree, and Walther accepted the honor.   See
Walther's letter to Fick, August 11, 1855, in *Walthers Briefe*, I, p. 99.

[60] The fathers of the older synods, particularly the Pennsylvania Ministerium, made most of their decisions with one eye on the ecclesiastical
leaders back home in Europe.   In addressing the Synod of the Pennsylvania
Ministerium in 1748 H. M. Muhlenberg said: "We preachers present here today
did not come to our congregations of our own accord.   We were called and
urged.   We must give an account before God and our conscience.   *We have
connections with our fathers in Europe.*"   Cf. Kraushaar, *Verfassungsformen*,
p. 226.   When Muhlenberg was asked why certain pastors were not invited
to the meeting, he replied by saying, "These men are under no consistory
and are under no obligation to give an account of their stewardship."
Kraushaar, *op. cit.*, p. 228.   The written instruction of Dr. Francke at Halle was
a part of Pastor Kurtz's contract with the congregation at Tulpehocken.
Cf. Kraushaar, *op. cit.*, p. 231.   In the constitution of 1781 candidates for the
ministry coming from Halle were favored in the procedure of admitting men
to ordination.   Kraushaar, *op. cit.*, p. 237.

[61] The evils of calls with a time limit are brought out with forceful
language by Pastor Brohm in an article published in *Der Lutheraner*, I (1845),
pp. 61—63 and 65—66.   "We can in no wise approve of a call with a time limit.
Such calls are altogether unworthy of a Lutheran congregation, because they
are in direct conflict with the doctrine of the divinity of the call;   because
they militate against the law of love;   and because they tend to destroy the
obedience which members of the flock owe to their pastors."   Cf. also Wyneken's

that is, that every pastor is called by God and placed in his respective parish by the Holy Ghost through the instrumentality of the local congregation, was a provision that greatly increased the respect for the office of the ministry. There were endless exhortations to respect the pastor. Many Missouri Synod churches had the words of Christ "He that heareth you heareth Me" embroidered on the antependia of their pulpits. This statement was also painted on the east walls of the churches before the eyes of the worshiping congregations.

The fact that the constitution provided for the training of ministers by Synod in Synod's own institutions and that a comparatively high standard of training was set very early surrounded the minister with a halo of learning. This was particularly important among the immigrants on the frontier.[62] At that time the average educa-

---

famous cry for help, *Die Noth der deutschen Lutheraner in Nordamerika*, reprinted in pamphlet form in Pittsburgh, 37 pages. Cf. *Der Lutheraner*, I (1844), pp. 31—32. Wyneken compares pastors whose calls have a time limit to cowhands ("Kuhhirten"). In Vol. III (1846), p. 8, Walther takes a decided stand against a call with a time limit. "Unfortunately it has become customary in our country to hire ministers for one year, even as we hire our servants and cattle herders. Many congregations have adopted this measure as a defense against vagabonds who tramp about our land in order to deceive our congregations. It would be far better if our congregations did not permit these untried and untested customers ('Gesellen') to preach a single sermon. With one sermon they can do irreparable damage to the souls of men. Even in emergencies these calls with a time limit cannot be justified. It is not proper for a pastor or a candidate of theology to accept such a call, because it is contrary to Scripture, contrary to ecclesiastical administration ('kirchliche Praxis'), and contrary to the dignity of the ministerial office ('streitet wider die Wuerde des Predigtamts'). Holy Scripture and the Church know only of a call for life ('Die Heilige Schrift und die Kirche weiss nur von einem Beruf auf Lebenszeit')." Incidentally, in this same article Walther opposes the system of licensing pastors, which was in vogue in Eastern synods, because the system tends to undermine confidence in the man who has been licensed. Walther would avoid everything that might detract from the dignity of the ministerial office.

[62] Cf. Pastor G. H. Loeber's lengthy report on the seminary in Perry County, *Der Lutheraner*, I (1845), pp. 93—95. All the instructors were graduates of German universities. The school combined the German Gymnasium and the subjects usually taught by the theological faculty in a German university. The subjects were: Greek, Latin, Hebrew, German, English, French, geography, history, arithmetic, geometry, drawing, music, church history, exegesis, dogmatics, symbolics, catechetics, logic, and psychology. The normal time to complete the course was nine years.

tion of the Methodist ministers was somewhere between the fifth and the eighth grade of an elementary school or its equivalent. The immigrant Lutheran on the frontier knew that his pastor was smart. No one on the frontier had an education that could approach that of his pastor. What his pastor said must be right. He had been at "college" nine years and was smarter than most doctors and lawyers. The prestige of a college education, especially among the Germans on the frontier, can hardly be overestimated. The permanency of the call coupled with the doctrine of the divinity of the call and a college education gave the Missouri Synod minister a position in his congregation which few men of his profession enjoyed.[63]

---

[63] Even as late as 1920 Sinclair Lewis made the claim that the Catholic priest and the Lutheran minister were the only educated persons in the typical small town of the Northwest.

CHAPTER SEVEN

====

CONCLUSIONS

THE PECULIAR TYPE of decentralized government adopted by the congregations which formed the Missouri Synod was different from any polity that had ever existed or was then existing in Germany. As indicated in Chapter II, the Christian layman and laywoman in the Lutheran Church of Germany played a rather insignificant part in handling the affairs of the local congregation. An association of congregations forming a synod in the American sense of the term was nonexistent. Aside from the fact that lawyers were appointed to act in conjunction with theologians in the consistory, laymen had counted for nothing in the management of provincial church groups.

The conclusion that the Missourians picked up the fundamentals of their church polity on American soil seemed very obvious. At a time when popular sovereignty was advanced as the panacea for political and economic ills a church body founded on the principle of congregational sovereignty in the land of the free could hardly escape the suspicion of being influenced by political theory in the formulation of its church polity. A friend of the Missourians, Pfarrer Loehe of Neuendettelsau, Bavaria, was perhaps the first man to draw the conclusion that seemed to be so close at hand. In his *Kirchliche Mittheilungen aus und ueber Nordamerika* he writes:

> Finally we do not wish to keep you in ignorance concerning something which has cut us to the quick and which also is of importance for the seminary at Fort Wayne. We notice with growing concern ("mit herzlichem Bedauern") that your synodical constitution, as it has now been adopted, does not follow the example of the first Christian congregation. We have good reason to fear that the strong admixture of democratic, independent, and congregational principles in your constitution will do greater damage than the interference of princes and governmental agencies in the Church of our homeland.[1]

---

[1] Vol. VI, 44 (September 8, 1847). This quotation is from a letter which Loehe wrote to the officials of the Missouri Synod and in which he transferred

Loehe called the government setup of the Fort Wayne constitutional convention American mob rule ("amerikanische Poebelherrschaft"). He feared that the tactics used in political elections would soon be applied in the selection of pastors if laymen were given the right of suffrage in the calling of a pastor. In a book which he published two years after the organization of the Missouri Synod he writes:

> Look at the composition of our congregations. How can it be said that they are competent to judge the ability and worthiness of candidates for the holy ministry? The candidates do not even come from their midst, to say nothing of the fact that the spirit of our times might drive laymen to apply the same pernicious tactics in the selection of a pastor which they now use in the election of a representative in the legislature. No; the unlimited right of suffrage on the part of the congregation is not only nonapostolic but also downright dangerous.[2]

J. A. A. Grabau, pastor of an immigrant church in Buffalo and founder of the Buffalo Synod, beheld the "new independent freedom of individual congregations in all its nakedness and misery." [3] Among the recent writers Carl Mauelshagen and W. G. Polack indicate a belief that the Missourians found their peculiar church polity in American political theory. Mauelshagen, *op. cit.*, writes:

> It [the Missouri Synod] is a product of the German religious revival in the first half of the nineteenth century transplanted to the United States, where it imbibed rather distinctly American democratic characteristics. The reaction of its leaders against the rationalistic influence of the Age of Enlightenment made for a reversion to the fundamental confessions of sixteenth-century Lutheranism, while their re-

---

the title of the Fort Wayne seminary to the Missouri Synod. The entire letter was published in Loehe's bulletin.

2 Wm. Loehe, *Aphorismen ueber die Neutestamentlichen Aemter und ihr Verhaeltnis zur Gemeinde*, p. 59: "Von welcher Art und Zusammensetzung sind unsre Gemeinden! Wie sollten sie im stande sein, ueber Befaehigung und Wuerdigkeit von Candidaten zu urtheilen, welche nicht einmal aus ihrer Mitte sind! Gar nichts zu sagen von dem Geiste unsrer Zeit, der bei der Wahl eines Presbyters zu denselben Wuehlereien treiben koennte wie bei der Wahl eines Landtagsdeputierten. Nein! Ein unbedingtes Wahlrecht der Gemeinde ist nicht nur unapostolisch, sondern auch hoechst gefaehrlich."

3 Document No. 3. In "Der Hirtenbrief des Herrn Pastor Grabau," p. 43. "Wenn wir die neue independendistische Freiheit der einzelnen Gemeinden erst recht in ihrer Bloesse und Elend sehen koennten."

ligious experience in America and contact with a democratic environment were responsible for a turn in doctrine and polity which differentiated it from its German prototype.[4]

Speaking of Sihler's and Lochner's astonishment at the strong opposition which some of his members showed to Walther's plan for a synod as outlined in the May meetings, St. Louis, 1846, W. G. Polack writes:

> They (Sihler and Lochner) did not understand the strongly democratic character of Walther's parishioners and the depth of the Missouri 'show me' spirit they had imbibed in a very short time.[5]

There are several factors which make connection between the genesis of Missouri's polity and existing American democratic theory rather improbable. The resemblance between the theory of congregational supremacy and American popular sovereignty is more apparent than real. Only male communicant members of the church who had reached their twenty-first year had the right to vote. Furthermore, matters of doctrine and conscience which assumed great importance in the immigrant Church were not subject to popular vote, but were decided on the sole authority of the Scriptures. In such matters the Word of God hovered as a supreme authority over the congregation and Synod. This authority, be it remembered, was wielded officially and effectively by the pastor and by the synodical officials. In a sermon delivered upon the occasion of the twenty-fifth anniversary of the founding of the Missouri Synod at the jubilee convention, St. Louis, 1872, Walther said, "Reverence and implicit obedience are due the ministry when the pastor teaches the Word of God." [6] In his second *Synodalrede* Walther addressed the young Synod in its meeting at St. Louis, June 21, 1848 on the topic "Why should and why can we do the work of our Lord cheerfully even though we have no power but the power of the Word?" [7] This doctrine was not only preached, it was generally accepted in the Missouri Synod. There was profound respect for the minister

[4] Carl Mauelshagen, *op. cit.*, p. 125.

[5] W. G. Polack, *The Building of a Great Church*, p. 67.

[6] Quoted from W. G. Polack, *The Story of C. F. W. Walther*, p. 128.

[7] *Synodal-Bericht der deutschen Ev.-Luth. Synode von Missouri, Ohio u. a. Staaten*, 1848. The entire address, which is very helpful in understanding the "democratic" element in Missouri Synod polity, is found on pp. 30—38. The quotations are from pp. 36—37.

and his opinion. Jokes commonly cracked at the expense of the American preacher were unknown among the German Lutherans.

Walther realized the tremendous check that was placed upon popular sovereignty by the authority of the Word. In the above-quoted *Synodalrede* he tells his hearers that the theory of congregational supremacy will not lead to popular popery ("Volks-pabstthum") or shameful rule of the people ("schimpfliche Volks-herrschaft"). He said:

> Don't worry that the adoption of our church polity will lead to an influx of the secular elements of political democracy into the Church or that an enslaving rule of the people, a popery of the people, will develop among us. . . . A shameful rule of the people can develop only when the people disregard the Word of God. . . . Whenever the pastor preaches, he stands before his congregation with the power of the Word, not as a hired servant but as an ambassador of the most high God. He speaks as Christ's representative.

The pastors themselves were convinced of their dignity. Already in their seminary days special effort was made to impress them with the dignity of the ministerial office.[8] The people accepted this dignity as a matter of course. Every pastor they had seen in Germany was a highly honored man, a *Standesperson.* Why should their minister in America be different from their minister in the homeland in point of honor?

The authority and power believed to be inherent in the Word of God, the permanent tenure of office for all ministers of the Gospel, the doctrine that all pastors are divinely called when properly called by the congregation — these doctrines served as very effective checks upon any mob rule or any "shameful rule of the people" ("schimpfliche Volksherrschaft"). As Walther said, they prevented the secular elements of political democracy from entering the polity of the Church. In addition, they gave the pastor a position in the church that more than counter-

---

[8] In the Keyl MSS., now in possession of Dr. L. Fuerbringer, the present writer found a MS. of an address delivered before the entire student group of Concordia Seminary, St. Louis — the future ministers of the Missouri Synod — either by Dr. Walther or by his understudy, Professor Pieper. The speaker asserted, "A pastor must be thoroughly imbued with the dignity and glory of the Christian ministry. This attitude is necessary for the proper administration of the ministerial office." ("Ein Prediger muss von der Hoheit und Herrlichkeit des christlichen Predigtamtes lebendig durchdrungen sein. Das ist durchaus noethig zu einer rechten Amtsfuehrung.") 4. Vortrag (no pages given).

balanced any influence that might have come from the direction of any political theory of popular sovereignty.

The manner in which the Missourians obtained their church polity precludes any connection between it and the secular elements of political theory. Political theorists derived their theory of popular sovereignty from the nature of man and the nature of society. From the days of John Locke empiricism had dominated political thinking on the subject of popular sovereignty. The power of reason in human affairs was unfettered by any authoritarian considerations.[9] The framers of the Missouri Synod form of government on the other hand were authoritarians to the bone.[10] True, their authority in constitutional matters was not so much the Word of God as it was the word of Luther and of the sixteenth- and seventeenth-century dogmaticians. The doctrine of the priesthood of all believers came from the writings of Martin Luther. These writings, not the Bible, were the source from which they took their polity. We have previously referred to the authoritarian habit of Walther and his congregation of searching for *Zeugnisse* of Luther every time a question of church polity was to be decided. This same habit was carried over into the Synod.

Furthermore, the time element makes it very unlikely that the Missourians imbibed their ideas of church government from existing political theory. While the future Missourians were still in Germany, there was no demand on the part of the pastors or the laymen for participation in the government of the Church. In their complaints against the Consistory and the *Cultusministerium* one looks in vain for a request for lay participation in government. As a matter of fact, they knew little, if anything,

---

[9] H. H. Maurer, *The American Journal of Sociology*, Vol. XXX, pp. 257 to 286, "Studies in the Sociology of Religion," "The Sociology of Protestantism," writes on p. 257: "The fathers of the modern social order were distinguished by an unreasonable animus against religion and a mountain-moving faith in reason." C. E. Merriam, *Political Science Quarterly*, Vol. LIII, pp. 328—349, "The Assumptions of Democracy," presents the two chief assumptions, both of which are diametrically opposite to basic beliefs of the Missouri Synod. Merriam mentions 1. the essential dignity of man; 2. a constant drive toward the perfectibility of mankind. The Missourians believed in the total depravity of mankind and the *sola gratia* as its only means of escape from the wrath to come.

[10] J. L. Gruber in *Erinnerungen* maintains stoutly that the only difference between the authoritarianism of the Missouri Synod and that of the Pope is one of degree, not of kind.

about it. Had they made such a request, Stephan himself would
have been quick to brand it as insubordination. During the years
of their connection with Stephan, as we have previously indicated,
they were carefully conditioned in favor of a highly centralized
episcopal form of church government.

The demand for lay participation in the government of the
Church did not come until September 19, 1839. The demand
came from a group of laymen led by Dr. Eduard Vehse. At that
time these men had been in America barely six months. Most of
this time they had spent arranging for lodging and shelter and
food. The request grew out of the catastrophe brought about
by Martin Stephan. Only a calamity of major proportions could
have shaken them sufficiently to demand a share in the government
of their Church. Even then the clerical party, including C. F. W.
Walther, stoutly resisted, and continued to resist, their demand for
almost a year and a half.[11] The removal of Martin Stephan on
May 30, 1839, and all the misery that followed that event gave the

---

[11] Vehse gives an account of the clergy's resistance to the laymen's
demands in his *Die Stephan'sche Auswanderung*, Leipzig, 1841. The minutes
of the pastors' meeting called "Protocoll des Ministeriums" and dated September 4, 1839, and September 9, 1839, are still extant. They are signed by all
the pastors, including C. F. W. Walther. The account of the September 9 meeting is particularly pertinent. According to these minutes it had come to the
attention of the ministerium that Dr. Vehse was trying to undermine the
confidence of the laymen in the leadership of the clergy and that he was
trying to effect a change in polity ("Verfassung"). Therefore the ministerium
found itself forced to send out a circular letter warning all members against
Vehse and informing everyone that there would be no change in polity.
In this circular the clergy declare their readiness to defend their way of
doing things ("unsere Amtsfuehrung") and the existing polity. The circular,
which is part of the minutes, plainly indicates that the clergy intended to
continue a government of the clergy and by the clergy. At that time the
ministerium had no thought of granting the laymen the slightest participation
in the government of the Church. F. A. Marbach in his manifesto, dated
March 3, 1841, and entitled "An meine unter Pastor Stephan mitausgewanderten
deutschen Landsleute," has a great deal to say about the government of the
clergy and by the clergy. Marbach claims that the essence of Stephanism
was the indescribable respect and honor which was shown to Martin Stephan.
His word was God's word. The entire spiritual life of the colonists was
corrupted by the homage paid to Stephan's word. "We have removed the
person of Stephan, but we have not swept out the essence of Stephanism
from our midst." Then he goes on to give his version of the church government as conducted by the clergy. "After Stephan's removal the ministerium
took his place. The ministerium removed the right of candidacy from certain
men, put pastors into office, governed the congregation, deliberated on the
incorporation of the Church, carried on correspondence in the name of the
congregation without informing a single soul of the congregation, expelled
recalcitrants, that is, those who told the real truth, warned officially against
Dr. Vehse, claiming that the devil was in him."

laymen the necessary jolt to press for lay participation in the government of the Church. This misery drove them into the writings of Luther, and here the laymen found the weapons which they needed to win the battle for congregational supremacy from the power-jealous pastors.

The influence of American political theory upon the constitutional forms of the Missouri Synod seems still less likely when one recognizes the attitude of synodical leaders toward the use of the English language. Walther, Wyneken, and Sihler believed that there was a relationship of cause and effect between the use of the English language and the deterioration of doctrine and polity among the non-German speaking Christian groups in America. Very early in the history of the building of Trinity Church, St. Louis, Walther pressed a resolution through the voters' meeting that the new church then under discussion should never be used except for divine services in the German language.[12] Shortly thereafter he persuaded the congregation to insert a "language paragraph" into the constitution. This paragraph forbade the use of any language but German in the public services. It was aimed primarily at the use of the English language.[13]

As far as their attitude toward the use of the English language by the "Easterners" ("Sendlinge") is concerned, it should

---

12 The Minutes of February 21, 1842, contain the following: "The suggestion of the pastor that in the church we are about to build, the German language only be used in the public services was accepted unanimously. This resolution shall be part of that document." By "document" the secretary was probably referring to the articles of incorporation which the congregation had under consideration at the time. ("Der Vortrag des Herrn Pastor, dass in der zu erbauenden Kirche allein in der deutschen Sprache Gottesdienst gehalten werden moechte, wurde einstimmig angenommen! Und es soll dies ein Paragraph jenes Documents sein.")

13 The entire meeting of April 3, 1843, was devoted to the question whether the "language paragraph" in the constitution should be unalterable and irrepealable. The language paragraph said that the German language only should be used in the public services. After a long discussion it was decided to make this paragraph unalterable and irrepealable "since we regard this church as a foundation for German Lutherans for the maintenance of divine services" ("weil wir unsre Kirche als eine Stiftung fuer deutsche Lutheraner zur Erhaltung ihres Gottesdienstes ansehen"). In the next meeting, April 10, 1843, it was decided to put the unalterable and irrepealable paragraph 14 (the language paragraph) into a testament. "Paragraph 14 soll testamentarisch als unveraenderlich verschrieben werden." Evidently some members had some scruples about the unalterability and irrepealability of this paragraph. In the next meeting, April 17, 1843, it was voted that "the unalterability and irrepealability should not be regarded as a divine command" ("Die Unveraenderlichkeit Paragraphs 14 soll nicht als ein goettliches Gebot angesehen werden").

be remembered that Loehe had impressed upon his "Sendlinge" his belief that there was an inherent relationship between language and faith.[14]

At that time Walther saw eye to eye with the "Sendlinge" on the correlation between language and purity of faith. He writes to Sihler under date of January 2, 1845:

> There seems to be less danger that the German language will be replaced in our congregations here in the West than in the East and in the middle States. The Lutheran congregations here are exclusively German. There is no desire for services in the English language. . . . I presume that it is not necessary for me to write you that we are making every effort to maintain the German language in our midst and to keep out the evil leaven that begins to permeate pure doctrine and polity with the coming of the English language.[15]

Wyneken, next to Walther and Sihler the most influential member of the young Synod, shared their view concerning the

---

[14] In his *Kirchliche Mittheilungen,* 1843, No. 8, Loehe admonishes Teacher Baumgarten to assist the German settlers in preserving their Church and nationality. In 1844, No. 1, Loehe writes an article on "Dangers Which Threaten the German Language in North America" ("Gefahren fuers Deutsche in Nord-Amerika"). 1844, No. 6: Since the German language and customs are "the vanguard for the Evangelical Lutheran faith," Pastor G. W. Hattstaedt, who was stationed in Michigan and who later became a member of the Missouri Synod, was not permitted to serve congregations where the English language was in use. 1844, No. 11, Loehe expressed the fear that with the introduction of the English language at the seminary in Columbus, Ohio, "the English spirit — that is, the Methodistic spirit — would prevail." One reason why Sihler, a Loehe "Sendling," left the Ohio Synod was the use of the English language as a medium of instruction at the seminary in Columbus. Cf. his *Lebenslauf,* II, p. 34. Also *Der Lutheraner,* II (1846), p. 42. In *Kirchliche Mittheilungen,* 1844, No. 11, Pastor Ernst reports Sihler's intention "never to preach English so long as he is in America."

[15] *Walthers Briefe,* I, pp. 13—14. "Dass wir alle mit dem groessten Ernste darauf denken, alles zu tun, um die deutsche Sprache zu erhalten und den boesen Sauerteig abzuweisen, der sich mit der englischen Sprache hier so leicht der reinen Lehre und Verfassung beimischt, bedarf wohl keiner Erwaehnung." In a letter to Sihler, dated May 10, 1849, *Briefe,* I, p. 58, Walther shows his concern about the training of future ministers in German ideals. He is suggesting the Rev. Craemer of Michigan for a professorship. "Ich halte Craemern durchaus fuer den rechten Mann, junge Leute zu erziehen zu echt deutschen und echt lutherischen Predigern." In a letter to Pastor H. C. Schwan, dated March 7, 1864, *Briefe,* I, p. 199, Walther advocates the calling of Rev. J. C. W. Lindemann as director of the teacher-training seminary at Addison, Illinois. He (Walther) is aware of the fact that Lindemann knows little English and music, but he says that is of little consequence. ("Was ihm abgeht, Musik, Englisch, ist durchaus so nebensaechlich, dass ich meine, man sollte darauf keine Ruecksicht nehmen.") As late as March, 1842, C. F. W. Walther did not know enough English to translate a letter which he had written in the name of Trinity Congregation to the Vestry of Christ Church, St. Louis.

correlation of language and faith. In his "Aufruf" he describes the dangers threatening the German Lutherans on the frontier, and among these he lists the following:

> The children follow in the footsteps of their parents. Some grow up without the least bit of schooling. Others go to English schools and merely learn the things which are necessary for this life.[16]

The language barrier made it next to impossible at least for the laymen of the frontier to do much imbibing of democratic political theory.

If the founders of the Missouri Synod derived their principle of congregational supremacy from American political thought, some special interest in popular political sovereignty would be evident; at least, one would suspect some favorable reference to it. During his early years in America — the years during which the principle of congregational supremacy was developed among the Saxons — it can hardly be said that Walther was ardently active in any form of politics.[17] He was a regular reader of the German daily paper *Anzeiger des Westens*.[18] Though he was a member

---

[16] *Zeitschrift fuer Protestantismus und Kirche*, V, p. 127.

[17] He became an American citizen on Monday, March 8, 1847. He could have become a citizen three years earlier as far as the naturalization law was concerned. *Die deutsche Tribuene*, a German-language newspaper published in St. Louis, printed the following news item under date of Wednesday, March 10, 1847: "Carl W. Weise, Johann G. Schmidt, Carl F. W. Walther und Johann Heid wurden am Montag von der Court of Common Pleas naturalisiert."

[18] J. L. Gruber, *op. cit.*, p. 118. "Walther seems to have been imperfectly acquainted with political affairs. Most probably he derived his political knowledge from the Democratic *Anzeiger des Westens*, which was read almost exclusively in his congregation, since the Republican *Westliche Post* was under the ban because of its antichurch attitude. It was for this reason that Walther and most of the members of his congregation belonged to the Democratic Party." ("Walther scheint auf politischem Gebiet schlecht beschlagen gewesen zu sein. Wahrscheinlich zog er seine ganze politische Weisheit aus dem demokratischen *Anzeiger des Westens*, der fast ausschliesslich in der Gemeinde gelesen wurde; denn die republikanische *Westliche Post* stand ihrer kirchenfeindlichen Stellung wegen auf dem Interdikt; daher kam es wohl, dass Walther und die meisten Gemeindeglieder zur demokratischen Partei gehoerten.")

The *Westliche Post* was edited by a "Forty-eighter." At one time Carl Schurz was its editor. In an article of the *North American Review* (1856), p. 248 ff., entitled "German Emigration to America," the statement is made that one half of the German-language newspapers in America is controlled by the "Forty-eighters." As a group the "Forty-eighters" were exceedingly irreligious and hostile to both Roman Catholics and Lutherans. Cf. J. F. Rhodes, *History of the United States*, 1910, I, p. 495. Though the *Anzeiger des Westens* was not as inimical to the Church as was the *Westliche Post*, it was known as the mouthpiece of religious and political liberalism and as the

of the Democratic Party, it can hardly be said that he was an ardent student of politics.[19] This much is certain, Walther was not at all impressed with the contentions of the "Forty-eighters." His unfriendly reference to the liberal Germans as "deutsche Dema-

---

leading representative of enlightened German thought in the Middle West. Cf. Carl Schneider, *op. cit.*, p. 30. In *Der Lutheraner*, XVII (1861), p. 68, Walther calls the political papers "tools of Satan." In a sermon preached November 27, 1862, and printed in *Der Lutheraner*, XIX (1863), pp. 81—83, Walther speaks of "the godless atheistic press."

[19] Walther's chief concern was with life after this present existence. He was *Jenseitigkeitstheologe* par excellence; and for that reason, if for no other, he would not be likely to become rabidly partisan in politics. His transmundane interest is brought out in a letter to his daughter, Magdalene, dated January 9, 1870, *Walthers Briefe*, II, p. 172. "Life in this world has value only in so far as it prepares us for a blessed eternity." ("Das Leben auf dieser Erde hat ja nur so viel Wert, soviel wir dadurch zur Seligkeit vorbereitet werden.") Walther's political activity can be understood from a *Bekanntmachung* which some of the members of Trinity Congregation inserted in *Der Anzeiger des Westens* of November 26, 1844. Heinrich Koch, in his *Anti-Pfaff*, had made one of his periodic attacks upon Walther, accusing him of political activity. Thereupon Walther's friends inserted the following: "Several members of the Ev. Lutheran Congregation in St. Louis feel the obligation to refute the abominable lies and misrepresentations which the last number of the *Anti-Pfaff* has spread among the public against Pastor C. F. W. Walther and against his congregation, which the editor of the *Anti-Pfaff* has called "Stephanists." The *Anti-Pfaff* has created the impression that members of Trinity have voted for Clay and Frelinghuysen at the command of Pastor Walther. If the *Anti-Pfaff* were active only in the field of religion, we would pay little attention to its lies, blasphemies, and mudslinging, since he who touches filth is bound to soil his fingers. However, since the editor of the *Anti-Pfaff* has the unrestrained audacity to stir up the German public against us also in political matters, we believe that we have the double obligation to call him by his right name. It is true, some of our members have voted for Clay and Frelinghuysen, but they have done so of their own free will and conviction, and not at the command of their pastor. Incidentally, the majority of the congregation is democratic and voted for Polk and Dallas.

"We believe that we are living in a free country, in which the methods of the Inquisition are taboo, where one can live and move and have his being as he sees fit, as long as he obeys the laws of the land. We can assure you with absolute confidence that Pastor Walther never has made a political public address and that in private conversation he has not declared himself for or against any party. He believes that such political activities are not in keeping with the dignity of his ministerial office. We therefore declare Mr. Heinrich Koch, the editor of the *Anti-Pfaff*, an abominable liar and defamer so long as he does not mention by name the men of whom he says that Pastor Walther commanded them to vote as they did." . . . Signed by several members of the congregation.

Cf. C. F. W. Walther, *Communismus und Socialismus*. In the late 1870's a daily paper in the interest of the labor class was begun. About the same time an organization for laborers ("Arbeiterverein") was called into being. Since the daily paper in question, *Die Volksstimme des Westens*, was predominantly communistic, and since some of the younger men of the church were subscribing to the paper, Walther thought it proper to give a set of four lectures to the men of his church. The lectures were published in a brochure of sixty pages. On page 7 he gives his views on politics: "It is true,

gogen" has already been mentioned. In 1852 he writes about "the fraud concerning liberty that is raging in this country."[20] In the same article he writes of "the capriciousness of the ever-changing multitude."[21] He is genuinely sorry that Loehe harbors the erroneous notion "that we have sacrificed the divine dignity of the holy ministry to democratic principles."[22] On January 8, 1860, he writes to A. C. Preus and speaks of "freedom-drunk America."[23] Wyneken's attitude toward current democratic ideology was much the same as Walther's. He uses the same phrases. As early as 1843 he speaks of

> the fraud concerning liberty which has been concocted by the unrestrained spirit of man and which is destroying all divine order.[24]

Any democratic political theories which the founders of the Missouri Synod might have entertained, they did not get from America, but from the same source from which they derived their theology and church polity, viz., from the writings of Martin Luther.[25] Walther's political democracy was not that of John Locke nor of Jean Jacques Rousseau.

---

my brethren, that politics are of no concern to theologians. Nor have ministers of the Gospel any business to hold forth on economic questions, even though they may affect human society. We haven't the least desire to do so. Read our church papers, and you will soon notice that we are not in the habit of discussing political and economic subjects. They do not belong to our profession and calling. However, if those who claim to be political writers dabble in religion, we would be cowards and traitors of the truth if we did not open our mouths." ("Gewiss, lieben Brueder, uns Theologen geht die Politik gar nichts an; auch was die oeconomischen Verhaeltnisse der menschlichen Societaet betrifft, so haben wir nicht dreinzureden, und es faellt uns auch gar nicht ein, es thun zu wollen. Man lese unsere Kirchenblaetter, und man wird bald finden, dass wir uns in diese Sachen gar nicht mischen. Es ist nicht unsers Amts und Berufs. Wenn aber freilich diejenigen, welche vorgeben, sie seien Politiker, sich in die Religion mischen, dann koennen wir nicht schweigen, oder wir werden Verraeter an der Wahrheit.")

20 *Der Lutheraner*, VIII (1852), p. 97: "der hier grassierende Freiheitsschwindel."

21 *Der Lutheraner*, VIII (1852), p. 97: "die Willkuer der veraenderlichen Menge."

22 *Der Lutheraner*, VIII (1852), p. 97: "wir haetten den falsch democratischen Grundsaetzen die goettliche Wuerde des Predigtamtes geopfert."

23 *Walthers Briefe*, I, p. 127: "das freiheitstrunkene Amerika."

24 Wyneken's "Aufruf" in *Zeitschrift fuer Protestantismus und Kirche*, V (1843), p. 157: "der alle goettliche Ordnung aufloesende Freiheitsschwindel des sich entfesselnden Menschengeistes."

25 This is particularly evident in the manner in which Walther became a States'-rights man. Strange as it may seem, his literal interpretation of Rom. 13:1 had much to do with his espousal of States' rights. He followed

14

Perhaps the strongest argument against any connection between contemporary American political theory and the genesis of decentralized church polity in the Missouri Synod is in the extreme exclusivism adopted first by the Stephanites in Germany and then by the Saxon congregations in St. Louis and Perry County. The utterly anti-Lutheran belief that they comprised the entire Church at the time of their emigration and that outside of their group there was no salvation has already been described. Dr. Marbach, the greatest Stephanite layman of them all, describes their exclusivism more precisely than even their bitterest enemies. After his bitter disillusionment under date of March 3, 1841, he writes as follows:

> A chief occupation of our group was to pass uncharitable judgments on all outsiders or on all such as had fallen into the disfavor of the leader.[26]
> In open defiance of all government and all divine and human laws and statutes and duties and under the thunder and lightning of our crackling condemnation of Europe we left the shores of our fatherland.[27]
> We announced to all Europe that Christ was leaving the old world with us, and to America that Christ was coming to her. To Europe, especially to those who were left behind on the scorched earth of God's disfavor, we announced fire and brimstone; to America we played ourselves up as bearers of grace, blessing, and salvation. And after all this had taken place we made our debut in St. Louis as the true Church.[28]

Luther most closely. The King James Version of Rom. 13:1 is less encouraging to States' rights than Martin Luther's translation. The English version reads: "Let every soul be subject unto the higher powers." Luther's translation has in it the concept of the *Kleinstaat*. It reads: "Jedermann sei untertain der Obrigkeit, die Gewalt ueber ihn hat." (Literally: "Let every soul be subject to that government which has power over him.") Walther's letter to the Rev. J. C. W. Lindemann, Cleveland, Ohio, April 27, 1861, in *Walthers Briefe*, I, pp. 162—164, reveals the fact that Walther took Luther's translation literally. He merely substituted Abraham Lincoln for Charles V and Governor Jackson of Missouri for Frederick the Wise and then followed Luther in his political thinking.

[26] Marbach, "An meine Landsleute." There are seventeen pages in this neatly handwritten document. They are not numbered, but according to actual count this quotation is from page 11. In the original it reads as follows: "Eine Hauptbeschaeftigung in der Gemeinschaft war das Richten ueber solche, die draussen waren, oder die sich die Ungnade des Ordenshauptes zugezogen hatten."

[27] Marbach, *op. cit.*, p. 12. "Unter Verhoehnung der Obrigkeit und aller goettlichen und menschlichen Ordnungen Rechte und Pflichten und unter dem Donner des von uns ueber Europa verkuendigten Gerichts zogen wir aus."

[28] Marbach, *op. cit.*, p. 15. "Wir verkuendigten Europa, dass Christus mit uns sich von ihm weg, und Amerika, dass er sich zu ihm wende, Ungnade und Zorn ueber Europa und alle Abtruennigen, die Gott in der Duerre zurueckgelassen, Gnade, Segen und Heil ueber Amerika durch uns."

The opposition of the Saxons to all mixed congregations, i. e., congregations composed of Lutherans and Reformed, did not come
into existence with the Fort Wayne constitution but was manifest
in the very beginning of Trinity Congregation.[29] The hostile attitude toward the Methodists exhibited by the editor of *Der Lutheraner* and by William Sihler in his pamphlet has been described
in a former chapter. The Baptists were particularly distasteful
to Wyneken.[30] The Lutheran General Synod was handled severely
by Wyneken in his "Aufruf" and by Sihler in a series of articles
in *Der Lutheraner*.[31] The Roman Catholics were bitterly opposed
by Wyneken [32] and by *Der Lutheraner*.[33] In view of the oppo-

[29] The paragraph in the Fort Wayne constitution which refused admission
into the Synod to a pastor who served a mixed congregation was merely the
codification of a policy which had been developed by the Saxons over a period
of six years. Schneider, *op. cit.*, p. 105, brings a letter from G. Wall, pastor of
a mixed congregation in St. Louis, to the Look Upward, Press Onward Society,
dated May 11, 1840. The following excerpt is significant. "Mr. Walther once
called on me, and I repaid him, with my dear brother, the Rev. Mr. Nollau,
his visit. I must confess that I have to regard him as a true Christian, but
at the same time as a man whose heart is too narrow towards other Christians,
and towards all other forms in the Church than he has among his Saxonians.
He thinks it the irremissible duty to condemn every doctrine which is against
their Symbolical Books. He thinks that every thorough true Christian must
consent with Luther, therefore or ergo — you may make conclusion after
conclusion. . . .'"

[30] In "Aufruf" published in *Zeitschrift fuer Protestantismus und Kirche*,
V, p. 148, Wyneken refers to the Baptists in the following words: "The Sacraments are regarded as mere signs in the shallowest sense of the word. The
baptism of children is decreasing daily in America, because it is regarded as
an unchristian abomination. Just think of it, there are 4,000,000 Baptists
who rave against infant baptism." ("Die Sakramente sind ihnen blosses
Zeichen im flachsten Sinn, und die Kindertaufe nimmt in Amerika immer
mehr ab als ein unchristlicher Greuel (!). . . . Ach wenn man weiss, dass
dort allein 4,000,000 Baptisten gegen die Kindertaufe wuethen!")

[31] *Der Lutheraner*, V (1849), pp. 97—100: Sermon on Baptism. *Der
Lutheraner*, V (1849): Second sermon on Baptism. Both were by Dr. Sihler.

[32] *Zeitschrift fuer Protestantismus und Kirche*, V (1843), pp. 148—152.
Part of Wyneken's "Aufruf."

[33] *Der Lutheraner*, II (1846), p. 82: Lutheran and Roman Catholic doctrine of Confession. *Der Lutheraner*, II (1846), p. 83. There is a long series
of articles beginning in *Der Lutheraner*, III, p. 20, entitled: "Does Old
Lutheranism Lead to Rome?" continued on pp. 27—29, 33—34, 39—42, 45—46,
60—62, 77—78, 79—80. The articles were written by the editor, C. F. W. Walther.

Heinrich H. Maurer, in *The American Journal of Sociology*, XXX (1925),
pp. 665—682, "Studies in the Sociology of Religion. IV. The Problems of the
Group Consensus; Founding the Missouri Synod," writes on p. 680: "Walther
did not find it necessary to consult either history or theology of the last two
centuries. With the seventeenth century his casebook of history closes, and
thus he performed for his group the decisive service of cutting it off from
Germany, from Europe, from time and space, from pietism, from rationalism,
from the old theology, from the new; from the Geistesgeschichte of the last

sition manifested by the Missourians against the more influential church organizations represented on the frontier it does not seem likely that they would imbibe anything in the way of polity from existing religious groups.

As to the genesis of the Missouri Synod's decentralized polity it is rather doubtful whether America contributed very much more than the stage upon which Luther's theories of church government were put into practice.* Led by Dr. Vehse from May 30 to December 11, 1839, and after his return to Germany by Dr. F. A. Marbach, a group of highly intelligent laymen propagandized the colony in behalf of laymen's participation in the government of the Church. At the suggestion of Stephan these laymen had studied the writings of Martin Luther for years while they were still in Germany. Their knowledge of Luther's writings was astonishing. Their claims for lay participation in the government of the Church were based primarily upon the earlier statements of Luther concerning the priesthood of all believers. At first the Saxon ministerium, including C. F. W. Walther, resisted

---

two centuries with all its troubles. To-day, to one of the best-informed minds of the group 'there has been little that is new since Aristotle.' In rationalizing its relation to what is left of the world and the devil, the group, with Walther, limited itself to the precedents of the first two, the sixteenth and the seventeenth centuries. In those centuries they are at home, these Middle Westerners; by rehearsing the experiences of those ages they learn; by tracing the pattern of the experience of those centuries they live; by applying those patterns to new situations they make history; and thus it is that while some history does not, some history does repeat itself. Such is the influence of Mr. Walther on the historical perspective of the group that it interprets the process of life in America in terms of the life of the early Christians in the Roman Empire and of the early Lutherans in the Holy Roman Empire of Charles V and of the seventeenth century. Without an appreciation of this fact, the mind of this group and the mind of the Middle West as far as they are concerned, are not intelligible and therefore apt to be misjudged."

* EDITOR'S NOTE. — C. F. W. Walther, in his address at the second convention of the Synod, in 1848, in which he at length discusses the constitution of the new body, with special reference to the paragraph on the advisory character of the Synod which his own Trinity Church had insisted must be included in the constitution, at the convention in 1847, speaks of the freedom which the members of the Church enjoyed in America and that any effort to restrict that freedom would be strongly opposed. He says: "In a republic such as the United States of America, in which the spirit of freedom and independence of men is nurtured from childhood, it could not be otherwise than that any effort, no matter how well meant, to restrict this freedom beyond the limitations which God Himself has drawn would arouse the opposition of many even toward such arrangements as they would have accepted if they had been allowed the liberty to accept or reject." *Synodical Report*, 1848, p. 9, col. 1.   W. G. P.

these laymen most vigorously, as already stated.[34]   In the winter of 1840 to 1841, however, the situation was threatening to get out of hand.   C. F. W. Walther was deposed from office by his Perry County congregation on account of its want of confidence in the ministry ("Misstrauen gegen das Amt").[35]   The clerical party was rapidly losing caste and disintegrating.   As previously pointed out, Pastor Buerger and Magister Wege espoused the cause of the lay party, while the influential Candidate Brohm began to straddle and the faith of Keyl and Loeber in the cause of the clericals was badly shaken.   The colonists generally were utterly confused.

In this extreme exigency Walther made a virtue of necessity and adopted a realistic course.   He accepted principles of church government which his lay opponents had gathered from the writings of Luther.[36]   To these he added from Luther certain provisions which safeguarded the dignity of the ministerial office: his transfer theory, the doctrine of the divinity of the call,[37] the absolute authority of the Word of God, and permanence of tenure.

---

[34] In Chapter IV of the present study reference has been made to the resistance of the clerics to the claims of the laymen.   The laymen's side of the story is given in Vehse's *Die Stephan'sche Auswanderung*.   The minutes of the ministerium, which were signed by all ministers, including C. F. W. Walther, prove that Vehse's account is substantially correct.   For well over a year the clerics, including C. F. W. Walther, were violently opposed to the participation of laymen in the government of the Church.   The clerics hint in rather strong language that the laymen's demands are "tricky devices of Satan" ("listige Anschlaege des Satans").   This remark is found in the minutes of the ministerium dated September 9, 1839.   In his manifesto "An Meine Landsleute," dated March 3, 1841, Marbach maintains that "the ministerium warned the congregations officially against Dr. Vehse, claiming 'that the devil was speaking through him' ('der Teufel rede aus ihm')."   As late as March 3, 1841, Marbach asked the question, seemingly without fear of contradiction, "Has this statement of the ministerium ever been officially recanted?"   ("Ist dies foermlich zurueckgenommen?")   Marbach's claims likewise receive strong support from the minutes of the ministerium.

[35] Loeber's letter to Guericke *et al*, dated April 28, 1841, and printed in Rudelbach und Guerickes *Zeitschrift*, II (1841), p. 114.   Loeber makes the statement of the loss of confidence in the ministry in connection with Walther's removal from office.

[36] It is highly significant that in the year 1850 Trinity Congregation, St. Louis, republished the great arsenal from which the lay party drew its weapons, namely, *Brief Dr. Martin Luthers von der Einsetzung der Kirchendiener* an den Rath zu Prag in Boehmen vom Jahr 1523, aus dem Lateinischen uebersetzt von Paulus Speratus als ein Wort zu seiner Zeit zur Rettung der theuren Lehre von dem geistlichen Priesterthum aller glaeubigen Christen.   The last part of the title is printed in heavy black type.   This letter, which covers thirty-two pages in the Trinity edition of 1850, contains all that is basic in the polity of the Missouri Synod.

[37] Walther, *Pastoraltheologie*.   The substance of this volume appeared originally in a long series of articles in *Lehre und Wehre*, a theological monthly

Thus the youngest of the clerical group gave evidence that he was a realistic thinker and that he knew how to wield doctrine. Two alternatives were open to him. One was to go back to Germany and possibly re-establish himself. The other was to stay in America and try to establish himself. Conditions under which he left the Fatherland made the former choice prohibitive. The latter involved a coming to terms with the opposing lay group. Walther chose this course. By this choice he accomplished something on American soil that Luther for various reasons had failed to achieve on German soil.

Divorced from contemporary church law and custom of Germany and freed from the nuisance of the Saxon *Polizeistaat,* in the practical atmosphere of the free American frontier, he devised a form of church government in which there was a nice balance between the power of the clergy and the power of the laymen. Essentially this form of government has remained intact for a hundred years.

What made this form of government succeed? Why did the Missouri Synod gradually outdistance its competitors? The answer to this question cannot be given in one sentence or even in one paragraph. At times the factors of success seem to be working independently of each other, and then again they are working in conjunction. It is difficult to say to what extent a certain factor should receive credit for the growth of the immigrant body. There is no doubt that there were circumstances which favored the Missouri Synod entirely aside from its peculiar church polity. The wave of immigrants from Germany pouring into the United States,[38] the steady stream of well-trained and well-disciplined

---

founded by Walther in 1855. The series was published from 1865 to 1871. In 1872 the first edition of the *Pastoraltheologie* was published. Pages 23—69 of the fifth edition are devoted to the doctrine of the call in its practical applications. Walther's basic assumption in the doctrine of the call is that the congregation is an instrument of God. When the congregation calls, God is calling. The individual layman, who is a priest in his own name, transfers his right to function publicly as a priest to the man who is chosen or called. The call makes the minister. There is no doubt that this doctrine gave dignity to the ministry in the eyes of the people, and it safeguarded the rights of the pastor.

[38] 1841 to 1850 the number of German immigrants was 434,626. 1851 to 1860 it was 951,667. See *Annual Report of the Commissioner General of Immigration to the Secretary of Labor,* June 30, 1930, United States Government Printing Office, p. 202. Of the total St. Louis population of 77,465 in 1850, 37,051 were native Americans, 23,774 were Germans, 11,257 were Irish, 2,933 were English, and the remainder of other extraction. Cf. *Encyclopedia of History*

ministers and teachers of Christian day schools pouring forth from
the Synod's own educational institutions,[39] a well-nurtured and
highly promoted system of Christian elementary education,[40] a

---

of St. Louis, II, p. 890. The *Anzeiger des Westens* in 1854 "boasted that there
were 40,000 Germans in this city" (St. Louis). In 1858 St. Louis had 14 German churches, 27 German societies, 2 German-language daily newspapers,
and 5 German weeklies. Cf. Schneider, *op. cit.*, p. 422.

[39] As already stated, the first institution of higher learning in the Missouri
Synod was founded in 1839 as a theological seminary and preparatory school
training students for the seminary. The preparatory school began an independent existence, locally removed from the seminary, in 1861. In 1855
a teachers' seminary for the training of teachers for parochial schools was
founded. These three schools, each representing a different type of higher
education, were not modeled after the existing patterns of American high
schools, colleges, normal schools, or theological seminaries. Higher education
in the Middle West, where these schools were located, can hardly be said to
have emerged at that time from the pioneering stage. Although there seems
to be some evidence that the American systems were considered, as a matter
of fact the founders of the Missouri Synod system of education modeled these
new institutions upon schools with which they were personally acquainted,
in which they had received their own training, and which were generally
acknowledged at the time, also by outstanding American educators
(e. g., Horace Mann), to be at the peak of educational achievement and
efficiency and superior to all other schools. Their models were the continental
European, and more specifically the German, classical Gymnasium, Lehrer-
seminar, and theological department of the university. This was an important
and far-reaching step. It tied the Missouri Synod institutions of higher learning into a powerful and stimulating educational tradition and helped to make
them effective educational institutions from the very beginning. There could
be little question of their superiority over the average Midwestern high schools
and colleges of that time.

Speaking before the triannual conference of the Missouri Synod instructors and school administrators, on July 29, 1940, W. H. Wente, Ph. D., said: "The
European classical Gymnasium of the last half of the nineteenth and the first
decades of the twentieth century was unquestionably a very successful
institution. Its success, however, it should be said, did not lie wholly, or even
partially, in its particular type of curricular organization and administration,
the feature to which Missouri Synod schools clung most steadfastly, but in its
very high level of teacher training and teacher competence, in its powerful
tradition, and in the general social and intellectual environment of the Germany of those years, into which its roots were sunk. Neither can it be denied
that our own schools, drawing their intellectual inspiration from these European models and the whole Gymnasium tradition, produced results of high
quality." Typewritten MS. of the address, p. 3.

[40] Walter H. Beck's *Lutheran Elementary Schools in the United States*,
contains a reliable and authoritative account of the origin of the elementary
Christian school system of the Missouri Synod on pages 101—118. C. F. W. Walther refers to the early days of the school system in his *Lebenslauf* of Buenger,
p. 57. "In the Saxon-Lutheran congregation it was the rule always to establish at once the office of teaching ('Schulamt') together with the office of
preaching ('Predigtamt'). Within a few days after the arrival of the first
division of the company of immigrants in St. Louis a school was founded there.
If no teacher could be appointed, it was a matter of course that the minister
took over, together with his ministerial office, the office of schoolmaster and

policy towards the language and culture of the immigrants that
made for group solidarity,[41] an exceedingly high type of leader-

administered both according to his ability." The constitution drawn up at
St. Louis and Fort Wayne in 1846 provided (II, 4) that only such congregations could be and remain members of Synod as made necessary provision
"for the Christian schooling of the children of the congregation."

Official supervision and direction on the part of the President of Synod
was provided in V, 7: "The President shall report . . . on his supervision of the
teaching, life, and ministry of pastors and teachers . . . also concerning the
orthodox character of church and school regulations and books." V, 18 of the
constitution read: "Pastors shall submit annual parochial reports concerning
. . . pupils in the schools, those from the congregation as well as of strangers."
According to III, 3 of the constitution, Synod shall concern itself with . . .
"the conscientious examination of candidates for the ministry and teaching."
The provisions of the constitution as well as subsequent reports and pronouncements of presidents indicate that "there was a definite, clearly defined,
well-organized, and virtually obligatory system of schools, which because of
its close identification with the Church as such was destined to grow and to
establish itself more firmly than was possible within other Lutheran bodies
where organization was less uniform and establishment of schools less
rigorously insisted upon." (Beck, *op. cit.*, p. 107.)

In his *Erinnerungen*, p. 17, Gruber describes Walther's contribution to
the parish-school system of the Missouri Synod with these words: "Walther
insisted with might and main on the establishment of a parish school by every
congregation. If a congregation was too weak to engage a teacher, then the
pastor had to do the schoolteaching."

[41] The professors, pastors, and teachers of the Missouri Synod were
largely the product of their German Lutheran frontier environment. They
were thoroughly familiar with the likes and dislikes, the mores and folk-
ways, in short, the life and culture of their people. They did relatively little
to disturb this culture. Wittingly or unwittingly they helped to maintain its
status quo. The fact that Walther and Sihler, to mention only two, saw
a correlation between orthodoxy and the German language, that every pastor
was thoroughly trained in the German language, and that the German
language played an important role in the virtually obligatory elementary
school system of the Synod helped more to maintain the German language
and German culture as the immigrants knew it at the time of their immigration
than any other single factor. The German language and the Christian
religion became identified in the minds of most Missouri Lutherans. The practical consequences were far-reaching. It enabled the second and third generation of Missourians to sit in the same pew and sing out of the same hymnbook. At the same time the cultural policy insulated the Missourians as a
group against the prevalent currents of thought. Culturally this state of
affairs was costly, but religiously it was of decided advantage.

Heinrich H. Maurer in *The American Journal of Sociology* XXXI (1925),
pp. 29—57, "Studies in the Sociology of Religion V, The Fellowship Law of
a Fundamentalist Group. The Missouri Synod." states on p. 51: "Undoubtedly
the fact that this church has identified itself with the language interest of
the family and the culture group has much to do with its growth and strength.
. . . It might easily be shown that in this quarter [Missouri Synod], more
than anywhere else, the German language has been effectively preserved unto
the third and fourth generation, not as a link with Germany and as an
insulator against America, but as an insulator of an older group life against
both. The strongest appeal of a separate linguistic and educational medium
has been for its value as a protection and a means of domestication and im-
munization against 'rationalism,' 'materialism,' 'indifferentism,' against the
paganism of the state schools ('Staatsschulen sind Heidenschulen')."

ship, particularly during the formative years of Synod,[42] long tenure of office of influential men, persistent interest in the social and economic well-being of the immigrants,[43] and heavy emphasis on the teaching activity of the pastors [44] — these were some of the factors which contributed to the rapid growth and unusual solidarity of the Missouri Synod.

However, immigration, cheap land, a fair supply of indigenous, well-trained pastors, interest in the social and economic well-being of their constituency, were factors that were present in other immigrant synods which had their field of activity on the American

[42] It was a remarkable coincidence that during its infancy the Missouri Synod had a triumvirate of leaders that put the body in a class by itself and definitely promoted its growth. A mere listing of their chief characteristics indicates the strength of leadership that was in this combination: the polite, refined, theologically thoroughly trained Saxon graduate of Leipzig at its height (C. F. W. Walther); the sympathetic, patient, and completely human Hannoverian graduate of Goettingen (F. C. D. Wyneken); the erudite, energetic, and somewhat stern doctor of philosophy from the young University of Berlin (Wm. Sihler) — men in their late thirties and early forties who seem to have complemented one another remarkably, and who were able to fit themselves into the frontier picture admirably.

[43] Throughout most of its history the Missouri Synod has been one of the most compact German-culture groups in the United States. Since it has kept aloof from all other culture groups, also from all other German-culture groups both in America and in Germany, it has been able to conserve its energy for intra-group activity. The interest of the group in the economic and social well-being of the immigrants is very noticeable in the minutes of Trinity Congregation, St. Louis. Members took their regular turns staying up nights with other members of the *Gemeinde* who were ill. The congregation had an *Armenkasse* which received regular contributions and from which regular grants-in-aid were made. Each case was discussed with sincerity and charity. As early as the fall of 1839 Pastor O. H. Walther announced to the congregation assembled in the basement of Christ Church (Episcopal) that there would be a meeting to discuss an *Unterstuetzungsverein*. Thirty years later Gruber, *Erinnerungen*, p. 8, sang the praises of Trinity and said, "A faith that worketh by love lived in the hearts of the members." For Walther's interest in the *Emigrantenmission* cf. his two letters to Pastor St. Keyl, one dated December 19, 1868, and the other March 18, 1869, in *Walthers Briefe*, II, pp. 141—142, 153, 155. In the "Haustafel" of Luther's Catechism, which "Haustafel" and which Catechism may be designated as one of the most powerful and far-reaching pedagogical agencies ever designed, the Missouri Synod was taught the ways of Lutheran economic paternalism. For the attitude of the pastors to the well-being of the members see Walther's *Pastorale*, pp. 276—277.

[44] The Missouri Synod has placed strong emphasis on teaching from its inception. *Lehre, reine Lehre, Lehrstand,* are prominent words in the Missouri vocabulary. Aside from his interest in promoting the elementary school of the parish the pastor is a teacher par excellence. The main objective of the sermon is to teach. Walther, *Pastorale*, p. 81: "The didactic element in the sermon is the most important. . . . No matter how rich a sermon may be in exhortation, in correction and comfort, if it is weak in doctrine, it is an empty, meager sermon. The exhortation, correction, and comfort of such a sermon is dangling in the air and has no foundation."

frontier. A share of the credit for the success of the Missouri Synod in group perpetuation and group promotion must no doubt be attributed to congregational and synodical polity. Though this polity was not made of contemporary German materials, much less of contemporary American materials, it was made in America, and it surely was tailor-made for the nineteenth-century American frontier.[45]

By putting real power into the laymen's hands the founders of the Missouri Synod nurtured and developed a sturdy and informed laity. The laymen learned by doing. The difficult problem of teaching men and women who had been brought up in the State Church of Germany the task of paying for the maintenance of the Church was solved by giving laymen the privilege and the duty of making important decisions in the Church.[46] The problem of getting laymen interested in the education of ministers was solved by giving laymen something to say about the institutions in which an indigenous ministry was trained.[47] The problem of generating interest in the well-being of the Church at home and

[45] The process of adapting Luther's principles of church government to American frontier conditions is graphically described by W. Sihler in a series of articles, *Lehre und Wehre*, III and IV (1857—1858), pp. 71 ff., 131 ff., 139 ff., entitled "Von Spaltungen in hiesigen lutherischen Gemeinden." Sihler gives advice on how to organize congregations and insure the consensus under prevailing difficulties "not with the help of oratory or by organizing a party or by emphasizing the authority of your office ('auf Amtsgewalt pochend'), not by forcing completed constitutions on congregations, but by discussing individual needs of the congregation and thus letting the constitution gradually grow out of the congregation ('nicht fertige Verfassung aufzwingen, sondern von Fall zu Fall mit der Gemeinde entscheiden und so eine Verfassung organisch aus der Gemeinde allmaehlich herauswachsen lassen . . . die Gemeinde zur Mitarbeit an der Selbstregierung erziehen')." Speaking of the Missouri Synod's polity fitting into the American situation, H. H. Maurer writes in *The American Journal of Sociology*, XXXI (1925), p. 56: "By an irony of fate, it [the Missouri Synod] rises in defense of the Jeffersonian state, the limited state, the thing that was begotten in the iniquity of rationalism." Cf. Mauelshagen, *op. cit.*, p. 204: "The Missouri Synod's congregational and synodical organization was less objectionable than that of any other to the German immigrant, who came to America prejudiced against the hierarchical and consistorial form of church administration and autocratic, political government."

[46] Cf. the minutes of Trinity Church in St. Louis with respect to the building of the first church.

[47] According to the reports of the synodical meetings many decisions regarding the seminary and college were made by the entire Synod in regular session. Buildings, location, appointment of faculty members, etc., were decided on the floor of Synod. At times laymen reported to Synod on the present state of affairs at Concordia Seminary. In the early history of the Synod usually three pastors and one layman formed the Board of Control.

abroad was brought nearer to solution by giving the laymen a voice in making decisions which affected this well-being. The zeal which the early Missouri Synod laymen showed for their Church in that they attended meeting after meeting was produced, no doubt, in part by the fact that these men knew that their decisions were final.

The power and authority given to the laymen, on the other hand, was not permitted in any way to undermine or affect adversely the authority and dignity of the holy ministry. The principle of pastoral leadership was honored. The provisions of congregational and synodical polity not only made effective leadership on the part of the pastor possible, but probable. Thus, the polity initiated by the Saxon laymen in the isolation of the frontier amidst trial and struggle a few months after their arrival on American soil was an important factor in the growth of the immigrant Church.

SOURCES

Books and Pamphlets

Abbott, Edith, *Historical Aspects of the Immigration Problem.* University of Chicago Press, Chicago, 1926.

> This is a collection of documents which provide source material for the student of immigration. It was made by the dean of the Graduate School of Social Service Administration, University of Chicago. The chapter entitled "The Attractions of Pioneer Life in Missouri" brings extracts from Gottfried Duden's *Bericht ueber eine Reise nach den westlichen Staaten Nordamerikas.*

Althaus, Paul, *Kirche und Staat nach lutherischer Lehre.* "Theologia militans." A. Deichertsche Buchhandlung, Leipzig, 1935.

Althaus, Paul, *Politisches Christentum.* Theologia militans. A. Deichertsche Buchhandlung, Leipzig, 1935.

Beck, Walter, *Lutheran Elementary Schools in the United States.* Concordia Publishing House, St. Louis, Mo., 1939.

Bente, Frederick, *American Lutheranism* (2 vols.). Concordia Publishing House, St. Louis, Mo., 1919.

Blegen, Theodore C., *Norwegian Migration to America, 1825—1850.* Norwegian American Historical Association, Northfield, Minn., 1931.

Blegen, Theodore C., *The Norwegian Migration to America: the American Transition.* Norwegian American Historical Association, Northfield, Minn., 1940.

Beschreibung der Feierlichkeiten, welche am dritten Jubelfeste der Augsburgischen Confession den 25., 26. und 27. Juni 1830 im Koenigreich Sachsen stattfanden. 858 pages. Verlag von Johann Friedrich Glueck, Leipzig, 1830.

Brandi, Karl, *Die deutsche Reformation.* Quelle und Meyer Verlag, Leipzig, 1927.

Brauer, Albert, *Lebensbild des weiland ehrwuerdigen Pastor Ernst August Brauer.* Concordia Publishing House, St. Louis, Mo., 1898.

> A biography of an early Concordia Seminary professor written by his son.

Buerger, Ernst, *Sendschreiben* an die evangelisch-lutherische Kirche zunaechst in Wisconsin, Missouri, Preussen und Sachsen. Koesslingsche Buchhandlung, Leipzig, 1846.

> An interpretation of the Saxon emigration by a participant.

Concordia Cyclopedia. A handbook of religious information, with special reference to the history, doctrine, work, and usages of the Lutheran Church. Edited by L. Fuerbringer, Th. Engelder, and P. E. Kretzmann, Concordia Publishing House, St. Louis, Mo., 1927.

Constitution and By-Laws of a Lutheran Congregation. Concordia Publishing House, St. Louis, Mo., 1897.

> The constitution of Old Trinity, St. Louis, Mo., translated into English by A. L. Graebner, served as a model for the congregations of the Missouri Synod.

Delitzsch, Franz, *Wissenschaft, Kunst und Judentum.* Grimma, 1838.

Deutelmoser, Arno, *Luther — Staat und Glaube.* Eugen Diederich-Verlag, Jena, 1937.

Dictionary of American Biography. (21 volumes.) Charles Scribner's Sons, New York, 1928—1944.

Diehm, Harold, *Luthers Lehre von den zwei Reichen.* Chr. Kaiser-Verlag, Muenchen, 1938.
> Doctoral dissertation, University of Tuebingen. A modern German study of Luther's attitude towards government. Well documented.

Documentary History of the Evangelical Lutheran Ministerium of Pennsylvania and Adjacent States. Board of Publications of the General Council, Philadelphia, 1898.

Ebenezer. Reviews of the work of the Missouri Synod during three quarters of a century. Concordia Publishing House, St. Louis, Mo., 1922.
> A *Festschrift,* written by various Missouri Synod pastors and professors and edited by W. H. T. Dau.

Eilfter Jahresbericht der saechsischen Bibel-Gesellschaft. Verlag von C. G. Gaertner, Dresden, 1825.
> Contains a complete sermon by Martin Stephan.

Elert, Werner, *Morphologie des Luthertums.* Band I: Theologie und Weltanschauung des Luthertums, hauptsaechlich im 16. und 17. Jahrhundert. Band II: Soziallehren und Sozialwirkungen des Luthertums. C. H. Becksche Verlagsbuchhandlung, Muenchen, 1931.
> An authoritative modern study of Lutheranism.

Elert, Werner, *Die Herrschaft Christi und die Herrschaft von Menschen.* "Theologia militans." A. Deichertsche Buchhandlung, Leipzig, 1936.

Encyclopedia Americana. Revised edition. Americana Corporation, New York, 1926.

Encyclopedia of the History of St. Louis. Four volumes. Edited by W. Hyde and H. Conard. New York, 1899.

Engelder, Th., Dallmann, W., Dau, W. H. T., *Walther and the Church.* Concordia Publishing House, St. Louis, Mo., 1939.
> Three former students of Dr. C. F. W. Walther collaborated in the production of this volume. An authoritative presentation of Walther's doctrines concerning the Church and the ministry.

Ernst, James, *Roger Williams New England Firebrand.* Macmillan, New York, 1932.

Ferm, Vergilius, *The Crisis in American Lutheran Theology.* The Century Co., New York, 1927.

Fischer, Ludwig, *Das falsche Maertyrerthum der Stephanisten.* Verlag von Wilhelm Kuenzel, Leipzig, 1839.
> A very keen and, on the whole, fair analysis of Stephanism by a contemporary.

Fritschel, G. J., *Quellen und Dokumente zur Geschichte der Iowa-Synode.* Wartburg Publishing House, Chicago, 1916.

Fritschel, G. J., *Aus den Tagen der Vaeter*. Wartburg Publishing House, Chicago, 1930.

Fritz, John H. C., *Pastoral Theology*. Concordia Publishing House, St. Louis, Mo., 1932.

> The dean of Concordia Seminary, St. Louis, has brought Walther's *Pastorale* up to date.

Glaubensbekenntnis der Gemeinde zu St. Johannis in Dresden. No author given. Ernst Blochmann Druckerei, Dresden, 1833.

> A somewhat wordy and expansive defense of Martin Stephan. This volume has been ascribed to a candidate of theology who was a member of Martin Stephan's church and who is said to have worked under the direction of Martin Stephan.

Grabau, John A., *Lebenslauf des ehrwuerdigen J. A. A. Grabau*. Volksblatt Publishing Company, Buffalo, N. Y., 1879.

> This is a biography of the founder of the Buffalo Synod written by his son.

Graebner, A. L. *Geschichte der lutherischen Kirche in Amerika*. Concordia Publishing House, St. Louis, Mo., 1892.

> Develops subject up to 1820. No footnotes to indicate sources.

Graebner, Theodore. *Handbook for Congregational Officers*. Concordia Publishing House, St. Louis, Mo., 1928.

Gruber, J. L., *Erinnerungen an Professor Walther und seine Zeit*. Lutheran Literary Board, Burlington, Iowa, 1930.

> The author was a Christian day school teacher in Walther's parish in St. Louis. Later he left the Missouri Synod.

Guenther, L., *Die Schicksale und Abenteuer der aus Sachsen ausgewanderten Stephanianer*. Verlag von C. Heinrich, Dresden, 1839.

> The Missouri Historical Association has made photostatic copies of this entire volume. The author seems to have been a man of rather limited mentality. He was participant in the emigration but left the colony and returned to Saxony soon after the arrival in St. Louis.

Guenther, Martin, *Dr. C. F. W. Walther. Lebensbild*. Lutherischer Concordia-Verlag, St. Louis, Mo., 1890.

> A Missouri Synod biography of Dr. C. F. W. Walther, which first appeared in Vols. 44 and 45 of *Der Lutheraner*. Written by a former student and colleague of Walther.

Haan, Wilhelm, *Kirchlich-statistisches Handbuch fuer das Koenigreich Sachsen, bearbeitet von Wilhelm Haan*. Carl Ramming Herausgeber, Dresden, 1838.

> Very valuable for a study of the parishes in which the Missouri Synod pastors served before their emigration.

Hanser, C. J. Otto, *Die Geschichte der Ersten Evangelisch-Lutherischen Dreieinigkeitsgemeinde zu St. Louis, Mo.* Concordia-Verlag, Saint Louis, Mo., 1889.

> A *Festschrift*.

Harless, Adolf von, *Das Verhaeltnis des Christenthums zu Cultur und Lebensfragen*. Verlag von Theodor Blaesing, Erlangen, 1866.

Harnack, Theodosius, *Die Kirche: ihr Amt, ihr Regiment.* First published in Nuernberg, 1862. Republished with a brief introductory note, Verlag von C. Bertelsmann, Guetersloh, 1934.

Hennig, Karl, *Die saechsische Erweckungsbewegung im Anfang des 19. Jahrhunderts.* Verlag von Theodor Weicher, Leipzig, 1929.
A doctoral dissertation at the University of Leipzig.

Herzog-Plitt, *Real-Encyclopaedie fuer protestantische Theologie und Kirche,* zweite Auflage. (21 Baende.) J. C. Hinrichsche Buchhandlung, Leipzig, 1884.
Contains an excellent article by Pastor Kummer of Dresden, Saxony, on Martin Stephan. Kummer had access to various archives in Dresden and surrounding territory. Unfortunately, his article was dropped in the third edition of Herzog-Plitt.

Hochstetter, Chr., *Geschichte der Evangelisch-Lutherischen Missouri-Synode.* Heinrich J. Naumann, Dresden, 1885.

Jacobs, Henry E., *History of the Evangelical Lutheran Church in the United States.* Vol. IV of "American Church History Series." The Christian Literature Company, New York, 1893.

Koehler, John P., *Geschichte der Allgemeinen Evangelisch-Lutherischen Synode von Wisconsin und anderen Staaten.* Northwestern Publishing House, Milwaukee, Wis., 1924.
Careful use of the documents.

Koestering, J. F., *Auswanderung der saechsischen Lutheraner im Jahre 1838.* A. Wiebusch and Son, St. Louis, Mo., 1867.
Reliable in those parts which are based on documentary evidence, Not so reliable in the parts that are based on tradition.

Koestlin, J. Th., *Martin Luther.*

Leben und Wirken des Ehrw. Ernst Gerhard Wilhelm Keyl. Concordia Publishing House, St. Louis, Mo., 1882.

Kraushaar, Chr. Otto, *Verfassungsformen der lutherischen Kirche Amerikas.* Verlag von C. Bertelsmann, Guetersloh, 1911.
Contains copies of constitutions and minutes of important meetings. Indispensable for a study of Lutheran polity in America.

Kretzmann, Karl, *The Atlantic District of the Evangelical Lutheran Synod of Missouri, Ohio, and Other States and Its Antecedents.* Erie Printing Company, Erie, Pa., 1932.

Krueger, Gustav, *Handbuch der Kirchengeschichte.* (Zwei Baende.) Erster Band: Altertum und Mittelalter. Zweiter Band: Reformation und Gegenreformation. Verlag von J. C. B. Mohr, Tuebingen, 1912.

Lau, Franz, *Kirchliche Ordnungen als Erziehungsmacht.* "Theologia militans." A. Deichertsche Buchhandlung, Leipzig, 1938.

Lewis, Sinclair, *Main Street.* Grosset and Dunlap Publishers, New York. Copyright by Harcourt Brace and Company, Inc. First printing, October, 1920.

Loeber, G. H., *Gaben fuer unsere Zeit aus dem Schatz der lutherischen Kirche und besonders aus Dr. Martin Luthers Geist-und Glaubensreichen Schriften,* 1834.

Lochner, Friedrich, *Predigten ueber die Episteln der Sonn- und Festtage des Kirchenjahres.* Verlag von Georg Brumder, Milwaukee, 1886.
Lochner belonged to the founding fathers of the Missouri Synod. His sermon on the national holiday of the United States is useful as source material for the present study.

Loehe, Wilhelm, *Zuruf aus der Heimat an die deutsch-lutherische Kirche Nordamerikas.* Stuttgart, 1845.

Loehe, Wilhelm, *Aphorismen ueber die neutestamentlichen Aemter und ihr Verhaeltnis zur Gemeinde.* Joh. Phil. Rawsche Buchhandlung, Nuernberg, 1849.

Loehe, Wilhelm, *Kirche und Amt.* Neue Aphorismen. Verlag von Theodor Blaesing, Erlangen, 1851.

Loehe, Wilhelm, *Der Evangelische Geistliche.* Zweiter unveraenderter Abdruck. Verlag von S. G. Liesching Stuttgart, 1852.
This is pastoral theology and portrays Loehe's concept of the ministry. Since Loehe differed from C. F. W. Walther on the office of the ministry, and since Loehe was instrumental in founding the Iowa Synod on American soil, this book helps understand certain phases of church polity of the Lutheran Church in America.

Luetkemueller, L. P. W., *Die Lehren und Umtriebe der Stephanisten.* Altenburg, 1838.

Luthers Werke. Weimar Edition.

Luthers Werke. St. Louis Edition.
Follows the Walch Edition.

Luther's Works with Introductions and Notes. A. J. Holman, Philadelphia, 1915—1932.

Luther, Martin, *Brief Dr. Martin Luthers von Einsetzung der Kirchendiener* an den Rath zu Prag in Boehmen vom Jahr 1523, aus dem Lateinischen uebersetzt von Paulus Speratus, herausgegeben von der Evangelisch-Lutherischen Gemeinde Ungeaenderter Augsburgischer Confession zu St. Louis, Missouri, 1850.

McNutt, William Roy, Crozier Theological Seminary, Chester, Pennsylvania, *Polity and Practice in Baptist Churches.* American Baptist Publication Society, Philadelphia, Pa., 1935.

Mauelshagen, Carl, *American Lutheranism Surrenders to the Forces of Conservatism.* University of Georgia, Division of Publications, Athens, Ga., 1936.

Meusel, Carl, *Kirchliches Handlexikon.* (Seven volumes.) Verlag von Justus Naumann, Leipzig, 1887.
A reliable work of reference by a superintendent of the Lutheran Church of Saxony.

Mezger, Georg, *Denkstein. Zum fuenfundsiebzigjaehrigen Jubilaeum der Missouri-Synode.* Concordia Publishing House, St. Louis, Mo., 1922.
A *Festschrift* containing essays by various contributors of the Missouri Synod. The article on the constitutional development (*Verfassung*) is by the editor, Dr. Mezger.

Morgan, J. B., *The Psychology of the Unadjusted School Child.* Revised edition, Macmillan Company, New York, 1937.

Morgan J. B., *The Psychology of Abnormal People.* Second edition, Longmans, Green and Company, New York, 1940.

Mowrer, Harriet R., *Personality Adjustment and Domestic Discord.* American Book Company, 1935.

Mueller, Karl, *Kirchengeschichte.* (Drei Baende.) Erste und zweite Auflage, Verlag von J. C. Mohr, Tuebingen, 1919.

Mueller, Karl, *Kirche, Gemeinde und Obrigkeit nach Luther.* Verlag von J. C. Mohr Tuebingen, 1910.

Neve, J. L., *Churches and Sects of Christendom.* The Lutheran Literary Board, Burlington, Iowa, 1940.

Neve-Allbeck, *History of the Lutheran Church in America.* Third edition, Lutheran Literary Board, Burlington, Iowa, 1934.

> This is a thoroughly revised edition of the 1916 *Brief History of the Lutheran Church in America,* by J. L. Neve. The third edition was done by Williard D. Allbeck.

Philipp, J. P. C., *Woerterbuch des chursaechsischen Kirchenrechts.* Verlag von Wilhelm Webel, Zeitz, 1803.

> Very useful in getting at the exact contemporary meaning of certain rules, laws, rescripts, and usages as they affected the polity of the Lutheran Church in Saxony.

Pieper, Franz, *Die evangelisch-lutherische Kirche die wahre sichtbare Kirche Gottes auf Erden.* Seminary Press, St. Louis, Mo., 1916.

Pleissner, G., *Die kirchlichen Fanatiker im Muldethale.* Verlag von Julius Helbig, Altenburg, 1839.

> This is a contemporary criticism of the Stephanists from the mildly rationalistic point of view. It shows how the Stephanists were a problem for the non-Stephanists. Contains many interesting details and sheds much light through side remarks.

Polack, W. G., *The Building of a Great Church.* Second edition, revised and enlarged, Concordia Publishing House, St. Louis, Mo., 1941.

Polack W. G., *The Story of C. F. W. Walther,* Concordia Publishing House, St. Louis, Mo., 1935.

Polenz, G. von, *Die oeffentliche Meinung und der Pastor Stephan.* Arnoldsche Buchhandlung, Dresden und Leipzig, 1840.

> The author is a former Stephanite. While he criticizes some of the things which Stephan did in Germany, he never becomes bitter. Most useful for a proper understanding of Stephan's development.

Publizisten, von einem Norddeutschen. *Der gegenwaertige Grenzstreit zwischen Staats- und Kirchengewalt.* Aus dem staatskirchenrechtlichen und legislativen Gesichtspunkt. Verlag von C. A. Schwetschke und Sohn, Halle, 1839.

Qualben, Lars P., *A History of the Christian Church.* Revised and enlarged edition, Thomas Nelson and Sons, New York, 1936.

> Gives a synoptic view. Very useful for background.

Qualben Lars P., *The Lutheran Church in Colonial America.* Thomas Nelson and Sons, New York, 1940.

Richter, Emil L., *Lehrbuch des katholischen und evangelischen Kirchenrechts.* Fuenfte umgearbeitete Auflage, Tauchnitz-Verlag, Leipzig, 1858.

An early nineteenth-century authority on church law.

Richter, Emil L., *Die evangelischen Kirchenordnungen des 16. Jahrhunderts.* Urkunden und Regesten. Landes-Industrie-Comptoir-Verlag, Weimar, 1846.

A heavy volume containing copies of various *Kirchenordnungen,* etc. In part superseded by Emil Sehling.

Religion in Geschichte und Gegenwart. Zweite Auflage. (Five volumes.) Verlag von J. C. B. Mohr, Tuebingen, 1930.

Some of the best German scholars collaborated in producing this very reliable work of reference.

Rhodes, James Ford, *History of the United States from Compromise of 1850.* (Eight volumes.) MacMillan, New York, 1893—1922.

Rhone, J. Magnus, *Norwegian American Lutheranism up to 1872.* Macmillan Company, New York, 1926.

This book is the result of work done on a doctoral dissertation at the Harvard Divinity School.

Rudelbach, A. G., *Die Grundveste der lutherischen Kirchenlehre und Friedenspraxis.* Streitschrift wider Dr. K. H. Sack in Bonn und Dr. F. C. Baur in Tuebingen. Verlag von B. Taugnitz, Leipzig, 1840.

Rudelbach, A. G., *Amtliches Gutachten ueber die Wiedereinfuehrung der Katechismusexamen im Koenigreich Sachsen.* Verlag von Justus Naumann, Dresden, 1841.

Sabine, George H., *A History of Political Theory.* Henry Holt and Company, New York, 1937.

Sadler, W. S., *The Mind at Mischief.* Sixth Printing. Funk and Wagnalls, New York, November, 1930.

Schaffer, Laurence F., *The Psychology of Adjustment.* Houghton Mifflin, Cambridge, 1936.

Schaeffer, C., and Brode, H., *Kirchenrecht.* Fuenfte Auflage, C. L. Hirschfeld Verlag, 1927.

Scharf, J. T., *History of St. Louis and County.* (2 volumes.) Philadelphia, 1883.

Scheibel, J. G., *Luthers Agende und die neue Preussische.* Verlag von K. F. Koehler, Leipzig, 1836.

Schmid, Heinrich, *Geschichte des Pietismus.* C. H. Becksche Buchhandlung, Noerdlingen, 1863.

Schneider, Carl E., *The German Church on the American Frontier.* Eden Publishing House, St. Louis, Mo., 1939.

A scholarly treatment of the documents. Very useful for background study of all German immigrants of the early nineteenth century.

Sehling, Emil, *Die Evangelischen Kirchenordnungen des 16. Jahrhunderts.* (Five large volumes.) Verlag von O. R. Reisland, Leipzig, 1902.

> Very useful for any study of the genesis of Lutheran polity.

Schaff-Herzog Encyclopedia of Religious Knowledge. Funk and Wagnalls, New York and London, 1909. "Church Government," Vol. III, pp. 92—96.

Sihler, Ernst G., *From the Maumee to the Thames and Tiber.* New York University Press, 1930.

> Interesting information on life in a Missouri Synod Lutheran parsonage in the middle of the nineteenth century.

Sihler, Wilhelm, *Evangelienpredigten.* Concordia Publishing House, St. Louis, Mo.

> A collection of sermons on the Gospels for the church year by the first Vice-President of the Missouri Synod.

Sihler, Wilhelm, *Lebenslauf.* Auf mehrfaches Begehren von ihm selbst beschrieben.

> Vol. I was published by Concordia Publishing House, St. Louis, Mo., 1879. Vol. II by Lutherischer Verlagsverein, New York, 1880.

Sihler, Wilhelm, *Zeit- und Gelegenheitspredigten.* Lutherischer Concordia-Verlag, St. Louis, Mo., 1883.

> The topics of these sermons were suggested by special problems or occasions. Many of them are "against" something: "Against Life Insurance" — "Against the Dance" — "Against the Lodges" — "God's Purpose in the Chicago Fire" (1871) — "Against Drunkenness." An example of Sihler's practical bent is to be found on page 362, where he suggests a game to be played by the young people as a substitute for dancing. These sermons are a great aid in understanding the first Vice-President of the Missouri Synod.

Sorenson, Herbert, *Psychology in Education.* McGraw Hill Book Company, New York, 1940.

Stahl, K., *Die Kirchenverfassung nach Lehre und Recht der Protestanten.* Zweite Ausgabe. Verlag von Theodor Blaesing, Erlangen, 1862.

Statistical Yearbook of the Evangelical Lutheran Synod of Missouri, Ohio, and Other States.

> Published annually by Concordia Publishing House, St. Louis, Mo. Reliable statistics on the Missouri Synod.

Steffens, D. H., *Doctor Carl Ferdinand Wilhelm Walther.* Lutheran Publication Society, Philadelphia, 1917.

Stephan, Horst, *Geschichte der evangelischen Theologie seit dem deutschen Idealismus.* Verlag von Alfred Toepelmann, Berlin, 1938.

> A history of German theology covering the years 1775 to 1930.

Stephan, Martin, *Der christliche Glaube* in einem vollstaendigen Jahrgange Predigten des Kirchenjahres 1824 ueber die gewoehnlichen Sonn- und Festtagsevangelien. Erster Theil 1825; zweiter Theil 1826. Gedruckt auf Kosten des Verfassers in der koeniglichen Hofbuchdruckerei, Dresden.

Stephan, Martin, *Predigt gehalten am Sonntage Jubilate, 1831*. Walthersche Buchhandlung, Dresden, 1831.
> This sermon does not come up to the standard of Stephan, but it was "auf vielfaeltiges Verlangen dem Druck uebergeben." It bears the imprimatur "von Ammon D."

Stephan, Martin, *Herzlicher Zuruf an alle evangelischen Christen*. Zwei Predigten gehalten am Reformationsfest und ersten Adventssonntage 1823. Koenigliche Hofbuchdruckerei, Dresden, 1823.
> In a long preface Stephan defends himself against Schwaermerei und Sektenwesen. Strong emphasis on "das heilige Amt."

Stephenson, George Malcolm, *A History of American Immigration, 1820—1924*. Ginn and Company, New York, 1926.

Stephenson, George, Malcolm, *The Founding of the Augustana Synod, 1850—1860*. Augustana Book Concern, Rock Island, Ill., 1927.

Stephenson, George Malcolm, *Religious Aspects of Swedish Immigration*. University of Minnesota Press, 1932.

Troeltsch, Ernst, *Die Restaurationsepoche am Anfange des 19. Jahrhunderts*. Gesammelte Schriften, IV, 1925.

Uckermann, Otto Baron von, *Sendschreiben an den Herrn Professor W. T. Krug*. Zum Besten der Casse des Dresdener Huelfs-Bibel-Vereins unter der Direction Sr. Hochwuerden des Herrn Pastor Stephan zu St. Johannis. Verlag von F. A. Eupel, Sondershausen, 1837.

Vehse, Carl Eduard, *Die Stephansche Auswanderung nach Amerika*. Dresden, 1840.

Verfassungsurkunde des Koenigreichs Sachsen. Verlag von C. C. Meinhold und Soehne, Dresden, 4. September 1831.
> No author given. Contains the basic laws of Saxony as of September 4, 1831.

Walther, C. F. W., *Briefe*. (Two volumes.) Edited by Walther's nephew, L. Fuerbringer. Concordia Publishing House, St. Louis, Mo., 1915 and 1916.
> Vol. I contains letters from 1841 to 1865; Volume II, from 1865 to 1871. Very useful for any study of early Missouri Synod history.

Walther, C. F. W., *Die Stimme unserer Kirche in der Frage von Kirche und Amt*. A. Deichertscher Verlag, Erlangen, 1852.

Walther, C. F. W., *Die rechte Gestalt einer vom Staat unabhaengigen Ortsgemeinde*. Sechste unveraenderte Auflage. Lutherischer Concordia-Verlag, St. Louis, Mo., 1890.

Walther, C. F. W., *Die rechte Unterscheidung von Gesetz und Evangelium*. 39 Abendvortraege. Concordia Publishing House, St. Louis, Mo., 1897.
> Very useful for an understanding of Walther's concept of the ministry. This book has been done into English by W. H. T. Dau under the title: *The Right Distinction Between Law and Gospel*. The addresses were originally given to the entire student group of Concordia Seminary, St. Louis.

Walther, C. F. W., *Communismus und Socialismus.* Druckerei der Synode von Missouri, Ohio und anderen Staaten, St. Louis, Mo., 1878.

A series of lectures which Walther delivered before the men of Old Trinity.

Walther, C. F. W., *Die Wucherfrage.* Druck von August Wiebusch und Sohn, St. Louis, Mo., 1869.

A discussion of interest, based on a tract by Martin Luther. Originally given in a series of lectures before the men of Old Trinity.

Walther, C. F. W., *Pastoraltheologie.* Fifth edition, Concordia Publishing House, St. Louis, Mo., 1906.

This was the standard text on pastoral theology in the Missouri Synod from 1875 to 1925. Originally the material in this book appeared in a long series of articles in *Lehre und Wehre.* In this book Walther tells the future ministers of the Synod how to conduct their office. The book is invaluable for a study of Missouri Synod polity. The book contains the usual amount of quotations from Luther and the Lutheran theologians of the sixteenth and seventeenth centuries.

Walther, C. F. W., *Lebenslauf des weiland ehrwuerdigen J. F. Buenger.* Dette-Verlag, St. Louis, Mo., 1882.

At the close of his life Walther writes a biography of his brother-in-law and gives his views on some of the facts concerning the Saxon immigration. In part an *apologia.*

Walther, C. F. W., *Gnadenjahr.* Predigten ueber die Evangelien des Kirchenjahrs. Lutherischer Concordia-Verlag, St. Louis, Mo., 1890.

Sermons that were preached during the period 1840—1883, most of them before 1850. The date is given after each sermon. Very useful for an understanding of the early Walther. Especially valuable when used in conjunction with the minutes of Old Trinity.

Walther, C. F. W., *Lutherische Brosamen.* Predigten und Reden, seit 1847, theils in Pamphletform, theils in Zeitschriften bereits erschienen, in einem Sammelband aufs neue dargeboten. M. C. Barthel, Generalagent der Deutschen Evangelisch-Lutherischen Synode von Missouri, Ohio, und anderen Staaten, St. Louis, Mo., 1876.

Contains *Gelegenheitspredigten* and *Gelegenheitsreden.*

Walther, C. F. W., *Licht des Lebens.* Ein Jahrgang von Evangelienpredigten. Concordia Publishing House, St. Louis, Mo., 1905.

Most of these sermons were preached before 1850. Every sermon is dated.

Walther, C. F. W., *Festklaenge.* Predigten ueber Festtexte des Kirchenjahrs. Concordia Publishing House, St. Louis, Mo., 1892.

These are holiday sermons. Most of them were preached before 1850.

Walther, C. F. W., *Amerikanisch-Lutherische Evangelien-Postille.* Lutherischer Concordia-Verlag, St. Louis, Mo., 1871.

Also translated into Norwegian and published in Bergen, 1878.

Walther, C. F. W., *Amerikanisch-Lutherische Epistel-Postille.* Lutherischer Concordia-Verlag, St. Louis, Mo., 1882.

Walther, C. F. W., *Church Membership.* Addresses and prayers at the meetings of the Evangelical Lutheran Joint Congregation of St. Louis, Missouri. Translated from the original German by Rudolph Prange, Concordia Publishing House, St. Louis, Mo., 1931.

Walther, Georg Conrad, *Neu-vermehrtes und vollstaendiges Corpus Juris Ecclesiastici Saxonici oder Churfl. Saechsische Kirchen-Schul-Ordnungen.* Walthersche Hofbuchhandlung, Dresden, 1773.
Very useful source material for a study of Lutheran polity in Saxony.

Walther, W., *Zur Wertung der deutschen Reformation.* Vortraege und Aufsaetze. A. Deichertscher Verlag, Leipzig, 1909.

Walter, Johannes von, *Die Geschichte des Christentums.* (Three volumes.) Verlag von C. Bertelsmann, Guetersloh, 1932—1935. Vol. I, Das Altertum. Vol. II, Das Mittelalter. Volume III, Die Reformation.

Waring, Luther Hess, *The Political Theories of Martin Luther.* G. Putnam's Sons, New York, 1910.
Grew out of a doctoral dissertation at George Washington University.

Weathered, Leslie D., *Psychology and Life.* Abingdon Press, New York. Sixth printing, September, 1937.

Wentz, Abdel Ross, *The Lutheran Church in American History.* United Lutheran Publication House, Philadelphia. Second edition, 1932.

Weller, Hieronymus, *Dr. Martin Luthers Anweisung zum rechten Studium der Theologie.* Aus dem Lateinischen uebersetzt von G. Schick. Zweite Auflage, Concordia Publishing House, St. Louis, Mo., 1881.

Ziehnert, J. C., *Praktisches evangelisches Kirchenrecht.* (Two volumes.) Verlag von F. W. Goedsche, Meissen, 1826.
Contains constitutional and administrative law as it affected the Lutheran pastor of Saxony during the first half of the nineteenth century. What Walther's *Pastorale* was to the Lutheran ministers of the Missouri Synod, Ziehnert's *Kirchenrecht* was to the Lutheran ministers of Saxony from 1825 to 1850.

Newspapers, Magazines, and Periodicals

Anzeiger des Westens, Der. Gedruckt und herausgegeben von H. Bimpage und W. Weber, 1835.

Concordia Historical Institute Quarterly, The. St. Louis, Mo., 1928.
Contains many reprints of MSS. in addition to articles pertaining to the history of the Missouri Synod.

Daily Evening Gazette. St. Louis, Missouri, 1839.

Daily Missouri Republican. St. Louis, Missouri, 1838.

Deutsche Tribuene, Die. St. Louis, Missouri, 1838.

Friedensbote, Der. Herausgegeben von dem Evangelischen Kirchenverein des Westens. St. Louis, Missouri, 1850.

Kirchliche Mittheilungen aus und ueber Nord-Amerika. Herausgegeben von Wilhelm Loehe und J. F. Wucherer, Nordlingen, 1843.
Very valuable and very rare. L. Fuerbringer has a complete file.

Lehre und Wehre. Concordia Publishing House, St. Louis, Mo., 1855.
A professional theological magazine.

Lutheraner, Der. Herausgegeben von C. F. W. Walther, St. Louis, Mo., 1844.
  Official periodical of the Missouri Synod since 1847.

Missouri Argus. St. Louis, Mo., 1839.

Missouri Historical Review, The. Published by the State Historical Society of Missouri, Columbia, Mo., 1906.

Niedners Zeitschrift fuer historische Theologie, 1863. No. 2.

North American Review, Boston, 1815. Vol. 41, p. 248 ff.: "German Emigration to America."

Political Science Quarterly, 53:328—349. September, 1938. C. E. Merriam: "The Assumptions of Democracy."

Zeitschrift fuer die gesamte Lutherische Theologie und Kirche. Herausgegeben von A. G. Rudelbach und H. E. F. Guericke. Leipzig, 1840.

Zeitschrift fuer Kirchengeschichte. Dritte Folge, LVIII (1939). Verlag von W. Kohlhammer in Stuttgart.

Zeitschrift fuer Protestantismus und Kirche. Herausgegeben von G. Chr. A. Harless. Erlangen, 1838.

Manuscript Material

"Absetzungserklaerung."
  This is a statement signed by the pastors in the colony in which they relieve Pastor Stephan of his office as bishop. Concordia Historical Institute possesses the rough draft and the final draft. The final draft closes with the following sentence: "So geschehen, Perry County an der Muendung des Brazo, den 30. Mai, 1839. Das Concil."

"Acta Ephoralia" den des Mysticismus und Separatismus beschuldigten Herrn Pfarrer Keyl betreffend. Eingegangen bei der Superintendentur Penig, 1836.
  Letters and rescripts of Superintendent O. Siebenhaar and the *Kultusministerium* pertaining to Pastor Keyl.

"Acta der evangel. Superintendentur Penig bei Chemnitz betreffend Wahl, Ordination und Amtseinfuehrung des sel. Professor Dr. C. F. W. Walther ins Pfarramt zu Braeunsdorf in Sachsen sowie den Zwist zwischen den Nagelschen Eheleuten, 1836 bis 1838."
  Extracts from the records of the superintendent pertaining to the ministry of C. F. W. Walther in Braeunsdorf, Saxony.

"Acta die Anstellung des Candidaten des Predigtamtes Otto Hermann Walther als Pfarrvicar in Langenchursdorf und Lauenberg betreffend." Superintendentur Waldenburg Litt. LII, No. 9, Rep. II, Vol. Lec. 1.
  Orders, rescripts, responses, etc., pertaining to the ministry of O. H. Walther in Langenchursdorf, Saxony. A typewritten copy from the original archives is in Concordia Historical Institute.

Buenger, J. F., "Reisetagebuch gefuehrt von J. F. Buenger."
  Entries are made from October 1, 1838, to December 21, 1838.

Buerger, Ernst Moritz. "Lebensgeschichte von Ernst Moritz Buerger, Pastor emeritus, von ihm selbst beschrieben."

>Very valuable unpublished autobiography, in possession of a grandson, Pastor E. J. Buerger, 219 West Wallace Avenue, Shawnee, Okla.

"Entwurf zu einer Gemeinde- und Vorsteher-Ordnung fuer die Gemeinde zu Frohna, Perry County, Missouri."

>This constitution was finally adopted March 31, 1844. A copy in Pastor E. G. W. Keyl's handwriting, signed by every voting member of the parish, is in the archives of the present congregation at Frohna.

"Fasciculus III."

>This is a bundle of documents sewed together with thread and protected by a semistiff cover. This particular fascicle contains the original minutes of the "Berathungs-Comite." Invaluable for a proper understanding of the emigration. There are a hundred pages, size 10×16.

"Fasciculus IV."

>This bundle contains the various constitutions ("Ordnungen") which Martin Stephan had formulated for the emigrant company.

"Fasciculus V."

>This bundle contains the papers pertaining to the investigations and the defense of Martin Stephan in Dresden. "Die Untersuchung des Herrn Pastor Stephans. Sein Mysticismus und Muckerei, Sectierungen, u. s. w. Kammerverhandlungen." These documents seem to have belonged to Marbach, who was Stephan's chief legal adviser during the trials before various courts in Saxony.

"Fasciculus VI."

>This bundle contains original copies of letters to and from Stephan. A transcript of the hearing of Sophie Hoeschel in the police court in Dresden after the arrest of Martin Stephan. Marbach's notes on the progress of the Altenburg Debate. A *Protokoll* of the pastors' meeting with Marbach shortly after March 3, 1841.

"Geschichte der Evangelisch-Lutherischen Gemeinde Ungeaenderter Augsburgischer Confession zu St. Louis, Missouri, von der Grundsteinlegung der Dreieinigkeits-Kirche (an der Lombard Strasse) an bis zur Grundsteinlegung der Immanuels-Kirche den 30. Juli, 1849."

>This history is in the handwriting of Pastor J. F. Buenger and was placed in the cornerstone of Immanuel Lutheran Church. A copy in the handwriting of Pastor Buenger is to be found in Concordia Historical Institute.

Guenther, Martin. "Kollegienhefte."

>Guenther was a student in the seminary at Altenburg. When the seminary was moved to St. Louis, in 1850, he moved with it. Later on he became professor at Concordia Seminary. These *Kollegienhefte* are his notebooks. They are extremely useful in the study of ministerial education in the Missouri Synod. His entire set of notebooks is now in possession of L. Fuerbringer. The titles are as follows: "Ad Lutheri locos theologicos." 3. September 1847 bis 1. August 1848. "Allgemeine Einleitung in die Naturlehre." 1852. "Annotationes ad Joh. Guil. Baieri Compendium theologiae positivae." 1851. "Die Christlich-Kirchliche Archaeologie." 1851. "Einleitung in das Neue Testament." 1850. "Ethik oder die Lehre von der tugendhaften Einrichtung des Gemueths." "Explication des Epheserbriefs." "Explicatio Evangelii Sancti Matthaei," den 2. Septem-

ber, 1850, Finis den 2. Maerz 1853. "Hermeneutica Sacra." 1850. "Katechetik." 1850. "Logik Einleitung. Von den philosophischen Wissenschaften und Kunstwoertern." 1850. "Metaphysik nach Crusius." 1851. "Praktische Philosophie oder Anweisung, vernuenftig zu leben." 1853. "Psychologie, Logik, Philosophie." 1849. "Repetitio Chemnitziana," hoc est propositiones de praecipuis christianae religionis capitibus excerptae ex locis theologicis.

"Hanewinckel, F."

A manuscript copy of documents pertaining to the founders of the Missouri Synod. These copies were made from the originals recorded in the various archives of Dresden. Rev. Hannewinckel, who was pastor of the Saxon Free Church in Dresden, combed the court records and the ecclesiastical archives for W. H. T. Dau. The result of his efforts is this 201-page hand-written book of documents, now in the hands of L. Fuerbringer.

"Kirchenbuch von Frohna, Perry County, Mo.," vom Okt. 1839 bis Sept. 1847.

Contains a record of baptisms, marriages, and funerals of the parish.

"Kirchenvorsteherordnung fuer die Gemeinde in Altenburg."

This is a constitution adopted November 14, 1842. Additions ("Zusaetze") were made in 1849.

Marbach, F. A. "An meine unter Pastor Stephan mitausgewanderten deutschen Landsleute."

This is a rather lengthy manifesto, in which Marbach criticizes the entire emigration project and suggests what ought to be done. Invaluable for an understanding of the pastors' attitudes toward lay participation in the government of the Church.

"Nachrichten an unsere Nachkommen."

A brief and somewhat patriotic history in MS. form. It is in the archives of Trinity Church, Altenburg, Perry County, Missouri.

"Olbers Erklaerung."

A statement signed by the pastors on board the *Olbers*, in which Martin Stephan is asked to assume the title and position of a bishop. Unbound MSS. in Concordia Historical Institute.

"Perry County Court Files 600 and 601."

The suit of Martin Stephan vs. Gotthold H. Loeber, E. G. W. Keyl, E. M. Buerger, Henry C. Bimpage, Fred. W. Barthel, F. A. Marbach, I. G. Palisch, and Gustavus Jaekel.

"Protokollbuch der Evangelisch-Lutherischen Gemeinde Ungeaenderter Augsburgischer Confession zu St. Louis, Mo."

The original book of minutes of Old Trinity. It begins with the meeting of December 16, 1839. One of the most valuable sources for the present study.

"Protokollbuch der Gemeinde zu Altenburg."

This is a book of minutes of the Altenburg congregation from November, 1846, to January, 1857. The minutes are not as complete and extensive as the minutes of Old Trinity in St. Louis, but they are very valuable.

"Protokoll des Ministeriums."

Minutes of the Saxon pastors' meetings September 4 and 9, 1839. Supplies the evidence for the pastors' (including C. F. W. Walther's) opposition to lay participation in government.

"Selma Erklaerung." Dated February 16, 1839.

This is a statement in which all immigrants aboard the Mississippi River ship *Selma* declare their absolute obedience to Bishop Stephan.

"Shiplists."

Photostatic copies of the lists of immigrants on the various ships of the immigrant company. The lists show the names, the place of residence from which the immigrant emigrated, age, and occupation. The originals are in the Port of Entry at New Orleans. The photostatic copies are the property of the Concordia Historical Society, St. Louis, Missouri.

Stephan, Martin. "Anweisung."

This is an order in which Martin Stephan authorized the payment, out of the common treasury, of $100 to every clergyman in the company shortly after arrival in St. Louis.

"Stephan's Ruecktrittserklaerung."

This is the resignation of Bishop Martin Stephan in Perry County, Missouri. Concordia Historical Institute has a German and an English copy. The German copy is signed in Stephan's own handwriting.

"Vermeldungsbuch."

A book in which Pastor Loeber wrote his formal announcements made to the congregation in the course of the service. It covers all the services from 1835 to 1846. Very valuable source material. In the archives of the congregation at Altenburg, Missouri.

Walther, C. F. W. "Letter to his brother O. H. Walther," dated March 4, 1840.

This is a long letter of ten closely written pages. It is a self-analysis and self-accusation of C. F. W. Walther making due allowance for the spiritual tribulations through which the writer was passing at the time the letter was written. Must be rated as of real value for an understanding of the "chaos in Missouri." The letter is to be found in the package labeled "Walther Letters" in Concordia Historical Institute. The folder containing this letter has a note on it: "Notizen zu Walthers Briefen."

Walther, O. H. "Zur Agende."

This is a *Vermeldungsbuch*. It was used in all the services of Old Trinity from the Second Sunday after Trinity (Dom. II, post Trinitatis), 1839, to the First Sunday after Epiphany, 1841. It is now in the private library of L. Fuerbringer.

Wente, W. H. "Recent Trends in American Education." Paper read before the triannual conference of the Missouri Synod instructors and school administrators, River Forest, Illinois. July, 1940.

This paper traces the development of Missouri Synod colleges and seminaries.

Printed Minutes and Reports

Exulantenlieder.
> Composed by O. H. Walther and sung by the immigrants.

Hirtenbrief des Herrn Pastor Grabau zu Buffalo nebst den zwischen ihm und mehreren lutherischen Pastoren in Missouri gewechselten Schriften. Der Oeffentlichkeit uebergeben als eine Protestation gegen Geltendmachung hierarchischer Grundsaetze innerhalb der lutherischen Kirche. Gedruckt von H. Ludwig und Co., New York, 1849.

Mittheilungen des Vereins fuer Geschichte und Altertumskunde zu Kahla und Roda. Kahla 1912. Hofbuchdruckerei J. Beck.
> This volume contains valuable letters written by Pastor G. H. Loeber from Perry County, Mo., to his relatives in Saxony during the years 1838 and 1839.

Proceedings of the Western District of the Missouri Synod, June 10—15, 1939.
> These minutes contain an essay written by F. Mayer, professor at Concordia Seminary, St. Louis, Missouri, on the topic: "The Ministry Is the Highest Office in the Church." This essay was part of the celebration of the hundredth anniversary of the Saxon immigration and brings the doctrine of Walther concerning the ministry clearly and authoritatively.

Protokoll ueber die Verhandlungen des Colloquiums gehalten in Buffalo, New York, vom 20. November bis 5. Dezember 1866. Colloquenten der Missouri Synode: Professor C. F. W. Walther, Pastor Dr. Wilhelm Sihler, Pastor H. C. Schwan und die Herren J. C. D. Roemer aus St. Louis, Missouri, J. Keil aus Pittsburgh, Pennsylvania, und John C. Theiss aus Altenburg, Missouri.

Synodalberichte der deutschen Ev.-Luth. Synode von Missouri, Ohio u. a. Staaten vom Jahre 1847 bis 1860.
> The synodical reports of the first ten years of the Synod's existence were published in a second edition by Concordia Publishing House, St. Louis, Missouri, in 1876. They are a valuable source for a study of early church government in the Missouri Synod.

U. S. Report, Commissioner General of Immigration, June 30, 1930. U. S. Government Printing Office.

TOPICAL INDEX

Altenburg Debate, Loeber's correspondence concerning 94; importance for emerging church polity 113; Schieferdecker's estimate of 113; Luther and Gerhard deciding factors in 113; Walther's Theses 115; nature of debate 116; results of 124, 125; doubts removed by 165

Amalia, capacity of ship 113; Walther legendary passenger 113

America, where Luther's church government theories function 212

Ammon, von, "most vicious" rationalist 19; examines Ernst M. Buerger 28

Anti-Pfaff, Der, St. Louis journal opposing priest rule 149; attacks Walther 157, 158; scurrilous attacks on Walther 177; Walther defended by Old Trinity against lies of 208

Antirationalists, "Erweckungsbewegung" coined by 21

Anzeiger des Westens, liberal St. Louis paper used by Sproede against Walther 104, 149; Old Trinity dedication advertised in 159; popular in Old Trinity 207; Democratic 207; Walther's political beliefs publicized by Old Trinity in 207

Arkansas, why considered as Stephanite colony site 71

Augustana Synod, numerical representation in 182

Australia, a considered site for the Stephanite colony 71; why not chosen 71

Baptists, polity of 182

Barthel, F. W., government employee and adherent of Stephan 41; first permanent treasurer of Missouri Synod 183; bitter against pastors, inconsiderate of congregational rights 192

Bavarians, sent to Michigan by Loehe 17; lacked leadership of Missouri Saxons 17

Beer gardens, frequented by St. Louis Germans 160, 161

Bible Societies 23; Dresden branch under control of M. Stephan 59

Brohm, Theodor Julius, marriage of 26; candidate under Stephanism 28; one of nine candidates in Stephanite Immigration 41; member of Stephan's emigration committee 60; lived with G. H. Loeber 92; confession in three parts by 103; aims of clerical party questioned by 111; candidate as successor to O. H. Walther 127

Buenger, J. F., forbears of 26; secondary education of 27; connection with Stephanism 28; loyalty to Stephan 41, 42; joined the Immigration 41; narrow concept of the Church 66; arrival at New York 112, 113; temporary successor of O. H. Walther 126; candidate as successor to O. H. Walther 127

Buerger, E. M., appointment to the ministry 1, 23, 31; use of Luther's writings 4; the wording of his call 20; his attitude toward Hahn 24; his courses at Leipzig 27; his examination *pro candidatura* 28; attitude toward aristocrats 31; favors the episcopacy of Stephan 32; his parish 34; joins the Immigration 41; loyalty to Stephan 41; becomes a Stephanite 59; forsakes Rudelbach 60; has trouble with Consistorium 78; has trouble with populace 79; resigns from congregation 94; confesses his guilt 103; confused by fall of Stephan 104; "colossal error" 106; joins lay party 109; plans return to Germany 117; espouses cause of lay party 213

Burger, George, present at Cleveland 1845, 174; deficient training 176; present at Fort Wayne 1846, 181

Caesaropapism 16

Call, time limit 196, 197

Calvinistic theocracy in Perry County community 92

16

"Korpsgeist" of 165; the beginning of the controversy with Buffalo 165; solidarity explained by training of ministers 166; Sihler suggests organization of Synod December 11, 1844, in letter to Walther 171; Walther favors organization of Synod, but fears the opposition in St. Louis and the West 172; Walther writes Ernst six characteristics of a desirable synod 173; its congregationalism is the result of experience with Stephanism 182; its congregationalism is not taken from American democracy 182, 183; balance-of-power theory between clergy and laity 183; Old Trinity's paragraph safeguarding the congregations' rights not adopted by Synod until 1854, 194; Missouri Synod's constitution different from anything then existing 193; attitude toward confessional writings of Lutheran church 195; constitution limits both powers of clergy and powers of laymen 195; authoritarians 203; doctrine of total depravity of man contrary to democratic theory 203; reasons for the success of 214-219; system of higher education defined 215; elementary system of education defined 215, 216; system of higher education different from anything existing in America 215; emphasis on teaching by the pastor 217

Missouri, prevailing lynch law makes committee on emigration skeptical about Missouri as a location for the colony 71

"Mixed congregations" consisted of Lutherans and Reformed, the Missouri Synod's policy toward them 190, 191

Moravians 22

Muhlenberg, H. M., fails to train ministers 166; kept his eye on the fathers in Halle 196

Nagel, Mrs., fanatical Stephanite 41

"New Measurism" in General Synod 163

New Orleans selected after long debate as port of entry by emigration committee 69

New York, strongly favored by the emigration as port of entry for the Stephanites; reasons for choosing New York opposed by M. Stephan 69-71

New York Ministerium a "Pastorensynode," but to a less degree than the Pennsylvania Ministerium 194, 195; attitude to Confessional Writings of Lutheran Church 195

"New Yorkers," a group that left New York under Oertel and joined the Saxons in Perry County 103

Nollau, L., pastor of Evangelical Church near St. Louis, makes personal attack on Walther 177

Numerical representation in the General Council 182; in the Augustana Synod 182

Oertel, Maximilian, leader of "New Yorkers," also called "Berliners" 103

Pastor, his relation to the school 26; his tasks 33; emphasis on preaching 33; obliged to send a sheaf of outlines each year to his superintendent 33; a "Standesperson" 34; he supervised the school 34; a privileged class 34; his income in Saxony 35; fees paid him 36; his remuneration in kind 36; had considerable control over the economic life of the parish 37; his standard of living 40; well educated even on the American frontier 198

"Pastorenkirchen," clergy-managed churches of Germany 193

Paulus, H. E. G., exegete of the rationalists, denied many traditional doctrines of Christianity 21; extreme radicalism losing its vigor 25

Pennsylvania Ministerium an association of ministers, not of congregations 181; no balance between the voting strength of clergy and that of the laity 182; a "Pastorensynode" 193-195; attitude to Confessional Writings of the Lutheran Church 195

Perry County, purchase of land in 86; payments for the land 90; political community of Stephanites in 92; housing conditions in the settlement 92; Calvinistic theocracy in 92; college built in hot summer of 1839, 166

Pietism 1, 18; pietistic group in Breslau 46; pietism opposed by M. Stephan 47

Polack, W. G., connects Missouri Synod's policy with American political theory 201

Tenure of office for pastors made permanent in the constitution of the Missouri Synod 184, 185

Theaters, German stock companies in St. Louis 160

Toledo, one of two ships used to take settlers from St. Louis to Perry County for expulsion of Stephan 88

Trautmann, J., pastor in Danbury, Ohio, present at Fort Wayne convention, July, 1846, 181

Trinity Congregation, St. Louis, opposes Donatism 106; fears priest craft 107; pastor not permitted to attend voters' meetings 107; principles of Altenburg Debate put into practice in 125-128; calls a successor to O. H. Walther 126-128; ratifies call extended to C. F. W. Walther after hearing his explanations of personal unworthiness 131; omits the celebration of Lord's Supper for four months in 1841, 131, 132; observes Lutheran principles of relationship between pastor and congregation 132; treats C. F. W. Walther with respect and kindness 132; observes dignity of the ministry 132; adopts a constitution ("Gemeindeordnung") 132 to 149; a mother church of the Missouri Synod 133; constitution used as model by Missouri Synod congregations 133; constitution based on quotations from M. Luther and John Gerhard 133; "Instruction for the elders" 134; responsibility of elders to congregation 134, 135; name "Kirchenrath" changed to "Gemeindevorstand" 134; congregation reserves right to nominate all candidates 134; plans for new church discussed 135; absentee "Vorsteher" are cited before congregation to give an account of their attitude 135; powers of elders largely administrative, not discretionary 135; constitution, or parts of it come up for discussion in no less than thirty-one meetings before it is finally adopted 136; name Trinity suggested by C. F. W. Walther 136; seal of congregation adopted 137; C. F. W. Walther reads quotations from Luther to congregation 136, 137; conditions of membership 137; minimum age of elders is set at twenty-five years 138;

minimum age for voters "majority" 138; copy of constitution recorded in courthouse 138; accepts all Symbolical Books of the Lutheran Church 138; constitution for poor fund read and discussed 139; testimonies from Luther, Johann Gerhard, and others which Vehse had gathered in his book read by C. F. W. Walther to voters 139; every member must be familiar with Augsburg Confession 139; Visitation Articles put on same level with Synodical Books 139; increase in ceremony for reception of new members suggested, discussed, and rejected 139, 140; no delegation of powers in calling pastors and teachers 140; trustees are held strictly accountable 140; purely Lutheran forms and purely Lutheran hymns to be used in 141; method of becoming a member defined 141; sufficient causes for removal of pastors or schoolteachers 141; certain paragraphs, among them the language paragraph, of the constitution are unalterable and irrepealable 141, 142; C. F. W. Walther makes an address about the importance of making and signing a constitution 143; connects orthodoxy with German language 143; members much concerned about their posterity 144; lodge paragraph adopted 144; knotty problem of signing the constitution 145-148; the "weak brethren" approach to the problem of signing the constitution is successful 147, 148; genuinely democratic methods used in adopting the constitution 148; plans and erects a new church 149-160; principles enunciated by C. F. W. Walther in the Altenburg Debate applied to building a church 149; committee on building site appointed 150; the purchase of a building site 151-153; plan for church building discussed 154-156; building committee has very few discretionary powers 156; bids opened in voters' meeting 156; contract for new church let at cost of $4,000.00 156; cornerstone laying is in Christ Church for fear of the populace 157; building committee consists entirely of laymen 158; only building committee can give orders to the contractor 158; rais-